HINDUISM AND BUDDHISM

VOLUME I

HINDUISM AND BUDDHISM

AN HISTORICAL SKETCH

BY

SIR CHARLES ELIOT

In three volumes

VOLUME I

LONDON

ROUTLEDGE & KEGAN PAUL LTD

Broadway House, 68-74 Carter Lane

First Published 1921
By Routledge & Kegan Paul Ltd.
Broadway House, 68-74 Carter Lane
London, EC4V 5EL
Reprinted 1954, 1957, 1962, 1968 and 1971
Printed in Great Britain
by Lowe & Brydone (Printers) Ltd., London

ISBN 0 7100 1328 0

PREFACE

The present work was begun in 1907 and was practically complete when the war broke out, but many circumstances such as the difficulty of returning home, unavoidable delays in printing and correcting proofs, and political duties have deferred its publication until now. In the interval many important books dealing with Hinduism and Buddhism have appeared, but having been resident in the Far East (with one brief exception) since 1912 I have found it exceedingly difficult to keep in touch with recent literature. Much of it has reached me only in the last few months and I have often been compelled to notice new facts and views in footnotes only, though I should have wished to modify the text.

Besides living for some time in the Far East, I have paid many visits to India, some of which were of considerable length, and have travelled in all the countries of which I treat except Tibet. I have however seen something of Lamaism near Darjeeling, in northern China and in Mongolia. But though I have in several places described the beliefs and practices prevalent at the present day, my object is to trace the history and development of religion in India and elsewhere with occasional remarks on its latest phases. I have not attempted to give a general account of contemporary religious thought in India or China and still less to forecast the possible result of present tendencies.

In the following pages I have occasion to transcribe words belonging to many oriental languages in Latin characters. Unfortunately a uniform system of transcription, applicable to all tongues, seems not to be practical at present. It was attempted in the *Sacred Books of the East*, but that system has fallen into disuse and is liable to be misunderstood. It therefore seems best to use for each language the method of transcription adopted by standard works in English dealing with each, for French and German transcriptions, whatever their merits may be as representations of the original sounds, are often misleading to English readers, especially in Chinese. For Chinese I have adopted Wade's system as used in Giles's *Dictionary*, for Tibetan the system of Sarat Chandra Das, for Pali that of the Pali Text Society and for Sanskrit that of Monier-Williams's *Sanskrit Dictionary*, except that I write ś instead of ṣ. Indian languages however offer many difficulties: it is often hard to decide whether Sanskrit or vernacular forms are more suitable and in dealing with Buddhist subjects whether Sanskrit or Pali words should be used. I have found it convenient to vary the form of proper names according as my remarks are based on Sanskrit or on Pali literature, but this obliges me to write the same word differently in different places, e.g. sometimes Ajâtaśatru and sometimes Ajâtasattu, just as in a book dealing with Greek and Latin mythology one might employ both Herakles and Hercules. Also many Indian names such as Ramayana, Krishna, nirvana have become Europeanized or at least are familiar to all Europeans interested in Indian literature. It seems pedantic to write them with their full and accurate complement of accents and dots and my general practice is to give such words in their accurate spelling (Râmâyaṇa, etc.) when they are first mentioned and also in the notes but usually to print them in their simpler and unaccented forms. I fear however that my practice in this matter is not entirely consistent since different parts of the book were written at different times.

My best thanks are due to Mr R. F. Johnston (author of *Chinese Buddhism*), to Professor W. J. Hinton of the University of Hong Kong and to Mr H. I. Harding of H.M. Legation at Peking for reading the proofs and correcting many errors: to Sir E. Denison Ross and Professor L. Finot for valuable information: and especially to Professor and Mrs Rhys Davids for much advice, though they are in no way responsible for the views which I have expressed and perhaps do not agree with them. It is superfluous for me to pay a tribute to these eminent scholars whose works are well known to all who are interested in Indian religion, but no one who has studied the early history of Buddhism or the Pali language can refrain from acknowledging a debt of gratitude to those who have made such researches possible by founding and maintaining during nearly forty years the Pali Text Society and rendering many of the texts still more accessible to Europe by their explanations and translations.

C. ELIOT.

TOKYO,
May, 1921.

LIST OF ABBREVIATIONS

The following are the principal abbreviations used:

Ep.Ind.	Epigraphia India.
E.R.E.	Encyclopedia of Religion and Ethics (edited by Hastings).
I.A.	Indian Antiquary.
J.A.	Journal Asiatique.
J.A.O.S.	Journal of the American Oriental Society.
J.R.A.S.	Journal of the Royal Asiatic Society.
P.T.S.	Pali Text Society.
S.B.E.	Sacred Books of the East (Clarendon Press).

CONTENTS

BOOK I

INTRODUCTION

BOOK II

EARLY INDIAN RELIGION: A GENERAL VIEW

BOOK III

PALI BUDDHISM

BOOK I

INTRODUCTION

INTRODUCTION

1. *Influence of Indian Thought in Eastern Asia*

PROBABLY the first thought which will occur to the reader who is acquainted with the matters treated in this work will be that the subject is too large. A history of Hinduism or Buddhism or even of both within the frontiers of India may be a profitable though arduous task, but to attempt a historical sketch of the two faiths in their whole duration and extension over Eastern Asia is to choose a scene unsuited to any canvas which can be prepared at the present day. Not only is the breadth of the landscape enormous but in some places it is crowded with details which cannot be omitted while in others the principal features are hidden by a mist which obscures the unity and connection of the whole composition. No one can feel these difficulties more than I do myself or approach his work with more diffidence, yet I venture to think that wide surveys may sometimes be useful and are needed in the present state of oriental studies. For the reality of Indian influence in Asia—from Japan to the frontiers of Persia, from Manchuria to Java, from Burma to Mongolia—is undoubted and the influence is one. You cannot separate Hinduism from Buddhism, for without it Hinduism could not have assumed its medieval shape and some forms of Buddhism, such as Lamaism, countenance Brahmanic deities and ceremonies, while in Java and Camboja the two religions were avowedly combined and declared to be the same. Neither is it convenient to separate the fortunes of Buddhism and Hinduism outside India from their history within it, for although the importance of Buddhism depends largely on its foreign conquests, the forms which it assumed in its new territories can be understood only by reference to the religious condition of India at the periods when successive missions were despatched.

This book then is an attempt to give a sketch of Indian thought or Indian religion—for the two terms are nearly equivalent in extent—and of its history and influence in Asia. I will not say in the world, for that sounds too ambitious and really adds little to the more restricted phrase. For ideas, like empires and races, have their natural frontiers. Thus Europe may be said to be non-Mohammedan. Although the essential principles of Mohammedanism seem in harmony with European monotheism, yet it has been deliberately rejected by the continent and often repelled by force. Similarly in the regions west of India[1], Indian religion is sporadic and exotic. I do not think that it had much influence on ancient Egypt, Babylon and Palestine or that it should be counted among the forces which shaped the character and teaching of Christ, though Christian monasticism and mysticism perhaps owed something to it. The debt of Manichæism and various Gnostic sects is more certain and more considerable, but these communities have not endured and were regarded as heretical while they lasted. Among the Neoplatonists of Alexandria and the Sufis of Arabia and Persia many seem to have listened to the voice of Hindu mysticism but rather as individuals than as leaders of popular movements.

But in Eastern Asia the influence of India has been notable in extent, strength and duration. Scant justice is done to her position in the world by those histories which recount the exploits of her invaders and leave the impression that her own people were a feeble, dreamy folk, sundered from the rest of mankind by their sea and mountain frontiers. Such a picture takes no account of the intellectual conquests of the Hindus. Even their political conquests were not contemptible and were remarkable for the distance if not for the extent of the territory occupied. For there were Hindu kingdoms in Java and Camboja and settlements in Sumatra[2] and even in Borneo, an island about as far from India as is Persia from Rome. But such military or commercial invasions are insignificant compared with the spread of Indian thought. The south-eastern region of Asia—both mainland and archipelago—owed its civilization almost entirely to India. In Ceylon, Burma, Siam, Camboja, Champa and Java,

[1] The frontier seems to be about Long. 65° E.

[2] See Coedes's views about Śrîvijaya in *B.E.F.E.O.* 1918, 6. The inscriptions of Rajendracola I (1012—1042 A.D) show that Hindus in India were not wholly ignorant of Indian conquests abroad.

religion, art, the alphabet, literature, as well as whatever science and political organization existed, were the direct gift of Hindus, whether Brahmans or Buddhists, and much the same may be said of Tibet, whence the wilder Mongols took as much Indian civilization as they could stomach. In Java and other Malay countries this Indian culture has been superseded by Islam, yet even in Java the alphabet and to a large extent the customs of the people are still Indian.

In the countries mentioned Indian influence has been dominant until the present day, or at least until the advent of Islam. In another large area comprising China, Japan, Korea, and Annam it appears as a layer superimposed on Chinese culture, yet not a mere veneer. In these regions Chinese ethics, literature and art form the major part of intellectual life and have an outward and visible sign in the Chinese written characters which have not been ousted by an Indian alphabet[1]. But in all, especially in Japan, the influence of Buddhism has been profound and penetrating. None of these lands can be justly described as Buddhist in the same sense as Burma or Siam but Buddhism gave them a creed acceptable in different forms to superstitious, emotional and metaphysical minds: it provided subjects and models for art, especially for painting, and entered into popular life, thought and language.

But what are Hinduism and Buddhism? What do they teach about gods and men and the destinies of the soul? What ideals do they hold up and is their teaching of value or at least of interest for Europe? I will not at once answer these questions by general statements, because such names as Hinduism and Buddhism have different meanings in different countries and ages, but will rather begin by briefly reviewing the development of the two religions. I hope that the reader will forgive me if in doing so I repeat much that is to be found in the body of this work.

One general observation about India may be made at the outset. Here more than in any other country the national mind finds its favourite occupation and full expression in religion. This quality is geographical rather than racial, for it is possessed by Dravidians as much as by Aryans. From the Raja to the peasant most Hindus have an interest in theology and often a

[1] But the Japanese syllabaries were probably formed under Indian influence.

passion for it. Few works of art or literature are purely secular: the intellectual and aesthetic efforts of India, long, continuous and distinguished as they are, are monotonous inasmuch as they are almost all the expression of some religious phase. But the religion itself is extraordinarily full and varied. The love of discussion and speculation creates considerable variety in practice and almost unlimited variety in creed and theory. There are few dogmas known to the theologies of the world which are not held by some of India's multitudinous sects[1] and it is perhaps impossible to make a single general statement about Hinduism, to which some sects would not prove an exception. Any such statements in this book must be understood as referring merely to the great majority of Hindus.

As a form of life and thought Hinduism is definite and unmistakeable. In whatever shape it presents itself it can be recognized at once. But it is so vast and multitudinous that only an encyclopedia could describe it and no formula can summarize it. Essayists flounder among conflicting propositions such as that sectarianism is the essence of Hinduism or that no educated Hindu belongs to a sect. Either can easily be proved, for it may be said of Hinduism, as it has been said of zoology, that you can prove anything if you merely collect facts which support your theory and not those which conflict with it. Hence many distinguished writers err by overestimating the phase which specially interests them. For one the religious life of India is fundamentally monotheistic and Vishnuite: for another philosophic Sivaism is its crown and quintessence: a third maintains with equal truth that all forms of Hinduism are tantric. All these views are tenable because though Hindu life may be cut up into castes and sects, Hindu creeds are not mutually exclusive and repellent. They attract and colour one another.

2. *Origin and Growth of Hinduism*

The earliest product of Indian literature, the Rig Veda, contains the songs of the Aryan invaders who were beginning

[1] Probably the Christian doctrine of the atonement or salvation by the death of a deity is an exception. I do not know of any Indian sect which holds a similar view. The obscure verse Rig Veda x. 13. 4 seems to hint at the self-sacrifice of a deity but the hymn about the sacrifice of Purusha (x. 90) has nothing to do with redemption or atonement.

to make a home in India. Though no longer nomads, they had little local sentiment. No cities had arisen comparable with Babylon or Thebes and we hear little of ancient kingdoms or dynasties. Many of the gods who occupied so much of their thoughts were personifications of natural forces such as the sun, wind and fire, worshipped without temples or images and hence more indefinite in form, habitation and attributes than the deities of Assyria or Egypt. The idea of a struggle between good and evil was not prominent. In Persia, where the original pantheon was almost the same as that of the Veda, this idea produced monotheism: the minor deities became angels and the chief deity a Lord of hosts who wages a successful struggle against an independent but still inferior spirit of evil. But in India the Spirits of Good and Evil are not thus personified. The world is regarded less as a battlefield of principles than as a theatre for the display of natural forces. No one god assumes lordship over the others but all are seen to be interchangeable—mere names and aspects of something which is greater than any god.

Indian religion is commonly regarded as the offspring of an Aryan religion, brought into India by invaders from the north and modified by contact with Dravidian civilization. The materials at our disposal hardly permit us to take any other point of view, for the literature of the Vedic Aryans is relatively ancient and full and we have no information about the old Dravidians comparable with it. But were our knowledge less one-sided, we might see that it would be more correct to describe Indian religion as Dravidian religion stimulated and modified by the ideas of Aryan invaders. For the greatest deities of Hinduism, Siva, Krishna, Râma, Durgâ and some of its most essential doctrines such as metempsychosis and divine incarnations, are either totally unknown to the Veda or obscurely adumbrated in it. The chief characteristics of mature Indian religion are characteristics of an area, not of a race, and they are not the characteristics of religion in Persia, Greece or other Aryan lands[1].

[1] It is possible (though not, I think, certain) that the Buddha called his principal doctrines *ariya* in the sense of Aryan not of noble. But even the Blessed One may not have been infallible in ethnography. When we call a thing British we do not mean to refer it to the ancient Britons more than to the Saxons or Normans. And was the Buddha an Aryan? See V. Smith, *Oxford History of India*, p. 47 for doubts.

Some writers explain Indian religion as the worship of nature spirits, others as the veneration of the dead. But it is a mistake to see in the religion of any large area only one origin or impulse. The principles which in a learned form are championed to-day by various professors represent thoughts which were creative in early times. In ancient India there were some whose minds turned to their ancestors and dead friends while others saw divinity in the wonders of storm, spring and harvest. Krishna is in the main a product of hero worship, but Śiva has no such historical basis. He personifies the powers of birth and death, of change, decay and rebirth—in fact all that we include in the prosaic word nature. Assuredly both these lines of thought—the worship of nature and of the dead—and perhaps many others existed in ancient India.

By the time of the Upanishads, that is about 600 B.C., we trace three clear currents in Indian religion which have persisted until the present day. The first is ritual. This became extraordinarily complicated but retained its primitive and magical character. The object of an ancient Indian sacrifice was partly to please the gods but still more to coerce them by certain acts and formulae[1]. Secondly all Hindus lay stress on asceticism and self-mortification, as a means of purifying the soul and obtaining supernatural powers. They have a conviction that every man who is in earnest about religion and even every student of philosophy must follow a discipline at least to the extent of observing chastity and eating only to support life. Severer austerities give clearer insight into divine mysteries and control over the forces of nature. Europeans are apt to condemn eastern asceticism as a waste of life but it has had an important moral effect. The weakness of Hinduism, though not of Buddhism, is that ethics have so small a place in its fundamental conceptions. Its deities are not identified with the moral law and the saint is above that law. But this dangerous doctrine is corrected by the dogma, which is also a popular conviction, that a saint must be a passionless ascetic. In India no religious teacher can expect a hearing unless he begins by renouncing the world.

Thirdly, the deepest conviction of Hindus in all ages is that salvation and happiness are attainable by knowledge. The corre-

[1] This is not altogether true of the modern temple ritual.

sponding phrases in Sanskrit are perhaps less purely intellectual than our word and contain some idea of effort and emotion. He who knows God attains to God, nay he is God. Rites and self-denial are but necessary preliminaries to such knowledge: he who possesses it stands above them. It is inconceivable to the Hindus that he should care for the things of the world but he cares equally little for creeds and ceremonies. Hence, side by side with irksome codes, complicated ritual and elaborate theology, we find the conviction that all these things are but vanity and weariness, fetters to be shaken off by the free in spirit. Nor do those who hold such views correspond to the anti-clerical and radical parties of Europe. The ascetic sitting in the temple court often holds that the rites performed around him are spiritually useless and the gods of the shrine mere fanciful presentments of that which cannot be depicted or described.

Rather later, but still before the Christian era, another idea makes itself prominent in Indian religion, namely faith or devotion to a particular deity. This idea, which needs no explanation, is pushed on the one hand to every extreme of theory and practice: on the other it rarely abolishes altogether the belief in ritualism, asceticism and knowledge.

Any attempt to describe Hinduism as one whole leads to startling contrasts. The same religion enjoins self-mortification and orgies: commands human sacrifices and yet counts it a sin to eat meat or crush an insect: has more priests, rites and images than ancient Egypt or medieval Rome and yet out does Quakers in rejecting all externals. These singular features are connected with the ascendancy of the Brahman caste. The Brahmans are an interesting social phenomenon without exact parallel elsewhere. They are not, like the Catholic or Moslem clergy, a priesthood pledged to support certain doctrines but an intellectual, hereditary aristocracy who claim to direct the thought of India whatever forms it may take. All who admit this claim and accord a nominal recognition to the authority of the Veda are within the spacious fold or menagerie. Neither the devil-worshipping aboriginee nor the atheistic philosopher is excommunicated, though neither may be relished by average orthodoxy.

Though Hinduism has no one creed, yet there are at least two doctrines held by nearly all who call themselves Hindus.

One may be described as polytheistic pantheism. Most Hindus are apparently polytheists, that is to say they venerate the images of several deities or spirits, yet most are monotheists in the sense that they address their worship to one god. But this monotheism has almost always a pantheistic tinge. The Hindu does not say the gods of the heathen are but idols, but it is the Lord who made the heavens: he says, My Lord (Râma, Krishna or whoever it may be) is all the other gods. Some schools would prefer to say that no human language applied to the Godhead can be correct and that all ideas of a personal ruler of the world are at best but relative truths. This ultimate ineffable Godhead is called Brahman[1].

The second doctrine is commonly known as metempsychosis, the transmigration of souls or reincarnation, the last name being the most correct. In detail the doctrine assumes various forms since different views are held about the relation of soul to body. But the essence of all is the same, namely that a life does not begin at birth or end at death but is a link in an infinite series of lives, each of which is conditioned and determined by the acts done in previous existences (karma). Animal, human and divine (or at least angelic) existences may all be links in the chain. A man's deeds, if good, may exalt him to the heavens, if evil may degrade him to life as a beast. Since all lives, even in heaven, must come to an end, happiness is not to be sought in heaven or on earth. The common aspiration of the religious Indian is for deliverance, that is release from the round of births and repose in some changeless state called by such names as union with Brahman, nirvana and many others.

[1] It is very unfortunate that English usage should make this word appear the same as Brahman, the name of a caste, and there is much to be said for using the old-fashioned word Brahmin to denote the caste, for it is clear, though not correct. In Sanskrit there are several similar words which are liable to be confused in English. In the nominative case they are:

(1) Brâhmaṇaḥ, a man of the highest caste.
(2) Brâhmaṇam, an ancient liturgical treatise.
(3) Brahma, the Godhead, stem Brahman, neuter.
(4) Brahmâ, a masculine nominative also formed from the stem Brahman and used as the name of a personal deity.

For (3) the stem Brahman is commonly used, as being distinct from Brahmâ, though liable to be confounded with the name of the caste.

3. *The Buddha*

As observed above, the Brahmans claim to direct the religious life and thought of India and apart from Mohammedanism may be said to have achieved their ambition, though at the price of tolerating much that the majority would wish to suppress. But in earlier ages their influence was less extensive and there were other currents of religious activity, some hostile and some simply independent. The most formidable of these found expression in Jainism and Buddhism both of which arose in Bihar in the sixth century[1] B.C. This century was a time of intellectual ferment in many countries. In China it produced Lao-tzŭ and Confucius: in Greece, Parmenides, Empedocles, and the sophists were only a little later. In all these regions we have the same phenomenon of restless, wandering teachers, ready to give advice on politics, religion or philosophy, to any one who would hear them.

At that time the influence of the Brahmans had hardly permeated Bihar, though predominant to the west of it, and speculation there followed lines different from those laid down in the Upanishads, but of some antiquity, for we know that there were Buddhas before Gotama and that Mahâvîra, the founder of Jainism, reformed the doctrine of an older teacher called Parśva.

In Gotama's youth Bihar was full of wandering philosophers who appear to have been atheistic and disposed to uphold the boldest paradoxes, intellectual and moral. There must however have been constructive elements in their doctrine, for they believed in reincarnation and the periodic appearance of superhuman teachers and in the advantage of following an ascetic discipline. They probably belonged chiefly to the warrior caste as did Gotama, the Buddha known to history. The Pitakas represent him as differing in details from contemporary teachers but as rediscovering the truth taught by his predecessors. They imply that the world is so constituted that there is only one way to emancipation and that from time to time superior

[1] For some years most scholars accepted the opinion that the Buddha died in 487 B.C. but the most recent researches into the history of the Saisunâga dynasty suggest that the date should be put back to 554 B.C. See Vincent Smith, *Oxford History of India*, p. 52.

minds see this and announce it to others. Still Buddhism does not in practice use such formulae as living in harmony with the laws of nature.

Indian literature is notoriously concerned with ideas rather than facts but the vigorous personality of the Buddha has impressed on it a portrait more distinct than that left by any other teacher or king. His work had a double effect. Firstly it influenced all departments of Hindu religion and thought, even those nominally opposed to it. Secondly it spread not only Buddhism in the strict sense but Indian art and literature beyond the confines of India. The expansion of Hindu culture owes much to the doctrine that the Good Law should be preached to all nations.

The teaching of Gotama was essentially practical. This statement may seem paradoxical to the reader who has some acquaintance with the Buddhist scriptures and he will exclaim that of all religious books they are the least practical and least popular: they set up an anti-social ideal and are mainly occupied with psychological theories. But the Buddha addressed a public such as we now find it hard even to imagine. In those days the intellectual classes of India felt the ordinary activities of life to be unsatisfying: they thought it natural to renounce the world and mortify the flesh: divergent systems of ritual, theology and self-denial promised happiness but all agreed in thinking it normal as well as laudable that a man should devote his life to meditation and study. Compared with this frame of mind the teaching of the Buddha is not unsocial, unpractical and mysterious but human, business-like and clear. We are inclined to see in the monastic life which he recommended little but a useless sacrifice but it is evident that in the opinion of his contemporaries his disciples had an easy time, and that he had no intention of prescribing any cramped or unnatural existence. He accepted the current conviction that those who devote themselves to the things of the mind and spirit should be released from worldly ties and abstain from luxury but he meant his monks to live a life of sustained intellectual activity for themselves and of benevolence for others. His teaching is formulated in severe and technical phraseology, yet the substance of it is so simple that many have criticized it as too obvious and jejune to be the basis of a religion. But when he first enunciated his theses some two thousand five hundred years ago, they were not obvious but revolutionary and little less than paradoxical.

The principal of these propositions are as follows. The existence of everything depends on a cause: hence if the cause of evil or suffering can be detected and removed, evil itself will be removed. That cause is lust and craving for pleasure[1]. Hence all sacrificial and sacramental religions are irrelevant, for the cure which they propose has nothing to do with the disease. The cause of evil or suffering is removed by purifying the heart and by following the moral law which sets high value on sympathy and social duties, but an equally high value on the cultivation of individual character. But training and cultivation imply the possibility of change. Hence it is a fatal mistake in the religious life to hold a view common in India which regards the essence of man as something unchangeable and happy in itself, if it can only be isolated from physical trammels. On the contrary the happy mind is something to be built up by good thoughts, good words and good deeds. In its origin the Buddha's celebrated doctrine that there is no permanent self in persons or things is not a speculative proposition, nor a sentimental lament over the transitoriness of the world, but a basis for religion and morals. You will never be happy unless you realize that you can make and remake your own soul.

These simple principles and the absence of all dogmas as to God or Brahman distinguish the teaching of Gotama from most Indian systems, but he accepted the usual Indian beliefs about Karma and rebirth and with them the usual conclusion that release from the series of rebirths is the *summum bonum*. This deliverance he called saintship (*arahattam*) or nirvana of which I shall say something below. In early Buddhism it is primarily a state of happiness to be attained in this life and the Buddha persistently refused to explain what is the nature of a saint after death. The question is unprofitable and perhaps he would have said, had he spoken our language, unmeaning. Later generations did not hesitate to discuss the problem but the Buddha's

[1] This is sometimes rendered simply by desire but *desire* in English is a vague word and may include feelings which do not come within the Pali *tanhâ*. The Buddha did not reprobate good desires. See Mrs Rhys David's *Buddhism*, p. 222 and *E.R.E.* s.v. Desire.

own teaching is simply that a man can attain before death to a blessed state in which he has nothing to fear from either death or rebirth.

The Buddha attacked both the ritual and the philosophy of the Brahmans. After his time the sacrificial system, though it did not die, never regained its old prestige and he profoundly affected the history of Indian metaphysics. It may be justly said that most of his philosophic as distinguished from his practical teaching was common property before his time, but he transmuted common ideas and gave them a currency and significance which they did not possess before. But he was less destructive as a religious and social reformer than many have supposed. He did not deny the existence nor forbid the worship of the popular gods, but such worship is not Buddhism and the gods are merely angels who may be willing to help good Buddhists but are in no wise guides to religion, since they need instruction themselves. And though he denied that the Brahmans were superior by birth to others, he did not preach against caste, partly because it then existed only in a rudimentary form. But he taught that the road to salvation was one and open to all who were able to walk in it[1], whether Hindus or foreigners. All may not have the necessary qualifications of intellect and character to become monks but all can be good laymen, for whom the religious life means the observance of morality combined with such simple exercises as reading the scriptures. It is clear that this lay Buddhism had much to do with the spread of the faith. The elemental simplicity of its principles—namely that religion is open to all and identical with morality—made a clean sweep of Brahmanic theology and sacrifices and put in its place something like Confucianism. But the innate Indian love for philosophizing and ritual caused generation after generation to add more and more supplements to the Master's teaching and it is only outside India that it has been preserved in any purity.

4. *Asoka*

Gotama spent his life in preaching and by his personal exertions spread his doctrines over Bihar and Oudh but for two

[1] It is practically correct to say that Buddhism was the first universal and missionary religion, but Mahâvîra, the founder of the Jains and probably somewhat slightly his senior, is credited with the same wide view.

centuries after his death we know little of the history of Buddhism. In the reign of Asoka (273–232 B.C.) its fortunes suddenly changed, for this great Emperor whose dominions comprised nearly all India made it the state religion and also engraved on rocks and pillars a long series of edicts recording his opinions and aspirations. Buddhism is often criticized as a gloomy and unpractical creed, suited at best to stoical and scholarly recluses. But these are certainly not its characteristics when it first appears in political history, just as they are not its characteristics in Burma or Japan to-day. Both by precept and example Asoka was an ardent exponent of the strenuous life. In his first edict he lays down the principle "Let small and great exert themselves" and in subsequent inscriptions he continually harps upon the necessity of energy and exertion. The Law or Religion (Dhamma) which his edicts enjoin is merely human and civic virtue, except that it makes respect for animal life an integral part of morality. In one passage he summarizes it as "Little impiety, many good deeds, compassion, liberality, truthfulness and purity." He makes no reference to a supreme deity, but insists on the reality and importance of the future life. Though he does not use the word *Karma* this is clearly the conception which dominates his philosophy: those who do good are happy in this world and the next but those who fail in their duty win neither heaven nor the royal favour. The king's creed is remarkable in India for its great simplicity. He deprecates superstitious ceremonies and says nothing of Nirvana but dwells on morality as necessary to happiness in this life and others. This is not the whole of Gotama's teaching but two centuries after his death a powerful and enlightened Buddhist gives it as the gist of Buddhism for laymen.

Asoka wished to make Buddhism the creed not only of India but of the world as known to him and he boasts that he extended his "conquests of religion" to the Hellenistic kingdoms of the west. If the missions which he despatched thither reached their destination, there is little evidence that they bore any fruit, but the conversion of Ceylon and some districts in the Himalayas seems directly due to his initiative.

5. *Extension of Buddhism and Hinduism beyond India*

This is perhaps a convenient place to review the extension of Buddhism and Hinduism outside India. To do so at this point implies of course an anticipation of chronology, but to delay the survey might blind the reader to the fact that from the time of Asoka onward India was engaged not only in creating but also in exporting new varieties of religious thought.

The countries which have received Indian culture fall into two classes: first those to which it came as a result of religious missions or of peaceful international intercourse, and second those where it was established after conquest or at least colonization. In the first class the religion introduced was Buddhism. If, as in Tibet, it seems to us mixed with Hinduism, yet it was a mixture which at the date of its introduction passed in India for Buddhism. But in the second and smaller class including Java, Camboja and Champa the immigrants brought with them both Hinduism and Buddhism. The two systems were often declared to be the same but the result was Hinduism mixed with some Buddhism, not *vice versâ*.

The countries of the first class comprise Ceylon, Burma and Siam, Central Asia, Nepal, China with Annam, Korea and Japan, Tibet with Mongolia. The Buddhism of the first three countries[1] is a real unity or in European language a church, for though they have no common hierarchy they use the same sacred language, Pali, and have the same canon. Burma and Siam have repeatedly recognized Ceylon as a sort of metropolitan see and on the other hand when religion in Ceylon fell on evil days the clergy were recruited from Burma and Siam. In the other countries Buddhism presents greater differences and divisions. It had no one sacred language and in different regions used either Sanskrit texts or translations into Chinese, Tibetan, Mongolian and the languages of Central Asia.

1. Ceylon. There is no reason to doubt that Buddhism was introduced under the auspices of Asoka. Though the invasions and settlements of Tamils have brought Hinduism into Ceylon,

[1] It may be conveniently and correctly called Pali Buddhism. This is better than Southern Buddhism or Hînayâna, for the Buddhism of Java which lies even farther to the south is not the same and there were formerly Hînayânists in Central Asia and China.

yet none of the later and mixed forms of Buddhism, in spite of some attempts to gain a footing, ever flourished there on a large scale. Sinhalese Buddhism had probably a closer connection with southern India than the legend suggests and Conjevaram was long a Buddhist centre which kept up intercourse with both Ceylon and Burma.

2. Burma. The early history of Burmese Buddhism is obscure and its origin probably complex, since at many different periods it may have received teachers from both India and China. The present dominant type (identical with the Buddhism of Ceylon) existed before the sixth century[1] and tradition ascribes its introduction both to the labours of Buddhaghosa and to the missionaries of Asoka. There was probably a connection between Pegu and Conjevaram. In the eleventh century Burmese Buddhism had become extremely corrupt except in Pegu but King Anawrata conquered Pegu and spread a purer form throughout his dominions.

3. Siam. The Thai race, who starting from somewhere in the Chinese province of Yünnan began to settle in what is now called Siam about the beginning of the twelfth century, probably brought with them some form of Buddhism. About 1300 the possessions of Râma Komhëng, King of Siam, included Pegu and Pali Buddhism prevailed among his subjects. Somewhat later, in 1361, a high ecclesiastic was summoned from Ceylon to arrange the affairs of the church but not, it would seem, to introduce any new doctrine. Pegu was the centre from which Pali Buddhism spread to upper Burma in the eleventh century and it probably performed the same service for Siam later. The modern Buddhism of Camboja is simply Siamese Buddhism which filtered into the country from about 1250 onwards. The older Buddhism of Camboja, for which see below, was quite different.

At the courts of Siam and Camboja, as formerly in Burma, there are Brahmans who perform state ceremonies and act as astrologers. Though they have little to do with the religion of the people, their presence explains the predominance of Indian rather than Chinese influence in these countries.

4. Tradition says that Indian colonists settled in Khotan during the reign of Asoka, but no precise date can at present be

[1] See Finot, *J.A.* 1912, II. 121–136.

fixed for the introduction of Buddhism into the Tarim basin and other regions commonly called Central Asia. But it must have been flourishing there about the time of the Christian era, since it spread thence to China not later than the middle of the first century. There were two schools representing two distinct currents from India. First the Sarvâstivâdin school, prevalent in Badakshan, Kashgar and Kucha, secondly the Mahâyâna in Khotan and Yarkand. The spread of the former was no doubt connected with the growth of the Kushan Empire but may be anterior to the conversion of Kanishka, for though he gave a great impetus to the propagation of the faith, it is probable that, like most royal converts, he favoured an already popular religion. The Mahâyâna subsequently won much territory from the other school.

5. As in other countries, so in China Buddhism entered by more than one road. It came first by land from Central Asia. The official date for its introduction by this route is 62 A.D. but it was probably known within the Chinese frontier before that time, though not recognized by the state. Secondly when Buddhism was established, there arose a desire for accurate knowledge of the true Indian doctrine. Chinese pilgrims went to India and Indian teachers came to China. After the fourth century many of these religious journeys were made by sea and it was thus that Bodhidharma landed at Canton in 520[1]. A third stream of Buddhism, namely Lamaism, came into China from Tibet under the Mongol dynasty (1280). Khubilai considered this the best religion for his Mongols and numerous Lamaist temples and convents were established and still exist in northern China. Lamaism has not perhaps been a great religious or intellectual force there, but its political importance was considerable, for the Ming and Manchu dynasties who wished to assert their rule over the Tibetans and Mongols by peaceful methods, consistently strove to win the goodwill of the Lamaist clergy.

The Buddhism of Korea, Japan and Annam is directly derived from the earlier forms of Chinese Buddhism but was not affected by the later influx of Lamaism. Buddhism passed from China into Korea in the fourth century and thence to Japan in

[1] There is no Indian record of Bodhidharma's doctrine and its origin is obscure, but it seems to have been a compound of Buddhism and Vedantism.

the sixth. In the latter country it was stimulated by frequent contact with China and the repeated introduction of new Chinese sects but was not appreciably influenced by direct intercourse with Hindus or other foreign Buddhists. In the twelfth and thirteenth centuries Japanese Buddhism showed great vitality, transforming old sects and creating new ones.

In the south, Chinese Buddhism spread into Annam rather late: according to native tradition in the tenth century. This region was a battlefield of two cultures. Chinese influence descending southwards from Canton proved predominant and, after the triumph of Annam over Champa, extended to the borders of Camboja. But so long as the kingdom of Champa existed, Indian culture and Hinduism maintained themselves at least as far north as Hué.

6. The Buddhism of Tibet is a late and startling transformation of Gotama's teaching, but the transformation is due rather to the change and degeneration of that teaching in Bengal than to the admixture of Tibetan ideas. Such admixture however was not absent and a series of reformers endeavoured to bring the church back to what they considered the true standard. The first introduction is said to have occurred in 630 but probably the arrival of Padma Sambhava from India in 747 marks the real foundation of the Lamaist church. It was reformed by the Hindu Atîśa in 1038 and again by the Tibetan Tsong-kha-pa about 1400.

The Grand Lama is the head of the church as reorganized by Tsong-kha-pa. In Tibet the priesthood attained to temporal power comparable with the Papacy. The disintegration of the government divided the whole land into small principalities and among these the great monasteries were as important as any temporal lord. The abbots of the Sakya monastery were the practical rulers of Tibet for seventy years (1270–1340). Another period of disintegration followed but after 1630 the Grand Lamas of Lhasa were able to claim and maintain a similar position.

Mongolian Buddhism is a branch of Lamaism distinguished by no special doctrines. The Mongols were partially converted in the time of Khubilai and a second time and more thoroughly in 1570 by the third Grand Lama.

7. Nepal exhibits another phase of degeneration. In Tibet Indian Buddhism passed into the hands of a vigorous national

priesthood and was not exposed to the assimilative influence of Hinduism. In Nepal it had not the same defence. It probably existed there since the time of Asoka and underwent the same phases of decay and corruption as in Bengal. But whereas the last great monasteries in Bengal were shattered by the Mohammedan invasion of 1193, the secluded valley of Nepal was protected against such violence and Buddhism continued to exist there in name. It has preserved a good deal of Sanskrit Buddhist literature but has become little more than a sect of Hinduism.

Nepal ought perhaps to be classed in our second division, that is those countries where Indian culture was introduced not by missionaries but by the settlement of Indian conquerors or immigrants. To this class belong the Hindu civilizations of Indo-China and the Archipelago. In all of these Hinduism and Mahayanist Buddhism are found mixed together, Hinduism being the stronger element. The earliest Sanskrit inscription in these regions is that of Vochan in Champa which is apparently Buddhist. It is not later than the third century and refers to an earlier king, so that an Indian dynasty probably existed there about 150–200 A.D. Though the presence of Indian culture is beyond dispute, it is not clear whether the Chams were civilized in Champa by Hindu invaders or whether they were hinduized Malays who invaded Champa from elsewhere.

8. In Camboja a Hindu dynasty was founded by invaders and the Brahmans who accompanied them established a counterpart to it in a powerful hierarchy, Sanskrit becoming the language of religion. It is clear that these invaders came ultimately from India but they may have halted in Java or the Malay Peninsula for an unknown period. The Brahmanic hierarchy began to fail about the fourteenth century and was supplanted by Siamese Buddhism. Before that time the state religion of both Champa and Camboja was the worship of Śiva, especially in the form called Mukhalinga. Mahayanist Buddhism, tending to identify Buddha with Śiva, also existed but enjoyed less of the royal patronage.

9. Religious conditions were similar in Java but politically there was this difference, that there was no one continuous and paramount kingdom. A considerable number of Hindus must have settled in the island to produce such an effect on its

language and architecture but the rulers of the states known to us were hinduized Javanese rather than true Hindus and the language of literature and of most inscriptions was Old Javanese, not Sanskrit, though most of the works written in it were translations or adaptations of Sanskrit originals. As in Camboja, Śivaism and Buddhism both flourished without mutual hostility and there was less difference in the status of the two creeds.

In all these countries religion seems to have been connected with politics more closely than in India. The chief shrine was a national cathedral, the living king was semi-divine and dead kings were represented by statues bearing the attributes of their favourite gods.

6. *New Forms of Buddhism*

In the three or four centuries following Asoka a surprising change came over Indian Buddhism, but though the facts are clear it is hard to connect them with dates and persons. But the change was clearly posterior to Asoka for though his edicts show a spirit of wide charity it is not crystallized in the form of certain doctrines which subsequently became prominent.

The first of these holds up as the moral ideal not personal perfection or individual salvation but the happiness of all living creatures. The good man who strives for this should boldly aspire to become a Buddha in some future birth and such aspirants are called Bodhisattvas. Secondly Buddhas and some Bodhisattvas come to be considered as supernatural beings and practically deities. The human life of Gotama, though not denied, is regarded as the manifestation of a cosmic force which also reveals itself in countless other Buddhas who are not merely his predecessors or destined successors but the rulers of paradises in other worlds. Faith in a Buddha, especially in Amitâbha, can secure rebirth in his paradise. The great Bodhisattvas, such as Avalokita and Mañjuśrî, are splendid angels of mercy and knowledge who are theoretically distinguished from Buddhas because they have indefinitely postponed their entry into nirvana in order to alleviate the sufferings of the world. These new tenets are accompanied by a remarkable development of art and of idealist metaphysics.

This new form of Buddhism is called Mahâyâna, or the

Great Vehicle, as opposed to the Small Vehicle or Hînayâna, a somewhat contemptuous name given to the older school. The idea underlying these phrases is that sects are merely coaches, all travelling on the same road to salvation though some may be quicker than others. The Mahayana did not suppress the Hinayana but it gradually absorbed the traffic.

The causes of this transformation were two-fold, internal or Indian and external. Buddhism was a living, that is changing, stream of thought and the Hindus as a nation have an exceptional taste and capacity for metaphysics. This taste was not destroyed by Gotama's dicta as to the limits of profitable knowledge nor did new deities arouse hostility because they were not mentioned in the ancient scriptures. The development of Brahmanism and Buddhism was parallel: if an attractive novelty appeared in one, something like it was soon provided by the other. Thus the Bhagavad-gîtâ contains the ideas of the Mahayana in substance, though in a different setting: it praises disinterested activity and insists on faith. It is clear that at this period all Indian thought and not merely Buddhism was vivified and transmuted by two great currents of feeling demanding, the one a more emotional morality the other more personal and more sympathetic deities.

I shall show in more detail below that most Mahayanist doctrines, though apparently new, have their roots in old Indian ideas. But the presence of foreign influences is not to be disputed and there is no difficulty in accounting for them. Gandhara was a Persian province from 530 to 330 B.C. and in the succeeding centuries the north-western parts of India experienced the invasions and settlements of numerous aliens, such as Greeks from the Hellenistic kingdoms which arose after Alexander's expedition, Parthians, Sakas and Kushans. Such immigrants, even if they had no culture of their own, at least transported culture, just as the Turks introduced Islam into Europe. Thus whatever ideas were prevalent in Persia, in the Hellenistic kingdoms, or in Central Asia may also have been prevalent in north-western India, where was situated the university town of Taxila frequently mentioned in the Jâtakas as a seat of Buddhist learning. The foreigners who entered India adopted Indian religions[1] and probably Buddhism more often

[1] This is proved by coins and also by the Besnagar inscription.

than Hinduism, for it was at that time predominant and disposed to evangelize without raising difficulties as to caste.

Foreign influences stimulated mythology and imagery. In the reliefs of Asoka's time, the image of the Buddha never appears, and, as in the earliest Christian art, the intention of the sculptors is to illustrate an edifying narrative rather than to provide an object of worship. But in the Gandharan sculptures, which are a branch of Græco-Roman art, he is habitually represented by a figure modelled on the conventional type of Apollo. The gods of India were not derived from Greece but they were stereotyped under the influence of western art to this extent that familiarity with such figures as Apollo and Pallas encouraged the Hindus to represent their gods and heroes in human or quasi-human shapes. The influence of Greece on Indian religion was not profound: it did not affect the architecture or ritual of temples and still less thought or doctrine. But when Indian religion and especially Buddhism passed into the hands of men accustomed to Greek statuary, the inclination to venerate definite personalities having definite shapes was strengthened[1].

Persian influence was stronger than Greek. To it are probably due the many radiant deities who shed their beneficent glory over the Mahayanist pantheon, as well as the doctrine that Bodhisattvas are emanations of Buddhas. The discoveries of Stein, Pelliot and others have shown that this influence extended across Central Asia to China and one of the most important turns in the fortunes of Buddhism was its association with a Central Asian tribe analogous to the Turks and called Kushans or Yüeh-chih, whose territories lay without as well as within the frontiers of modern India and who borrowed much of their culture from Persia and some from the Greeks. Their great king Kanishka is a figure in Buddhist annals second only to Asoka. Unfortunately his date is still a matter of discussion. The majority of scholars place his accession about 78 A.D. but

[1] I do not think that this view is disproved by the fact that Patañjali and the scholiasts on Pâṇini allude to images for they also allude to Greeks. For the contrary view see Sten Konow in *I.A.* 1909, p. 145. The facts are (*a*) The ancient Brahmanic ritual used no images. (*b*) They were used by Buddhism and popular Hinduism about the fourth century B.C. (*c*) Alexander conquered Bactria in 329 B.C. But allowance must be made for the usages of popular and especially of Dravidian worship of which at this period we know nothing.

some put it rather later[1]. The evidence of numismatics and of art indicates that he came towards the end of his dynasty rather than at the beginning and the tradition which makes Aśvaghosha his contemporary is compatible with the later date.

Some writers describe Kanishka as the special patron of Mahayanism. But the description is of doubtful accuracy. The style of religious art known as Gandharan flourished in his reign and he convened a council which fixed the canon of the Sarvâstivâdins. This school was reckoned as Hinayanist and though Aśvaghosha enjoys general fame in the Far East as a Mahayanist doctor, yet his undoubted writings are not Mahayanist in the strict sense of the word[2]. But a more ornate and mythological form of religion was becoming prevalent and perhaps Kanishka's Council arranged some compromise between the old and the new.

After Aśvaghosha comes Nâgârjuna who may have flourished any time between 125 and 200 A.D. A legend which makes him live for 300 years is not without significance, for he represents a movement and a school as much as a personality and if he taught in the second century A.D. he cannot have been the *founder* of Mahayanism. Yet he seems to be the first great name definitely connected with it and the ascription to him of numerous later treatises, though unwarrantable, shows that his authority was sufficient to stamp a work or a doctrine as orthodox Mahayanism. His biographies connect him with the system of idealist or nihilistic metaphysics expounded in the literature (for it is more than a single work) called Prajñâpâramitâ, with magical practices (by which the power of summoning Bodhisattvas or deities is specially meant) and with the worship of Amitâbha. His teacher Saraha, a foreigner, is said to have been the first who taught this worship in India. In this there may be a kernel of truth but otherwise the extant accounts of Nâgârjuna are too legendary to permit of historical deductions. He was perhaps the first eminent exponent of Mahayanist metaphysics, but the train of thought was not new: it was the result of applying to the external world the same destructive logic which Gotama applied to the soul and the result had considerable analogies to Śankara's version of the Vedanta. Whether in the

[1] Few now advocate an earlier date such as 58 B.C.

[2] His authorship of *The Awakening of Faith* must be regarded as doubtful.

second century A.D. the leaders of Buddhism already identified themselves with the sorcery which demoralized late Indian Mahayanism may be doubted, but tradition certainly ascribes to Nâgârjuna this corrupting mixture of metaphysics and magic.

The third century offers a strange blank in Indian history. Little can be said except that the power of the Kushans decayed and that northern India was probably invaded by Persians and Central Asian tribes. The same trouble did not affect southern India and it may be that religion and speculation flourished there and spread northwards, as certainly happened in later times. Many of the greatest Hindu teachers were Dravidians and at the present day it is in the Dravidian regions that the temples are most splendid, the Brahmans strictest and most respected. It may be that this Dravidian influence affected even Buddhism in the third century A.D., for Aryadeva the successor of Nâgârjuna was a southerner and the legends told of him recall certain Dravidian myths. Bodhidharma too came from the South and imported into China a form of Buddhism which has left no record in India.

7. *Revival of Hinduism*

In 320 a native Indian dynasty, the Guptas, came to the throne and inaugurated a revival of Hinduism, to which religion we must now turn. To speak of the revival of Hinduism does not mean that in the previous period it had been dead or torpid. Indeed we know that there was a Hindu reaction against the Buddhism of Asoka about 150 B.C. But, on the whole, from the time of Asoka onwards Buddhism had been the principal religion of India, and before the Gupta era there are hardly any records of donations made to Brahmans. Yet during these centuries they were not despised or oppressed. They produced much literature[1]: their schools of philosophy and ritual did not decay and they gradually made good their claim to be the priests of India's gods, whoever those gods might be. The difference between the old religion and the new lies in this. The Brâhmaṇas and Upanishads describe practices and doctrines of considerable

[1] Much of the Ramayana and Mahabharata must have been composed during this period, both poems (especially the latter) consisting of several strata.

variety but still all the property of a privileged class in a special region. They do not represent popular religion nor the religion of India as a whole. But in the Gupta period Hinduism began to do this. It is not a system like Islam or even Buddhism but a parliament of religions, of which every Indian creed can become a member on condition of observing some simple rules of the house, such as respect for Brahmans and theoretical acceptance of the Veda. Nothing is abolished: the ancient rites and texts preserve their mysterious power and kings perform the horse-sacrifice. But side by side with this, deities unknown to the Veda rise to the first rank and it is frankly admitted that new revelations more suited to the age have been given to mankind.

Art too enters on a new phase. In the early Indian sculptures deities are mostly portrayed in human form, but in about the first century of our era there is seen a tendency to depict them with many heads and limbs and this tendency grows stronger until in mediæval times it is predominant. It has its origin in symbolism. The deity is thought of as carrying many insignia, as performing more actions than two hands can indicate; the worshipper is taught to think of him as appearing in this shape and the artist does not hesitate to represent it in paint and stone.

As we have seen, the change which came over Buddhism was partly due to foreign influences and no doubt they affected most Indian creeds. But the prodigious amplification of Hinduism was mainly due to the absorption of beliefs prevalent in Indian districts other than the homes of the ancient Brahmans. Thus south Indian religion is characterized when we first know it by its emotional tone and it resulted in the mediæval Sivaism of the Tamil country. In another region, probably in the west, grew up the monotheism of the Bhâgavatas, which was the parent of Vishnuism.

Hinduism may be said to fall into four principal divisions which are really different religions: the Smârtas or traditionalists, the Sivaites, the Vishnuites and the Śâktas. The first, who are still numerous, represent the pre-buddhist Brahmans. They follow, so far as modern circumstances permit, the ancient ritual and are apparent polytheists while accepting pantheism as the higher truth. Vishnuites and Sivaites however are monotheists in the sense that their minor deities are not essentially different from the saints of Roman and Eastern Christianity but their monotheism has a pantheistic tinge. Neither sect denies the existence of the rival god, but each makes its own deity God, not only in the theistic but in the pantheistic sense and regards the other deity as merely an influential angel. From time to time the impropriety of thus specially deifying one aspect of the universal spirit made itself felt and then Vishnu and Śiva were adored in a composite dual form or, with the addition of Brahmâ, as a trinity. But this triad had not great importance and it is a mistake to compare it with the Christian trinity. Strong as was the tendency to combine and amalgamate deities, it was mastered in these religions by the desire to have one definite God, personal inasmuch as he can receive and return love, although the Indian feeling that God must be all and in all continually causes the conceptions called Vishnu and Śiva to transcend the limits of personality. This feeling is specially clear in the growth of Râma and Krishna worship. Both of these deities were originally ancient heroes, and stories of love and battle cling to them in their later phases. Yet for their respective devotees each becomes God in every sense, God as lover of the soul, God as ruler of the universe and the God of pantheism who is all that exists and can exist.

For some time before and after the beginning of our era, north-western India witnessed a great fusion of ideas and Indian, Persian and Greek religion must have been in contact at the university town of Taxila and many other places. Kashmir too, if somewhat too secluded to be a meeting-place of nations, was a considerable intellectual centre. We have not yet sufficient documents to enable us to trace the history and especially the chronology of thought in these regions but we can say that certain forms of Vishnuism, Śivaism and Buddhism were all evolved there and often show features in common. Thus in all we find the idea that the divine nature is manifested in four forms or five, if we count the Absolute Godhead as one of them[1].

I shall consider at length below this worship of Vishnu and

[1] *E.g.* the Vyûhas of the Pâncarâtras, the five Jinas of the Mahayanists and the five Sadâśiva tattvas. See Gopinâtha Rao, *Elements of Indian Iconography*, vol. III. p. 363.

Śiva and here will merely point out that it differs from the polytheism of the Smârtas. In their higher phases all Hindu religions agree in teaching some form of pantheism, some laying more and some less stress on the personal aspect which the deity can assume. But whereas the pantheism of the Smârtas grew out of the feeling that the many gods of tradition must all be one, the pantheism of the Vishnuites was not evolved out of pre-buddhist Brahmanism and is due to the conviction that the one God must be everything. It is Indian but it grew up in some region outside Brahmanic influence and was accepted by the Brahmans as a permissible creed, but many legends in the Epics and Puranas indicate that there was hostility between the old-fashioned Brahmans and the worshippers of Râma, Krishna and Śiva before the alliance was made.

Śâktism[1] also was not evolved from ancient Brahmanism but is different in tone from Vishnuism and Sivaism. Whereas they start from a movement of thought and spiritual feeling, Śâktism has for its basis certain ancient popular worships. With these it has combined much philosophy and has attempted to bring its teaching into conformity with Brahmanism, but yet remains somewhat apart. It worships a goddess of many names and forms, who is adored with sexual rites and the sacrifice of animals, or, when the law permits, of men. It asserts even more plainly than Vishnuism that the teaching of the Vedas is too difficult for these latter days and even useless, and it offers to its followers new scriptures called Tantras and new ceremonies as all-sufficient. It is true that many Hindus object to this sect, which may be compared with the Mormons in America or the Skoptsy in Russia, and it is numerous only in certain parts of India (especially Bengal and Assam) but since a section of Brahmans patronize it, it must be reckoned as a phase of Hinduism and even at the present day it is an important phase.

There are many cults prevalent in India, though not recognized as sects, in which the worship of some aboriginal deity is accepted in all its crudeness without much admixture of philosophy, the only change being that the deity is described

[1] I draw a distinction between Śâktism and Tantrism. The essence of Śâktism is the worship of a goddess with certain rites. Tantrism means rather the use of spells, gestures, diagrams and various magical or sacramental rites, which accompanies Śâktism but may exist without it.

as a form, incarnation or servant of some well-known god and that Brahmans are connected with this worship. This habit of absorbing aboriginal superstitions materially lowers the average level of creed and ritual. An educated Brahman would laugh at the idea that village superstitions can be taken seriously as religion but he does not condemn them and, as superstitions, he does not disbelieve in them. It is chiefly owing to this habit that Hinduism has spread all over India and its treatment of men and gods is curiously parallel. Princes like the Manipuris of Assam came under Hindu influence and were finally recognized as Kshattiyas with an imaginary pedigree, and on the same principle their deities are recognized as forms of Siva or Durga. And Siva and Durga themselves were built up in past ages out of aboriginal beliefs, though the cement holding their figures together is Indian thought and philosophy, which are able to see in grotesque rustic godlings an expression of cosmic forces.

Though this is the principal method by which Hinduism has been propagated, direct missionary effort has not been wanting. For instance a large part of Assam was converted by the preaching of Vishnuite teachers in the sixteenth century and the process still continues[1]. But on the whole the missionary spirit characterizes Buddhism rather than Hinduism. Buddhist missionaries preached their faith, without any political motive, wherever they could penetrate. But in such countries as Camboja, Hinduism was primarily the religion of the foreign settlers and when the political power of the Brahmans began to wane, the people embraced Buddhism. Outside India it was perhaps only in Java and the neighbouring islands that Hinduism (with an admixture of Buddhism) became the religion of the natives.

Many features of Hinduism, its steady though slow conquest of India, its extraordinary vitality and tenacity in resisting the attacks of Mohammedanism, and its small power of expansion beyond the seas are explained by the fact that it is a mode of life as much as a faith. To be a Hindu it is not sufficient to hold the doctrine of the Upanishads or any other scriptures: it is necessary to be a member of a Hindu caste and observe

[1] According to *Census of India*, 1911, *Assam*, p. 47, about 80,000 animists were converted to Hinduism in Goalpara between 1901 and 1911 by a Brahman called Sib Narayan Swami.

its regulations. It is not quite correct to say that one must be born a Hindu, since Hinduism has grown by gradually hinduizing the wilder tribes of India and the process still continues. But a convert cannot enter the fold by any simple ceremony like baptism. The community to which he belongs must adopt Hindu usages and then it will be recognized as a caste, at first of very low standing but in a few generations it may rise in the general esteem. A Hindu is bound to his religion by almost the same ties that bind him to his family. Hence the strength of Hinduism in India. But such ties are hard to knit and Hinduism has no chance of spreading abroad unless there is a large colony of Hindus surrounded by an appreciative and imitative population[1].

In the contest between Hinduism and Buddhism the former owed the victory which it obtained in India, though not in other lands, to this assimilative social influence. The struggle continued from the fourth to the ninth century, after which Buddhism was clearly defeated and survived only in special localities. Its final disappearance was due to the destruction of its remaining monasteries by Moslem invaders but this blow was fatal only because Buddhism was concentrated in its monkhood. Innumerable Hindu temples were destroyed, yet Hinduism was at no time in danger of extinction.

The Hindu reaction against Buddhism became apparent under the Gupta dynasty but Mahayanism in its use of Sanskrit and its worship of Bodhisattvas shows the beginnings of the same movement. The danger for Buddhism was not persecution but tolerance and obliteration of differences. The Guptas were not bigots. It was probably in their time that the oldest Puranas, the laws of Manu and the Mahabharata received their final form. These are on the whole text-books of Smârta Hinduism and two Gupta monarchs celebrated the horse sacrifice. But the Mahabharata contains several episodes which justify the exclusive worship of either Vishnu or Siva, and the architecture of the Guptas suggests that they were Vishnuites. They also bestowed favours on Buddhism which was not yet decadent, for Vasubandhu and Asanga, who probably lived in the fourth century, were constructive thinkers. It is true that their

[1] It is said that in Burma Hindu settlers become absorbed in the surrounding Buddhists. *Census of India*, 1911, I. p. 120.

additions were of the dangerous kind which render an edifice top-heavy but their works show vitality and had a wide influence[1]. The very name of Asanga's philosophy—Yogâcârya—indicates its affinity to Brahmanic thought, as do his doctrines of Alayavijñâna and Bodhi, which permit him to express in Buddhist language the idea that the soul may be illumined by the deity. In some cases Hinduism, in others Buddhism, may have played the receptive part but the general result—namely the diminution of differences between the two—was always the same.

The Hun invasions were unfavourable to religious and intellectual activity in the north and, just as in the time of Moslim inroads, their ravages had more serious consequences for Buddhism than for Hinduism. The great Emperor Harsha (†647), of whom we know something from Bâṇa and Hsüan Chuang, became at the end of his life a zealous but eclectic Buddhist. Yet it is plain from Hsüan Chuang's account that at this time Buddhism was decadent in most districts both of the north and south.

This decadence was hastened by an unfortunate alliance with those forms of magic and erotic mysticism which are called Śâktism[2]. It is difficult to estimate the extent of the corruption, for the singularity of the evil, a combination of the austere and ethical teaching of Gotama with the most fantastic form of Hinduism, arrests attention and perhaps European scholars have written more about it than it deserves. It did not touch the Hinayanist churches nor appreciably infect the Buddhism of the Far East, nor even (it would seem) Indian Buddhism outside Bengal and Orissa. Unfortunately Magadha, which was both the home and last asylum of the faith, was also very near the regions where Śâktism most flourished. It is, as I have often noticed in these pages, a peculiarity of all Indian sects that in matters of belief they are not exclusive nor hostile to novelties. When a new idea wins converts it is the instinct of the older sects to declare that it is

[1] The life and writings of Vasubandhu illustrate the transition from the Hina- to the Mahayana. In the earlier part of his life he wrote the Abhidharmakośa which is still used by Mahayanists in Japan as a text-book, though it does not go beyond Hinayanism. Later he became a Mahayanist and wrote Mahayanist works.

[2] As already mentioned, I think Śâktism is the more appropriate word but Tantrism is in common use by the best authorities.

compatible with their teaching or that they have something similar and just as good. It was in this fashion that the Buddhists of Magadha accepted Śâktist and tantric ideas. If Hinduism could summon gods and goddesses by magical methods, they could summon Bodhisattvas, male and female, in the same way, and these spirits were as good as the gods. In justice it must be said that despite distortions and monstrous accretions the real teaching of Gotama did not entirely disappear even in Magadha and Tibet.

8. *Later Forms of Hinduism*

In the eighth and ninth centuries this degenerate Buddhism was exposed to the attacks of the great Hindu champions Kumârila and Śankara, though it probably endured little persecution in our sense of the word. Both of them were Smârtas or traditionalists and laboured in the cause not of Vishnuism or Śivaism but of the ancient Brahmanic religion, amplified by many changes which the ages had brought but holding up as the religious ideal a manhood occupied with ritual observances, followed by an old age devoted to philosophy. Śankara was the greater of the two and would have a higher place among the famous names of the world had not his respect for tradition prevented him from asserting the originality which he undoubtedly possessed. Yet many remarkable features of his life work, both practical and intellectual, are due to imitation of the Buddhists and illustrate the dictum that Buddhism did not disappear from India[1] until Hinduism had absorbed from it all the good that it had to offer. Śankara took Buddhist institutions as his model in rearranging the ascetic orders of Hinduism, and his philosophy, a rigorously consistent pantheism which ascribed all apparent multiplicity and difference to illusion, is indebted to Mahayanist speculation. It is remarkable that his opponents stigmatized him as a Buddhist in disguise and his system, though it is one of the most influential lines of

[1] In India proper there are hardly any Buddhists now. The Kumbhipathias, an anti-Brahmanic sect in Orissa, are said to be based on Buddhist doctrines and a Buddhist mission in Mysore, called the Sakya Buddhist Society, has met with some success. See *Census of India*, 1911, I. pp. 122 and 126.

thought among educated Hindus, is anathematized by some theistic sects[1].

Śankara was a native of southern India. It is not easy to combine in one picture the progress of thought in the north and south, and for the earlier centuries our information as to the Dravidian countries is meagre. Yet they cannot be omitted, for their influence on the whole of India was great. Greeks, Kushans, Huns, and Mohammedans penetrated into the north but, until after the fall of Vijayanagar in 1565, no invader professing a foreign religion entered the country of the Tamils. Left in peace they elaborated their own version of current theological problems and the result spread over India. Buddhism and Jainism also flourished in the south. The former was introduced under Asoka but apparently ceased to be the dominant religion (if it ever was so) in the early centuries of our era. Still even in the eleventh century monasteries were built in Mysore. Jainism had a distinguished but chequered career in the south. It was powerful in the seventh century but subsequently endured considerable persecution. It still exists and possesses remarkable monuments at Sravana Belgola and elsewhere.

But the characteristic form of Dravidian religion is an emotional theism, running in the parallel channels of Vishnuism and Śivaism and accompanied by humbler but vigorous popular superstitions, which reveal the origin of its special temperament. For the frenzied ecstasies of devil dancers (to use a current though inaccurate phrase) are a primitive expression of the same sentiment which sees in the whole world the exulting energy and rhythmic force of Siva. And though the most rigid Brahmanism still flourishes in the Madras Presidency there is audible in the Dravidian hymns a distinct note of anti-sacerdotalism and of belief that every man by his own efforts can come into immediate contact with the Great Being whom he worships.

The Vishnuism and Śivaism of the south go back to the early centuries of our era, but the chronology is difficult. In both there is a line of poet-saints followed by philosophers and teachers and in both a considerable collection of Tamil hymns esteemed as equivalent to the Veda. Perhaps Śivaism was

[1] See the quotation in Schomerus, *Der Śaiva Siddhânta*, p. 20 where a Śaiva Hindu says that he would rather see India embrace Christianity than the doctrine of Śankara.

dominant first and Vishnuism somewhat later but at no epoch did either extinguish the other. It was the object of Śankara to bring these valuable but dangerous forces, as well as much Buddhist doctrine and practice, into harmony with Brahmanism.

Islam first entered India in 712 but it was some time before it passed beyond the frontier provinces and for many centuries it was too hostile and aggressive to invite imitation, but the spectacle of a strong community pledged to the worship of a single personal God produced an effect. In the period extending from the eighth to the twelfth centuries, in which Buddhism practically disappeared and Islam came to the front as a formidable though not irresistible antagonist, the dominant form of Hinduism was that which finds expression in the older Puranas, in the temples of Orissa and Khajarao and the Kailâsa at Ellora. It is the worship of one god, either Siva or Vishnu, but a monotheism adorned with a luxuriant mythology and delighting in the manifold shapes which the one deity assumes. It freely used the terminology of the Sânkhya but the first place in philosophy belonged to the severe pantheism of Śankara which, in contrast to this riotous exuberance of legend and sculpture, sees the highest truth in one Being to whom no epithets can be applied.

In the next epoch, say the twelfth to the seventeenth centuries, Indian thought clearly hankers after theism in the western sense and yet never completely acquiesces in it. Mythology, if still rampant according to our taste, at least becomes subsidiary and more detachable from the supreme deity, and this deity, if less anthropomorphic than Allah or Jehovah, is still a being who loves and helps souls, and these souls are explained in varying formulae as being identical with him and yet distinct.

It can hardly be by chance that as the Hindus became more familiar with Islam their sects grew more definite in doctrine and organization especially among the Vishnuites who showed a greater disposition to form sects than the Sivaites, partly because the incarnations of Vishnu offer an obvious ground for diversity. About 1100 A.D.[1] the first great Vaishnava sect was founded by Râmânuja. He was a native of the Madras country and claimed to be the spiritual descendant of the early Tamil

[1] Some think that the sect called Nimâvats was earlier.

saints. In doctrine he expressly accepted the views of the ancient Bhâgavatas, which had been condemned by Śankara, and he affirmed the existence of one personal deity commonly spoken of as Nârâyaṇa or Vâsudeva.

From the time of Śankara onwards nearly all Hindu theologians of the first rank expounded their views by writing a commentary on the Brahma Sûtras, an authoritative but singularly enigmatic digest of the Upanishads. Śankara's doctrine may be summarized as absolute monism which holds that nothing really exists but Brahman and that Brahman is identical with the soul. All apparent plurality is due to illusion. He draws a distinction between the lower and higher Brahman which perhaps may be rendered by God and the Godhead. In the same sense in which individual souls and matter exist, a personal God also exists, but the higher truth is that individuality, personality and matter are all illusion. But the teaching of Râmânuja rejects the doctrines that the world is an illusion and that there is a distinction between the lower and higher Brahman and it affirms that the soul, though of the same substance as God and emitted from him rather than created, can obtain bliss not in absorption but in existence near him.

It is round these problems that Hindu theology turns. The innumerable solutions lack neither boldness nor variety but they all try to satisfy both the philosopher and the saint and none achieve both tasks. The system of Śankara is a masterpiece of intellect, despite his disparagement of reasoning in theology, and could inspire a fine piety, as when on his deathbed he asked forgiveness for having frequented temples, since by so doing he had seemed to deny that God is everywhere. But piety of this kind is unfavourable to public worship and even to those religious experiences in which the soul seems to have direct contact with God in return for its tribute of faith and love. In fact the Advaita philosophy countenances emotional theism only as an imperfect creed and not as the highest truth. But the existence of all sects and priesthoods depends on their power to satisfy the religious instinct with ceremonial or some better method of putting the soul in communication with the divine. On the other hand pantheism in India is not a philosophical speculation, it is a habit of mind: it is not enough for the Hindu that his God is lord of all things: he must *be* all things and the soul in its endeavour to reach God must obtain deliverance from the fetters not only of matter but of individuality. Hence Hindu theology is in a perpetual oscillation illustrated by the discrepant statements found side by side in the Bhagavad-gîtâ and other works. Indian temperament and Indian logic want a pantheistic God and a soul which can transcend personality, but religious thought and practice imply personality both in the soul and in God. All varieties of Vishnuism show an effort to reconcile these double aspirations and theories. The theistic view is popular, for without it what would become of temples, worshippers and priests? But I think that the pantheistic view is the real basis of Indian religious thought.

The qualified monism of Râmânuja (as his system is sometimes called) led to more uncompromising treatment of the question and to the affirmation of dualism, not the dualism of God and the Devil but the distinctness of the soul and of matter from God. This is the doctrine of Madhva, another southern teacher who lived about a century after Râmânuja and was perhaps directly influenced by Islam. But though the logical outcome of his teaching may appear to be simple theism analogous to Islam or Judaism, it does not in practice lead to this result but rather to the worship of Krishna. Madhva's sect is still important but even more important is another branch of the spiritual family of Râmânuja, starting from Râmânand who probably flourished in the fourteenth century[1].

Râmânuja, while in some ways accepting innovations, insisted on the strict observance of caste. Râmânand abandoned this, separated from his sect and removed to Benares. His teaching marks a turning-point in the history of modern Hinduism. Firstly he held that caste need not prevent a man from rightly worshipping God and he admitted even Moslims as members of his community. To this liberality are directly traceable the numerous sects combining Hindu with Mohammedan doctrines, among which the Kabir Panthis and the Sikhs are the most conspicuous. But it is a singular testimony to the tenacity of Hindu ideas that though many teachers holding most diverse opinions have declared there is no caste before God, yet caste has generally reasserted itself among their

[1] The determination of his precise date offers some difficulties. See for further discussion Book v.

followers as a social if not as a religious institution. The second important point in Râmânand's teaching was the use of the vernacular for religious literature. Dravidian scriptures had already been recognized in the south but it is from this time that there begins to flow in the north that great stream of sacred poetry in Hindi and Bengali which waters the roots of modern popular Hinduism. Among many eminent names which have contributed to it, the greatest is Tulsi Das who retold the Ramayana in Hindi and thus wrote a poem which is little less than a Bible for millions in the Ganges valley.

The sects which derive from the teaching of Râmânand mostly worship the Supreme Being under the name of Râma. Even more numerous, especially in the north, are those who use the name of Krishna, the other great incarnation of Vishnu. This worship was organized and extended by the preaching of Vallabha and Caitanya (c. 1500) in the valley of the Ganges and Bengal, but was not new. I shall discuss in some detail below the many elements combined in the complex figure of Krishna but in one way or another he was connected with the earliest forms of Vishnuite monotheism and is the chief figure in the Bhagavad-gîtâ, its earliest text-book. Legend connects him partly with Muttra and partly with western India but, though by no means ignored in southern India, he does not receive there such definite and exclusive adoration as in the north. The Krishnaite sects are emotional, and their favourite doctrine that the relation between God and the soul is typified by passionate love has led to dubious moral results.

This Krishnaite propaganda, which coincided with the Reformation in Europe, was the last great religious movement in India. Since that time there has been considerable activity of a minor kind. Protests have been raised against abuses and existing communities have undergone changes, such as may be seen in the growth of the Sikhs, but there has been no general or original movement. The absence of such can be easily explained by the persecutions of Aurungzeb and by the invasions and internal struggles of the eighteenth century. At the end of that century Hinduism was at its lowest but its productive power was not destroyed. The decennial census never fails to record the rise of new sects and the sudden growth of others which had been obscure and minute.

Any historical treatment of Hinduism inevitably makes Vishnuism seem more prominent than other sects, for it offers more events to record. But though Sivaism has undergone fewer changes and produced fewer great names, it must not be thought of as lifeless or decadent. The lingam is worshipped all over India and many of the most celebrated shrines, such as Benares and Bhubaneshwar, are dedicated to the Lord of life and death. The Śivaism of the Tamil country is one of the most energetic and progressive forms of modern Hinduism, but in doctrine it hardly varies from the ancient standard of the Tiruvacagam.

9. *European Influence and Modern Hinduism*

The small effect of European religion on Hinduism is remarkable. Islam, though aggressively hostile, yet fused with it in some sects, for instance the Sikhs, but such fusions of Indian religion and Christianity as have been noted[1] are microscopic curiosities. European free thought and Deism have not fared better, for the Brahmo Samaj which was founded under their inspiration has only 5504 adherents[2]. In social life there has been some change: caste restrictions, though not abolished, are evaded by ingenious subterfuges and there is a growing feeling against child-marriage. Yet were the laws against sati and human sacrifice repealed, there are many districts in which such practices would not be forbidden by popular sentiment.

It is easy to explain the insensibility of Hinduism to European contact: even Islam had little effect on its stubborn vitality, though Islam brought with it settlers and resident rulers, ready to make converts by force. But the British have shown perfect toleration and are merely sojourners in the land who spend their youth and age elsewhere. European exclusiveness and Indian ideas about caste alike made it natural to regard them as an isolated class charged with the business of Government but divorced from the intellectual and religious life of other classes. Previous experience of Moslims and other invaders disposed the Brahmans to accept foreigners as rulers

[1] The Kadianis and Chet Ramis in the N. W. Provinces are mentioned but even here the fusion seems to be chiefly between Islam and Christianity. See also the article Râdhâ Soâmi in *E.R.E.*

[2] According to the Census of 1911.

without admitting that their creeds and customs were in the least worthy of imitation. European methods of organization and advertisement have not however been disdained.

The last half century has witnessed a remarkable revival of Hinduism. In the previous decades the most conspicuous force in India, although numerically weak, was the already mentioned Brahmo Samaj, founded by Ram Mohun Roy in 1828. But it was colourless and wanting in constructive power. Educated opinion, at least in Bengal, seemed to be tending towards agnosticism and social revolution. This tendency was checked by a conservative and nationalist movement, which in all its varied phases gave support to Indian religion and was intolerant of European ideas. It had a political side but there was nothing disloyal in its main idea, namely, that in the intellectual and religious sphere, where Indian life is most intense, Indian ideas must not decay. No one who has known India during the last thirty years can have failed to notice how many new temples have been built and how many old ones repaired. Almost all the principal sects have founded associations to protect and extend their interests by such means as financial and administrative organization, the publication of periodicals and other literature, annual conferences, lectures and the foundation of religious houses or quasi-monastic orders. Several societies have been founded not restricted to any particular sect but with the avowed object of defending and promoting strict Hinduism. Among such the most important are, first the Bharat Dharma Mahamandala, under the distinguished presidency of the Maharaja of Darbhanga: secondly the movement started by Ramakrishna and Swami Vivekananda and adorned by the beautiful life and writings of Sister Nivedita (Miss Noble) and thirdly the Theosophical Society under the leadership of Mrs Besant. It is remarkable that Europeans, both men and women, have played a considerable part in this revival. All these organizations are influential: the two latter have done great service in defending and encouraging Hinduism, but I am less sure of their success in mingling Eastern and Western ideas or in popularizing Hinduism among Europeans.

Somewhat different, but described by the Census of 1911 as "the greatest religious movement in India of the past half century" is the Arya Samaj, founded in 1875 by Swami Dayanand. Whereas the movements mentioned above support

Sanâtana Dharma or Orthodox Hinduism in all its shapes, the Arya Samaj aims at reform. Its original programme was a revival of the ancient Vedic religion but it has since been perceptibly modified and tends towards conciliating contemporary orthodoxy, for it now prohibits the slaughter of cattle, accords a partial recognition to caste, affirms its belief in karma and apparently approves a form of the Yoga philosophy. Though it is not yet accepted as a form of orthodox Hinduism, it seems probable that concessions on both sides will produce this result before long. It numbers at present only about a quarter of a million but is said to be rapidly increasing, especially in the United Provinces and Panjab, and to be remarkable for the completeness and efficiency of its organization. It maintains missionary colleges, orphanages and schools. Affiliated to it is a society for the purification (shuddhi) of Mohammedans, Christians and outcasts, that is for turning them into Hindus and giving them some kind of caste. It would appear that those who undergo this purification do not always become members of the Ṡamaj but are merged in the ordinary Hindu community where they are accepted without opposition if also without enthusiasm.

10. *Change and Permanence in Buddhism*

Thus we have a record of Indian thought for about 3000 years. It has directly affected such distant points as Balkh, Java and Japan and it is still living and active. But life and action mean change and such wide extension in time and space implies variety. We talk of converting foreign countries but the religion which is transplanted also undergoes conversion or else it cannot enter new brains and hearts. Buddhism in Ceylon and Japan, Christianity in Scotland and Russia are not the same, although professing to reverence the same teachers. It is easy to argue the other way, but it can only be done by setting aside as non-essential differences of great practical importance. Europeans are ready enough to admit that Buddhism is changeable and easily corrupted but it is not singular in that respect[1]. I doubt if Lhasa and Tantrism are further from

[1] There are curious survivals of paganism in out of the way forms of Christianity. Thus animal sacrifices are not extinct among Armenians and Nestorians. See *E.R.E.* article "Prayer for the Dead" at the end.

the teaching of Gotama than the Papacy, the Inquisition, and the religion of the German Emperor, from the teaching of Christ.

A religion is the expression of the thought of a particular age and cannot really be permanent in other ages which have other thoughts. The apparent permanence of Christianity is due first to the suppression of much original teaching, such as Christ's turning the cheek to the smiter and Paul's belief in the coming end of the world, and secondly to the adoption of new social ideals which have no place in the New Testament, such as the abolition of slavery and the improved status of women.

Buddhism arising out of Brahmanism suggests a comparison with Christianity arising out of Judaism, but the comparison breaks down in most points of detail. But there is one real resemblance, namely that Buddhism and Christianity have both won their greatest triumphs outside the land of their birth. The flowers of the mind, if they can be transplanted at all, often flourish with special vigour on alien soil. Witness the triumphs of Islam in the hands of the Turks and Mughals, the progress of Nestorianism in Central Asia, and the spread of Manichæism in both the East and West outside the limits of Persia. Even so Lamaism in Tibet and Amidism in Japan, though scholars may regard them as singular perversions, have more vitality than any branch of Buddhism which has existed in India since the seventh century. But even here the parallel with Christian sects is imperfect. It would be more complete if Palestine had been the centre from which different phases of Christianity radiated during some twelve centuries, for this is the relation between Indian and foreign Buddhism. Lamaism is not the teaching of the Buddha travestied by Tibetans but a late form of Indian Buddhism exported to Tibet and modified there in some external features (such as ecclesiastical organization and art) but not differing greatly in doctrine from Bengali Buddhism of the eleventh century. And even Amidism appears to have originated not in the Far East but in Gandhara and the adjacent lands. Thus the many varieties of Buddhism now existing are due partly to local colour but even more to the workings of the restless Hindu mind which during many centuries after the Christian era continued to invent for it novelties in metaphysics and mythology.

The preservation of a very ancient form of Buddhism in

Ceylon[1] is truly remarkable, for if in many countries Buddhism has shown itself fluid and protean, it here manifests a stability which can hardly be paralleled except in Judaism. The Sinhalese, unlike the Hindus, had no native propensity to speculation. They were content to classify, summarize and expound the teaching of the Pitakas without restating it in the light of their own imagination. Whereas the most stable form of Christianity is the Church of Rome, which began by making considerable additions to the doctrine of the New Testament, the most stable form of Buddhism is neither a transformation of the old nor a protest against innovation but simply the continuation of a very ancient sect in strange lands[2]. This ancient Buddhism, like Islam which is also simple and stable, is somewhat open to the charge of engaging in disputes about trivial details[3], but alike in Ceylon, Burma and Siam, it has not only shown remarkable persistence but has become a truly national religion, the glory and comfort of those who profess it.

11. *Rebirth and the Nature of the Soul*

The most characteristic doctrine of Indian religion—rarely absent in India and imported by Buddhism into all the countries which it influenced—is that called metempsychosis, the transmigration of the soul or reincarnation. The last of these terms best expresses Indian, especially Buddhist, ideas but still the usual Sanskrit equivalent, *Saṃsâra,* means migration. The body breaks up at death but something passes on and migrates to another equally transitory tenement. Neither Brahmans nor Buddhists seem to contemplate the possibility that the human soul may be a temporary manifestation of the Eternal Spirit which comes to an end at death—a leaf on a tree or a momentary ripple on the water. It is always regarded as passing through many births, a wave traversing the ocean.

Hindu speculation has never passed through the materialistic phase, and the doctrine that the soul is annihilated at death is extremely rare in India. Even rarer perhaps is the

[1] The Buddhism of Siam and Burma is similar but in Siam it is a mediæval importation and the early religious history of Burma is still obscure.

[2] Although stability is characteristic of the Hinayana its later literature shows a certain movement of thought phases of which are marked by the Questions of Milinda, Buddhaghosa's works and the Abhidhammattha Sangaha.

[3] *E.g.* the way a monastic robe should be worn and the Sîmâ.

doctrine that it usually enters on a permanent existence, happy or otherwise. The idea underlying the transmigration theory is that every state which we call existence must come to an end. If the soul can be isolated from all the accidents and accessories attaching to it, then there may be a state of permanence and peace but not a state comparable with human existence, however enlarged and glorified. But why does not this conviction of impermanence lead to the simpler conclusion that the end of physical life is the end of all life? Because the Hindus have an equally strong conviction of continuity: everything passes away and changes but it is not true to say of anything that it arises from nothing or passes into nothing. If human organisms (or any other organisms) are mere machines, if there is nothing more to be said about a corpse than about a smashed watch, then (the Hindu thinks) the universe is not continuous. Its continuity means for him that there is something which eternally manifests itself in perishable forms but does not perish with them any more than water when a pitcher is broken or fire that passes from the wood it has consumed to fresh fuel.

These metaphors suggest that the doctrine of transmigration or reincarnation does not promise what we call personal immortality. I confess that I cannot understand how there can be personality in the ordinary human sense without a body. When we think of a friend, we think of a body and a character, thoughts and feelings, all of them connected with that body and many of them conditioned by it. But the immortal soul is commonly esteemed to be something equally present in a new born babe, a youth and an old man. If so, it cannot be a personality in the ordinary sense, for no one could recognize the spirit of a departed friend, if it is something which was present in him the day he was born and different from all the characteristics which he acquired during life. The belief that we shall recognize our friends in another world assumes that these characteristics are immortal, but it is hard to understand how they can be so, especially as it is also assumed that there is nothing immortal in a dog, which possesses affection and intelligence, but that there is something immortal in a new born infant which cannot be said to possess either.

In one way metempsychosis raises insuperable difficulties to the survival of personality, for if you become someone else, especially an animal, you are no longer yourself according to any ordinary use of language. But one of the principal forms taken by the doctrine in India makes a modified survival intelligible. For it is held that a new born child brings with it as a result of actions done in previous lives certain predispositions and these after being developed and modified in the course of that child's life are transmitted to its next existence.

As to the method of transmission there are various theories, for in India the belief in reincarnation is not so much a dogma as an instinct innate in all and only occasionally justified by philosophers, not because it was disputed but because they felt bound to show that their own systems were compatible with it. One explanation is that given by the Vedânta philosophy, according to which the soul is accompanied in its migrations by the *Sûkshmaśarîra* or subtle body, a counterpart of the mortal body but transparent and invisible, though material. The truth of this theory, as of all theories respecting ghosts and spirits, seems to me a matter for experimental verification, but the Vedânta recognizes that in our experience a personal individual existence is always connected with a physical substratum.

The Buddhist theory of rebirth is somewhat different, for Buddhism even in its later divagations rarely ceased to profess belief in Gotama's doctrine that there is no such thing as a soul—by which is meant no such thing as a permanent unchanging self or *âtman*. Buddhists are concerned to show that transmigration is not inconsistent with this denial of the *âtman*. The ordinary, and indeed inevitable translation of this word by soul leads to misunderstanding for we naturally interpret it as meaning that there is nothing which survives the death of the body and *a fortiori* nothing to transmigrate. But in reality the denial of the *âtman* applies to the living rather than to the dead. It means that in a living man there is no permanent, unchangeable entity but only a series of mental states, and since human beings, although they have no *âtman*, certainly exist in this present life, the absence of the *âtman* is not in itself an obstacle to belief in a similar life after death or before birth. Infancy, youth, age and the state immediately after death may form a series of which the last two are as intimately connected as any other two. The Buddhist teaching is that when men die in whom the desire for another life exists—as it exists in all except saints—then desire, which is really the creator of the world, fashions another being, conditioned by the character and merits of the being which has just come to an end. Life is like fire: its very nature is to burn its fuel. When one body dies, it is as if one piece of fuel were burnt: the vital process passes on and recommences in another and so long as there is desire of life, the provision of fuel fails not. Buddhist doctors have busied themselves with the question whether two successive lives are the same man or different men, and have illustrated the relationship by various analogies of things which seem to be the same and yet not the same, such as a child and an adult, milk and curds, or fire which spreads from a lamp and burns down a village, but, like the Brahmans, they do not discuss why the hypothesis of transmigration is necessary. They had the same feeling for the continuity of nature, and more than others they insisted on the principle that everything has a cause. They held that the sexual act creates the conditions in which a new life appears but is not an adequate cause for the new life itself. And unless we accept a materialist explanation of human nature, this argument is sound: unless we admit that mind is merely a function of matter, the birth of a mind is not explicable as a mere process of cell development: something pre-existent must act upon the cells.

Europeans in discussing such questions as the nature of the soul and immortality are prone to concentrate their attention on death and neglect the phenomena of birth, which surely are equally important. For if a soul survives the death of this complex of cells which is called the body, its origin and development must, according to all analogy, be different from those of the perishable body. Orthodox theology deals with the problem by saying that God creates a new soul every time a child is born[1] but free discussion usually ignores it and taking an adult

[1] I believe this to be the orthodox explanation but it is open to many objections.

(1) It is a mere phrase. If to create means to produce something out of nothing, then we have never seen such an act and to ascribe a sudden appearance to such an act is really no explanation. Perhaps an act of imagination or a dream may justly be called a creation, but the relation between a soul and its Creator is not usually regarded as similar to the relation between a mind and its fancies.

(2) The responsibility of God for the evil of the world seems to be greatly increased, if he is directly responsible for every birth of a child in unhappy conditions.

(3) Animals are not supposed to have souls. Therefore the production of an

as he is, asks what are the chances that any part of him survives death. Yet the questions, what is destroyed at death and how and why, are closely connected with the questions what comes into existence at birth and how and why. This second series of questions is hard enough, but it has this advantage over the first that whereas death abruptly closes the road and we cannot follow the soul one inch on its journey beyond, the portals of birth are a less absolute frontier. We know that every child has passed through stages in which it could hardly be called a child. The earliest phase consists of two cells, which unite and then proceed to subdivide and grow. The mystery of the process by which they assume a human form is not explained by scientific or theological phrases. The complete individual is assuredly not contained in the first germ. The microscope cannot find it there and to say that it is there potentially, merely means that we know the germ will develop in a certain way. To say that a force is manifesting itself in the germ and assuming the shape which it chooses to take or must take is also merely a phrase and metaphor, but it seems to me to fit the facts[1].

The doctrines of pre-existence and transmigration (but not, I think, of karma which is purely Indian) are common among savages in Africa and America, nor is their wide distribution strange. Savages commonly think that the soul wanders during sleep and that a dead man's soul goes somewhere: what more natural than to suppose that the soul of a new born infant comes from somewhere? But among civilized peoples such ideas are in most cases due to Indian influence. In India they seem

animal's mind is not explained by this theory and it seems to be assumed that such a complex mind as a dog's can be explained as a function of matter, whereas there is something in a child which cannot be so explained.

(4) If a new immortal soul is created every time a birth takes place, the universe must be receiving incalculably large additions. For some philosophies such an idea is impossible. (See Bradley, *Appearance and Reality*, p. 502. "The universe is incapable of increase. And to suppose a constant supply of new souls, none of which ever perished, would clearly land us in the end in an insuperable difficulty.") But even if we do not admit that it is impossible, it at least destroys all analogy between the material and spiritual worlds. If all the bodies that ever lived continued to exist separately after death, the congestion would be unthinkable. Is a corresponding congestion in the spiritual world really thinkable?

[1] This seems to be the view of the Chândogya Up. vi. 12. As the whole world is a manifestation of Brahman, so is the great banyan tree a manifestation of the subtle essence which is also present in its minute seeds.

indigenous to the soil and not imported by the Aryan invaders, for they are not clearly enunciated in the Rig Veda, nor formulated before the time of the Upanishads[1]. They were introduced by Buddhism to the Far East and their presence in Manichæism, Neoplatonism, Sufiism and ultimately in the Jewish Kabbala seems a rivulet from the same source. Recent research discredits the theory that metempsychosis was an important feature in the earlier religion of Egypt or among the Druids[2]. But it played a prominent part in the philosophy of Pythagoras and in the Orphic mysteries, which had some connection with Thrace and possibly also with Crete. A few great European intellects[3]—notably Plato and Virgil—have given it undying expression, but Europeans as a whole have rejected it with that curiously crude contempt which they have shown until recently for Oriental art and literature.

Considering how fixed is the belief in immortality among Europeans, or at least the desire for it, the rarity of a belief in pre-existence or transmigration is remarkable. But most people's expectation of a future life is based on craving rather than on reasoned anticipation. I cannot myself understand how anything that comes into being can be immortal. Such immortality is unsupported by a single analogy nor can any instance be quoted of a thing which is known to have had an

[1] The Brihad Ar. Up. knows of samsâra and karma but as matters of deep philosophy and not for the vulgar: but in the Buddhist Pitakas they are assumed as universally accepted. The doctrine must therefore have been popularized after the composition of the Upanishad. But some allowance must be made for the fact that the Upanishads and the earliest versions of the Buddhist Suttas were produced in different parts of India.

[2] Yet many instances are quoted from Celtic and Teutonic folklore to the effect that birds and butterflies are human souls, and Cæsar's remarks about the Druids may not be wholly wrong.

[3] Several other Europeans of eminence have let their minds play with the ideas of metempsychosis, pre-existence and karma, as for instance Giordano Bruno, Swedenborg, Goethe, Lessing, Lavater, Herder, Schopenhauer, Ibsen, von Helmont, Lichtenberg and in England such different spirits as Hume and Wordsworth. It would appear that towards the end of the eighteenth century these ideas were popular in some literary circles on the continent. See Bertholet, *The Transmigration of Souls*, pp. 111 ff. Recently Professor McTaggart has argued in favour of the doctrine with great lucidity and persuasiveness. Huxley too did not think it absurd. See his *Romanes Lecture, Evolution and Ethics, Collected Essays*, vol. IX. p. 61. As Deussen observes, Kant's argument which bases immortality on the realization of the moral law, attainable only by an infinite process of approximation, points to transmigration rather than immortality in the usual sense.

origin and yet is even apparently indestructible[1]. And is it possible to suppose that the universe is capable of indefinite increase by the continual addition of new and eternal souls? But these difficulties do not exist for theories which regard the soul as something existing before as well as after the body, truly immortal *a parte ante* as well as *a parte post* and manifesting itself in temporary homes of human or lower shape. Such theories become very various and fall into many obscurities when they try to define the nature of the soul and its relation to the body, but they avoid what seems to me the contradiction of the created but immortal soul.

The doctrine of metempsychosis is also interesting as affecting the relations of men and animals. The popular European conception of "the beasts which perish" weakens the arguments for human immortality. For if the mind of a dog or chimpanzee contains no element which is immortal, the part of the human mind on which the claim to immortality can be based must be parlously small, since *ex hypothesi* sensation, volition, desire and the simpler forms of intelligence are not immortal. But in India where men have more charity and more philosophy this distinction is not drawn. The animating principle of men, animals and plants is regarded as one or at least similar, and even matter which we consider inanimate, such as water, is often considered to possess a soul. But though there is ample warrant in both Brahmanic and Buddhist literature for the idea that the soul may sink from a human to an animal form or *vice versâ* rise, and though one sometimes meets this belief in modern life[2], yet it is not the most prominent aspect of metempsychosis in India and the beautiful precept of ahimsâ or not injuring living things is not, as Europeans imagine, founded on the fear of eating one's grandparents but rather on the humane and enlightened feeling that all life is one and that men who devour beasts are not much above the level of the beasts who devour one another. The feeling has grown stronger with time. In the Vedas animal sacrifices are prescribed and they are even now used in the worship of some

[1] The chemical elements are hardly an exception. Apparently they have no beginning and no end but there is reason to suspect that they have both.

[2] I know well-authenticated cases of Burmese and Indians thinking that the soul of a dead child had passed into an animal.

deities. In the Epics the eating of meat is mentioned. But the doctrine that it is wrong to take animal life was definitely adopted by Buddhism and gained strength with its diffusion.

One obvious objection to all theories of rebirth is that we do not remember our previous existences and that, if they are connected by no thread of memory, they are for all practical purposes the existences of different people. But this want of memory affects not only past existences but the early phases of this existence. Does any one deny his existence as an infant or embryo because he cannot remember it[1]? And if a wrong could be done to an infant the effects of which would not be felt for twenty years, could it be said to be no concern of the infant because the person who will suffer in twenty years time will have no recollection that he was that infant? And common opinion in Eastern Asia, not without occasional confirmation from Europe, denies the proposition that we cannot remember our former lives and asserts that those who take any pains to sharpen their spiritual faculties can remember them. The evidence for such recollection seems to me better than the evidence for most spiritualistic phenomena[2].

Another objection comes from the facts of heredity. On the whole we resemble our parents and ancestors in mind as well as in body. A child often seems to be an obvious product of its parents and not a being come from outside and from another life. This objection of course applies equally to the creation theory. If the soul is created by an act of God, there seems to be no reason why it should be like the parents, or, if he causes it to be like them, he is made responsible for sending children into the world with vicious natures. On the other hand if parents literally make a child, mind as well as body, there seems to be no reason why children should ever be unlike their parents, or brothers and sisters unlike one another, as they

[1] Or again, when I wake up in the morning I am conscious of my identity because innumerable circumstances remind me of the previous day. But if I wake up suddenly in the night with a toothache which leaves room for no thought or feeling except the feeling of pain, is the fact that I experience the pain in any way lessened if for the moment I do not know who or where I am?

[2] I believe that a French savant, Colonel Rochas, has investigated in a scientific spirit cases in which hypnotized subjects profess to remember their former births and found that these recollections are as clear and coherent as any revelations about another world which have been made by Mrs Piper or other mediums. But I have not been able to obtain any of Col. Rochas's writings.

undoubtedly sometimes are. An Indian would say that a soul[1] seeking rebirth carries with it certain potentialities of good and evil and can obtain embodiment only in a family offering the necessary conditions. Hence to some extent it is natural that the child should be like its parents. But the soul seeking re-birth is not completely fixed in form and stiff: it is hampered and limited by the results of its previous life, but in many respects it may be flexible and free, ready to vary in response to its new environment.

But there is a psychological and temperamental objection to the doctrine of rebirth, which goes to the root of the matter. Love of life and the desire to find a field of activity are so strong in most Europeans that it might be supposed that a theory offering an endless vista of new activities and new chances would be acceptable. But as a rule Europeans who discuss the question say that they do not relish this prospect. They may be willing to struggle until death, but they wish for repose—conscious repose of course—afterwards. The idea that one just dead has not entered into his rest, but is beginning another life with similar struggles and fleeting successes, similar sorrows and disappointments, is not satisfying and is almost shocking[2]. We do not like it, and not to like any particular view about the destinies of the soul is generally, but most illogically, considered a reason for rejecting it[3].

12.

It must not however be supposed that Hindus like the prospect of transmigration. On the contrary from the time of the Upanishads and the Buddha to the present day their religious ideal corresponding to salvation is emancipation and

[1] I use the word *soul* merely for simplicity, but Buddhists and others might demur to this phraseology.

[2] But for a contrary view see *Reincarnation, the Hope of the World* by Irving S. Cooper. Even the Bṛihad Aran. Upan. (IV. 4. 3. 4) speaks of new births as new and more beautiful shapes which the soul fashions for itself as a goldsmith works a piece of gold.

[3] The increase of the human population of this planet does not seem to me a serious argument against the doctrine of rebirth for animals, and the denizens of other worlds may be supplying an increasing number of souls competent to live as human beings.

deliverance, deliverance from rebirth and from the bondage of desire which brings about rebirth. Now all Indian theories as to the nature of transmigration are in some way connected with the idea of *Karma*, that is the power of deeds done in past existences to condition or even to create future existences. Every deed done, whether good or bad, affects the character of the doer for a long while, so that to use a metaphor, the soul awaiting rebirth has a special shape, which is of its own making, and it can find re-embodiment only in a form into which that shape can squeeze.

These views of rebirth and karma have a moral value, for they teach that what a man gets depends on what he is or makes himself to be, and they avoid the difficulty of supposing that a benevolent creator can have given his creatures only one life with such strange and unmerited disproportion in their lots. Ordinary folk in the East hope that a life of virtue will secure them another life as happy beings on earth or perhaps in some heaven which, though not eternal, will still be long. But for many the higher ideal is renunciation of the world and a life of contemplative asceticism which will accumulate no karma so that after death the soul will pass not to another birth but to some higher and more mysterious state which is beyond birth and death. It is the prevalence of views like this which has given both Hinduism and Buddhism the reputation of being pessimistic and unpractical.

It is generally assumed that these are bad epithets, but are they not applicable to Christian teaching? Modern and medieval Christianity—as witness many popular hymns—regards this world as vain and transitory, a vale of tears and tribulation, a troubled sea through whose waves we must pass before we reach our rest. And choirs sing, though without much conviction, that it is weary waiting here. This language seems justified by the Gospels and Epistles. It is true that some utterances of Christ suggest that happiness is to be found in a simple and natural life of friendliness and love, but on the whole both he and St Paul teach that the world is evil or at least spoiled and distorted: to become a happy world it must be somehow remade and transfigured by the second coming of Christ. The desires and ambitions which are the motive power of modern Europe are, if not wrong, at least vain and do not even seek for true peace and happiness. Like Indian teachers, the early Christians tried to create a right temper rather than to change social institutions. They bade masters and slaves treat one another with kindness and respect, but they did not attempt to abolish slavery.

Indian thought does not really go much further in pessimism than Christianity, but its pessimism is intellectual rather than emotional. He who understands the nature of the soul and its successive lives cannot regard any single life as of great importance in itself, though its consequences for the future may be momentous, and though he will not say that life is not worth living. Reiterated declarations that all existence is suffering do, it is true, seem to destroy all prospect of happiness and all motive for effort, but the more accurate statement is, in the words of the Buddha himself, that all clinging to physical existence involves suffering. The earliest Buddhist texts teach that when this clinging and craving cease, a feeling of freedom and happiness takes their place and later Buddhism treated itself to visions of paradise as freely as Christianity. Many forms of Hinduism teach that the soul released from the body can enjoy eternal bliss in the presence of God and even those severer philosophers who do not admit that the released soul is a personality in any human sense have no doubt of its happiness.

The opposition is not so much between Indian thought and the New Testament, for both of them teach that bliss is attainable but not by satisfying desire. The fundamental contrast is rather between both India and the New Testament on the one hand and on the other the rooted conviction of European races[1], however much Christian orthodoxy may disguise their expression of it, that this world is all-important. This conviction finds expression not only in the avowed pursuit of pleasure and ambition but in such sayings as that the best religion is the one which does most good and such ideals as self-realization or the full development of one's nature and powers. Europeans as a rule have an innate dislike and mistrust of the doctrine that the world is vain or unreal. They can accord some sympathy to a dying man who sees in due perspective the unimportance of his past life or to a poet who under the starry

[1] Perhaps Russians in this as in many other matters think somewhat differently from other Europeans.

heavens can make felt the smallness of man and his earth. But such thoughts are considered permissible only as retrospects, not as principles of life: you may say that your labour has amounted to nothing, but not that labour is vain. Though monasteries and monks still exist, the great majority of Europeans instinctively disbelieve in asceticism, the contemplative life and contempt of the world: they have no love for a philosopher who rejects the idea of progress and is not satisfied with an ideal consisting in movement towards an unknown goal. They demand a religion which theoretically justifies the strenuous life. All this is a matter of temperament and the temperament is so common that it needs no explanation. What needs explanation is rather the other temperament which rejects this world as unsatisfactory and sets up another ideal, another sphere, another standard of values. This ideal and standard are not entirely peculiar to India but certainly they are understood and honoured there more than elsewhere. They are professed, as I have already observed, by Christianity, but even the New Testament is not free from the idea that saints are having a bad time now but will hereafter enjoy a triumph, parlously like the exuberance of the wicked in this world. The Far East too has its unworldly side which, though harmonizing with Buddhism, is native. In many ways the Chinese are as materialistic as Europeans, but throughout the long history of their art and literature, there has always been a school, clear-voiced if small, which has sung and pursued the joys of the hermit, the dweller among trees and mountains who finds nature and his own thoughts an all-sufficient source of continual happiness. But the Indian ideal, though it often includes the pleasures of communion with nature, differs from most forms of the Chinese and Christian ideal inasmuch as it assumes the reality of certain religious experiences and treats them as the substance and occupation of the highest life. We are disposed to describe these experiences as trances or visions, names which generally mean something morbid or hypnotic. But in India their validity is unquestioned and they are not considered morbid. The sensual scheming life of the world is sick and ailing; the rapture of contemplation is the true and healthy life of the soul. More than that it is the type and foretaste of a higher existence compared with which this world is worthless or rather nothing at all. This view has been held in India for nearly three thousand years: it has been confirmed by the experience of men whose writings testify to their intellectual power and has commanded the respect of the masses. It must command our respect too, even if it is contrary to our temperament, for it is the persistent ideal of a great nation and cannot be explained away as hallucination or charlatanism. It is allied to the experiences of European mystics of whom St Teresa is a striking example, though less saintly persons, such as Walt Whitman and J. A. Symonds, might also be cited. Of such mysticism William James said "the existence of mystical states absolutely overthrows the pretension of non-mystical states to be the sole and ultimate dictators of what we may believe[1]."

These mystical states are commonly described as meditation but they include not merely peaceful contemplation but ecstatic rapture. They are sometimes explained as union with Brahman[2], the absorption of the soul in God, or its feeling that it is one with him. But this is certainly not the only explanation of ecstasy given in India, for it is recognized as real and beneficent by Buddhists and Jains. The same rapture, the same sense of omniscience and of ability to comprehend the scheme of things, the same peace and freedom are experienced by both theistic and non-theistic sects, just as they have also been experienced by Christian mystics. The experiences are real but they do not depend on the presence of any special deity, though they may be coloured by the theological views of individual thinkers[3]. The earliest Buddhist texts make right rapture (sammâ samâdhi) the end and crown of the eight-fold path but offer no explanation of it. They suggest that it is something wrought by the mind for itself and without the co-operation or infusion of any external influence.

13.

Indian ideas about the destiny of the soul are connected with equally important views about its nature. I will not presume to

[1] *Varieties of Religious Experience*, p. 427. The chapter contains many striking instances of these experiences, collected mostly in the west.

[2] Compare *St Teresa's Orison of Union*, W. James, *l.c.* p. 408.

[3] Indian devotees understand how either Śiva or Krishna is all in all, and thus too St Teresa understood the mystery of the Trinity. See W. James, *l.c.* p. 411.

say what is the definition of the soul in European philosophy but in the language of popular religion it undoubtedly means that which remains when a body is arbitrarily abstracted from a human personality, without enquiring how much of that personality is thinkable without a material substratum. This popular soul includes mind, perception and desire and often no attempt is made to distinguish it from them. But in India it is so distinguished. The soul (âtman or purusha) *uses* the mind and senses: they are its instruments rather than parts of it. Sight, for instance, serves as the spectacles of the soul, and the other senses and even the mind (manas) which is an intellectual *organ* are also instruments. If we talk of a soul passing from death to another birth, this according to most Hindus is a soul accompanied by its baggage of mind and senses, a subtle body indeed, but still gaseous not spiritual. But what is the soul by itself? When an English poet sings of death that it is "Only the sleep eternal in an eternal night" or a Greek poet calls it ἀτέρμονα νήγρετον ὕπνον we feel that they are denying immortality. But Indian divines maintain that deep sleep is one of the states in which the soul approaches nearest to God: that it is a state of bliss, and is unconscious not because consciousness is suspended but because no objects are presented to it. Even higher than dreamless sleep is another condition known simply as the fourth state[1], the others being waking, dream-sleep and dreamless sleep. In this fourth state thought is one with the object of thought and, knowledge being perfect, there exists no contrast between knowledge and ignorance. All this sounds strange to modern Europe. We are apt to say that dreamless sleep is simply unconsciousness[2] and that the so-called fourth state is imaginary or unmeaning. But to follow even popular speculation in India it is necessary to grasp this truth, or assumption, that when discursive thought ceases, when the mind and the senses are no longer active, the result is not unconsciousness equivalent to non-existence but the highest and purest state of the soul, in which, rising above thought and feeling, it enjoys the untrammelled bliss of its own nature[3].

[1] Turîya or caturtha.

[2] Indians were well aware even in early times that such a state might be regarded as equivalent to annihilation. Br. Ar. Up. II. 4. 13; Chând. Up. VIII. ii. 1.

[3] The idea is not wholly strange to European philosophy. See the passage from the *Phaedo* quoted by Sir Alfred Lyall. "Thought is best when the mind is gathered

If these views sound mysterious and fanciful, I would ask those Europeans who believe in the immortality of the soul what, in their opinion, survives death. The brain, the nerves and the sense organs obviously decay: the soul, you may say, is not a product of them, but when they are destroyed or even injured, perceptive and intellectual processes are inhibited and apparently rendered impossible. Must not that which lives for ever be, as the Hindus think, independent of thought and of sense-impressions?

I have observed in my reading that European philosophers are more ready to talk about soul and spirit than to define them [1] and the same is true of Indian philosophers. The word most commonly rendered by soul is *âtman*[2] but no one definition can be given for it, for some hold that the soul is identical with the Universal Spirit, others that it is merely of the same nature, still others that there are innumerable souls uncreate and eternal, while the Buddhists deny the existence of a soul *in toto*. But most Hindus who believe in the existence of an âtman or soul agree in thinking that it is the real self and essence of all human beings (or for that matter of other beings): that it is eternal *a parte ante* and *a parte post*: that it is not subject to variation but passes unchanged from one birth to another: that youth and age, joy and sorrow, and all the accidents of human life are affections, not so much of the soul as of the envelopes and limitations which surround it during its pilgrimage: that the soul, if it can be released and disengaged from these envelopes, is in itself knowledge and bliss, knowledge meaning the immediate and intuitive knowledge of God. A proper comprehension of this point of view will make us chary of labelling Indian thought as pessimistic on the ground that it promises the soul something which we are inclined to call unconsciousness.

In studying oriental religions sympathy and a desire to agree if possible are the first requisites. For instance, he who

into herself and none of these things trouble her—neither sounds nor sights nor pain nor any pleasure—when she has as little as possible to do with the body and has no bodily sense or feeling, but is aspiring after being."

[1] Mr Bradley (*Appearance and Reality*, p. 498) says "Spirit is a unity of the manifold in which the externality of the manifold has utterly ceased." This seems to me one of the cases in which Mr Bradley's thought shows an interesting affinity to Indian thought.

[2] But also sometimes *purusha*.

says of a certain ideal "this means annihilation and I do not like it" is on the wrong way. The right way is to ascertain what many of our most intelligent brothers mean by the cessation of mental activity and why it is for them an ideal.

14. *Eastern Pessimism and Renunciation*

But the charge of pessimism against Eastern religions is so important that we must consider other aspects of it, for though the charge is wrong, it is wrong only because those who bring it do not use quite the right word. And indeed it would be hard to find the right word in a European language. The temperament and theory described as pessimism are European. They imply an attitude of revolt, a right to judge and grumble. Why did the Deity make something out of nothing? What was his object? But this is not the attitude of Eastern thought: it generally holds that we cannot imagine nothing: that the world process is without beginning or end and that man must learn how to make the best of it.

The Far East purged Buddhism of much of its pessimism. There we see that the First Truth about suffering is little more than an admission of the existence of evil, which all religions and common sense admit. Evil ceases in the saint: nirvana in this life is perfect happiness. And though striving for the material improvement of the world is not held up conspicuously as an ideal in the Buddhist scriptures (or for that matter in the New Testament), yet it is never hinted that good effort is vain. A king should be a good king.

Renunciation is a great word in the religions of both Europe and Asia, but in Europe it is almost active. Except to advanced mystics, it means abandoning a natural attitude and deliberately assuming another which it is difficult to maintain. Something similar is found in India in the legends of those ascetics who triumphed over the flesh until they become very gods in power[1]. But it is also a common view in the East that he who renounces ambition and passion is not struggling against the world and the devil but simply leading a natural life. His passions indeed

[1] Even when low class yogis display the tortures which they inflict on their bodies, their object I think is not to show what penances they undergo but simply that pleasure and pain are alike to them.

obey his will and do not wander here and there according to their fancy, but his temperament is one of acquiescence not resistance. He takes his place among the men, beasts and plants around him and ceasing to struggle finds that his own soul contains happiness in itself.

Most Europeans consider man as the centre and lord of the world or, if they are very religious, as its vice-regent under God. He may kill or otherwise maltreat animals for his pleasure or convenience: his task is to subdue the forces of nature: nature is subservient to him and to his destinies: without man nature is meaningless. Much the same view was held by the ancient Greeks and in a less acute form by the Jews and Romans. Swinburne's line

> Glory to man in the highest, for man is the master of things

is overbold for professing Christians but it expresses both the modern scientific sentiment and the ancient Hellenic sentiment.

But such a line of poetry would I think be impossible in India or in any country to the East of it. There man is thought of as a part of nature not its centre or master[1]. Above him are formidable hosts of deities and spirits, and even European engineers cannot subdue the genii of the flood and typhoon: below but still not separated from him are the various tribes of birds and beasts. A good man does not kill them for pleasure nor eat flesh, and even those whose aspirations to virtue are modest treat animals as humble brethren rather than as lower creatures over whom they have dominion by divine command.

This attitude is illustrated by Chinese and Japanese art. In architecture, this art makes it a principle that palaces and temples should not dominate a landscape but fit into it and adapt their lines to its features. For the painter, flowers and animals form a sufficient picture by themselves and are not felt to be inadequate because man is absent. Portraits are frequent but a common form of European composition, namely a group of figures subordinated to a principal one, though not unknown, is comparatively rare.

How scanty are the records of great men in India! Great

[1] The sense of human dignity was strongest among the early Buddhists. They (or some sects of them) held that an arhat is superior to a god (or as we should say to an angel) and that a god cannot enter the path of salvation and become an arhat.

buildings attract attention but who knows the names of the architects who planned them or the kings who paid for them? We are not quite sure of the date of Kâlidâsa, the Indian Shakespeare, and though the doctrines of Śankara, Kabir, and Nânak still flourish, it is with difficulty that the antiquary collects from the meagre legends clinging to their names a few facts for their biographies. And Kings and Emperors, a class who in Europe can count on being remembered if not esteemed after death, fare even worse. The laborious research of Europeans has shown that Asoka and Harsha were great monarchs. Their own countrymen merely say "once upon a time there was a king" and recount some trivial story.

In fact, Hindus have a very weak historical sense. In this they are not wholly wrong, for Europeans undoubtedly exaggerate the historical treatment of thought and art[1]. In science, most students want to know what is certain in theory and useful in practice, not what were the discarded hypotheses and imperfect instruments of the past. In literature, when the actors and audience are really interested, the date of Shakespeare and even the authorship of the play cease to be important[2]. In the same way Hindus want to know whether doctrines and speculations are true, whether a man can make use of them in his own religious experiences and aspirations. They care little for the date, authorship, unity and textual accuracy of the Bhagavad-gîtâ. They simply ask, is it true, what can I get from it? The European critic, who expects nothing of the sort from the work, racks his brains to know who wrote it and when, who touched it up and why?

The Hindus are also indifferent to the past because they do not recognize that the history of the world, the whole cosmic

[1] Cf. Bosanquet, *Gifford Lectures*, 1912, p. 78. "History is a hybrid form of experience incapable of any considerable degree of being or trueness. The doubtful story of successive events cannot amalgamate with the complete interpretation of the social mind, of art, or of religion. The great things which are necessary in themselves, become within the narrative contingent or ascribed by most doubtful assumptions of insight to this actor or that on the historical stage. The study of Christianity is the study of a great world experience: the assignment to individuals of a share in its development is a problem for scholars whose conclusions, though of considerable human interest, can never be of supreme importance."

[2] The Chinese critic Hsieh Ho who lived in the sixth century of our era said: "In Art the terms ancient and modern have no place." This is exactly the Indian view of religion.

process, has any meaning or value. In most departments of Indian thought, great or small, the conception of τέλος or purpose is absent, and if the European reader thinks this a grave lacuna, let him ask himself whether satisfied love has any τέλος. For Hindus the world is endless repetition not a progress towards an end. Creation has rarely the sense which it bears for Europeans. An infinite number of times the universe has collapsed in flaming or watery ruin, æons of quiescence follow the collapse and then the Deity (he has done it an infinite number of times) emits again from himself worlds and souls of the same old kind. But though, as I have said before, all varieties of theological opinion may be found in India, he is usually represented as moved by some reproductive impulse rather than as executing a plan. Śankara says boldly that no motive can be attributed to God, because he being perfect can desire no addition to his perfection, so that his creative activity is mere exuberance, like the sport of young princes, who take exercise though they are not obliged to do so.

Such views are distasteful to Europeans. Our vanity impels us to invent explanations of the Universe which make our own existence important and significant. Nor does European science altogether support the Indian doctrine of periodicity. It has theories as to the probable origin of the solar system and other similar systems, but it points to the conclusion that the Universe as a whole is not appreciably affected by the growth or decay of its parts, whereas Indian imagination thinks of universal cataclysms and recurring periods of quiescence in which nothing whatever remains except the undifferentiated divine spirit.

Western ethics generally aim at teaching a man how to act: Eastern ethics at forming a character. A good character will no doubt act rightly when circumstances require action, but he need not seek occasions for action, he may even avoid them, and in India the passionless sage is still in popular esteem superior to warriors, statesmen and scientists.

15. *Eastern Polytheism*

Different as India and China are, they agree in this that in order not to misapprehend their religious condition we must make our minds familiar with a new set of relations. The relations of religion to philosophy, to ethics, and to the state, as well as the relations of different religions to one another, are not the same as in Europe. China and India are pagan, a word which I deprecate if it is understood to imply inferiority but which if used in a descriptive and respectful sense is very useful. Christianity and Islam are organized religions. They say (or rather their several sects say) that they each not only possess the truth but that all other creeds and rites are wrong. But paganism is not organized: it rarely presents anything like a church united under one head: still more rarely does it condemn or interfere with other religions unless attacked first. Buddhism stands between the two classes. Like Christianity and Islam it professes to teach the only true law, but unlike them it is exceedingly tolerant and many Buddhists also worship Hindu or Chinese gods.

Popular religion in India and China is certainly polytheistic, yet if one uses this word in contrast to the monotheism of Islam and of Protestantism the antithesis is unjust, for the polytheist does not believe in many creators and rulers of the world, in many Allahs or Jehovahs, but he considers that there are many spiritual beings, with different spheres and powers, to the most appropriate of whom he addresses his petitions. Polytheism and image-worship lie under an unmerited stigma in Europe. We generally assume that to believe in one God is obviously better, intellectually and ethically, than to believe in many. Yet Trinitarian religions escape being polytheistic only by juggling with words, and if Hindus and Chinese are polytheists so are the Roman and Oriental Churches, for there is no real distinction between praying to the Madonna, Saints and Angels, and propitiating minor deities. William James[1] has pointed out that polytheism is not theoretically absurd and is practically the religion of many Europeans. In some ways it is more intelligible and reasonable than monotheism. For if there is only one personal God, I do not understand how anything that can be called a person can be so expanded as to be capable of hearing and answering the prayers of the whole world. Anything susceptible of such extension must be more than a person. Is it

[1] *The Varieties of Religious Experience*, pp. 525–527 and *A Pluralistic Universe*, p. 310.

not at least equally reasonable to assume that there are many spirits, or many shapes taken by the superpersonal world spirit, with which the soul can get into touch?

The worship of images cannot be recommended without qualification, for it seems to require artists capable of making a worthy representation of the divine. And it must be confessed that many figures in Indian temples, such as the statues of Kâlî, seem repulsive or grotesque, though a Hindu might say that none of them are so strange in idea or so horrible in appearance as the crucifix. But the claim of the iconoclast from the times of the Old Testament onwards that he worships a spirit whereas others worship wood and stone is true only of the lowest phases of religion, if even there. Hindu theologians distinguish different kinds of *avatâras* or ways in which God descends into the world: among them are incarnations like Krishna, the presence of God in the human heart and his presence in a symbol or image (*arcâ*). It may be difficult to decide how far the symbol and the spirit are kept separate either in the East or in Europe, but no one can attend a great car-festival in southern India or the feast of Durgâ in Bengal without feeling and in some measure sharing the ecstasy and enthusiasm of the crowd. It is an enthusiasm such as may be evoked in critical times by a king or a flag, and as the flag may do duty for the king and all that he stands for, so may the image do duty for the deity.

16. *The Extravagance of Hinduism*

What I have just said applies to India rather than to China and so do the observations which follow. India is the most religious country in the world. The percentage of people who literally make religion their chief business, who sacrifice to it money and life itself (for religious suicide is not extinct), is far greater than elsewhere. Russia[1] probably comes next but the other nations fall behind by a long interval. Matter of fact respectable people—Chinese as well as Europeans—call this attitude extravagance and it sometimes deserves the name, for since there is no one creed or criterion in India, all sorts of

[1] And in Russia there are sects which prescribe castration and suicide.

aboriginal or decadent superstitions command the respect due to the name of religion.

This extravagance is both intellectual and moral. No story is too extraordinary to be told of Hindu gods. They are the magicians of the universe who sport with the forces of nature as easily as a conjuror in a bazaar does tricks with a handful of balls. But though the average Hindu would be shocked to hear the Puranas described as idle tales, yet he does not make his creed depend on their accuracy, as many in Europe make Christianity depend on miracles. The value of truth in religion is rated higher in India than in Europe but it is not historical truth. The Hindu approaches his sacred literature somewhat in the spirit in which we approach Milton and Dante. The beauty and value of such poems is clear. The question whether they are accurate reports of facts seems irrelevant. Hindus believe in progressive revelation. Many Tantras and Vishnuite works profess to be better suited to the present age than the Vedas, and innumerable treatises in the vernacular are commonly accepted as scripture.

Scriptures in India[1] are thought of as words not writings. It is the sacred sound not a sacred book which is venerated. They are learnt by oral transmission and it is rare to see a book used in religious services. Diagrams accompanied by letters and a few words are credited with magical powers, but still tantric spells are things to be recited rather than written. This view of scripture makes the hearer uncritical. The ordinary layman hears parts of a sacred book recited and probably admires what he understands, but he has no means of judging of a book as a whole, especially of its coherency and consistency.

The moral extravagance of Hinduism is more serious. It is kept in check by the general conviction that asceticism, or at least temperance, charity and self-effacement are the indispensable outward signs of religion, but still among the great religions of the world there is none which countenances so many hysterical, immoral and cruel rites. A literary example will illustrate the position. It is taken from the drama Mâdhava and Mâlatî written about 730 A.D., but the incidents of the plot might happen in any native state to-day, if European supervision were removed. In it Mâdhava, a young Brahman, surprises a priest

[1] This, of course, does not apply to Buddhism in China, Japan and Tibet.

of the goddess Châmundâ who is about to immolate Mâlatî. He kills the priest and apparently the other characters consider his conduct natural and not sacrilegious. But it is not suggested that either the police or any ecclesiastical authority ought to prevent human sacrifices, and the reason why Mâdhava was able to save his beloved from death was that he had gone to the uncanny spot where such rites were performed to make an offering of human flesh to demons.

In Buddhism religion and the moral law are identified, but not in Hinduism. Brahmanical literature contains beautiful moral sayings, especially about unselfishness and self-restraint, but the greatest popular gods such as Vishnu and Śiva are not identified with the moral law. They are super-moral and the God of philosophy, who *is* all things, is also above good and evil. The aim of the philosophic saint is not so much to choose the good and eschew evil as to draw nearer to God by rising above both.

Indian literature as a whole has a strong ethical and didactic flavour, yet the great philosophic and religious systems concern themselves little with ethics. They discuss the nature of the external world and other metaphysical questions which seem to us hardly religious: they clearly feel a peculiar interest in defining the relation of the soul to God, but they rarely ask why should I be good or what is the sanction of morality. They are concerned less with sin than with ignorance: virtue is indispensable, but without knowledge it is useless.

17. *The Hindu and Buddhist Scriptures*

The history and criticism of Hindu and Buddhist scriptures naturally occupy some space in this work, but two general remarks may be made here. First, the oldest scriptures are almost without exception compilations, that is collections of utterances handed down by tradition and arranged by later generations in some form which gives them apparent unity. Thus the Rig Veda is obviously an anthology of hymns and some three thousand years later the Granth or sacred book of the Sikhs was compiled on the same principle. It consists of poems by Nanak, Kabir and many other writers but is treated with extraordinary respect as a continuous and consistent revelation. The Brahmanas and Upanishads are not such obvious compilations yet on careful inspection the older[1] ones will be found to be nothing else. Thus the Brihad Aranyaka Upanishad, though possessing considerable coherency, is not only a collection of such philosophic views as commended themselves to the doctors of the Taittiriya school, but is formed by the union of three such collections. Each of the first two collections ends with a list of the teachers who handed it down and the third is openly called a supplement. One long passage, the dialogue between Yâjnavalkya and his wife, is incorporated in both the first and the second collection. Thus our text represents the period when the Taittirîyas brought their philosophic thoughts together in a complete form, but that period was preceded by another in which slightly different schools each had their own collection and for some time before this the various maxims and dialogues must have been current separately. Since the conversation between Yajnavalkya and Maitreyi occurs in almost the same form in two collections, it probably once existed as an independent piece.

In Buddhist literature the composite and tertiary character of the Sutta Pitaka is equally plain. The various Nikayas are confessedly collections of discourses. The two older ones seem dominated by the desire to bring before the reader the image of the Buddha preaching: the Samyutta and Anguttara emphasize the doctrine rather than the teacher and arrange much the same matter under new headings. But it is clear that in whatever form the various sermons, dialogues and dissertations appear, that form is not primary but presupposes compilers dealing with an oral tradition already stereotyped in language. For long passages such as the tract on morality and the description of progress in the religious life occur in several discourses and the amount of matter common to different Suttas and Nikayas is surprising. Thus nearly the whole of the long Sutta describing the Buddha's last days and death[2], which at first sight seems to be a connected narrative somewhat different from other Suttas, is found scattered in other parts of the Canon.

[1] This is not true of the more modern Upanishads which are often short treatises specially written to extol a particular deity or doctrine.

[2] Mahâparinibbâna sutta. See the table of parallel passages prefixed to Rhys Davids's translation, *Dialogues of the Buddha*, II. 72.

Thus our oldest texts whether Brahmanic or Buddhist are editions and codifications, perhaps amplifications, of a considerably older oral teaching. They cannot be treated as personal documents similar to the Koran or the Epistles of Paul.

The works of middle antiquity such as the Epics, Puranas, and Mahayanist sutras were also not produced by one author. Many of them exist in more than one recension and they usually consist of a nucleus enveloped and sometimes itself affected by additions which may exceed the original matter in bulk. The Mahâbhârata and Prajñâpâramitâ are not books in the European sense: we cannot give a date or a table of contents for the first edition[1]: they each represent a body of literature whose composition extended over a long period. As time goes on, history naturally grows clearer and literary personalities become more distinct, yet the later Puranas are not attributed to human authors and were susceptible of interpolation even in recent times. Thus the story of Genesis has been incorporated in the Bhavishya Purana, apparently after Protestant missionaries had begun to preach in India.

The other point to which I would draw attention is the importance of relatively modern works, which supersede the older scriptures, especially in Hinduism. This phenomenon is common in many countries, for only a few books such as the Bhagavad-gîtâ, the Gospels and the sayings of Confucius have a portion of the eternal and universal sufficient to outlast the wear and tear of a thousand years. Vedic literature is far from being discredited in India, though some Tantras say openly that it is useless. It still has a place in ritual and is appealed to by reforming sects. But to see Hinduism in proper perspective we must remember that from the time of the Buddha till now, the composition of religious literature in India has been almost uninterrupted and that almost every century has produced works accepted by some sect as infallible scripture. For most Vishnuites the Bhagavad-gîtâ is the beginning of sacred literature and the Nârâyaṇîya[2] is also held in high esteem: the philosophy of each sect is usually determined by a commentary on the Brahma Sutras: the Bhagavata Purana (perhaps in a vernacular

[1] Much the same is true of the various editions of the Vinaya and the Mahâvastu. These texts were produced by a process first of collection and then of amplification.

[2] The latter part of Mahâbhârata XII.

paraphrase) and the Ramayana of Tulsi Das are probably the favourite reading of the laity and for devotional purposes may be supplemented by a collection of hymns such as the Namghosha, copies of which actually receive homage in Assam. The average man—even the average priest—regards all these as sacred works without troubling himself with distinctions as to *śruti* and *smṛiti*, and the Vedas and Upanishads are hardly within his horizon.

In respect of sacred literature Buddhism is more conservative than Hinduism, or to put it another way, has been less productive in the last fifteen hundred years. The Hinayanists are like those Protestant sects which still profess not to go beyond the Bible. The monks read the Abhidhamma and the laity the Suttas, though perhaps both are disposed to use extracts and compendiums rather than the full ancient texts. Among the Mahayanists the ancient Vinaya and Nikayas exist only as literary curiosities. The former is superseded by modern manuals, the latter by Mahayanist Sutras such as the Lotus and the Happy Land, which are however of respectable antiquity. As in India, each sect selects rather arbitrarily a few books for its own use, without condemning others but also without according to them the formal recognition received by the Old and New Testaments among Christians.

No Asiatic country possesses so large a portion of the critical spirit as China. The educated Chinese, however much they may venerate their classics, think of them as we think of the masterpieces of Greek literature, as texts which may contain wrong readings, interpolations and lacunae, which owe whatever authority they possess to the labours of the scholars who collected, arranged and corrected them. This attitude is to some extent the result of the attempt made by the First Emperor about 200 B.C. to destroy the classical literature and to its subsequent laborious restoration. At a time when the Indians regarded the Veda as a verbal revelation, certain and divine in every syllable, the Chinese were painfully recovering and repiecing their ancient chronicles and poems from imperfect manuscripts and fallible memories. The process obliged them to enquire at every step whether the texts which they examined were genuine and complete: to admit that they might be defective or paraphrases of a difficult original. Hence the

Chinese have sound principles of criticism unknown to the Hindus and in discussing the date of an ancient work or the probability of an alleged historical event they generally use arguments which a European scholar can accept.

Chinese literature has a strong ethical and political flavour which tempered the extravagance of imported Indian ideas. Most Chinese systems assert more or less plainly that right conduct is conduct in harmony with the laws of the State and the Universe.

18. *Morality and Will*

It is dangerous to make sweeping statements about the huge mass of Indian literature, but I think that most Buddhist and Brahmanic systems assume that morality is merely a means of obtaining happiness[1] and is not obedience to a categorical imperative or to the will of God. Morality is by inference raised to the status of a cosmic law, because evil deeds will infallibly bring evil consequences to the doer in this life or in another. But it is not commonly spoken of as such a law. The usual point of view is that man desires happiness and for this morality is a necessary though insufficient preparation. But there may be higher states which cannot be expressed in terms of happiness.

The will receives more attention in European philosophy than in Indian, whether Buddhist or Brahmanic, which both regard it not as a separate kind of activity but as a form of thought. As such it is not neglected in Buddhist psychology: will, desire and struggle are recognized as good provided their object is good, a point overlooked by those who accuse Buddhism of preaching inaction[2].

Schopenhauer's doctrine that will is the essential fact in the universe and in life may appear to have analogies to Indian thought: it would be easy for instance to quote passages from the Pitakas showing that *taṇhâ*, thirst, craving or desire, is the

[1] Though European religions emphasize man's duty to God, they do not exclude the pursuit of happiness: e.g. Westminster Shorter Catechism (1647), Question 1, "What is the chief end of man? *A*. Man's chief end is to glorify God and to enjoy him for ever."

[2] Mrs Rhys Davids has brought out the importance of the will for Buddhist ethics in several works. See *J.R.A.S.* 1898, p. 47 and *Buddhism*, pp. 221 ff. See also Maj. Nik. 19 for a good example of Buddhist views as to the necessity and method of cultivating the will.

force which makes and remakes the world. But such statements must be taken as generalizations respecting the world as it is rather than as implying theories of its origin, for though *taṇhâ* is a link in the chain of causation, it is not regarded as an ultimate principle more than any other link but is made to depend on feeling. The Mâyâ of the Vedânta is not so much the affirmation of the will to live as the illusion that we have a real existence apart from Brahman, and the same may be said of Ahaṃkâra in the Sânkhya philosophy. It is the principle of egoism and individuality, but its essence is not so much self-assertion as the *mistaken* idea that this is *mine*, that *I* am happy or unhappy.

There is a question much debated in European philosophy but little argued in India, namely the freedom of the will. The active European feeling the obligation and the difficulties of morality is perplexed by the doubt whether he really has the power to act as he wishes. This problem has not much troubled the Hindus and rightly, as I think. For if the human will is not free, what does freedom mean? What example of freedom can be quoted with which to contrast the supposed non-freedom of the will? If in fact it is from the will that our notion of freedom is derived, is it not unreasonable to say that the will is not free? Absolute freedom in the sense of something regulated by no laws is unthinkable. When a thing is conditioned by external causes it is dependent. When it is conditioned by internal causes which are part of its own nature, it is free. No other freedom is known. An Indian would say that a man's nature is limited by Karma. Some minds are incapable of the higher forms of virtue and wisdom, just as some bodies are incapable of athletic feats. But within the limits of his own nature a human being is free. Indian theology is not much hampered by the mad doctrine that God has predestined some souls to damnation, nor by the idea of Fate, except in so far as Karma is Fate. It is Fate in the sense that Karma inherited from a previous birth is a store of rewards and punishments which must be enjoyed or endured, but it differs from Fate because we are all the time making our own karma and determining the character of our next birth.

The older Upanishads hint at a doctrine analogous to that of Kant, namely that man is bound and conditioned in so far as he is a part of the world of phenomena but free in so far as the self within him is identical with the divine self which is the creator of all bonds and conditions. Thus the Kaushîtaki Upanishad[1] says, "He it is who causes the man whom he will lead upwards from these worlds to do good works and He it is who causes the man whom he will lead downwards to do evil works. He is the guardian of the world, He is the ruler of the world, He is the Lord of the world and He is myself." Here the last words destroy the apparent determinism of the first part of the sentence. And similarly the Châdogya Upanishad says, "They who depart hence without having known the Self and those true desires, for them there is no freedom in all worlds. But they who depart hence after knowing the Self and those true desires, for them there is freedom in all worlds[2]."

Early Buddhist literature asserts uncompromisingly that every state of consciousness has a cause and in one of his earliest discourses the Buddha argues that the Skandhas, including mental states, cannot be the Self because we have not free will to make them exactly what we choose[3]. But throughout his ethical teaching it is I think assumed that, subject to the law of karma, conscious action is equivalent to spontaneous action. Good mental states can be made to grow and bad mental states to decrease until the stage is reached when the saint knows that he is free. It may perhaps be thought that the early Buddhists did not realize the consequences of applying their doctrine of causation to psychology and hence never faced the possibility of determinism. But determinism, fatalism, and the uselessness of effort formed part of the paradoxical teaching of Makkhali Gosala reported in the Pitakas and therefore well known. If neither the Jains nor the Buddhists allowed themselves to be embarrassed by such denials of free will, the inference is that in some matters at least the Hindus had strong common sense and declined to accept any view which takes away from man the responsibility and lordship of his own soul.

[1] Kaush. Up. III. 8.

[2] The words are kâmacâra and akâmacâra. Chând. Up. 8. 1—6.

[3] Mahâvag. I. 6. *E.g.* Ajâtasattu (Dig. Nik. 2, *ad fin.*) would have obtained the eye of truth, had he not been a parricide. The consequent distortion of mind made higher states impossible.

19. *The Origin of Evil*

The reader will have gathered from what precedes that Hinduism has little room for the Devil[1]. Buddhism being essentially an ethical system recognizes the importance of the Tempter or Mâra, but still Mâra is not an evil spirit who has spoilt a good world. In Hinduism, whether pantheistic or polytheistic, there is even less disposition to personify evil in one figure, and most Indian religious systems are disposed to think of the imperfections of the world as suffering rather than as sin.

Yet the existence of evil is the chief reason for the existence of religion, at least of such religions as promise salvation, and the explanation of evil is the chief problem of all religions and philosophies, and the problem which they all alike are conspicuously unsuccessful in solving. I can assign no reason for rejecting as untenable the idea that the ultimate reality may be a duality—a good and an evil spirit—or even a plurality[2], but still it is unthinkable for me and I believe for most minds. If there are two ultimate beings, either they must be complementary and necessary one to the other, in which case it seems to me more correct to describe them as two aspects of one being, or if they are quite separate, my mind postulates (but I do not know why) a third being who is the cause of them both.

The problem of evil is not quite the same for Indian and European pantheists. The European pantheist holds that since God is all things or in all things, evil is only something viewed out of due perspective: that the world would be seen to be perfect, if it could be seen as a whole, or that evil will be eliminated in the course of development. But he cannot explain why the partial view of the world which human beings are obliged to take shows the existence of obvious evil. The Hindus think that it is possible and better for the soul to leave the vain show of the world and find peace in union with God. They are therefore not concerned to prove that the world is good, although they cannot explain why God allows it to exist. The Upanishads

[1] But all general statements about Hinduism are liable to exceptions. The evil spirit Duḥsaha described in the Mârkandeya Purâna (chaps. L and LI) comes very near the Devil.

[2] I can understand that the immediate reality is a duality or plurality and that the one spirit may appear in many shapes.

contain some myths and parables about the introduction of evil but they do not say that a naturally good world was spoilt[1]. They rather imply that increasing complexity involves the increase of evil as well as of good. This is also the ground thought of the Aggañña Sutta, the Buddhist Genesis (Dig. Nik. xxvii.).

I think that the substance of much Indian pantheism—late Buddhist as well as Brahmanic—is that the world, the soul and God (the three terms being practically the same) have two modes of existence: one of repose and bliss, the other of struggle and trouble. Of these the first mode is the better and it is only by mistake[2] that the eternal spirit adopts the latter. But both the mistake and the correction of it are being eternally repeated. Such a formulation of the Advaita philosophy would no doubt be regarded in India as wholly unorthodox. Yet orthodoxy admits that the existence of the world is due to the coexistence of Mâyâ (illusion) with Brahman (spirit) and also states that the task of the soul is to pass beyond Mâyâ to Brahman. If this is so, there is either a real duality (Brahman and Mâyâ) or else Mâyâ is an aspect of Brahman, but an aspect which the soul should transcend and avoid, and for whose existence no reason whatever is given. The more theistic forms of Indian religion, whether Sivaite or Vishnuite, tend to regard individual souls and matter as eternal. By the help of God souls can obtain release from matter. But here again there is no explanation why the soul is contaminated by matter or ignorance.

It is clearly illogical to condemn the Infinite as bad or a mistake. Buddhism is perhaps sometimes open to this charge because on account of its exceedingly cautious language about nirvana it fails to set it up as a reality contrasted with the world of suffering. But many varieties of Indian religion do

[1] *E.g.* Chând. Up. v. 1. 2. Bri. Ar. Up. i. 3. In the Pâñcarâtra we do hear of a jñânabhraṃsa or a fall from knowledge analogous to the fall of man in Christian theology. Souls have naturally unlimited knowledge but this from some reason becomes limited and obscured, so that religion is necessary to show the soul the right way. Here the ground idea seems to be not that any devil has spoilt the world but that ignorance is necessary for the world process, for otherwise mankind would be one with God and there would be no world. See Schrader, *Introd. to the Pâñcarâtra*, pp. 78 and 83.

[2] The Śatapatha Brâhmana has a curious legend (xi. 1. 6. 8 ff.) in which the Creator admits that he made evil spirits by mistake and smites them. In the Kârikâ of Gauḍapâda, 2. 19 it is actually said: Mayaishâ tasya devasya yayâ sammohitaḥ svayam.

emphatically point to the infinite reality behind and beyond Mâyâ. It is only Mâyâ which is unsatisfactory because it is partial.

Another attempt to make the Universe intelligible regards it as an eternal rhythm playing and pulsing outwards from spirit to matter (pravritti) and then backwards and inwards from matter to spirit (nirvritti). This idea seems implied by Śankara's view that creation is similar to the sportive impulses of exuberant youth and the Bhagavad-gîtâ is familiar with *pravritti* and *nirvritti*, but the double character of the rhythm is emphasized most clearly in Śâkta treatises. Ordinary Hinduism concentrates its attention on the process of liberation and return to Brahman, but the Tantras recognize and consecrate both movements, the outward throbbing stream of energy and enjoyment (bhukti) and the calm returning flow of liberation and peace. Both are happiness, but the wise understand that the active outward movement is right and happy only up to a certain point and under certain restrictions.

That great poet Tulsi Das hints at an explanation of the creation or of God's expansion of himself which will perhaps commend itself to Europeans more than most Indian ideas, namely that the bliss enjoyed by God and the souls whom he loves is greater than the bliss of solitary divinity[1].

20. *Church and State*

I will now turn to another point, namely the relations of Church and State. These are simplest in Buddhism, which teaches that the truth is one, that all men ought to follow it and that all good kings should honour and encourage it. This is also the Christian position but Buddhism has almost always been tolerant and has hardly ever countenanced the doctrine that

[1] He does not say this expressly and it requires careful statement in India where it is held strongly that God being perfect cannot add to his bliss or perfection by creating anything. Compare Dante, *Paradiso*, XXIX. 13—18:

Non per aver a sè di bene acquisto,
 ch' esser non può, ma perchè suo splendore
 potesse risplendendo dir: subsisto.
In sua eternità di tempo fuore,
 fuor d' ogni altro comprender, come i piacque,
 s' aperse in nuovi amor l' eterno amore.

error should be suppressed by force[1]. Buddhism does not claim to cover the whole field of religion as understood in Europe: if people like to propitiate spirits in the hope of obtaining wealth and crops, it permits them to do so. In Japan and Tibet Buddhism has played a more secular role than in other countries, analogous to the struggles of the mediæval European church for temporal authority. In Japan the great monasteries very nearly became the chief military as well as the chief political power and this danger was averted only by the destruction of Hieizan and other large establishments in the sixteenth century. What was prevented in Japan did actually happen in Tibet, for the monasteries became stronger than any of the competing secular factions and the principal sect set up an ecclesiastical government singularly like the Papacy. In southern countries, such as Burma and Ceylon, Buddhism made no attempt to interfere in politics. This aloofness is particularly remarkable in Siam and Camboja, where state festivals are usually conducted by Brahmans not by Buddhist ecclesiastics. In Siam, as formerly in Burma, the king being a Buddhist is in some ways the head of the Church. He may reform lax discipline or incorrect observances, but apparently not of his own authority but merely as an executive power enforcing the opinion of the higher clergy.

Buddhism and Hinduism both have the idea that the monk or priest is a person who in virtue of ordination or birth lives on a higher level than others. He may teach and do good but irrespective of that it is the duty of the laity to support the priesthood. This doctrine is preached by Hinduism in a stronger form than by Buddhism. The intellectual superiority of the Brahmans as a caste was sufficiently real to ensure its acceptance and in politics they had the good sense to rule by serving, to be ministers and not kings. In theory and to a considerable extent in practice, the Brahmans and their gods are not an *imperium in imperio* but an *imperium super imperium*. The position was possible only because, unlike the Papacy and unlike the Lamas of Tibet, they had no Pope and no hierarchy. They produced no à'Beckets or Hildebrands and no Inquisition. They did not quarrel with science but monopolized it.

In India kings are expected to maintain the priesthood and

[1] The history of Japan and Tibet offers some exceptions.

the temples yet Hinduism rarely assumes the form of a state religion[1] nor does it admit, as state religions generally have to admit, that the secular arm has a co-ordinate jurisdiction in ecclesiastical matters. Yet it affects every department of social life and a Hindu who breaks with it loses his social status. Hindu deities are rarely tribal gods like Athene of Athens or the gods of Mr Kipling and the German Emperor. There are thousands of shrines specially favoured by a divine presence but the worshippers think of that presence not as the protector of a race or city but as a special manifestation of a universal though often invisible power. The conquests of Mohammedans and Christians are not interpreted as meaning that the gods of Hinduism have succumbed to alien deities.

The views prevalent in China and Japan as to the relations of Church and State are almost the antipodes of those described. In those countries it is the hardly dissembled theory of the official world that religion is a department of government and that there should be regulations for gods and worship, just as there are for ministers and etiquette. If we say that religion is identified with the government in Tibet and forms an *imperium super imperium* in India, we may compare its position in the Far East to native states under British rule. There is no interference with creeds provided they respect ethical and social conventions: interesting doctrines and rites are appreciated: the Government accepts and rewards the loyal co-operation of the Buddhist and Taoist priesthoods but maintains the right to restrict their activity should it take a wrong political turn or should an excessive increase in the number of monks seem a public danger. The Chinese Imperial Government successfully claimed the strangest powers of ecclesiastical discipline, since it promoted and degraded not only priests but deities. In both China and Japan there has often been a strong current of feeling in the official classes against Buddhism but on the other hand it often had the support of both emperors and people, and princes not infrequently joined the clergy, especially when it was desirable for them to live in retirement. Confucianism and Shintoism, which are ethical and ceremonial rather than doctrinal, have been in the past to some extent a law to the governments of China and Japan, or more accurately an aspect of those governments. But for many cen-

[1] There are some exceptions, *e.g.* ancient Camboja, the Sikhs and the Marathas.

turies Far Eastern statesmen have rarely regarded Buddhism and Taoism as more than interesting and legitimate activities, to be encouraged and regulated like educational and scientific institutions.

21. *Public Worship and Ceremonial*

In no point does Hinduism differ from western religions more than in its public worship and, in spite of much that is striking and interesting, the comparison is not to the advantage of India. It is true that temple worship is not so important for the Hindus as Church services are for the Christian. They set more store on home ceremonies and on contemplation. Still the temples of India are so numerous, so conspicuous and so crowded that the religion which maintains them must to some extent be judged by them.

At any rate they avoid the faults of public worship in the west. The practice of arranging the congregation in seats for which they pay seems to me more irreligious than the slovenliness of the heathen and makes the whole performance resemble a very dull concert.

Protestant services are in the main modelled on the ritual of the synagogue. They are meetings of the laity at which the scriptures are read, prayers offered, sermons preached and benedictions pronounced. The clergy play a principal but not exclusive part. The rites of the Roman and Eastern Churches have borrowed much from pagan ceremonial but still they have not wholly departed from the traditions of the synagogue. These have also served as a model for Mohammedan ritual which differs from the Jewish in little but its almost military regularity.

But with all this the ordinary ritual of Hindu temples[1] has nothing in common. It derives from another origin and follows other lines. The temple is regarded as the court of a prince and the daily ceremonies are the attendance of his courtiers on him. He must be awakened, fed, amused and finally put to bed. This conception of ritual prevailed in Egypt but in India there is no

[1] But there are other kinds of worship, such as the old Vedic sacrifices which are still occasionally performed, and the burnt offerings (homa) still made in some temples. There are also tantric ceremonies and in Assam the public worship of the Vishnuites has probably been influenced by the ritual of Lamas in neighbouring Buddhist countries.

trace of it in Vedic literature and perhaps it did not come into fashion until Gupta times. Although the laity may be present and salute the god, such worship cannot be called congregational. Yet in other ways a Hindu temple may provide as much popular worship as a Nonconformist chapel. In the corridors will generally be found readers surrounded by an attentive crowd to whom they recite and expound the Mahabharata or some other sacred text. At festivals and times of pilgrimage the precincts are thronged by a crowd of worshippers the like of which is hardly to be seen in Europe, worshippers not only devout but fired with an enthusiasm which bursts into a mighty chorus of welcome when the image of the god is brought forth from the inner shrine.

The earlier forms of Buddhist ceremonial are of the synagogue type (though in no way derived from Jewish sources) for, though there is no prayer, they consist chiefly of confession, preaching and reading the scriptures. But this puritanic severity could not be popular and the veneration of images and relics was soon added to the ritual. The former was adopted by Buddhism earlier than by the Brahmans. The latter, though a conspicuous feature of Buddhism in all lands, is almost unknown to Hinduism. In their later developments Buddhist and Christian ceremonies show an extraordinary resemblance due in my opinion chiefly to convergence, though I do not entirely exclude mutual influence. Both Buddhism and Roman Catholicism accepted pagan ritual with some reservations and refinements. The worship has for its object an image or a shrine containing a relic which is placed in a conspicuous position at the end of the hall of worship[1]. Animal sacrifices are rejected but offerings of flowers, lights and incense are permitted, as well as the singing of hymns. It is not altogether strange if Buddhist and Catholic rituals starting from the same elements ended by producing similar scenic effects.

Yet though the scenic effect may be similar, there is often a difference in the nature of the rite. Direct invocations are not wanting in Tibetan and Far Eastern Buddhism but many services consist not of prayers but of the recitation of scripture

[1] This position is of great importance as tending to produce a similar arrangement of religious paraphernalia. The similarity disappears when Buddhist ceremonies are performed round Stûpas out of doors.

by which merit is acquired. This merit is then formally transferred by the officiants to some special object, such as the peace of the dead or the prosperity of a living suppliant.

The later phases of both Hinduism and Buddhism are permeated by what is called Tantrism[1], that is to say the endeavour to attain spiritual ends by ritual acts such as gestures and the repetition of formulæ. These expedients are dangerous and may become puerile, but those who ridicule them often forget that they may be termed sacramental with as much propriety as magical and are in fact based on the same theory as the sacraments of the Catholic Church. When a child is made eligible for salvation by sprinkling with water, by the sign of the cross and by the mantra "In the Name of the Father," etc., or when the divine spirit is localized in bread and wine and worshipped, these rites are closely analogous to tantric ceremonial.

The Buddhist temples of the Far East are in original intention copies of Indian edifices and in the larger establishments there is a daily routine of services performed by resident monks. But the management of religious foundations in these countries has been much influenced by old pagan usages as to temples and worship which show an interesting resemblance to the customs of classical antiquity but have little in common with Buddhist or Christian ideas. A Chinese municipal temple is a public building dedicated to a spirit or departed worthy. If sacrifices are offered in it, they are not likely to take place more than three or four times a year. Private persons may go there to obtain luck by burning a little incense or still more frequently to divine the future: public meetings and theatrical performances may be held there, but anything like a congregational service is rare. Just so in ancient Rome a temple might be used for a meeting of the Senate or for funeral games.

22. *The Worship of the Reproductive Forces*

One aspect of Indian religions is so singular that it demands notice, although it is difficult to discuss. I mean the worship of the generative forces. The cult of a god, or more often of a goddess, who personifies the reproductive and also the destruc-

[1] As explained elsewhere, I draw a distinction between Tantrism and Śâktism.

tive powers of nature (for it is not only in India that the two activities are seen to be akin) existed in many countries. It was prominent in Babylonia and Asia Minor, less prominent but still distinctly present in Egypt and in many cases was accompanied by hysterical and immoral rites, by mutilations of the body and offerings of blood. But in most countries such deities and rites are a matter of ancient history: they decayed as civilization grew: in China and Japan, as formerly in Greece and Rome, they are not an important constituent of religion. It is only in India and to some extent in Tibet, which has been influenced by India, that they have remained unabashed until modern times.

If it is right to regard with veneration the great forces of nature, fire, sun and water, a similar feeling towards the reproductive force cannot be unphilosophic or immoral. Nor does the idea that the supreme deity is a mother rather than a father, though startling, contain anything unseemly. Yet it is an undoubted fact that all the great religions except Hinduism, though they may admit a Goddess of Mercy—Kuan-yin or the Madonna—agree in rejecting essentially sexual deities. Modern Europe is probably prudish to excess, but the general practice of mankind testifies that words and acts too nearly connected with sexual things cannot be safely permitted in the temple. This remark would indeed be superfluous were it not that many millions of our Hindu fellow-citizens are of a contrary opinion.

Such practices prevail chiefly among the Śâktas in Bengal and Assam but similar licence is permitted (though the theoretical justification and theological setting are different) in some Vishnuite sects. Both are reprobated by the majority of respectable Hindus, but both find educated and able apologists. And though it may be admitted that worship of the linga may exist without bad effects, moral or intellectual, yet I think that these effects make themselves felt so soon as a sect becomes distinctly erotic. Anyone who visits two such different localities as Kamakhya in Assam and Gokul near Muttra must be struck with the total absence in the shrines of anything that can be called beautiful, solemn or even terrible. The general impression is of something diseased, unclean and undignified. The figure of the Great Goddess of life and death might have fired[1] the

[1] It does not seem to me to have given much inspiration to Rossetti in his *Astarte Syriaca*.

invention of artists but as a matter of fact her worship has paralyzed their hands and brains.

Nor can I give much praise to the Tantras as literature[1]. It is true that, as some authors point out, they contain fine sayings about God and the soul. But in India such things form part of the common literary stock and do not entitle the author to the praise which he would win elsewhere, unless his language or thoughts show originality. Such originality I have not found in those Tantras which are accessible. The magical and erotic parts may have the melancholy distinction of being unlike other works but the philosophical and theological sections could have been produced by any Hindu who had studied these branches of Indian literature.

23. *Hinduism in Practice*

After reviewing the characteristics of a religion it is natural to ask what is its effect on those who profess it. Buddhism, Christianity and Islam offer materials for answering such a question, since they are not racial religions. In historical times they have been accepted by peoples who did not profess them previously and we can estimate the consequences of such changes. But Hinduism has racial or geographical limits. It proselytizes, but hardly outside the Indian area: it is difficult to distinguish it from Indian custom, as the gospel is distinguished from the practice of Europe: it is superfluous to enquire what would be its effect on other countries, since it shows no desire to impose itself on them and they none to accept it. It is, like Shinto in Japan, not a religion which has moulded the national character but the national character finding expression in religion. Shinto and Hinduism are also alike in perpetuating ancient beliefs and practices which seem anachronisms but otherwise they are very different, for many races and languages have contributed their thoughts and hopes to the ocean of Hinduism and they all had an interest in speculation and mysticism unknown to the Japanese.

The fact that Hinduism is something larger and more comprehensive than what we call a religion is one reason why it contains much of dubious moral value. It is analogous not to

[1] But in justice to the Tantras it should be mentioned that the Mahâ-nirvâṇa Tantra, x. 79, prohibits the burning of widows.

Christianity but to European civilization which produces side by side philanthropy and the horrors of war, or to science which has given us the blessings of surgery and the curse of explosives. There is a deep-rooted idea in India that a man's daily life must be accompanied by religious observances and regulated by a religious code, by no means of universal application but still suitable to his particular class. An immoral occupation need not be irreligious: it simply requires gods of a special character. Hence we find Thugs killing and robbing their victims in the name of Kali. But though the Hindu is not at ease unless his customs are sanctioned by his religion, yet religion in the wider sense is not bound by custom, for the founders of many sects have declared that before God there is no caste. A Hindu may devote himself to religion and abandon the world with all its conventions, but if like most men he prefers to live in the world, it is his duty to follow the customs and usages sanctioned for his class and occupation. Thus as Sister Nivedita has shown in her beautiful writings, cooking, washing and all the humble round of domestic life become one long ritual of purification and prayer in which the entertainment of a guest stands out as a great sacrifice. But though religion may thus give beauty and holiness to common things, yet inasmuch as it sanctifies what it finds rather than prescribes what should be, it must bear the blame for foolish and even injurious customs. Child marriages have nothing to do with the creed of Hinduism, yet many Hindus, especially Hindu women, would feel it irreligious, as well as a social disgrace, to let a daughter become adult without being married.

A comparison of Indian Mohammedans and Hindus suggests that the former are more warlike and robust, the latter more intellectual and ingenious. The fact that some Mohammedans belong to hardy tribes of invaders must be taken into account but Islam deserves the credit of having introduced a simple and fairly healthy rule of life which does not allow every caste to make its own observances into a divine law. Yet it would seem that the medical and sanitary rules of Hinduism deserve less abuse than they generally receive. Col. King, Sanitary Commissioner of the Madras Presidency, is quoted as saying in a lecture[1]: "The Institutes of Vishnu and the Laws of Manu fit

[1] See *Asiatic Review*, July, 1916, p. 33.

in excellently with the bacteriology, parasitology and applied hygiene of the West. The hygiene of food and water, private and public conservancy, disease suppression and prevention, are all carefully dealt with."

Hinduism certainly has proved marvellously stimulating to the intellect or—shall we put it the other way?—is the product of profound, acute, and restless minds. It cannot be justly accused of being enervating or melancholy, for many Hindu states were vigorous and warlike[1] and the accounts of early travellers indicate that in pre-mohammedan days the people were humane, civilized and contented. It created an original and spiritual art, for Indian art, more than any other, is the direct product of religion and not merely inspired by it. In ages when original talent is rare this close relation has disadvantages for it tends to make all art symbolic and conventional. An artist must not represent a deity in the way that he thinks most effective: the proportions, attitude and ornaments are all prescribed, not because they suit a picture or statue but because they mean something.

Indian literature is also directly related to religion. Its extent is well-nigh immeasurable. I will not alarm the reader with statistics of the theological and metaphysical treatises which it contains. A little of such goes a long way even when they are first-rate, but India may at least boast of having more theological works which, if considered as intellectual productions, must be placed in the first class than Europe. Nor are religious writings of a more human type absent—the language of heart to heart and of the heart to God. The Ramayana of Tulsi Das and the Tiruvwçagam are extolled by Groâse, Grierson and Pope (all of them Christians, I believe) as not only masterpieces of literature but as noble expressions of pure devotion, and the poems of Kabir and Tukaram, if less considerable as literary efforts, show the same spiritual quality. Indian poetry, even when nominally secular, is perhaps too much under religious influence to suit our taste and the long didactic and philosophic harangues which interrupt the action of the Mahabharata seem to us inartistic, yet to those who take the pains to familiarize themselves with what at first is strange, the Mahabharata is, I think, a greater poem than the *Iliad*. It should not be regarded

[1] *E.g.* Vijayanagar, the Marathas and the states of Rajputana.

as an epic distended and interrupted by interpolated sermons but as the scripture of the warrior caste, which sees in the soldier's life a form of religion.

I have touched in several places on the defects of Hinduism. They are due partly to its sanction of customs which have no necessary connection with it and partly to its extravagance, which in the service of the gods sees no barriers of morality or humanity. But suttee, human sacrifices and orgies strike the imagination and assume an importance which they have not and never had for Hinduism as a whole. If Hinduism were really bad, so many great thoughts, so many good lives could not have grown up in its atmosphere. More than any other religion it is a quest of truth and not a creed, which must necessarily become antiquated: it admits the possibility of new scriptures, new incarnations, new institutions. It has no quarrel with knowledge or speculation: perhaps it excludes materialists, because they have no common ground with religion, but it tolerates even the Sânkhya philosophy which has nothing to say about God or worship. It is truly dynamic and in the past whenever it has seemed in danger of withering it has never failed to bud with new life and put forth new flowers.

More than other religions, Hinduism appeals to the soul's immediate knowledge and experience of God. It has sacred books innumerable but they agree in little but this, that the soul can come into contact and intimacy with its God, whatever name be given him and even if he be superpersonal. The possibility and truth of this experience is hardly questioned in India and the task of religion is to bring it about, not to promote the welfare of tribes and states but to effect the enlightenment and salvation of souls.

The love of the Hindus for every form of argument and philosophizing is well known but it is happily counterbalanced by another tendency. Instinct and religion both bring them into close sympathy with nature. India is in the main an agricultural country[1] and nearly three-quarters of the population are villagers whose life is bound up with the welfare of plants and animals and lies at the mercy of rivers that overflow or skies that withhold the rain. To such people nature-myths and sacred

[1] According to the census of 1911 no less than 72 per cent. of the population live by agriculture.

animals appeal with a force that Europeans rarely understand. The parrots that perch on the pinnacles of the temple and the oxen that rest in the shade of its courts are not intruders but humble brothers of mankind, who may also be the messengers of the gods.

24. *Buddhism in Practice*

As I said above, it is easier to estimate the effects of Buddhism than of Hinduism, for its history is the chronicle of a great missionary enterprise and there are abundant materials for studying the results of its diffusion.

Even its adversaries must admit that it has many excellent qualities. It preaches morality and charity and was the first religion to proclaim to the world—not to a caste or country—that these are the foundation of that Law which if kept brings happiness. It civilized many nations, for instance the Tibetans and Mongols. It has practised toleration and true unworldliness, if not without any exception[1], at least far more generally than any other great religion. It has directly encouraged art and literature and, so far as I know, has never opposed the progress of knowledge. But two charges may be brought against it which deserve consideration. First that its pessimistic doctrines and monastic institutions are, if judged by ordinary standards, bad for the welfare of a nation: second that more than any other religion it is liable to become corrupt.

In all Buddhist lands, though good laymen are promised the blessings of religion, the monastic and contemplative life is held up as the ideal. In Christendom, this ideal is rejected by Protestants and for the Roman and Oriental Churches it is only one among others. Hence every one's judgment of Buddhism must in a large measure depend on what he thinks of this ideal. Monks are not of this world and therefore the world hateth

[1] The chief exceptions are: (*a*) the Tibetan church has acquired and holds power by political methods. It is an exact parallel to the Papacy, but it has never burnt people. (*b*) In mediæval Japan the great monasteries became fortified castles with lands and troops of their own. They fought one another and were a menace to the state. Later the Tokugawa sovereigns had the assistance of the Buddhist clergy in driving out Christianity but I do not think that their action can be compared either in extent or cruelty with the Inquisition. (*c*) In China Buddhism was in many reigns associated with a dissolute court and palace intrigues. This led to many scandals and great waste of money.

them. If they keep to themselves, they are called lazy and useless. If they take part in secular matters, they meet with even severer criticism. Yet can any one doubt that what is most needed in the present age is more people who have leisure and ability to think?

Whatever evil is said of Buddhist monks is also said of Mt Athos and similar Christian establishments. I am far from saying that this depreciation of the cloistered life is just in either case but any impartial critic of monastic institutions must admit that their virtues avoid publicity and their faults attract attention. In all countries a large percentage of monks are indolent: it is the temptation which besets all but the elect. Yet the Buddhist ideal of the man who has renounced the world leaves no place for slackness, nor I think does the Christian. Buddhist monks are men of higher aspirations than others: they try to make themselves supermen by cultivating not the forceful and domineering part of their nature but the gentle, charitable and intelligent part. The laity treat them with the greatest respect provided that they set an example of a life better than most men can live. A monastic system of this kind is found in Burma. I do not mean that it is not found in other Buddhist lands, but I cite an instance which I have seen myself and which has impressed most observers favourably.

The Burmese monks are not far from the ideal of Gotama, yet perhaps by adhering somewhat strictly to the letter of his law they have lost something of the freedom which he contemplated. In his time there were no books: the mind found exercise and knowledge in conversation. A monastery was not a permanent residence, except during the rainy season, but merely a halting-place for the brethren who were habitually wanderers, continually hearing and seeing something new. Hermits and solitary dwellers in the forests were not unknown but assuredly the majority of the brethren had no intention of secluding themselves from the intellectual life of the age. What would Gotama have done had he lived some hundreds or thousands of years later? I see no reason to doubt that he would have encouraged the study of literature and science. He would probably have praised all art which expresses noble and spiritual ideas, while misdoubting representations of sensuous beauty.

The second criticism—that Buddhists are prone to corrupt

their faith—is just, for their courteous acquiescence in other creeds enfeebles and denaturalizes their own. In Annam, Korea and some parts of China though there are temples and priests more or less deserving the name of Buddhist, there is no idea that Buddhism is a distinct religion or mode of life. Such statements as that the real religion of the Burmese is not Buddhism but animism are, I think, incorrect, but even the Burmese are dangerously tolerant.

This weakness is not due to any positive defect, since Buddhism provides for those who lead the higher life a strenuous curriculum and for the laity a system of morality based on rational grounds and differing little from the standard accepted in both Europe and China, except that it emphasizes the duties of mankind to animals. The weakness comes from the absence of any command against superstitious rites and beliefs. When the cardinal principles of Buddhism are held strongly these accessories do not matter, but the time comes when the creeper which was once an ornament grows into the walls of the shrine and splits the masonry. The faults of western religions are mainly faults of self-assertion—such as the Inquisition and opposition to science. The faults of Indian religions are mainly tolerance of what does not belong to them and sometimes of what is not only foreign to them but bad in itself.

Buddhism has been both praised and blamed as a religion which acknowledges neither God nor the soul[1] and its acceptance in its later phases of the supernatural has been regarded as proving the human mind's natural need of theism. But it is rather an illustration of that craving for personal though superhuman help which makes Roman Catholics supplement theism with the worship of saints.

[1] See for instance Huxley's striking definition of Buddhism in his *Romanes Lecture*, 1893. "A system which knows no God in the western sense; which denies a soul to man: which counts the belief in immortality a blunder and the hope of it a sin: which refuses any efficacy to prayer and sacrifice: which bids men look to nothing but their own efforts for salvation: which in its original purity knew nothing of vows of obedience and never sought the aid of the secular arm: yet spread over a considerable moiety of the old world with marvellous rapidity and is still with whatever base admixture of foreign superstitions the dominant creed of a large fraction of mankind." But some of this is too strongly phrased. Early Buddhism counted the desire for heaven as a hindrance to the highest spiritual life, but if a man had not attained to that plane and was bound to be reborn somewhere, it did not question that his natural desire to be reborn in heaven was right and proper.

On the whole it is correct to say that Buddhism (except perhaps in very exceptional sects) has always taken and still takes a point of view which has little in common with European theism. The world is not thought of as the handiwork of a divine personality nor the moral law as his will. The fact that religion can exist without these ideas is of capital importance[1]. But any statements implying that Buddhism divorces morality from the doctrine of immortality may be misunderstood for it teaches that just as an old man may suffer for the follies of his youth, so faults committed in one life may be punished in another. Rewards and punishments in another world were part of the creed of Asoka and tradition represents the missionaries who converted Ceylon as using this simple argument[2]. It would not however be true to say that Buddhism makes the value of morality contingent on another world. The life of an Arhat which includes the strictest morality is commended on its own account as the best and happiest existence.

European assertions about Buddhism often imply that it sets up as an ideal and goal either annihilation or some condition of dreamy bliss. Modern Buddhists who mostly neglect Nirvana as something beyond their powers, just as the ordinary Christian does not say that he hopes to become a saint, lose much of the Master's teaching but do it less injustice than such misrepresentations. The Buddha did not describe Nirvana as something to be won after death, but as a state of happiness attainable in this life by strenuous endeavour—a state of perfect peace but compatible with energy, as his own example showed.

25. *Interest of Indian Thought for Europe*

We are now in a better position to answer the question asked at the beginning of this introduction, Is Indian thought of value or at least of interest for Europe?

[1] It may of course be denied that Buddhism is a religion. In this connection some remarks of Mr Bradley are interesting. "The doctrine that there cannot be a religion without a personal God is to my mind entirely false" (*Essays on Truth and Reality*, p. 432). "I cannot accept a personal God as the ultimate truth" (*ib.* 449). "There are few greater responsibilities which a man can take on himself than to have proclaimed or even hinted that without immortality all religion is a cheat, all morality a self-deception" (*Appearance and Reality*, p. 510).

[2] Mahâvaṃsa, XII. 29, XIV. 58 and 64. Dîpavaṃsa, XII. 84 and 85, XIII. 7 and 8.

Let me confess that I cannot share the confidence in the superiority of Europeans and their ways which is prevalent in the west. Whatever view we take of the rights and wrongs of the recent war, it is clearly absurd for Europe as a whole to pose in the presence of such doings as a qualified instructor in humanity and civilization. Many of those who are proudest of our fancied superiority escape when the chance offers from western civilization and seek distraction in exploration, and many who have spent their lives among what they consider inferior races are uneasy when they retire and settle at home. In fact European civilization is not satisfying and Asia can still offer something more attractive to many who are far from Asiatic in spirit. Yet though most who have paid even a passing visit to the East feel its charm, the history, art and literature of Asia are still treated with ignorant indifference in cultured circles—an ignorance and indifference which are extraordinary in Englishmen who have so close a connection with India and devote a disproportionate part of their education to ancient Greece and Rome. I have heard a professor of history in an English university say that he thought the history of India began with the advent of the British and that he did not know that China had any history at all. And Matthew Arnold in speaking of Indian thought[1] hardly escaped meriting his own favourite epithets of condemnation, Philistine and *saugrenu*.

Europeans sometimes mention it as an amazing and almost ridiculous circumstance that an educated Chinese can belong to three religions, Confucianism, Taoism and Buddhism. But I find this attitude of mind eminently sensible. Confucianism is an admirable religion for State ceremonies and College chapels. By attending its occasional rites one shows a decent respect for Heaven and Providence and commits oneself to nothing. And though a rigid Confucianist may have the contempt of a scholar and statesman for popular ideas, yet the most devout Buddhist and Taoist can conform to Confucianism without scruple, whereas many who have attended an English coronation service must have wondered at the language which they seemed to approve of by their presence. And in China if you wish to water the aridity of Confucianism, you can find in Buddhism or Taoism whatever you want in the way of emotion or philosophy and you will not

[1] *Essays in Criticism.* Second series. Amiel.

be accused of changing your religion because you take this refreshment. This temper is not good for creating new and profound religious thought, but it is good for sampling and appreciating the "varieties of religious experience" which offer their results as guides for this and other lives.

For religion is systematized religious experience and this experience depends on temperament. There can therefore be no one religion in the European sense and it is one of the Hindus' many merits that they recognize this. Some people ask of religion forgiveness for their sins, others communion with the divine: most want health and wealth, many crave for an explanation of life and death. Indian religion accommodates itself to these various needs. Nothing is more surprising than the variety of its phases except the underlying unity.

This power of varying in sympathetic response to the needs of many minds and growing in harmony with the outlook of successive ages, is a contrast to the pretended *quod semper, quod ubique, quod ab omnibus*[1] of Western Churches, for in view of their differences and mutual hostility it can only be called a pretence. Indians recognize that only the greatest and simplest religious questions can be asked now in the same words that came to the lips more than two thousand years ago and even if the questions are the same, the answers of the thoughtful are still as widely divergent as the pronouncements of the Buddha and the Brahmans. But nearly all the propositions contained in a European creed involve matters of history or science which are obviously affected by research and discovery as much as are astronomy or medicine, and not only are the propositions out of date but they mostly refer to problems which have lost their interest. But Indian religion eschews creeds and will not die with the spread of knowledge. It will merely change and enter a new phase of life in which much that is now believed and practised will be regarded as the gods and rites of the Veda are regarded now.

I do not think that there is much profit in comparing religions, which generally means exalting one at the expense of the others, but rather that it is interesting and useful to learn what others, especially those least like ourselves, think of these

[1] This definition of orthodoxy is due to St Vincent of Lerins. *Quod ubique, quod semper, quod ab omnibus creditum est.*

matters. And in religious questions Asia has a distinct right to be heard.

For if Europeans have any superiority over Asiatics, it lies in practical science, finance and administration, not in thought or art. If one were collecting views about philosophy and religion in Europe, one would not begin by consulting financiers and engineers, and the policeman who stands in the middle of the street and directs the traffic to this side and that is not intellectually superior to those who obey him as if he were something superhuman. Europeans in Asia are like such a policeman: their gifts are authority and power to organize: in other respects their superiority is imaginary.

I do not think that Christianity will ever make much progress in Asia, for what is commonly known by that name is not the teaching of Christ but a rearrangement of it made in Europe and like most European institutions practical rather than thoughtful. And as for the teaching of Christ himself, the Indian finds it excellent but not ample or satisfying. There is little in it which cannot be found in some of the many scriptures of Hinduism and it is silent on many points about which they speak, if not with convincing authority, at least with suggestive profundity. Neither do I think that Europe is likely to adopt Buddhist or Brahmanic methods of thought on any large scale. Theosophical and Buddhist societies have my sympathy but it is sympathy with lonely workers in an unpopular cause and I am not sure that they always understand what they try to teach. There is truth at the bottom of the dogma that all Buddhas must be born and teach in India: Asiatic doctrine may commend itself to European minds but it fits awkwardly into European life.

But this is no reason for refusing to accord to Indian religion at least the same attention that we give to Plato and Aristotle. Every idea which is held strongly by any large body of men is worthy of respectful examination, although I do not think that because an opinion is widespread it is therefore true. Thus the idea that in the remote past there was some kind of paradise or golden age and that the span of human life was once much longer than now is found among most nations. Yet research and analogy suggest that it is without foundation. The fact that about half the population of the world has come under the influence of

Hindu ideas gives Indian thought historical importance rather than authority. The claim of India to the attention of the world is that she, more than any other nation since history began, has devoted herself to contemplating the ultimate mysteries of existence and, in my eyes, the fact that Indian thought diverges widely from our own popular thought is a positive merit. In intellectual and philosophical pursuits we want new ideas and Indian ideas are not familiar or hackneyed in the west, though I think that more European philosophers and mystics have arrived at similar conclusions than is generally supposed.

Indian religions have more spirituality and a greater sense of the Infinite than our western creeds and more liberality. They are not merely tolerant but often hold that the different classes of mankind have their own rules of life and suitable beliefs and that he who follows such partial truths does no wrong to the greater and all-inclusive truths on which his circumstances do not permit him to fix his attention. And though some Indian religions may sanction bad customs, sacrifice of animals and immoral rites, yet on the whole they give the duty of kindness to animals a prominence unknown in Europe and are more penetrated with the idea that civilization means a gentle and enlightened temper—an idea sadly forgotten in these days of war. Their speculative interest can hardly be denied. For instance, the idea of a religion without a personal God may seem distasteful or absurd but the student of human thought must take account of it and future generations may not find it a useless notion. It is certain that in Asia we find Buddhist Churches which preach morality and employ ritual and yet are not theistic, and also various systems of pantheism which, though they may use the word God, obviously use it in a sense which has nothing in common with Christian and Mohammedan ideas.

India's greatest contribution to religion is not intellectual, as the mass of commentaries and arguments produced by Hindus might lead us to imagine, but the persistent and almost unchallenged belief in the reality and bliss of certain spiritual states which involve intuition. All Indians agree that they are real, even to the extent of offering an alternative superior to any ordinary life of pleasure and success, but their value for us is lessened by the variety of interpretations which they receive and which make it hard to give a more detailed definition than that above. For some they are the intuition of a particular god, for others of divinity in general. For Buddhists they mean a new life of knowledge, freedom and bliss without reference to a deity.

But apart from such high matters I believe that the mental training preliminary to these states—what is called meditation and concentration—is well worth the attention of Europeans. I am not recommending trances or catalepsy: in these as in other matters the Hindus are probably prone to exaggerate and the Buddha himself in his early quest for truth discarded trances as an unsatisfactory method. But the reader can convince himself by experiment that the elementary discipline which consists in suppressing "discursive thought" and concentrating the mind on a particular object—say a red flower—so that for some time nothing else is present to the mind and the image of the flower is seen and realized in all its details, is most efficacious for producing mental calm and alertness. By such simple exercises the mind learns how to rest and refresh itself. Its quickness of apprehension and its retentive power are considerably increased, for words and facts imprinted on it when by the suppression of its ordinary activities it has thus been made a *tabula rasa* remain fixed and clear.

Such great expressions of emotional theism as the Râmâyana of Tulsi Das are likely to find sympathetic readers in Europe, but the most original feature of Indian thought is that, as already mentioned, it produces systems which can hardly be refused the name of religion and yet are hardly theistic. The Buddha preached a creed without reference to a supreme deity and the great Emperor Asoka, the friend of man and beast, popularized this creed throughout India. Even at the present day the prosperous and intelligent community of Jains follow a similar doctrine and the Advaita philosophy diverges widely from European theism. It is true that Buddhism invented gods for itself and became more and more like Hinduism and that the later Vedantist and Śivaite schools have a strong bent to monotheism. Yet all Indian theism seems to me to have a pantheistic tinge[1] and India is certainly the classic land of

[1] I know that this statement may encounter objections, but I believe that few Indians would be surprised at the proposition that God is all things. Some might deny it, but as a familiar error.

Pantheism. The difficulties of Pantheism are practical: it does not lend itself easily to popular cries and causes and it finds it hard to distinguish and condemn evil[1]. But it appeals to the scientific temper and is not repulsive to many religious and emotional natures. Indeed it may be said that in monotheistic creeds the most thoughtful and devout minds often tend towards Pantheism, as witness the Sufis among Moslims, the Kabbalists among the Jews and many eminent mystics in the Christian Church. In India, the only country where the speculative interest is stronger than the practical, it is a common form of belief and it is of great importance for the history and criticism of religion to see how an idea which in Europe is hardly more than philosophic theory works on a large scale.

Later Buddhism—the so-called Mahayana—may be justly treated as one of the many varieties of Indian religion, not more differentiated from others than is for instance the creed of the Sikhs. The speculative side of early Buddhism (which was however mainly a practical movement) may be better described as an Indian critique of current Indian views. The psychology of the Pitakas has certainly enough life to provoke discussion still, for it receives both appreciative treatment and uncompromising condemnation at the hands of European scholars. To set it aside as not worth the labour spent on elucidating it, seems to me an error of judgment. As a criticism of the doctrine developed in the Upanishads, it is acute and interesting, even if we hold the Upanishads to be in the right, and no serious attempt to analyze the human mind can be without value, for though the facts are before every human being such attempts are rare. It is singular that so many religions should prescribe and prophecy for the soul without being able to describe its nature. Hesitation and diffidence in defining the Deity seem proper and natural but it is truly surprising that people are not agreed as to the essential facts about their own consciousness, their selves, souls, minds and spirits: whether these are the same or different: whether they are entities or aggregations. The Buddha's answers to these questions cannot be dismissed as ancient or outlandish, for they are practically the conclusions arrived at

[1] But orthodox Christianity really falls into the same difficulty. For if God planned the redemption of the world and we are saved by the death of Christ, then the Chief Priests, Judas, Pilate and the soldiers who crucified Christ are at least the instruments of salvation.

by a distinguished modern psychologist, William James, who says in his *Psychology*[1], "The states of consciousness are all that psychology requires to do her work with. Metaphysics or theology may prove the soul to exist, but for psychology the hypothesis of such a substantial principle of unity is superfluous" and again "In this book the provisional solution which we have reached must be the final one: The thoughts themselves are the thinkers."

Equally in sympathy with Buddhist ideas is the philosophy of M. Bergson, which holds that movement, change, becoming is everything and that there is nothing else: no things that move and change and become[2]. Huxley too, speaking of idealism, said "what Berkeley does not seem to have so clearly perceived is that the non-existence of a substance of mind is equally arguable....It is a remarkable indication of the subtlety of Indian speculation that Gautama should have seen deeper than the greatest of modern idealists[3]."

Even Mr Bradley says "the soul is a particular group of psychical events in so far as those events are taken merely as happening in time[4]." There is a smack of the Pitakas about this, although Mr Bradley's philosophy as a whole shows little sympathy for Buddhism but a wondrous resemblance both in thought and language to the Vedânta. This is the more remarkable because there is no trace in his works of Sanskrit learning or even of Indian influence at second hand. A peculiarly original and independent mind seems to have worked its way to many of the doctrines of the Advaita, without entirely adopting its general conclusions, for I doubt if Śankara would have said "the positive relation of every appearance as an adjective to reality and the presence of reality among its appearances in different degrees and with different values—this double truth we have found to be the centre of philosophy." But still this is the gist of many Vedantic utterances both early[5] and late. Gauḍapâda states that the world of appearance is due to *svabhâva* or

[1] Wm James, *Psychology*, pp. 203 and 216.

[2] I quote this epitome from Wildon Carr's Henri Bergson, *The Philosophy of Change*, because the phraseology is thoroughly Buddhist and appears to have the approval of M. Bergson himself.

[3] *Romanes Lecture*, 1893.

[4] *Appearance*, p. 298.

[5] Thus the Śvetâśvatara Up. says that the whole world is filled with the parts or limbs of God and metaphors like sparks from a fire or threads from a spider seem an attempt to express the same idea. Br. Ar. Up. 2. 1. 20; Mund. Up. 2. 1. 1.

the essential nature of Brahman and I imagine that the thought here is the same as when Mr Bradley says that the Absolute is positively present in all appearances.

Among many coincidences both in thought and expression, I note the following. Mr Bradley[1] says "The Perfect...means the identity of idea and existence, accompanied by pleasure" which is almost the verbal equivalent of *saccidânanda*. "The universe is one reality which appears in finite centres." "How there can be such a thing as appearance we do not understand." In the same way Vedantists and Mahayanists can offer no explanation of Mâyâ or whatever is the power which makes the universe of phenomena. Again he holds that neither our bodies nor our souls (as we commonly understand the word) are truly real[2] and he denies the reality of progress "For nothing perfect, nothing genuinely real can move." And his discussion of the difficulty of reconciling the ideas of God and the Absolute and specially the phrase "short of the Absolute, God cannot rest and having reached that goal he is lost and religion with him" is an epitome of the oscillations of philosophic Hinduism which feels the difficulty far more keenly than European religion, because ideas analogous to the Absolute are a more vital part of religion (as distinguished from metaphysics) in India than in Europe[3].

Nor can Indian ideas as to Maya and the unreality of matter be dismissed as curious dreams of mystical brains, for the most recent phases of Physics—a science which changes its fundamental ideas as often as philosophy—tend to regard matter as

[1] *Appearance*, p. 244; *Essays on Truth*, p. 409; *Appearance*, p. 413. Though the above quotations are all from Mr Bradley I might have added others from Mr Bosanquet's *Gifford Lectures* and from Mr McTaggart.

[2] "The plurality of souls in the Absolute is therefore appearance and their existence not genuine...souls like their bodies, are as such nothing more than appearance....Neither (body and soul) is real in the end: each is merely phenomenal." *Appearance*, pp. 305–307.

[3] Since I wrote this I have read Mr Wells' book *God the Invisible King*. Mr Wells knows that he is indebted to oriental thought and thinks that European religion in the future may be so too, but I do not know if he realizes how nearly his God coincides with the Mahayanist conception of a Bodhisattva such as Avalokita or Mañjuśrî. These great beings have, as Bodhisattvas, a beginning: they are not the creators of the world but masters and conquerors of it and helpers of mankind: they have courage and eternal youth and Mañjuśrî "bears a sword, that clean discriminating weapon." Like most Asiatics, Mr Wells cannot allow his God to be crucified and he draws a distinction between God and the Veiled Being, very like that made by Indians between Îśvara and Brahman

electrical charges in motion. This theory is a phrase rather than an explanation, but it has a real affinity to Indian phrases which say that Brahman or Śakti (which are forces) produce the illusion of the world.

I am not venturing here on any general comparison of European and Indian thought. My object is merely to point out that the latter contains many ideas to which British philosophers find themselves led and from which, when they have discovered them in their own way, they do not shrink. It can hardly then be without interest to see how these ideas have been elaborated, often more boldly and thoroughly, in Asia.

BOOK II

EARLY INDIAN RELIGION
A GENERAL VIEW

BOOK II

In this book I shall briefly sketch the condition of religion in India prior to the rise of Buddhism and in so doing shall be naturally led to indicate several of the fundamental ideas of Hinduism. For few old ideas have entirely perished: new deities, new sects and new rites have arisen but the main theories of the older Upanishads still command respect and modern reformers try to justify their teaching from the ancient texts.

But I do not propose to discuss in detail the religion of the Vedic hymns for, so far as it can be distinguished from later phases, it looks backward rather than forward. It is important to students of comparative mythology, of the origins of religion, of the Aryan race. But it represents rather what the Aryans brought into India than what was invented in India, and it is this latter which assumes a prominent place in the intellectual history of the world as Hinduism and Buddhism. The ancient nature gods of the wind and the dawn have little place in the mental horizon of either the Buddha or Bhagavad-gîtâ and even when the old names remain, the beings who bear them generally have new attributes. Still, Vedic texts are used in modern worship and in many respects there is a real continuity of thought.

In the first chapter I enquire whether there is any element common to the religions of India and to the countries of Eastern Asia and find that the worship of nature spirits and the veneration of ancestors prevail throughout the whole of this vast region and have not been suppressed by Buddhism or Brahmanism. Then coming to the purely Indian sphere, I have thought it might not be amiss to give an epitome of such parts of Indian history as are of importance for religion. Next I endeavour to explain how the social institutions of India and the unique position acquired by the Brahman aristocracy have determined the character of Hindu religion—protean and yet unmistakeably Indian in all its phases—and I also investigate the influence of the belief in rebirth, which from the time of the Upanishads onwards dominates Indian thought. In the fourth and fifth chapters I trace the survival of some ancient ideas and show how many attributes of the Vedic gods can be found in modern deities who are at first sight widely different and how theories of salvation by sacrifice or asceticism or knowledge have been similarly persistent. In the sixth chapter I attempt to give a picture of religious life, both Brahmanic and non-Brahmanic, as it existed in India about the time when the Buddha was born. Of the non-Brahmanic sects which then flourished most have disappeared, but one, namely the Jains, has survived and left a considerable record in literature and art. I have therefore devoted a chapter to it here.

My object in this book is to discuss the characteristics of Indian religion which are not only fundamental but ancient. Hence this is not the place to dwell on Bhakti or relatively modern theistic sects, however great their importance in later Hinduism may be.

CHAPTER I

RELIGIONS OF INDIA AND EASTERN ASIA

The countries with which this work deals are roughly speaking India with Ceylon; Indo-China with parts of the Malay Archipelago; Japan and China with the neighbouring regions such as Tibet and Mongolia. All of them have been more or less influenced by Hinduism and Buddhism and in hardly any of them is Mohammedanism the predominant creed[1], though it may have numerous adherents. The rest of Asia is mainly Mohammedan or Christian and though a few Buddhists may be found even in Europe (as the Kalmuks) still neither Hinduism nor Buddhism has met with general acceptance west of India.

In one sense, the common element in the religion of all these countries is the presence of Indian ideas, due in most cases to Buddhism which is the export form of Hinduism, although Brahmanic Hinduism reached Camboja and the Archipelago. But this is not the element on which I wish now to insist. I would rather enquire whether apart from the diffusion of ideas which has taken place in historical times, there is any common substratum in the religious temperament of this area, any fund of primitive, or at least prehistoric ideas, shared by its inhabitants. Such common ideas will be deep-seated and not obvious, for it needs but little first-hand acquaintance with Asia to learn that all generalizations about the spirit of the East require careful testing and that such words as Asiatic or oriental do not connote one type of mind. For instance in China and Japan the control of the state over religion is exceptionally strong: in India it is exceptionally weak. The religious temperaments of these nations differ from one another as much as the Mohammedan and European temperaments and the fact that many races have adopted Buddhism and re-

[1] The Malay countries are the only exception.

fashioned it to their liking does not indicate that their mental texture is identical. The cause of this superficial uniformity is rather that Buddhism in its prime had no serious rivals in either activity or profundity, but presented itself to the inhabitants of Eastern Asia as pre-eminently the religion of civilized men, and was often backed by the support of princes. Yet one cannot help thinking that its success in Eastern Asia and its failure in the West are not due merely to politics and geography but must correspond with some racial idiosyncrasies. Though it is hard to see what mental features are common to the dreamy Hindus and the practical Chinese, it may be true that throughout Eastern Asia for one reason or another such as political despotism, want of military spirit, or on the other hand a tendency to regard the family, the clan or the state as the unit, the sense of individuality is weaker than in Western Asia or Europe, so that pantheism and quietism with their doctrines of the vanity of the world and the bliss of absorption arouse less opposition from robust lovers of life. This is the most that can be stated and it does not explain why there are many Buddhists in Japan but none in Persia.

But apart from Buddhism and all creeds which have received a name, certain ideas are universal in this vast region. One of them is the belief in nature spirits, beings who dwell in rocks, trees, streams and other natural objects and possess in their own sphere considerable powers of doing good or ill. The Nagas, Yakshas and Bhutas of India, the Nats of Burma, the Peys of Siam, the Kami of Japan and the Shen of China are a few items in a list which might be indefinitely extended. In many countries this ghostly population is as numerous as the birds of the forest: they haunt every retired spot and perch unseen under the eaves of every house. Theology has not usually troubled itself to define their status and it may even be uncertain whether respect is shown to the spirits inhabiting streams and mountain peaks or to the peaks and streams themselves[1].

They may be kindly (though generally requiring punctilious attention), or mischievous, or determined enemies of mankind.

[1] Thus Motoori (quoted in Aston's *Shintō*, p. 9) says "Birds, beasts, plants and trees, seas and mountains and all other things whatsoever which deserve to be dreaded and revered for the extraordinary and pre-eminent powers which they possess are called *Kami*."

But infinite as are their variations, the ordinary Asiatic no more doubts their existence than he doubts the existence of animals. The position which they enjoy, like their character, is various, for in Asia deities like men have careers which depend on luck. Many of them remain mere elves or goblins, some become considerable local deities. But often they occupy a position intermediate between real gods and fairies. Thus in southern India, Burma and Ceylon may be seen humble shrines, which are not exactly temples but the abodes of beings whom prudent people respect. They have little concern with the destinies of the soul or the observance of the moral law but much to do with the vagaries of rivers and weather and with the prosperity of the village. Though these spirits may attain a high position within a certain district (as for instance Maha Saman, the deity of Adam's Peak in Ceylon) they are not of the same stuff as the great gods of Asia. These latter are syntheses of many ideas, and centuries of human thought have laboured on their gigantic figures. It is true that the mental attitude which deifies the village stream is fundamentally the same as that which worships the sun, but in the latter case the magnitude of the phenomenon deified sets it even for the most rustic mind in another plane. Also the nature gods of the Veda are not quite the same as the nature spirits which the Indian peasants worship to-day and worshipped, as the Pitakas tell us, in the time of the Buddha. For the Vedic deities are such forces as fire and light, wind and water. This is nature worship but the worship of nature generalized, not of some bold rock or mysterious rustling tree. It may be that a migratory life, such as the ancient Aryans at one time led, inclined their minds to these wider views, since neither the family nor the tribe had an abiding interest in any one place. Thus the ancestors of the Turks in the days before Islam worshipped the spirits of the sky, earth and water, whereas the more civilized but sedentary Chinese had genii for every hamlet, pool and hillock.

It is difficult to say whether monotheism is a development of this nature worship or has another origin. In Japanese religion the monotheistic tendency is markedly absent. The sun-goddess is the principal deity but remains simply *prima inter pares*. But in the ancient religion of China, T'ien or

Heaven, also called Shang-ti, the supreme ruler, though somewhat shadowy and impersonal, does become an omnipotent Providence without even approximate rivals. Other superhuman beings are in comparison with him merely angels. Unfortunately the early history of Chinese religion is obscure and the documents scanty. In India however the evolution of pantheism or theism (though usually with a pantheistic tinge) out of the worship of nature forces seems clear. These gods or forces are seen to melt into one another and to be aspects of one another, until the mind naturally passes on to the idea that they are all manifestations of one force finding expression in human consciousness as well as in physical phenomena. The animist and pantheist represent different stages but not different methods of thought. For the former, every natural object which impresses him is alive; the latter concurs in this view, only he thinks the universe is instinct with one and the same life displaying itself in infinite variety.

One difficulty incidental to the treatment of Asiatic religions in European languages is the necessity, or at any rate the ineradicable habit, of using well-known words like God and soul as the equivalents of Asiatic terms which have not precisely the same content and which often imply a different point of view. For practical life it is wise and charitable to minimize religious differences and emphasize points of agreement. But this willingness to believe that others think as we do becomes a veritable vice if we are attempting an impartial exposition of their ideas. If the English word God means the deity of ordinary Christianity, who is much the same as Allah or Jehovah—that is to say the creator of the world and enforcer of the moral law—then it would be better never to use this word in writing of the religions of India and Eastern Asia, for the concept is almost entirely foreign to them. The nature spirits of which we have been speaking are clearly not God: when an Indian peasant brings offerings to the tomb of a deceased brigand or the Emperor of China promotes some departed worthy to be a deity of a certain class, we call the ceremony deification, but there is not the smallest intention of identifying the person deified with the Supreme Being, and odd as it may seem, the worship of such "gods" is compatible with monotheism or atheism. In China, Shang-ti is less definite than

God[1] and it does not appear that he is thought of as the creator of the world and of human souls. Even the greater Hindu deities are not really God, for those who follow the higher life can neglect and almost despise them, without, however, denying their existence. On the other hand Brahman, the pantheos of India, though equal to the Christian God in majesty, is really a different conception, for he is not a creator in the ordinary sense: he is impersonal and though not evil, yet he transcends both good and evil. He might seem merely a force more suited to be the subject matter of science than of religion, were not meditation on him the occupation, and union with him the goal, of many devout lives. And even when Indian deities are most personal, as in the Vishnuite sects, it will be generally found that their relations to the world and the soul are not those of the Christian God. It is because the conception of superhuman existence is so different in Europe and Asia that Asiatic religions often seem contradictory or corrupt: Buddhism and Jainism, which we describe as atheistic, and the colourless respectable religion of educated Chinese, become in their outward manifestations unblushingly polytheistic.

Similar difficulties and ambiguities attend the use of the word soul, for Buddhism, which is supposed to hold that there is no soul, preaches retribution in future existences for acts done in this, and seeks to terrify the evil doer with the pains of hell; whereas the philosophy of the Brahmans, which inculcates a belief in the soul, seems to teach in some of its phases that the disembodied and immortal soul has no consciousness in the ordinary human sense. Here language is dealing with the same problems as those which we describe by such phrases as the soul, immortality and continuous existence, but it is striving to express ideas for which we have little sympathy and no adequate terminology. They will be considered later.

But one attitude towards that which survives death is almost universal in Eastern Asia and also easily intelligible. It finds expression in the ceremonies known as ancestor worship. This practice has attracted special attention in China, where it is the commonest and most conspicuous form of religious

[1] This impersonality is perhaps a later characteristic. The original form of the Chinese character for T'ien Heaven represented a man. The old Finnish and Samoyede names for God—Ukko and Num—perhaps belong to this stage of thought.

observance, but it is equally prevalent among the Hindus, though less prominent because it is only one among the many rites which engage the attention of that most devout nation. It is one of the main constituents in the religions of Indo-China and Japan, though the best authorities think that it was not the predominant element in the oldest form of Shinto. It is less prominent among the Tibeto-Burmese tribes but not absent, for in Tibet there are both good and evil ghosts who demand recognition by appropriate rites. It is sometimes hard to distinguish it from the worship of natural forces. For instance in China and southern India most villages have a local deity who is often nameless. The origin of such deities may be found either in a departed worthy or in some striking phenomenon or in the association of the two.

The cult of ghosts may be due to either fear or affection, and both motives are found in Eastern Asia. But though abundant examples of the propitiation of angry spirits can be cited, respect and consideration for the dead are the feelings which usually inspire these ceremonies at the present day and form the chief basis of family religion. There is no need to explain this sentiment. It is much stronger in Asia than in Europe but some of its manifestations may be paralleled by masses and prayers for the dead, others by the care bestowed on graves and by notices *in memoriam*. As a rule both in China and India only the last three generations are honoured in these ceremonies. The reason is obvious: the more ancient ancestors have ceased to be living memories. But it might be hard to find a theoretical justification for neglecting them and it is remarkable that in all parts of Asia the cult of the dead fits very awkwardly into the official creeds. It is not really consistent with any doctrine of metempsychosis or with Buddhist teaching as to the impermanence of the Ego. In China may be found the further inconsistency that the spirit of a departed relative may receive the tribute of offerings and salutations called ancestor worship, while at the same time Buddhist services are being performed for his deliverance from hell. But of the wide distribution, antiquity and strength of the cult there can be no doubt. It is anterior not only to Brahmanism but to the doctrines of transmigration and karma, and the main occupation of Buddhist priests in China and Japan is the performance of ceremonies supposed to benefit the dead. Even within Buddhism these practices cannot be dismissed as a late or foreign corruption. In the Khuddaka-pâṭha which, if not belonging to the most ancient part of the Buddhist canon, is at least pre-Christian and purely Indian, the dead are represented as waiting for offerings and as blessing those who give them. It is also curious that a recent work called *Raymond* by Sir O. Lodge (1916) gives a view of the state after death which is substantially that of the Chinese. For its teaching is that the dead retain their personality, concern themselves with the things of this world, know what is going to happen here and can to some extent render assistance to the living[1]. Also (and this point is specially remarkable) burning and mutilation of the body seem to inconvenience the dead.

Early Chinese works prescribe that during the performance of ancestral rites, the ghosts are to be represented by people known as the personators of the dead who receive the offerings and are supposed to be temporarily possessed by spirits and to be their mouthpieces. Possession by ghosts or other spirits is, in popular esteem, of frequent occurrence in India, China, Japan and Indo-China. It is one of the many factors which have contributed to the ideas of incarnation and deification, that is, that gods can become men and men gods. In Europe the spheres of the human and divine are strictly separated: to pass from one to the other is exceptional: a single incarnation is regarded as an epoch-making event of universal importance. But in Asia the frontiers are not thus rigidly delimitated, nor are God and man thus opposed. The ordinary dead become powers in the spirit world and can bless or injure here: the great dead become deities: in another order of ideas, the dead immediately become reincarnate and reappear on earth: the gods take the shape of men, sometimes for the space of a human life, sometimes for a shorter apparition. Many teachers in India have been revered as partial incarnations of Vishnu and most of the higher clergy in Tibet claim to be Buddhas or Bodhisattvas manifest in the flesh. There is no proof that the doctrine of metempsychosis existed in Eastern Asia independently of Indian influence but the ready acceptance accorded to it was largely due to the prevalent feeling that the

[1] See the account of the Faunus message in this book.

worlds of men and spirits are divided by no great gulf. It is quite natural to step into the spirit world and back again into this.

It will not have escaped the reader's attention that many of the features which I have noticed as common to the religions of Eastern Asia—such as the worship of nature spirits and ancestors—are not peculiar to those countries but are almost, if not quite, universal in certain stages of religious development. They can, for instance, be traced in Europe. But whereas they exist here as survivals discernible only to the eye of research and even at the beginning of the Christian era had ceased to be the obvious characteristics of European paganism, in Asia they are still obvious. Age and logic have not impaired their vigour, and official theology, far from persecuting them, has accommodated its shape to theirs. This brings us to another point where the linguistic difficulty again makes itself felt, namely, that the word religion has not quite the same meaning in Eastern Asia as in Mohammedan and Christian lands. I know of no definition which would cover Christianity, Buddhism, Confucianism and the superstitions of African savages, for the four have little community of subject matter or aim. If any definition can be found it must I think be based on some superficial characteristic such as ceremonial. Nor is there any objection to refusing the title of religion to Buddhism and Confucianism, except that an inconvenient lacuna would remain in our vocabulary, for they are not adequately described as philosophies. A crucial instance of the difference in the ideas prevalent in Europe and Eastern Asia is the fact that in China many people belong to two or three religions and it would seem that when Buddhism existed in India the common practice was similar. Paganism and spiritual religion can co-exist in the same mind provided their spheres are kept distinct. But Christianity and Islam both retain the idea of a jealous God who demands not only exclusive devotion but also exclusive belief: to believe in other Gods is not only erroneous; it is disobedience and disloyalty. But such ideas have little currency in Eastern Asia, especially among Buddhists. The Buddha is not a creator or a king but rather a physician. He demands no allegiance and for those who disobey him the only punishment is continuance of the disease. And though Indian deities may claim personal and exclusive devotion, yet in defining and limiting belief their priests are less exacting than Papal or Moslim doctors. Despite sectarian formulas, the Hindu cherishes broader ideas such as that all deities are forms and passing shapes of one essence; that all have their proper places and that gods, creeds and ceremonies are necessary helps in the lower stages of the religious life but immaterial to the adept.

It does not follow from this that Hindus are lukewarm or insincere in their convictions. On the contrary, faith is more intense and more widely spread among them than in Europe. Nor can it be said that their religion is something detachable from ordinary life: the burden of daily observances prescribed and duly borne seems to us intolerable. But Buddhism and many forms of Hinduism present themselves as methods of salvation with a simplicity and singleness of aim which may be paralleled in the Gospels but only rarely in the national churches of Europe. The pious Buddhist is one who moulds his life and thoughts according to a certain law: he is not much concerned with worshipping the gods of the state or city, but has nothing against such worship: his aims and procedure have nothing to do with spirits who give wealth and children or avert misfortune. But since such matters are of great interest to mankind, he is naturally brought into contact with them and he has no more objection to a religious service for procuring rain than to a scientific experiment for the same purpose. Similarly Confucians follow a system of ethics which is sufficient for a gentleman and accords a decorous recognition to a Supreme Being and ancestral spirits. Much concession to superstition would be reprehensible according to this code but if a Confucian honours some deity either for his private objects or because it is part of his duties as a magistrate, he is not offending Confucius. He is simply engaging in an act which has nothing to do with Confucianism. The same distinction often applies in Indian religion but is less clear there, because both the higher doctrine as well as ordinary ceremonial and mythology are described under one name as Hinduism. But if a native of southern India occasionally sacrifices a buffalo to placate some village spirit, it does not follow that all his religious notions are of this barbarous type.

Asiatic ideas as to the relations between religions are

illustrated by an anecdote related to me in Assam. Christianity has made many converts among the Khasis, a non-Hindu tribe of that region, and a successful revival meeting extending over a week was once held in a district of professing Christians. When the week was over and the missionaries gone, the Khasis performed a ceremony in honour of their tribal deities. Their pastors regarded this as a woeful lapse from grace but no disbelief in Christianity or change of faith was implied. The Khasis had embraced Christianity in the same spirit that animated the ancient disciples of the Buddha: it was the higher law which spoke of a new life and of the world to come. But it was not understood that it offered to take over the business of the local deities, to look after crops and pigs and children, to keep smallpox, tigers and serpents in order. Nobody doubted the existence of spirits who regulate these matters, while admitting that ethics and the road to heaven were not in their department, and therefore it was thought wise to supplement the Christian ceremonies by others held in their honour and thus let them see that they were not forgotten and run no risk of incurring their enmity.

My object in this chapter is to point out at the very beginning that in Asia the existence of a duly labelled religion, such as Buddhism or Confucianism, does not imply the suppression of older nameless beliefs, especially about nature spirits and ghosts. In China and many other countries we must not be surprised to find Buddhists honouring spirits who have nothing to do with Buddhism. In India we must not suppose that the doctrines of Râmânuja or any other great teacher are responsible for the crudities of village worship, nor yet rashly assume that the villager is ignorant of them.

CHAPTER II

HISTORICAL

It may be useful to insert here a brief sketch of Indian history, but its aim is merely to outline the surroundings in which Hindu religion and philosophy grew up. It, therefore, passes lightly over much which is important from other points of view and is intended for reference rather than for continuous reading.

An indifference to history, including biography, politics and geography, is the great defect of Indian literature. Not only are there few historical treatises[1] but even historical allusions are rare and this curious vagueness is not peculiar to any age or district. It is as noticeable among the Dravidians of the south as among the speakers of Aryan languages in the north. It prevails from Vedic times until the Mohammedan conquest, which produced chronicles though it did not induce Brahmans to write them in Sanskrit. The lacuna is being slowly filled up by the labours of European scholars who have collected numerous data from an examination of inscriptions, monuments and coins, from the critical study of Hindu literature, and from research in foreign, especially Chinese, accounts of ancient India.

At first sight the history of India seems merely a record of invasions, the annals of a land that was always receptive and fated to be conquered. The coast is poor in ports and the nearest foreign shore distant. The land frontiers offer more temptation to invaders than to emigrants. The Vedic Aryans, Persians, Greeks and hordes innumerable from Central Asia poured in century after century through the passes of the north-western mountains and after the arrival of Vasco da Gama other hordes came from Europe by sea. But the armies and fleets of India

[1] The chief exception in Sanskrit is the Râjataranginî, a chronicle of Kashmir composed in 1148 A.D. There are also a few panegyrics of contemporary monarchs, such as the Harshacarita of Bâṇa, and some of the Puranas (especially the Matsya and Vâyu) contain historical material. See Vincent Smith, *Early History of India*, chap. I, sect. II, and *Pargiter Dynasties of the Kali Age*. The Greek and Roman accounts of Ancient India have been collected by McCrindle in six volumes 1877–1901.

can tell no similar story of foreign victories. This picture however neglects the fact that large parts of Indo-China and the Malay Archipelago (including Camboja, Champa, Java and even Borneo) received not only civilization but colonists and rulers from India. In the north too Nepal, Kashmir, Khotan and many other districts might at one time or another be legitimately described as conquered or tributary countries. It may indeed be justly objected that Indian literature knows nothing of Camboja and other lands where Indian buildings have been discovered[1] and that the people of India were unconscious of having conquered them. But Indian literature is equally unconscious of the conquests made by Alexander, Kanishka and many others. Poets and philosophers were little interested in the expeditions of princes, whether native or foreign. But if by India is meant the country bounded by the sea and northern mountains it undoubtedly sent armies and colonists to regions far beyond these limits, both in the south-east and the north, and if the expansion of a country is to be measured not merely by territorial acquisition but by the diffusion of its institutions, religion, art and literature, then "the conquests of the Dhamma," to use Asoka's phrase, include China, Japan, Tibet and Mongolia.

The fact that the Hindus paid no attention to these conquests and this spread of their civilization argues a curious lack of interest in national questions and an inability to see or utilize political opportunities which must be the result of temperament rather than of distracting invasions. For the long interval between the defeat of the Huns in 526 A.D. and the raids of Mahmud of Ghazni about 1000 A.D. which was almost entirely free from foreign inroads, seems precisely the period when the want of political ideas and constructive capacity was most marked. Nor were the incursions always destructive and sterile. The invaders, though they had generally more valour than culture of their own, often brought with them foreign art and ideas, Hellenic, Persian or Mohammedan. Naturally the northern districts felt their violence most as well as the new influences which they brought, whereas the south became the focus of Hindu politics and culture which radiated thence northwards again. Yet, on the whole, seeing how vast is the

[1] The inscriptions of the Chola Kings however (c. 1000 A.D.) seem to boast of conquests to the East of India. See Coedès "Le royaume de Çrîvijaya" in *B.E.F.E.O.* 1918

area occupied by the Hindus, how great the differences not only of race but of language, it is remarkable how large a measure of uniformity exists among them (of course I exclude Mohammedans) in things religious and intellectual. Hinduism ranges from the lowest superstition to the highest philosophy but the stages are not distributed geographically. Pilgrims go from Badrinath to Ramesvaram: the Vaishnavism of Trichinopoly, Muttra and Bengal does not differ in essentials, the worship of the linga can be seen almost anywhere. And though India has often been receptive, this receptivity has been deliberate and discriminating. Great as was the advance of Islam, the resistance offered to it was even more remarkable and at the present day it cannot be said that in the things which most interest them Indian minds are specially hospitable to British ideas.

The relative absence of political unity seems due to want of interest in politics. It is often said that the history of India in pre-Mohammedan times is an unintelligible or, at least, unreadable, record of the complicated quarrels and varying frontiers of small states. Yet this is as true of the history of the Italian as of the Indian peninsula. The real reason why Indian history seems tedious and intricate is that large interests are involved only in the greatest struggles, such as the efforts to repulse the Huns or Mohammedans.

The ordinary wars, though conducted on no small scale, did not involve such causes or principles as the strife of Roundheads with Cavaliers. With rare exceptions, states and empires were regarded as the property of their monarchs. Religion claimed to advise kings, like other wealthy persons, as to their duties and opportunities, and ministers became the practical rulers of kingdoms just as a steward may get the management of an estate into his hands. But it rarely occurred to Hindus that other persons in the estate had any right to a share in the government, or that a Raja could be dispossessed by anybody but another Raja. Of that, indeed, there was no lack. Not only had every sovereign to defend himself against the enemies in his own house but external politics seemed based on the maxim that it is the duty of a powerful ruler to increase his territory by direct and unprovoked attacks on his neighbours. There is hardly a king of eminence who did not expand his power in this way, and the usual history of a royal house is successful aggression followed by collapse when weaker hands were unable to hold the inherited handful. Even moderately long intervals of peace are rare. Yet all the while we seem to be dealing not with the expansion or decadence of a nation, but with great nobles who add to their estates or go bankrupt.

These features of Indian politics are illustrated by the Arthaśâstra, a manual of state-craft attributed to Câṇakya, the minister of Candragupta and sometimes called the Indian Macchiavelli. Its authenticity has been disputed but it is now generally accepted by scholars as an ancient work composed if not in the fourth century, at least some time before the Christian era. It does not, like Manu and other Brahmanic law-books, give regulations for an ideal kingdom but frankly describes the practice of kings. The form of state contemplated is a small kingdom surrounded by others like it and war is assumed to be their almost normal relation, but due to the taste or policy of kings, not to national aspirations or economic causes. Towards the Brahmans a king has certain moral obligations, towards his subjects and fellow monarchs none. It is assumed that his object is to obtain money from his subjects, conquer his neighbours, and protect himself by espionage and severe punishments against the attacks to which he is continually exposed, especially at the hands of his sons. But the author does not allow his prince a life of pleasure: he is to work hard and the first things he has to attend to are religious matters.

The difficulty of writing historical epitomes which are either accurate or readable is well known and to outline the events which have occurred in the vast area called India during the last 2500 years is a specially arduous task, for it is almost impossible to frame a narrative which follows the fortunes of the best known Hindu kingdoms and also does justice to the influence of southern India and Islam. It may be useful to tabulate the principal periods, but the table is not continuous and even when there is no gap in chronology, it often happens that only one political area is illuminated amid the general darkness and that this area is not the same for many centuries.

1. From about 500 to 200 B.C. Magadha (the modern Bihar) was the principal state and the dominions of its great king Asoka were almost the same as British India to-day.

2. In the immediately succeeding period many invaders entered from the north-west. Some were Greeks and some

Iranians but the most important were the Kushans who ruled over an Empire embracing both north-western India and regions beyond it in Afghanistan and Central Asia. This Empire came to an end in the third century A.D. but the causes of its collapse are obscure.

3. The native Hindu dynasty of the Guptas began to rule in 320 A.D. Its dominions included nearly all northern India but it was destroyed by the invasions of the Huns in the fifth and sixth centuries.

4. The Hindu Emperor Harsha (606–647 A.D.) practically reconstituted the Gupta Empire but his dominions split up after his death. At the same time another Empire which extended from Gujarat to Madras was founded by Pulakeśin, a prince from the south, a region which though by no means uncivilized had hitherto played a small part in the general history of India.

5. From 650 to 1000 A.D. India was divided among numerous independent kingdoms. There was no central power but Bengal and the Deccan were more prominent than previously.

6. After 1000 A.D. the conquests of Mohammedan invaders became important and the Hindu states of northern and central India collapsed or grew weak. But the Hindus held out in Rajputana, Orissa, and above all in Vijayanagar.

7. In 1526 came the invasion of the Mughals, who founded an Empire which at its zenith (1556–1707) included all India except the extreme south. In its decadence the Marathas and Sikhs became powerful and Europeans began to intervene.

It is generally agreed that at a period which, though not fixed, was anterior to 1000 B.C.[1] a body of invaders known as Aryans and nearly akin to the ancient Iranians entered India through the north-western mountains. They found there other tribes not deficient in civilization but unable to offer any effective resistance. These tribes who retired southwards are commonly known as Dravidians[2] and possibly represent an earlier invasion of central-Asiatic tribes allied to the remote

[1] Very different opinions have been held as to whether this date should be approximately 1500 B.C. or 3000 B.C. The strong resemblance of the hymns of the Ṛig Veda to those of the Avesta is in favour of the less ancient date, but the date of the Gathas can hardly be regarded as certain.

[2] Linguistically there seems to be two distinct divisions, the Dravidians and the Munda (Kolarian).

ancestors of the Turks and Mongols[1]. At the time when the earlier hymns of the Ṛig Veda were composed, the Aryans apparently lived in the Panjab and did not know the sea, the Vindhya mountains or the Narbudda river. They included several tribes, among whom five are specially mentioned, and we hear that a great battle was fought on the Ravi, in which a confederation of ten kings who wished to force a passage to the east was repulsed by Sudas, chief of the Tritsus. Still the south-eastern movement, across the modern United Provinces to the borders of Bengal, continued and, so far as our records go, it was in this direction rather than due south or south-west, that the Aryans chiefly advanced[2]. When the Brâhmaṇas and earlier Upanishads were composed (c. 800–600 B.C.) the principal political units were the kingdoms of the Pancâlas and Kurus in the region of Delhi. The city of Ayodhyâ (Oudh) is also credited with a very ancient but legendary history.

The real history of India begins with the life of the Buddha who lived in the sixth century B.C.[3] At that time the small states of northern India, which were apparently oligarchies or monarchies restricted by the powers of a tribal council, were in process of being absorbed by larger states which were absolute monarchies and this remained the normal form of government in both Hindu and Moslim times. Thus Kosala (or Oudh) absorbed the kingdom of Benares but was itself conquered by Magadha or Bihar, the chief city of which was Pataliputra or

[1] The affinity between the Dravidian and Ural-Altaic groups of languages has often been suggested but has met with scepticism. Any adequate treatment of this question demands a comparison of the earliest forms known in both groups and as to this I have no pretension to speak. But circumstances have led me to acquire at different times some practical acquaintance with Turkish and Finnish as well as a slight literary knowledge of Tamil and having these data I cannot help being struck by the general similarity shown in the structure both of words and of sentences (particularly the use of gerunds and the constructions which replace relative sentences) and by some resemblances in vocabulary. On the other hand the pronouns and consequently the conjugation of verbs show remarkable differences. But the curious Brahui language, which is classed as Dravidian, has negative forms in which *pa* is inserted into the verb, as in Yakut Turkish, *e.g.* Yakut *bis-pa-ppin*, I do not cut; Brahui *khan-pa-ra*, I do not see. The plural of nouns in Brahui uses the suffixes *k* and *t* which are found in the Finnish group and in Hungarian.

[2] See the legend in the Śat. Brâh. I. 4. 1. 14 ff.

[3] This much seems sure but whereas European scholars were till recently agreed that he died about 487 B.C. it is now suggested that 543 may be nearer the true date. See Vincent Smith in *Oxford History of India*, 1920, p. 48.

Patna, destined to become the capital of India. We also know that at this period and for about two centuries later the Persian Empire had two satrapies within the limits of modern India, one called "India," including the country east of the Indus and possibly part of the Panjab, and the other called Gândhâra (Peshawar) containing Takshaśilâ[1], a celebrated university. The situation of this seat of learning is important, for it was frequented by students from other districts and they must have felt there in early times Persian and afterwards Hellenistic influence. There are clear signs of Persian influence in India in the reign of Asoka. Of Magadha there is little to be said for the next century and a half, but it appears to have remained the chief state of northern India.

In 327 B.C. Alexander the Great after over-throwing the Persian Empire invaded India, where he remained only nineteen months. He probably intended to annex Sind and the Panjab permanently to his Empire but he died in 323 and in the next year Candragupta, an exiled scion of the royal house of Magadha, put an end to Macedonian authority in India and then seized the throne of his ancestors. He founded the Maurya dynasty under which Magadha expanded into an Empire comprising all India except the extreme south. Seleucus Nicator, who had inherited the Asiatic possessions of Alexander and wished to assert his authority, came into collision with Candragupta but was completely worsted and about 303 B.C. concluded a treaty by which he ceded the districts of Kabul, Herat and Kandahar. Shortly afterwards he sent as his ambassador to the court of Pataliputra a Greek named Megasthenes who resided there for a considerable time and wrote an account of the country still extant in a fragmentary form. The grandson of Candragupta was Asoka, the first ruler of all India (c. 273–231 B.C.). His Empire extended from Afghanistan almost to Madras and was governed with benevolent but somewhat grandmotherly despotism. He was an ardent Buddhist and it is mainly owing to his efforts, which are described in more detail below, that Buddhism became during some centuries the dominant faith in India. Asoka's Empire broke up soon after his death in circumstances which are not clear, for we now enter upon one of

[1] Pali Takkasila. Greek Taxila. It was near the modern Rawal Pindi and is frequently mentioned in the Jâtakas as an ancient and well-known place.

those chaotic periods which recur from time to time in Indian history and we have little certain information until the fourth century A.D. Andhra, a region including large parts of the districts now called the Northern Circars, Hyderabad and Central Provinces, was the first to revolt from the Mauryas and a dynasty of Andhra kings[1], who claimed to belong to the Śâtavâhana family, ruled until 236 A.D. over varying but often extensive territories. What remained of the Maurya throne was usurped in 184 B.C. by the Sungas who in their turn were overthrown by the Kaṇvas. These latter could not withstand the Andhras and collapsed before them about 27 B.C.

Alexander's invasion produced little direct effect, and no allusion to it has been found in Indian literature. But indirectly it had a great influence on the political, artistic and religious development of the Hindus by preparing the way for a series of later invasions from the north which brought with them a mixed culture containing Hellenic, Persian and other elements. During some centuries India, as a political region, was not delimitated on the north-western side as it is at present and numerous principalities rose and fell which included Indian territory as well as parts of Afghanistan.

These states were of at least three classes, Hellenistic, Persian or Parthian, and Scythian, if that word can be properly used to include the Sakas and Kushans.

Bactria was a Persian satrapy before Alexander's invasion but when he passed through it on his way to India he founded twelve cities and settled a considerable number of his soldiers in them. It formed part of the Empire of Seleucus but declared itself independent in 250 B.C. about the same time that the Parthians revolted and founded the Empire of the Arsacidae. The Bactrian kings bore Greek names and in 209 Antiochus III made peace with one of them called Euthydemus, in common cause against the nomads who threatened Western Asia. Demetrius, the son of this Euthydemus, appears to have conquered Kabul, the Panjab and Sind (c. 190 B.C.) but his reign was troubled by the rebellion of a certain Eukratides and it is probable that many small and contending frontier-states, of which we have a confused record, were ruled by the relatives of one or other of these two princes. The most important of

[1] Most of them are known by the title of Śâtakarṇi.

them was Menander, apparently king of the Kabul valley. About 155 he made an incursion to the east, occupied Muttra and threatened Pataliputra itself but was repulsed. He is celebrated in Buddhist literature as the hero of the Questions of Milinda but his coins, though showing some Buddhist emblems, indicate that he was also a worshipper of Pallas. Shortly after this Hellenic influence in Bactria was overwhelmed by the invasion of the Yüeh-chih, though the Greek principalities in the Panjab may have lasted considerably longer.

In the reign of Mithridates (c. 171–138 B.C.) the Parthian Empire was limitrophe with India and possibly his authority extended beyond the Indus. A little later the Parthian dependencies included two satrapies, Aracosia and the western Panjab with capitals at Kandahar and Taxila respectively. In the latter ruled kings or viceroys one of whom called Gondophores (c. 20 A.D.) is celebrated on account of his legendary connection with the Apostle Thomas.

More important for the history of India were the conquests of the Sakas and Yüeh-chih, nomad tribes of Central Asia similar to the modern Turkomans[1]. The former are first heard of in the basin of the river Ili, and being dislodged by the advance of the Yüeh-chih moved southwards reaching north-western India about 150 B.C. Here they founded many small principalities, the rulers of which appear to have admitted the suzerainty of the Parthians for some time and to have borne the title of satraps. It is clear that western India was parcelled out among foreign princes called Sakas, Yavanas, or Pallavas whose frontiers and mutual relations were constantly changing. The most important of these principalities was known as the Great Satrapy which included Surashṭra (Kathiawar) with adjacent parts of the mainland and lasted until about 395 A.D.

The Yüeh-chih started westwards from the frontiers of China about 100 B.C. and, driving the Sakas before them, settled in Bactria. Here Kadphises, the chief of one of their tribes, called the Kushans, succeeded in imposing his authority on the others who coalesced into one nation henceforth known by the tribal name. The chronology of the Kushan Empire is one of the vexed questions of Indian history and the dates given

[1] But perhaps not in language. Recent research makes it probable that the Kushans or Yüeh-chih used an Iranian idiom.

below are stated positively only because there is no space for adequate discussion and are given with some scepticism, that is desire for more knowledge founded on facts. Kadphises I (c. 15–45 A.D.) after consolidating his Empire led his armies southwards, conquering Kabul and perhaps Kashmir. His successor Kadphises II (c. 45–78 A.D.) annexed the whole of north-western India, including northern Sind, the Panjab and perhaps Benares. There was a considerable trade between India and the Roman Empire at this period and an embassy was sent to Trajan, apparently by Kanishka (c. 78–123), the successor of Kadphises. This monarch played a part in the later history of Buddhism comparable with that of Asoka in earlier ages[1]. He waged war with the Parthians and Chinese, and his Empire which had its capital at Peshawar included Afghanistan, Bactria, Kashgar, Yarkand, Khotan[2] and Kashmir. These dominions, which perhaps extended as far as Gaya in the east, were retained by his successors Huvishka (123–? 140 A.D.) and Vasudeva (? 140–178 A.D.), but after this period the Andhra and Kushan dynasties both collapsed as Indian powers, although Kushan kings continued to rule in Kabul. The reasons of their fall are unknown but may be connected with the rise of the Sassanids in Persia. For more than a century the political history of India is a blank and little can be said except that the kingdom of Surashṭra continued to exist under a Saka dynasty.

Light returns with the rise of the Gupta dynasty, which roughly marks the beginning of modern Hinduism and of a reaction against Buddhism. Though nothing is known of the fortunes of Pataliputra, the ancient imperial city of the Mauryas, during the first three centuries of our era, it continued to exist. In 320 a local Raja known as Candragupta I increased his dominions and celebrated his coronation by the institution of the Gupta era. His son Samudra Gupta continued his conquests and in the course of an extraordinary campaign, concluded about 340 A.D., appears to have received the submission of almost the whole peninsula. He made no attempt to retain all

[1] Fleet and Franke consider that Kanishka preceded the two Kadphises and began to reign about 58 B.C.

[2] He appears to have been defeated in these regions by the Chinese general Pan-Chao about 90 A.D. but to have been more successful about fifteen years later.

this territory but his effective authority was exercised in a wide district extending from the Hugli to the rivers Jumna and Chambal in the west and from the Himalayas to the Narbudda. His son Candragupta II or Vikramâditya added to these possessions Malwa, Gujarat and Kathiawar and for more than half a century the Guptas ruled undisturbed over nearly all northern India except Rajputana and Sind. Their capital was at first Pataliputra, but afterwards Kausambi and Ayodhya became royal residences.

The fall of the Guptas was brought about by another invasion of barbarians known as Hûnas, Ephthalites[1] or White Huns and apparently a branch of the Huns who invaded Europe. This branch remained behind in Asia and occupied northern Persia. They invaded India first in 455, and were repulsed, but returned about 490 in greater force and overthrew the Guptas. Their kings Toramâṇa and Mihiragula were masters of northern India till 540 and had their local capital at Sialkot in the Panjab, though their headquarters were rather in Bamyin and Balkh. The cruelties of Mihiragula provoked a coalition of Hindu princes. The Huns were driven to the north and about 565 A.D. their destruction was completed by the allied forces of the Persians and Turks. Though they founded no permanent states their invasion was important, for many of them together with kindred tribes such as the Gurjaras (Gujars) remained behind when their political power broke up and, like the Sakas and Kushans before them, contributed to form the population of north-western India, especially the Rajput clans.

The defeat of the Huns was followed by another period of obscurity, but at the beginning of the seventh century Harsha (606–647 A.D.), a prince of Thanesar, founded after thirty-five years of warfare a state which though it did not outlast his own life emulated for a time the dimensions and prosperity of the Gupta Empire. We gather from the account of the Chinese pilgrim Hsüan Chuang, who visited his court at Kanauj, that the kings of Bengal, Assam and Ujjain were his vassals but that the Panjab, Sind and Kashmir were independent. Kalinga, to the south of Bengal, was depopulated but Harsha was not able to subdue Pulakeśin II, the Câlukya king of the Deccan.

Let us now turn for a moment to the history of the south.

[1] Or Hephthalites. The original name seems to have been something like Haptal.

It is even more obscure both in events and chronology than that of the north, but we must not think of the Dravidian countries as uninhabited or barbarous. Even the classical writers of Europe had some knowledge of them. King Pandion (Pândya) sent a mission to Augustus in 20 B.C.[1] Pliny[2] speaks of Modura (Madura) and Ptolemy also mentions this town with about forty others. It is said[3] that there was a temple dedicated to Augustus at Muziris, identified with Cranganore. From an early period the extreme south of the peninsula was divided into three states known as the Pândya, Cera and Cola kingdoms[4]. The first corresponded to the districts of Madura and Tinnevelly. Cera or Kerala lay on the west coast in the modern Travancore. The Cola country included Tanjore, Trichinopoly, Madras, with the greater part of Mysore. From the sixth to the eighth century A.D. a fourth power was important, namely the Pallavas, who apparently came from the north of the Madras Presidency. They had their capital at Conjeevaram and were generally at war with the three kingdoms. Their king, Narasimha-Varman (625–645 A.D.) ruled over part of the Deccan and most of the Cola country but after about 750 they declined, whereas the Colas grew stronger and Rajaraja (985–1018) whose dominions included the Madras Presidency and Mysore made them the paramount power in southern India, which position they retained until the thirteenth century.

As already mentioned, the Deccan was ruled by the Andhras from 220 B.C. to 236 A.D., but for the next three centuries nothing is known of its history until the rise of the Câlukya dynasty at Vatapi (Badami) in Bijapur. Pulakeśin II of this dynasty (608–642), a contemporary of Harsha, was for some time successful in creating a rival Empire which extended from Gujarat to Madras, and his power was so considerable that he exchanged embassies with Khusru II, King of Persia, as is depicted in the frescoes of Ajanta. But in 642 he was defeated and slain by the Pallavas.

With the death of Pulakeśin and Harsha begins what has been called the Rajput period, extending from about 650 to

[1] Strabo XV. 4. 73. [2] *Hist. Nat.* VI. 23. (26).

[3] For authorities see Vincent Smith, *Early History of India*, 1908, p. 401.

[4] The inscriptions of Asoka mention four kingdoms, Pândya, Keralaputra, Cola and Satiyaputra.

1000 A.D. and characterized by the existence of numerous kingdoms ruled by dynasties nominally Hindu, but often descended from northern invaders or non-Hindu aboriginal tribes. Among them may be mentioned the following:

1. Kanauj or Pancâla. This kingdom passed through troublous times after the death of Harsha but from about 840 to 910 A.D. under Bhoja (or Mihira) and his son, it became the principal power in northern India, extending from Bihar to Sind. In the twelfth century it again became important under the Gaharwar dynasty.

2. Kanauj was often at war with the Palas of Bengal, a line of Buddhist kings which began about 730 A.D. Dharmapala (c. 800 A.D.) was sufficiently powerful to depose the king of Kanauj. Subsequently the eastern portion of the Pala kingdom separated itself under a rival dynasty known as the Senas.

3. The districts to the south of the Jumna known as Jejâkabhukti (Bundelkhand) and Cedi (nearly equivalent to our Central Provinces) were governed by two dynasties known as Candels and Kalacuris. The former are thought to have been originally Gonds. They were great builders and constructed among other monuments the temples of Khajarao. Kîrtivarman Chandel (1049–1100) greatly extended their territories. He was a patron of learning and the allegorical drama Prabodhacandrodaya was produced at his court.

4. The Paramara (Pawar) dynasty of Malwa were likewise celebrated as patrons of literature and kings Munja (974–995) and Bhoja (1018–1060) were authors as well as successful warriors.

5. Though the Câlukyas of Vatapi were temporarily crushed by the Pallavas their power was re-established in 655 and continued for a century. The Eastern Câlukyas, another branch of the same family, established themselves in Vengi between the Kistna and Godaveri. Here they ruled from 609 to 1070 first as viceroys of the Western Câlukyas and then as an independent power till they were absorbed by the Colas. Yet another branch settled in Gujarat.

6. The Câlukyas of Vatapi were overthrown by the Râshṭrakûṭas who were masters of the Deccan from about 750 to 972, and reigned first at Nasik and then at Manyakheta (Malkhed). Krishna I of this dynasty excavated the Kailasa

temple at Ellora (c. 760) but many of his successors were Jains. During the ninth century the Râshṭrakûṭas seem to have ruled over most of western India from Malwa to the Tungabhadra.

7. The Râshṭrakûṭas collapsed before a revival of the Câlukya dynasty which reappears from 993 to 1190 as the Câlukyas of Kalyani (in the Nizam's dominions). The end of this dynasty was partly due to the usurpation of a Jain named Bijjala in whose reign the sect of the Lingâyats arose.

We must now turn to an event of great historical importance although its details are not relevant to the subject of this book, namely the Mohammedan conquest. Three periods in it may be recognized. First, the conquest of Sind in 712 A.D. by the Arabs, who held it till the eleventh century but without disturbing or influencing India beyond their immediate neighbourhood. Secondly, the period of invasions and dynasties which are commonly called Turki (c. 1000–1526 A.D.). The progress of Islam in Central Asia coincided with the advance to the west and south of vigorous tribes known as Turks or Mongols, and by giving them a religious and legal discipline admirably suited to their stage of civilization, it greatly increased their political efficiency. The Moslim invaders of India started from principalities founded by these tribes near the north-western frontier with a military population of mixed blood and a veneer of Perso-Arabic civilization, and apart from the greater invasions, there were incursions and settlements of Turkis, Afghans and Mongols. The whole period was troublous and distracted. The third period was more significant and relatively stable. Baber, a Turkish prince of Fergana, captured Delhi in 1526 and founded the power of the Mughals, which during the seventeenth century deserved the name of the Indian Empire.

The first serious Moslim incursions were those of Mahmud of Ghazni, who between 997 and 1030 made many raids in which he sacked Kanauj, Muttra, Somnath and many other places but without acquiring them as permanent possessions. Only the Panjab became a Moslim province. In 1150 the rulers of Ghor, a vassal principality near Herat, revolted against Ghazni and occupied its territory, whence the chieftain commonly called Muhammad of Ghor descended on India and subdued Hindustan as well as the Panjab (1175–1206). One of his slaves named Kutb-ud-Din Ibak became his general and viceroy and, when Muhammad died, founded at Delhi the dynasty known as Slave Sultans. They were succeeded by the Khilji Sultans (1290–1318) the most celebrated of whom was the capable but ferocious Ala-ud-Din and these again by the Tughlak dynasty. Muhammad Adil, the second of this line, attempted to move the capital from Delhi to Daulatabad in the Deccan. In 1398 northern India was convulsed by the invasion of Timur who only remained a few months but sacked Delhi with terrible carnage. Many years of confusion followed, and a dynasty known as the Saiyids ruled in greatly diminished territories. But in 1451 arose the Lodi or Afghan dynasty which held the Panjab, Hindustan and Bundelkhand until the advent of the Mughals. These five royal houses do not represent successive invasions from the west. Their founders, though of diverse origin, were all leaders engaged in the troubled politics of northern India, and they all reigned at Delhi, round which a tradition of Empire thus grew up. But the succession was disputed in almost every case; out of thirty-four kings twelve came to a violent end and not one deserved to be called Emperor of India. They were confronted by a double array of rivals, firstly Hindu states which were at no period all reduced to subjection, and, secondly, independent Mohammedan states, for the governors in the more distant provinces threw off their allegiance and proclaimed themselves sovereigns. Thus Bengal from the time of its first conquest by Muhammad Bakhtyar had only a nominal connection with Delhi and declared itself independent in 1338. When Timur upset the Tughlak dynasty, the states of Jaunpur, Gujarat, Malwa and Khandesh became separate kingdoms and remained so until the time of Akbar. In the south one of Muhammad Adil's generals founded the Bahmani dynasty which for about a century (1374–1482) ruled the Deccan from sea to sea. It then split up into five sultanates with capitals at Bidar, Bijapur, Golkonda, Ahmadnagar and Elichpur.

In the twelfth century, the Hindu states were not quite the same as those noticed for the previous period. Kanauj and Gujarat were the most important. The Palas and Senas ruled in Bengal, the Tomaras at Delhi, the Chohans in Ajmer and subsequently in Delhi too. The Mohammedans conquered all these states at the end of the twelfth century. Their advance was naturally less rapid towards the south. In the Deccan the old Hindu dynasties had been replaced by the Hoysalas (c. 1117–1310 A.D.) and the Yadavas (1180–1309 A.D.) with capitals at Halebid and Daulatabad respectively. Both were destroyed by Malik Kafur, the slave general of Sultan Ala-ud-Din, but the spirit of the Deccan was not broken and within a few years the brothers Bukka and Harihara founded the state of Vijayanagar, "the never-to-be-forgotten Empire" as a native scholar has aptly termed it, which for more than two centuries was the centre of Hindu political power. The imposing ruins of its capital may still be seen at Hampi on the Tungabhadra and its possessions comprised everything to the south of this, and, at times, also territory to the north, for throughout its existence it was engaged in warfare with the Bahmani dynasty or the five sultanates. Among its rulers the most notable was Krishnadeva (1509–1529) but the arrogance and weakness of his successors provoked the five Moslim Sultans to form a coalition. They collected an immense army, defeated the troops of Vijayanagar at the battle of Taliḳota and sacked the city (1565).

In two other districts the Hindus were able to retain political independence until the time of Akbar, namely Orissa and Rajputana. In the former the best known name is Anantavarman Colaganga (1076–1147) who built the temple of Jagannath at Puri, established the Eastern Ganga dynasty and ruled from the Godaveri to the Ganges. The Mohammedans never occupied Rajputana, and though they captured the principal fortresses, they did not retain them. The State of Mewar can even boast that it never made any but a nominal and honourable submission to the Sultans of Delhi. Akbar incorporated the Rajputs in his Empire and by his considerate treatment secured their support.

The history of the Mughals may be divided into three periods. In the first Baber acquired (1526 A.D.) the dominions of the Lodi dynasty as well as Jaunpur, but his death was followed by a troubled interval and it was not till the second period (1556–1707) comprising the reigns of Akbar, Jehangir, Shah Jehan and Aurungzeb that the Empire was securely established. Akbar made himself master of practically all India north of the Godaveri and his liberal policy did much to conciliate his Hindu subjects. He abolished the poll tax levied from non-Moslims and the tax on pilgrimages. The reform of revenue administration was entrusted to an orthodox Hindu, Todar Mall. Among the Emperor's personal friends were Brahmans and Rajputs, and the principal Hindu states (except Mewar) sent daughters to his harem. In religion he was eclectic and loved to hear theological argument. Towards the end of his life he adopted many Hindu usages and founded a new religion which held as one of its principal tenets that Akbar was God's Viceregent. His successors, Jehangir and Shah Jehan, were also tolerant of Hinduism, but Aurungzeb was a fanatical Moslim and though he extended his rule over all India except the extreme south, he alienated the affection of his Hindu subjects by reimposing the poll tax and destroying many temples. The Rajputs, Sikhs and Marathas all rebelled and after his death the Empire entered into the third period in which it rapidly disintegrated. Hindu states, like the Maratha confederacy and Rajputana, asserted themselves. Mohammedan governors declared their independence in Oudh, Bengal, the Nizam's dominions and elsewhere: Persians and Afghans raided the Panjab: French and English contended for the possession of southern India.

It would be outside the purpose of this book even to outline the establishment of British authority, but I may mention that direct European influence began to be felt in the sixteenth century, for Vasco da Gama arrived in Calicut in 1498 and Goa was a Portuguese possession from 1510 onwards. Nor can we linger over the fortunes of the Marathas who took the place of Vijayanagar as the Hindu opposition to Mohammedanism. They are, however, important for us in so far as they show that even in matters political the long Moslim domination had not broken the spirit of the Hindus. About 1660 a chieftain named Sivaji, who was not merely a successful soldier but something of a fanatic with a belief in his divine mission, founded a kingdom in the western Ghats and, like the Sikh leaders, almost created a nation, for it does not appear that before his time the word Maratha (Mahârâshṭra) had any special ethnic significance. After half a century the power of his successors passed into the hands of their Brahman ministers, known as Peshwas, who became the heads of a confederacy of Maratha chiefs, including the Rajas of Gwalior, Berar and

Orissa, Indore and Baroda. About 1760 the Marathas were practically masters of India and though the Mughal Emperor nominally ruled at Delhi, he was under their tutelage. They had a chance of reviving the glories of Asoka and the Guptas, but, even apart from the intervention of Europeans, they were distracted by jealousy and quarrels.

CHAPTER III

GENERAL CHARACTERISTICS OF INDIAN RELIGION

1

In the first chapter we enquired whether there are any religious ideas common to Eastern Asia as a whole and found that they amount to little more than a background of nature worship and ancestor worship almost universally present behind the official creeds. Also the conception of a religious system and its relation to beliefs which do not fall within it are not quite the same in these countries as in Europe, so that the inhabitants sometimes follow more than one religion.

Let us now examine the characteristics common to Indian creeds. They are numerous and striking. A prolonged study of the multitudinous sects in which Indian religion manifests itself makes the enquirer feel the truth of its own thesis that plurality is an illusion and only the one substratum real. Still there are divergent lines of thought, the most important of which are Hinduism and Buddhism. Though decadent Buddhism differed little from the sects which surrounded it, early Buddhism did offer a decided contrast to the Brahmanic schools in its theories as to human nature as well as in ignoring tradition and sacerdotalism. We may argue that Buddhism is merely Vaishnavism or Śaivism in travelling dress, but its rejection of Brahmanic authority is of capital importance. It is one of the reasons for its success outside India and its disappearance in India meant that it could not maintain this attitude. Yet many features of Buddhism are due to the fact that Hinduism, and not Islam or Christianity, was the national expression of religion in India and also many features of Hinduism may be explained by the existence of this once vigorous antagonist.

Hinduism[1] has striking peculiarities which distinguish it

[1] Hinduism is often used as a name for the mediæval and modern religion of India, and Brahmanism for the older pre-Buddhist religion. But one word is needed as a general designation for Indian religion and Hinduism seems the better of the two for this purpose.

from Christianity, Islam and even from Buddhism. It recognizes no one master and all unifying principles known to other creeds seem here to be absent. Yet its unity and vitality are clear and depend chiefly on its association with the Brahman caste. We cannot here consider the complex details of the modern caste system but this seems the place to examine the position of the Brahmans, for, from the dawn of Sanskrit literature until now, they have claimed to be the guides of India in all matters intellectual and religious and this persistent claim, though often disputed, has had a great measure of success.

The institution of caste is social rather than religious and has grown gradually: we know for instance that in the time of the Buddha it had not attained to anything like its present complexity and rigidity. Its origin is explicable if we imagine that the Indo-Aryans were an invading people with an unusual interest in religion. The Kshatriyas and Vaiśyas mark the distinction between the warriors or nobles and the plebs which is found in other Aryan communities, and the natives whom the Aryans conquered formed a separate class, recognized as inferior to all the conquerors. This might have happened in any country. The special feature of India is the numerical, social and intellectual strength of the priestly caste. It is true that in reading Sanskrit literature we must remember that most of it is the work of Brahmans and discount their proclivity to glorify the priesthood, but still it is clear that in India the sacerdotal families acquired a position without parallel elsewhere and influenced its whole social and political history. In most countries powerful priesthoods are closely connected with the Government under which they flourish and support the secular authority. As a result of this alliance, kings and the upper classes generally profess and protect orthodoxy, and revolutionary movements in religion generally come from below. But in ancient India though the priests were glad enough to side with the kings, the nobles during many centuries were not ready to give up thinking for themselves. The Hindu's capacity for veneration and the small inclination of the Brahmans to exercise direct government prevented revolts against sacerdotal tyranny from assuming the proportions we should expect, but whereas in many countries history records the attempts of priests to become kings, the position is here reversed. The national proclivity towards all that is religious, metaphysical, intellectual and speculative made all agree in regarding the man of knowledge who has the secret of intercourse with the other world as the highest type. The priests tended to become a hereditary guild possessed of a secret professional knowledge. The warrior caste disputed this monopoly and sought with less learning but not inferior vigour to obtain the same powers. They had some success during a considerable period, for Buddhism, Jainism and other sects all had their origin in the military aristocracy and had it remained purely Hindu, it would perhaps have continued the contest. But it was partly destroyed by Turanian invaders and partly amalgamated with them, so that in 500 A.D. whereas the Brahmans were in race and temperament very much what they were in 500 B.C. the Kshatriyas were different. It is interesting to see how this continuity of race brought triumph to the Brahmans in the theological sphere. At one time the Buddhists and even the Jains seemed to be competitors for the first place, but there are now hardly any Indian Buddhists in India[1] and less than a million and a half of Jains, whereas Hinduism has more than 217 million adherents. The power of persistence and resistance displayed by the priestly caste is largely due to the fact that they were householders not collected in temples or monasteries but distributed over the country in villages, intensely occupied with the things of the mind and soul, but living a simple family life. The long succession of invasions which swept over northern India destroyed temples, broke up monasteries and annihilated dynasties, but their destructive force had less effect on these communities of theologians whose influence depended not on institutions or organization but on their hereditary aptitudes. Though the modern Brahmans are not pure in race, still the continuity of blood and tradition is greater among them than in the royal families of India. Many of these belong to districts which were formerly without the pale of Hinduism: many more are the descendants of the northern hordes who century after century invaded India: few can bring forward any good evidence of Kshatriya descent. Hence in India kings have

[1] Excluding Burma the last Census gives over 300,000. These are partly inhabitants of frontier districts, which are Indian only in the political sense, and partly foreigners residing in India.

never attained a national and representative position like the Emperors of China and Japan or even the Sultans of Turkey. They were never considered as the high priests of the land or a quasi-divine epitome of the national qualities: the people tended to regard them as powerful and almost superhuman beings, but somewhat divorced from the moral standard and ideals of their subjects. In early times there was indeed the idea of a universal Emperor, the Cakravartin, analogous to the Messiah but, by a characteristic turn of thought, he was thought of less as a deliverer than as a type of superman, recurring at intervals. But monarchs who even approximated to this type were rare, and some of the greatest of them were in early ages Buddhists and in later Mohammedans, so that they had not the support of the priesthood and as time went on it became less and less possible to imagine all India rendering sympathetic homage to one sovereign.

In the midst of a perturbed flux of dynasties, usually short lived, often alien, only occasionally commanding the affection and respect of the population, the Brahmans have maintained for at least two millenniums and a half their predominant position as an intellectual aristocracy. They are an aristocracy, for they boldly profess to be by birth better than other men. Although it is probable that many clans have entered the privileged order without genealogical warrant, yet in all cases birth is claimed[1]. And though the Brahmans have aristocratic faults, such as unreasonable pride of birth, still throughout their long history they have produced in every age men of intelligence, learning and true piety, in numbers sufficient to make their claims to superiority seem reasonable. In all ages they have been sensual, ambitious and avaricious, but in all ages penetrated by the conviction that desire is a plague and gratification unsatisfying. It is the intelligent sensualist and

[1] Only tradition preserves the memory of an older and freer system, when warriors like Viśvâmitra were able by their religious austerities to become Brahmans. See Muir's *Sanskrit texts*, vol. I. pp. 296–479 on the early contests between Warriors and Brahmans. We hear of Kings like Janaka of Videha and Ajâtaśatru of Kâśi who were admitted to be more learned than Brahmans but also of Kings like Vena and Nahusha who withstood the priesthood "and perished through want of submissiveness." The legend of Paraśurâma, an incarnation of Vishnu as a Brahman who destroyed the Kshatriya race, must surely have some historical foundation, though no other evidence is forthcoming of the events which it relates.

politician who are bound to learn that passion and office are vanity.

A Brahman is not necessarily a priest. Although they have continually and on the whole successfully claimed a monopoly of sacred science, yet at the present day many follow secular callings and probably this was so in early periods. And though many rites can be performed by Brahmans only, yet by a distinction which it is difficult for Europeans to grasp, the priests of temples are not necessarily and, in many places, not usually Brahmans. The reason perhaps is that the easy and superstitious worship offered in temples is considered trivial and almost degrading in comparison with the elaborate ceremonial and subtle speculation which ought to occupy a Brahman's life.

In Europe we are accustomed to associate the ideas of sacerdotalism, hierarchy and dogma, mainly because they are united in the greatest religious organization familiar to us, the Roman Catholic Church. But the combination is not necessary. Hinduism is intensely sacerdotal but neither hierarchical nor dogmatic: Mohammedanism is dogmatic but neither sacerdotal nor hierarchical: Buddhism is dogmatic and also somewhat hierarchical, since it has to deal with bodies of men collected in monasteries where discipline is necessary, but except in its most corrupt forms it is not sacerdotal. The absence of the hierarchical idea in Hinduism is striking. Not only is there no Pope, but there is hardly any office comparable with a Bishopric[1]. The relationships recognized in the priesthood are those springing from birth and the equally sacred ties uniting teacher and pupil. Hence there is little to remind us of the organization of Christian Churches. We have simply teachers expounding their sacred books to their scholars, with such combination of tradition and originality as their idiosyncrasies may suggest, somewhat after the theory of congregational churches. But that resemblance is almost destroyed by the fact that both teachers and pupils belong to clans, connected by descent and accepted by the people as a superior order of mankind. Even in the most modern sects the descendants of the founder often receive special reverence.

Though the Brahmans have no ecclesiastical discipline, they

[1] In southern India and in Assam the superiors of monasteries sometimes exercise a quasi-episcopal authority.

do not tolerate the interference of kings. Buddhist sovereigns have summoned councils, but not so Hindu monarchs. They have built temples, paid priests to perform sacrifices and often been jealous of them but for the last two thousand years they have not attempted to control them within their own sphere or to create a State Church. And the Brahmans on their side have kept within their own province. It is true that they have succeeded in imposing—or in identifying themselves with—a most exacting code of social, legal and religious prescriptions, but they have rarely aimed at temporal power or attempted to be more than viziers. They have of course supported pious kings and received support—especially donations—from them, and they have enjoyed political influence as domestic chaplains to royal families, but they have not consented to any such relations between religion and the state as exist (or existed) in England, Russia, Mohammedan countries or China. At the ancient coronation ceremony the priest who presented the new ruler to his subjects said, "This is your King, O people: The King of us Brahmans is Soma[1]."

2

These facts go far to explain some peculiar features of Hinduism. Compared with Islam or Christianity its doctrines are extraordinarily fluid, multiform and even inconsistent: its practice, though rarely lax, is also very various in different castes and districts. The strangeness of the phenomenon is diminished if one considers that the uniformity and rigidity of western creeds are due to their political more than to their religious character. Like the wind, the spirit bloweth where it listeth: it is governed by no laws but those which its own reverence imposes: it lives in changing speculation. But in Europe it has been in double bondage to the logic of Greece and the law of Rome. India deals in images and metaphor: Greece in dialectic. The original thought of Christianity had something of this Indian quality, though more sober and less fantastic, with more limitation and less imagination. On this substratum the Greeks reared their edifices of dialectic and when the quarrels of theologians began to disturb politics, the state treated the whole question from a legal point of view. It

[1] Śat. Brâhm. v. 3. 3. 12 and v. 4. 2. 3.

was assumed that there must be a right doctrine which the state should protect or even enforce, and a wrong doctrine which it should discourage or even forbid. Hence councils, creeds and persecutions. The whole position is logical and legal. The truth has been defined: those who do not accept it harm not only themselves but others: therefore they should be restrained and punished.

But in religious matters Hindus have not proceeded in this way as a rule. They have adopted the attitude not of a judge who decides, but of the humane observer who sees that neither side is completely right or completely wrong and avoids expressing his opinion in a legal form. Hindu teachers have never hesitated to proclaim their views as the whole and perfect truth. In that indeed they do not yield to Christian theologians but their pronouncements are professorial rather than judicial and so diverse and yet all so influential that the state, though bound to protect sound doctrine, dare not champion one more than the other. Religious persecution is rare. It is not absent but the student has to search for instances, whereas in Christian Europe they are among the most conspicuous facts of history.

Restless, subtle and argumentative as Hindu thought is, it is less prone than European theology to the vice of distorting transcendental ideas by too stringent definition. It adumbrates the indescribable by metaphors and figures. It is not afraid of inconsistencies which may illustrate different aspects of the infinite, but it rarely tries to cramp the divine within the limits of a logical phrase. Attempts to explain how the divine and human nature were combined in Christ convulsed the Byzantine Empire and have fettered succeeding generations with their stiff formulæ. It would be rash to say that the ocean of Hindu theological literature contains no speculations about the incarnations of Vishnu similar to the views of the Nestorians, Monophysites and Catholics, but if such exist they have never attracted much interest or been embodied in well-known phrases[1]. The process by which a god can be born as a man, while continuing to exist as a god, is not described in quasi-legal language. Similarly the Soma offered in sacrifices is a god as well as a drink. But though the ritual of this sacrifice has

[1] The Mârkaṇḍeya Purâṇa discusses the question how Kṛishṇa could become a man.

produced an infinity of discussion and exegesis, no doctrine like transubstantiation or consubstantiation has assumed any prominence.

The Hindu has an extraordinary power of combining dogma and free thought, uniformity and variety. For instance it is held that the Vedas are a self-existent, eternal revelation made manifest to ancient sages and that their correct recitation ensures superhuman results. Yet each Veda exists in several recensions handed down by oral tradition in separate schools, and though the exact text and pronunciation are matters of the utmost importance, diversities of opinion respecting them are tolerated and honoured. Further, though the early scriptures were preserved with scrupulous care the canon was never closed. It is impossible to say how many Upanishads there are, nor does a Hindu think the less of an Upanishad because it is not found in a certain list. And in mediæval and modern times these ancient sacred books have been replaced for all except Brahmans by more recent Sanskrit works, or by a vernacular literature which, though having no particular imprimatur, claims the same authority as the Vedas[1].

The only essential tenets of Hinduism are recognition of the Brahman caste and divine authority of the Vedas. Those who publicly deny these doctrines as the Buddhists, Jains and Sikhs have done, put themselves outside the pale, but the recognition required to ensure orthodoxy or at least to avoid excommunication must not be compared with that implied by such phrases as recognizing the authority of the Bible, or the supremacy of the Pope. The utmost latitude of interpretation is allowed and the supposed followers of the Veda comprise sects whose beliefs seem to have no relation to one another or to the Veda, philosophic atheists and demonolaters whose religious ideas hardly rise above those of African savages.

One explanation may be, that every nation insists on liberty at the expense of logic in the matters which interest it most. We do this in politics. It might be difficult to make an untravelled oriental understand how parliamentary institutions can continue for a day, how socialists and republicans can take

[1] See for instance *The Holy Lives of the Azhvars* by Alkondavilli Govindâcârya. Mysore, 1902, pp. 215–216. "The Dravida Vedas have thus as high a sanction and authority as the Girvana (*i.e.* Sanskrit) Vedas."

part in the government of a monarchical country, and why the majority do not muzzle the opposition. Yet Englishmen prefer to let this curious illogical muddle continue rather than tolerate some symmetrical and authoritative system which would check free speech and individuality. It is the same in Indian religion. In all ages the Hindu has been passionately devoted to speculation. He will bear heavy burdens in the way of priestly exaction, social restrictions, and elaborate ceremonies, but he will not allow secular or even ecclesiastical authority to cramp and school his religious fancy, nor will he be deterred from sampling an attractive form of speculation merely because it is pronounced unorthodox by the priesthood, and the priesthood, being themselves Hindus, are discreet in the use of anathemas. They insist not so much on particular doctrines and rites as on the principle that whatever the doctrine, whatever the rite, they must be the teachers and officiants. In critical and revolutionary times the Brahmans have often assured their pre-eminence by the judicious recognition of heresies. In all ages there has been a conservative clique which restricted religion to ceremonial observances. Again and again some intellectual or emotional outburst has swept away such narrow limits and proclaimed doctrines which seemed subversive of the orthodoxy of the day. But they have simply become the orthodoxy of the morrow, under the protection of the same Brahman caste. The assailants are turned into champions, and in time the bold reformers stiffen into antiquated saints.

Hinduism has not been made but has grown. It is a jungle not a building. It is a living example of a great national paganism such as might have existed in Europe if Christianity had not become the state religion of the Roman Empire, if there had remained an incongruous jumble of old local superstitions, Greek philosophy and oriental cults such as the worship of Mithra or Serapis. Yet the parallel is not exact, for in Rome many of the discordant religious elements remained exotic, whereas in India they all, whatever their origin, became Indian and smack of the soil. There was wanting in European paganism the bond of union supplied by the Brahmans who by sometimes originating, sometimes tolerating and adapting, have managed to set their seal upon all Indian beliefs.

3

Thus the dominance of the Brahmans and their readiness to countenance every cult and doctrine which can attract worshippers explains the diversity of Indian religion, but are there no general characteristics which mark all its multiple forms? There are, and they apply to Buddhism as well as Hinduism, but in attempting to formulate them it is well to say that Indian religion is as wilful and unexpected in its variations as human nature itself and that all generalizations about it are subject to exceptions. If we say that it preaches asceticism and the subjection of the flesh, we may be confronted with the Vallabhâcâryas who inculcate self-indulgence; if we say that it teaches reincarnation and successive lives, we may be told that the Lingâyats[1] do not hold that doctrine. And though we might logically maintain that these sects are unorthodox, yet it does not appear that Hindus excommunicate them. Still, it is just to say that the doctrines mentioned are characteristic of Hinduism and are repudiated only by eccentric sects.

Perhaps the idea which has had the widest and most penetrating influence on Indian thought is that conception of the Universe which is known as Saṃsâra, the world of change and transmigration. The idea of rebirth and the wandering of souls from one body to another exists in a fragmentary form among savage tribes in many countries, but in India it makes its appearance as a product of ripening metaphysics rather than as a survival. It plays no part in the Vedic hymns: it first acquires importance in the older Upanishads but more as a mystery to be communicated to the elect than as a popular belief and to some extent as the special doctrine of the military class rather than of the Brahmans. At the time of the Buddha, however, it had passed beyond this stage and was as integral a part of popular theology as is the immortality of the soul in Europe.

Such expressions as the transmigration of souls or metempsychosis imperfectly represent Indian ideas. They are incorrect as descriptions of Buddhist dogmas, which start by denying the existence of a soul, and they are not entirely suitable

[1] I am inclined to believe that the Lingâyat doctrine really is that Lingâyats dying in the true faith do not transmigrate any more.

to those Vedantic schools which regard transmigration as part of the illusory phenomenal world. The thought underlying the doctrine is rather that as a child grows into youth and age, so the soul passes from life to life in continuity if not in identity. Whatever the origin of the idea may have been, its root in post-Vedic times is a sense of the transitoriness but continuity of everything. Nothing is eternal or even permanent: not even the gods, for they must die, not even death, for it must turn into new life.

This view of life is ingrained in Indian nature. It is not merely a scientific or philosophical speculation, but it summarizes the outlook of ordinary humanity. In Europe the average religious man thanks or at least remembers his Creator. But in India the Creator has less place in popular thought. There is a disinclination to make him responsible for the sufferings of the world, and speculation, though continually occupied with the origins of things, rarely adopts the idea familiar to Christians and Mohammedans alike, that something was produced out of nothing by the divine fiat. Hindu cosmogonies are various and discordant in details, but usually start with the evolution or emanation of living beings from the Divinity and often a reproductive act forms part of the process, such as the hatching of an egg or the division of a Divinity into male and female halves. In many accounts the Deity brings into being personages who continue the work of world-making and such entities as mind, time and desire are produced before the material world. But everything in these creation stories is figurative. The faithful are not perplexed by the discrepancies in the inspired narratives, and one can hardly imagine an Indian sect agitated by the question whether God made the world in six literal days.

All religious doctrines, especially theories about the soul, are matters of temperament. A race with more power of will and more delight in life might have held that the soul is the one agent that can stand firm and unshaken midst the flux of circumstance. The intelligent but passive Hindu sees clearly that whatever illusions the soul may have, it really passes on like everything else and continueth not in one stay. He is disposed to think of it not as created with the birth of the body, but as a drop drawn from some ocean to which it is destined to return.

As a rule he considers it to be immortal but he does not emphasize or value personality in our sense. In previous births he has already been a great many persons and he will be a great many more. Whatever may be the thread between these existences it is not individuality. And what he craves is not eternal personal activity, but unbroken rest in which personality, even if supposed to continue, can have little meaning.

The character of the successive appearances or tenements of the soul is determined by the law of Karma, which even more than metempsychosis is the basis of Indian ideas about the universe. Karma is best known as a term of the Buddhists, who are largely responsible both for the definition and wide diffusion of the doctrine. But the idea is Brahmanic as well as Buddhist and occurs in well-known passages of the Upanishads, where it is laid down that as a man acts so shall he be in the next life[1]. The word (which means simply *deed*) is the accepted abbreviation for the doctrine that all deeds bring upon the doer an accurately proportionate consequence either in this existence, or, more often, in a future birth. At the end of a man's life his character or personality is practically the sum of his acts, and when extraneous circumstances such as worldly position disappear, the soul is left with nothing but these acts and the character they have formed as, in Indian language, the fruit of life and it is these acts and this character which determine its next tenement. That tenement is simply the home which it is able to occupy in virtue of the configuration and qualities which it has induced in itself. It cannot complain.

One aspect of the theory of Saṃsâra which is important for the whole history of Indian thought is its tendency towards pessimism. This tendency is specially definite and dogmatic in Buddhism, but it is a marked characteristic of the Indian temperament and appears in almost every form of devotion and speculation. What salvation or the desire to be saved is to the ordinary Protestant, Mukti or Moksha, deliverance, is to the ordinary Hindu. In Buddhism this desire is given a dogmatic basis for it is declared that all existence in all possible worlds necessarily involves dukkha or suffering[2] and this view

[1] *E.g.* Brih.-Âr. III. 2. 13 and IV. 4. 2–6.

[2] This is the accepted translation of *dukkha* but perhaps it is too strong, and *uneasiness*, though inconvenient for literary reasons, gives the meaning better.

seems to have met with popular as well as philosophic assent. But the desire for release and deliverance is based less on a contemplation of the woes of life than on a profound sense of its impermanence and instability[1]. Life is not the preface to eternity, as religious Europeans think: the Hindu justly rejects the notion that the conduct of the soul during a few score years can fix its everlasting destiny. Every action is important for it helps to determine the character of the next life, but this next life, even if it should be passed in some temporary heaven, will not be essentially different from the present. Before and behind there stretches a vista of lives, past, present and to come, impermanent and unsatisfying, so that future existences are spoken of not as immortality but as repeated death.

4

This sense of weary reiteration is increased by two other doctrines, which are prevalent in Hinduism, though not universal or uncontested. The first of them identifies the human soul with the supreme and only Being. The doctrine of Saṃsâra holds that different forms of existence may be phases of the same soul and thus prepares the way for the doctrine that all forms of existence are the same and all souls parts of, or even identical with the Âtman or Self, the divine soul which not only pervades the world but *is* the world. Connected with this doctrine is another, namely, that the whole world of phenomena is Mâyâ or illusion. Nothing really exists except the supreme Âtman: all perception of plurality and difference is illusion and error: the reality is unity, identity and rest. The development of these ideas leads to some of the principal systems of philosophy and will claim our attention later. At present I merely give their outlines as indicative of Hindu thought and temperament. The Indian thinks of this world as a circular and unending journey, an ocean without shore, a shadow play without even a plot. He feels more strongly than the European that change is in itself an evil and he finds small satisfaction in action for its own sake. All his higher aspirations bid him extricate him-

[1] The old Scandinavian literature with its gods who must die is equally full of this sense of impermanence, but the Viking temperament bade a man fight and face his fate.

self from this labyrinth of repeated births, this phantasmagoria of fleeting, unsubstantial visions and he has generally the conviction that this can be done by knowledge, for since the whole Saṃsâra is illusion, it collapses and ceases so soon as the soul knows its own real nature and its independence of phenomena. This conviction that the soul in itself is capable of happiness and in order to enjoy needs only the courage to know itself and be itself goes far to correct the apathy which is the great danger of Indian thought. It is also just to point out that from the Upanishads down to the writings of Rabindranath Tagore in the present day Indian literature from time to time enunciates the idea that the whole universe is the manifestation of some exuberant force giving expression to itself in joyous movement. Thus the Taittirîya Upanishad (III. 6) says: "Bliss is Brahman, for from bliss all these beings are born, by bliss when born they live, into bliss they enter at their death."

It is remarkable that Indian thought, restless and speculative as it is, hardly ever concerns itself with the design, object or end of the world. The notion of Τέλος plays little part in its cosmogony or ethics[1]. The Universe is often regarded as a sport, a passing whim of the divine Being, almost a mistake. Those legends which describe it as the outcome of a creative act, generally represent the creator as moved by some impulse to multiply himself rather than as executing some deliberate if mysterious plan. Legends about the end of the world and the establishment of a better order are rare. Hindu chronology revels in periods, whose enormous length though expressed in figures leaves no real impression on the mind, days and nights of Brahma, Kalpas, Manvantaras and Yugas, in which gods and worlds are absorbed into the supreme essence and born again. But there is no finality about these catastrophes: the destruction of the whole universe is as certain as the death of a mouse and to the philosopher not more important[2]. Everything is periodic: Buddhas, Jinas and incarnations of all sorts

[1] But see Rabindrannath Tagore: Sadhana, especially the Chapter on Realization.

[2] Cf. Shelley's lines in Hellas:—

"Worlds on worlds are rolling ever
From creation to decay,
Like the bubbles on a river
Sparkling, bursting, borne away."

are all members of a series. They all deserve great respect and are of great importance in their own day, but they are none of them final, still less are they able to create a new heaven and earth or to rise above the perpetual flux of Saṃsâra. The Buddhists look forward to the advent of Maitreya, the future Buddha, and the Hindus to the reappearance of Vishnu as Kalkî, who, sword in hand and mounted on a white horse, will purge India of barbarians, but these future apparitions excite only a feeble interest in the popular conscience and cannot be compared in intensity with such ideas as the Jewish Messiah.

It may seem that Indian religion is dreamy, hopeless, and unpractical, but another point of view will show that all Indian systems are intensely practical and hopeful. They promise happiness and point out the way. A mode of life is always prescribed, not merely by works on law and ceremony but by theological and metaphysical treatises. These are not analogous to the writings of Kant or Schopenhauer and to study them as if they were, is like trying to learn riding or cricket by reading handbooks. The aphorisms of the Sânkhya and Vedânta are meant to be read under the direction of a teacher who will see that the pupil's mind is duly prepared not only by explanation but by abstinence and other physical training. Hindu religions are unpractical only in so far that they decline to subordinate themselves to human life. It is assumed that the religious man who is striving towards a goal beyond this world is ready to sacrifice the world without regret and in India the assumption is justified surprisingly often.

As mentioned already the word god has more than one meaning. In India we have at least two different classes of divinities, distinguished in the native languages. First there is Brahman the one self-existent, omnipresent, superpersonal spirit from whom all things emanate and to whom all things return. The elaboration of this conception is the most original feature of Indian theology, which tends to regard Brahman as not merely immanent in all things, but as being all things, so that the soul liberated from illusion can see that it is one with him and that nothing else exists. Very different is the meaning of Deva: this signifies a god (which is not the same as God, though our language insufficiently distinguishes the two) roughly comparable with the gods of classical mythology[1]. How little sense of divinity it carries with it is seen by the fact that it became the common form of address to kings and simply equivalent to Your Majesty. In later times, though Śiva is styled Mahâdeva, it was felt that the great sectarian gods, who are for their respective worshippers the personal manifestations in which Brahman makes himself intelligible, required some name distinguishing them from the hosts of minor deities. They are commonly spoken of by some title signifying the Lord: thus Śiva is Îśvara, Vishnu and his incarnations are more often styled Bhagavad.

From the Vedic hymns onwards the gods of India have been polymorphic figures not restricted by the limitations of human personality. If a Jew or a Moslim hears new views about God, he is disposed to condemn them as wrong. The Hindu's inclination is to appropriate them and ascribe to his own deity the novel attributes, whether they are consistent with the existing figure or not. All Indian gods are really everything. As the thought of the worshipper wanders among them they turn into one another. Even so sturdy a personality as Indra is declared to be the same as Agni and as Varuṇa, and probably every deity in the Vedic pantheon is at some time identified with another deity. But though in one way the gods seem vague and impersonal, in another the distinction between gods and men is slight. The Brâhmaṇas tell us that the gods were originally mortal and obtained immortality by offering sacrifices: the man who sacrifices like them makes for himself an immortal body in the abode of the gods and practically becomes a Deva and the bliss of great sages is declared equal to the bliss of the gods[2]. The human and divine worlds are not really distinct, and as in China and Japan, distinguished men are deified. The deification of Buddha takes place before our eyes as we follow the course of history: the origin of Krishna's godhead is more obscure but it is probable that he was a deified local hero. After the period of the Brâhmaṇas the theory that deities manifest themselves to the world in avatâras or descents, that is in our idiom incarnations, becomes part of popular theology.

[1] Nevertheless *deva* is sometimes used in the Upanishads as a designation of the supreme spirit.

[2] *E.g.* Brih.-Âr. Up. IV. 3. 33 and the parallel passages in the Taittirîya and other Upanishads.

There are other general characteristics of Indian religion which will be best made clear by more detailed treatment in succeeding chapters. Such are, firstly, a special theory of sacrifice or ritual which, though totally rejected by Buddhism, has survived to modern times. Secondly, a belief in the efficacy of self-mortification as a means of obtaining super-human powers or final salvation. Thirdly, an even more deeply rooted conviction that salvation can be obtained by knowledge. Fourthly, there is the doctrine that faith or devotion to a particular deity is the best way to salvation, but this teaching, though it seems natural to our minds, does not make its appearance in India until relatively late. It is not so peculiarly Indian as the other ideas mentioned, but even at the outset it is well to insist on its prevalence during the last two thousand years because a very false impression may be produced by ignoring it.

There also runs through Indian religion a persistent though inconspicuous current of non-theistic thought. It does not deny the existence of spirits but it treats them as being, like men, subject to natural laws, though able, like men, to influence events. The ultimate truth for it is not pantheism but fixed natural laws of which no explanation is offered. The religion of the Jains and the Sânkhya philosophy belong to this current. So did the teaching of several ancient sects, such as the Âjîvikas, and strictly speaking Buddhism itself. For the Buddha is not an Avatâra or a messenger but a superman whose exceptional intelligence sees that the Wheel of Causation and the Four Truths are part of the very nature of things. It is strange too that asceticism, sacrifices and modern tantric rites which seem to us concerned with the relations between man and God are in India penetrated by a non-theistic theory, namely that there are certain laws which can be studied and applied, much like electricity, and that then spirits can be coerced to grant what the ascetic or sacrificer desires. At the same time such views are more often implied than formulated. The Dharma is spoken of as the teaching of the Buddha rather than as Cosmic Order like the Tao of the Chinese and though tantric theory assumes the existence of certain forces which can be used scientifically, the general impression produced by tantric works is that they expound an intricate mythology and ritual.

CHAPTER IV

VEDIC DEITIES AND SACRIFICES

1

OUR knowledge of early Indian religion is derived almost entirely from literature. After the rise of Buddhism this is supplemented to some extent by buildings, statues and inscriptions, but unlike Egypt and Babylonia, pre-Buddhist India has yielded no temples, images or other religious antiquities, nor is it probable that such will be discovered. Certainly the material for study is not scanty. The theological literature of India is enormous: the difficulty is to grasp it and select what is important. The enquirer is confronted with a series of encyclopædic works of great bulk and considerable antiquity, treating of every aspect of religion which interested the Brahmans. But he continually feels the want of independent testimony to check their statements. They set forth the views of their authors but whether those views met with general acceptance outside the Brahmanic caste and influenced Indian life as a whole or whether classes, such as the military caste, or regions, such as western India and Dravidian India, had different views, it is often hard to say. Even more serious is the difficulty of chronology which affects secular as well as religious literature. The feats of Hindus in the matter of computing time show in the most extravagant form the peculiarities of their mental temperament, for while in their cosmogonies æons whose length the mind can hardly grasp are tabulated with the names of their superhuman rulers there are few[1] dates in the pre-Mohammedan history which can be determined from purely Indian sources. The fragments of obscure Greek writers and the notes of a travelling Chinaman furnish more trustworthy data about important epochs in the history of the Hindus than the whole of their gigantic literature, in which there has been found no mention of Alexander's invasion and only scattered allusions to the conquests of the

[1] The principal one is the date of Asoka, deducible from an inscription in which he names contemporary Seleucid monarchs.

Sakas, Kushans and Hûnas. We can hardly imagine doubt as to the century in which Shakespeare or Virgil lived, yet when I first studied Sanskrit the greatest of Indian dramatists, Kalidasa, was supposed to have lived about 50 B.C. His date is not yet fixed with unanimity but it is now generally placed in the fifth or sixth century A.D.

This chronological chaos naturally affects the value of literature as a record of the development of thought. We are in danger of moving in a vicious circle: of assigning ideas to an epoch because they occur in a certain book, while at the same time we fix the date of the book in virtue of the ideas which it contains. Still we may feel some security as to the sequence, if not the exact dates, of the great divisions in Indian religious literature such as the period of the Vedic hymns, the period of the Brâhmaṇas, the rise of Buddhism, the composition of the two great epics, and the Puranas. If we follow the opinion of most authorities and accept the picture of Indian life and thought contained in the Pali Tripitaka as in the main historical, it seems to follow that both the ritual system of the Brâhmaṇas and the philosophic speculations of the Upanishads were in existence by 500 B.C.[1] and sufficiently developed to impress the public mind with a sense of their futility. Some interval of mental growth seems to separate the Upanishads from the Brâhmaṇas and a more decided interval separates the Brâhmaṇas from the earlier hymns of the Rig Veda, if not from the compilation of the whole collection[2]. We may hence say that the older Upanishads and Brâhmaṇas must have been composed between 800 and 500 B.C. and the hymns of the Rig Veda hardly later than 1000 B.C. Many authorities think the earlier hymns must date from 2000 rather than 1000 B.C. but the resemblance of the Rig Veda to the Zoroastrian Gathas (which are generally regarded as considerably later than

[1] *E.g.* a learned Brahman is often described in the Sutta Pitaka as "a repeater (of the sacred words) knowing the mystic verses by heart, one who had mastered the three Vedas, with the indices, the ritual, the phonology, the exegesis and the legends as a fifth."

[2] There had been time for misunderstandings to arise. Thus the Śatapatha Brâhmaṇa sees in the well-known verse "who is the God to whom we shall offer our sacrifices" an address to a deity named Ka (Sanskrit for *who*) and it would seem that an old word, *uloka*, has been separated in several passages into two words, *u* (a meaningless particle) and *loka*.

1000 B.C.) is plain, and it will be strange if the two collections prove to be separated by an interval of many centuries. But the stage of social and religious culture indicated in the Vedic hymns may have begun long before they were composed, and rites and deities common to Indians and Iranians existed before the reforms of Zoroaster[1].

It may seem that everything is uncertain in this literature without dates or authors and that the growth of religion in India cannot be scientifically studied. The difficulties are indeed considerable but they are materially reduced by the veneration in which the ancient scriptures were held, and by the retentiveness of memory and devotion to grammar, if not to history, which have characterized the Brahmans for at least twenty-five centuries. The authenticity of certain Vedic texts is guaranteed not only by the quotations found in later works, but by treatises on phonetics, grammar and versification as well as by indices which give the number of words in every book, chapter and verse. We may be sure that we possess not perhaps the exact words of the Vedic poets, but what were believed about 600 B.C. to be their exact words, and there is no reason to doubt that this is a substantially correct version of the hymns as recited several centuries earlier[2].

In drawing any deductions from the hymns of the Rig Veda it must be remembered that it is the manual of the Hotri priests[3]. This does not affect the age or character of the single pieces: they may have been composed at very different dates and they are not arranged in the order in which the priest recites them. But the liturgical character of the compilation does somewhat qualify its title to give a complete picture of religion. One could not throw doubt on a ceremony of the Church, still less on a popular custom, because it was not

[1] Recent scholars are disposed to fix the appearance of Zoroaster between the middle of the seventh century and the earlier half of the sixth century B.C. But this date offers many difficulties. It makes it hard to explain the resemblances between the Gathas and the Ṛig Veda and how is it that respectable classical authorities of the fourth century B.C. quoted by Pliny attribute a high antiquity to Zoroaster?

[2] This applies chiefly to the three Saṃhitâs or collections of hymns and prayers. On the other hand there was no feeling against the composition of new Upanishads or the interpolation and amplification of the Epics.

[3] The Hotri recites prayers while other priests perform the act of sacrifice. But there are several poems in the Ṛig Veda for which even Indian ingenuity has not been able to find a liturgical use.

mentioned in the missal, and we cannot assume that ideas or usages not mentioned in the Rig Veda did not exist at the time when it was composed.

We have no other Sanskrit writings contemporary with the older parts of the Rig Veda, but the roots of epic poetry stretch far back and ballads may be as old as hymns, though they neither sought nor obtained the official sanction of the priesthood. Side by side with Vedic tradition, unrecorded Epic tradition built up the figures of Śiva, Râma and Krishna which astonish us by their sudden appearance in later literature only because their earlier phases have not been preserved.

The Vedic hymns were probably collected and arranged between 1000 and 500 B.C. At that period rites and ceremonies multiplied and absorbed man's mind to a degree unparalleled in the history of the world and literature occupied itself with the description or discussion of this dreary ceremonial. Buddhism was a protest against the necessity of sacrifices and, though Buddhism decayed in India, the sacrificial system never recovered from the attack and assumed comparatively modest proportions. But in an earlier period, after the composition of the Vedic hymns and before the predominance of speculation, skill in ceremonial was regarded as the highest and indeed only science and the ancient prayers and poems of the race were arranged in three collections to suit the ritual. These were the Rig Veda, containing metrical prayers: the Yajur Veda (in an old and new recension known as the Black and the White) containing formulæ mainly in prose to be muttered during the course of the sacrifice: and the Sâma Veda, a book of chants, consisting almost entirely of verses taken from the Rig Veda and arranged for singing. The Rig Veda is clearly older than the others: its elements are anterior to the Brahmanic liturgy and are arranged in less complete subservience to it than in the Yajur and Sâma Vedas.

The restriction of the words Veda and Vedic to the collection of hymns, though convenient, is not in accordance with Indian usage, which applies the name to a much larger body of religious literature. What we call the Rig Veda is strictly speaking the mantras of the Rig Veda or the Ṛig-Veda-Saṃhitâ: besides this, there are the Brâhmaṇas or ceremonial treatises, the Âraṇyakas and Upanishads containing philosophy and speculation, the

Sûtras or aphoristic rules, all comprised in the Veda or Śruti (hearing), that is the revelation heard directly by saints as opposed to Smṛiti (remembering) or tradition starting from human teachers. Modern Hindus when not influenced by the language of European scholars apply the word Veda especially to the Upanishads.

For some time only three[1] Vedas were accepted. But the Epics and the Puranas know of the fourfold Veda and place the Atharva Veda on a level with the other three. It was the manual of two ancient priestly families, the Atharvans and Angirasas, whose speciality was charms and prophylactics rather than the performance of the regular sacrifices. The hymns and magic songs which it contains were probably collected subsequently to the composition of the Brâhmaṇas, but the separate poems are older and, so far as can be judged from their language, are intermediate between the Rig Veda and the Brâhmaṇas. But the substance of many of the spells must be older still, since the incantations prescribed show a remarkable similarity to old German, Russian and Lettish charms. The Atharva also contains speculative poems and, if it has not the freshness of the Rig Veda, is most valuable for the history of Indian thought and civilization.

I will not here enquire what was the original home of the Aryans or whether the resemblances shown by Aryan languages justify us in believing that the ancestors of the Hindus, Greeks, Kelts, Slavs, etc., belonged to a single race and physical type. The grounds for such a belief seem to me doubtful. But a comparison of language, religion and customs makes it probable that the ancestors of the Iranians and Hindus dwelt together in some region lying to the north of India and then, in descending southwards, parted company and wandered, one band westwards to Persia and the other to the Panjab and south-east[2]. These latter produced the poets of the Rig Veda. Their home is indicated by their acquaintance with the Himalayas, the Kabul river, the Indus and rivers of the Panjab, and the Jamna. The Ganges, though known, apparently lay beyond their sphere,

[1] Thus the Pali Pitakas speak of the Tevijjâ or threefold knowledge of the Brahmans.

[2] Or it may be that the ancestors of the Persians were also in the Panjab and retired westwards.

but the geography of the Atharva extends as far as Benares and implies a practical knowledge of the sea, which is spoken of somewhat vaguely in the Rig Veda. It is probable that the oldest hymns were composed among the rivers of the Panjab, but the majority somewhat further to the east, in the district of Kurukshetra or Thanesar. At some period subsequent to the Aryan immigration there was a great struggle between two branches of the same stock, related in a legendary form as the contest between the Kauravas and Pâṇḍavas. Some have thought that we have here an indication of a second invasion composed of Aryans who remained in the mountainous districts north of the Hindu Kush when the first detachment moved south and who developed there somewhat different customs. It is also possible that the Atharva Veda may represent the religious ideas of these second invaders. In several passages the Mahâbhârata speaks of the Atharva as the highest Veda and represents the Pâṇḍavas as practising polyandry, a custom which still prevails among many Himalayan tribes.

The Rig Veda depicts a life not far advanced in material arts but, considering the date, humane and civilized. There were no towns but merely villages and fortified enclosures to be used as refuges in case of necessity. The general tone of the hymns is kindly and healthy; many of them indeed have more robust piety than interest. There are few indications of barbarous customs. The general impression is of a free and joyous life in which the principal actors are chiefs and priests, though neither have become tyrannical.

The composition of this anthology probably extended over several centuries and comprised a period of lively mental growth. It is therefore natural that it should represent stages of religious development which are not contemporaneous. But though thought is active and exuberant in these poems they are not altogether an intellectual outburst excited by the successful advance into India. The calm of settlement as well as the fire of conquest have left their mark on them and during the period of composition religion grew more boldly speculative but also more sedentary, formal and meticulous. The earliest hymns bear traces of quasi-nomadic life, but the writers are no longer nomads. They follow agriculture as well as pasturage, but they are still contending with the aborigines: still expanding and moving on. They mention no states or capitals: they revere rivers and mountains but have no shrines to serve as religious centres, as repositories and factories of tradition. Legends and precepts have of course come down from earlier generations, but are not very definite or cogent: the stories of ancient sages and warriors are vague and wanting in individual colour.

2

The absence of sculpture and painting explains much in the character of the Vedic deities. The hymn-writers were devout and imaginative, not content to revere some undescribed being in the sky, but full of mythology, metaphor and poetry and continually singling out new powers for worship. Among many races the conceptions thus evolved acquire solidity and permanence by the aid of art. An image stereotypes a deity, worshippers from other districts can see it and it remains from generation to generation as a conservative and unifying force. Even a stone may have something of the same effect, for it connects the deity with the events, rites and ideas of a locality. But the earliest stratum of Vedic religion is worship of the powers of nature—such as the Sun, the Sky, the Dawn, the Fire—which are personified but not localized or depicted. Their attributes do not depend at all on art, not much on local or tribal custom but chiefly on imagination and poetry, and as this poetry was not united in one collection until a later period, a bard was under no obligation to conform to the standards of his fellows and probably many bards sang without knowing of one another's existence.

Such a figure as Agni or Fire—if one can call him a figure—illustrates the fluid and intangible character of Vedic divinities. He is one of the greatest in the Pantheon, and in some ways his godhead is strongly marked. He blesses, protects, preserves, and inspires: he is a divine priest and messenger between gods and men: he "knows all generations." Yet we cannot give any definite account of him such as could be drawn up for a Greek deity. He is not a god of fire, like Vulcan, but the Fire itself regarded as divine. The descriptions of his appearance are not really anthropomorphic but metaphorical imagery depicting shining, streaming flames. The hymns tell us that he has a tawny beard and hair: a flaming head or three heads: three tongues or seven: four eyes or a thousand. One poem says that he faces in all directions: another that he is footless and headless. He is called the son of Heaven and Earth, of Tvashṭri and the Waters, of the Dawn, of Indra-Vishnu. One singer says that the gods generated him to be a light for the Aryans, another that he is the father of the gods. This multiple origin becomes more definite in the theory of Agni's three births: he is born on earth from the friction of fire sticks, in the clouds as lightning, and in the highest heavens as the Sun or celestial light. In virtue of this triple birth he assumes a triune character: his heads, tongues, bodies and dwellings are three, and this threefold nature has perhaps something to do with the triads of deities which become frequent later and finally develop into the Trimûrti or Brahmâ, Vishnu, and Siva. But there is nothing fixed or dogmatic in this idea of Agni's three births. In other texts he is said to have two, one in Heaven and one on Earth, and yet another turn of fancy ascribes to him births innumerable because he is kindled on many hearths. Some of the epithets applied to him become quasi-independent. For instance, Agni Vaiśvânara—All men's fire—and Agni Tanunapat, which seems to mean son of himself, or fire spontaneously generated, are in a later period treated almost as separate deities. Mâtariśvan is sometimes a name of Agni and sometimes a separate deity who brings Agni to mankind.

In the same way the Rig Veda has not one but many solar deities. Mitra, Sûrya, Savitri, and perhaps Puśan, Bhaga, Vivasvat and Vishnu, are all loose personifications of certain functions or epithets of the sun. Deities are often thought of in classes. Thus we have the Maruts, Rudras and Vasus. We hear of Prajâpati in the singular, but also of the Prajâpatis or creative forces.

Not only does Agni tend to be regarded as more than one: he is identified with other gods. We are told he is Varuṇa and Mitra, Savitri and Indra. "Thou art Varuṇa when born," says one hymn, "thou becomest Mitra when kindled. In thee, O son of strength, are all the gods[1]." Such identifications are common in the Vedas. Philosophically, they are an early manifestation of the mental bias which leads to pantheism, metempsychosis,

[1] R.V. v. 3. 1.

and the feeling that all things and persons are transitory and partial aspects of the one reality. But evidently the mutability of the Vedic gods is also due to their nature: they are bundles of epithets and functions without much personal or local centre. And these epithets and functions are to a large extent, the same. All the gods are bright and swift and helpful: all love sacrifices and bestow wealth, sons and cows. A figure like Agni enables us to understand the many-sided, inconsistent presentment of Siva and Vishnu in later times. A richer mythology surrounds them but in the fluidity of their outline, their mutability and their readiness to absorb or become all other deities they follow the old lines. Even a deity like Gaṇeśa who seems at first sight modern and definite illustrates these ancient characteristics. He has one or five heads and from four to sixteen arms: there are half a dozen strange stories of his birth and wonderful allegories describing his adventures. Yet he is also identified with all the Gods and declared to be the creator, preserver and destroyer of the Universe, nay the Supreme Spirit itself[1].

In Soma, the sacred plant whose juice was offered in the most solemn sacrifices, we again find the combination of natural phenomena and divinity with hardly any personification. Soma is not a sacred tree inhabited by some spirit of the woods but the Lord of immortality who can place his worshippers in the land of eternal life and light. Some of the finest and most spiritual of the Vedic hymns are addressed to him and yet it is hard to say whether they are addressed to a person or a beverage. The personification is not much more than when French writers call absinthe "La fée aux yeux verts." Later, Soma was identified with the moon, perhaps because the juice was bright and shining. On the other hand Soma worship is connected with a very ancient but persistent form of animism, for the Vedic poets celebrate as immortal the stones under which the plant is pressed and beg them to bestow wealth and children. Just so at the present day agricultural and other implements receive the salutations and prayers of those who use them. They are not gods in any ordinary sense but they are potent forces.

[1] See the Gaṇeśâtharvaśîrsha Upan. and Gopinatha Rao. *Hindu Iconography*, vol. I. pp. 35–67.

But some Vedic deities are drawn more distinctly, particularly Indra, who having more character has also lasted longer than most of his fellows, partly because he was taken over by Buddhism and enrolled in the retinue of the Buddha. He appears to have been originally a god of thunder, a phenomenon which lends itself to anthropomorphic treatment. As an atmospheric deity, he conquers various powers of evil, particularly Vritra, the demon of drought. The Vedas know of evil spirits against whom the gods wage successful war but they have no single personification of evil in general, like our devil, and few malevolent deities. Of these latter Rudra, the prototype of Siva, is the most important but he is not wholly malevolent for he is the god of healing and can take away sickness as well as cause it. Indian thought is not inclined to dualism, which is perhaps the outcome of a practical mind desiring a certain course and seeing everywhere the difficulties which the Evil One puts in the way of it, but rather to that pantheism which tends to subsume both good and evil under a higher unity.

Indra was the tutelary deity of the invading Aryans. His principles would delight a European settler in Africa. He protects the Aryan colour and subjects the black skin: he gave land to the Aryans and made the Dâsyus (aborigines) subject to them: he dispersed fifty thousand of the black race and rent their citadels[1]. Some of the events with which he is connected, such as the battles of King Sudas, may have a historical basis. He is represented as a gigantic being of enormous size and vigour and of gross passions. He feasts on the flesh of bulls and buffaloes roasted by hundreds, his potations are counted in terms of lakes, and not only nerve him for the fray but also intoxicate him[2]. Under the name of Sakka, Indra figures largely in the Buddhist sûtras, and seems to have been the chief popular deity in the Buddha's lifetime. He was adopted into the new creed as a sort of archangel and heavenly defender of the faith. In the epics he is still a mighty deity and the lord of paradise. Happiness in his heaven is the reward of the pious warrior after death. The Mahâbhârata and the Puranas, influenced perhaps

[1] See R.V. III. 34. 9. i. 130. 8; IV. 26. 2. vi. 18. 3; IV. 16. 13.

[2] In one singular hymn (R.V. x. 119) Indra describes his sensations after drinking freely, and in the Śatapatha Brâhmaṇa (v. 5. 4. 9 and XII. 7. 1. 11) he seems to be represented as suffering from his excesses and having to be cured by a special ceremony.

by Buddhism, speak of a series of Indras, each lasting for a cycle, but superseded when a new heaven and earth appear. In modern Hinduism his name is familiar though he does not receive much worship. Yet in spite of his long pre-eminence there is no disposition to regard him as the supreme and only god. Though the Rig Veda calls him the creator and destroyer of all things[1], he is not God in our sense any more than other deities are. He is the personification of strength and success, but he is not sufficiently spiritual or mystical to hold and satisfy the enquiring mind.

3

One of the most interesting and impressive of Vedic deities is Varuṇa, often invoked with a more shadowy double called Mitra. No myths or exploits are related of him but he is the omnipotent and omniscient upholder of moral and physical law. He established earth and sky: he set the sun in heaven and ordained the movements of the moon and stars: the wind is his breath and by his law the heavens and earth are kept apart. He perceives all that exists in heaven and earth or beyond, nor could a man escape him though he fled beyond the sky. The winkings of men's eyes are all numbered by him[2]: he knows all that man does or thinks. Sin is the infringement of his ordinances and he binds sinners in fetters. Hence they pray to him for release from sin and he is gracious to the penitent. Whereas the other deities are mainly asked to bestow material boons, the hymns addressed to Varuṇa contain petitions for forgiveness. He dwells in heaven in a golden mansion. His throne is great and lofty with a thousand columns and his abode has a thousand doors. From it he looks down on the doings of men and the all-seeing sun comes to his courts to report.

There is much in these descriptions which is unlike the attributes ascribed to any other member of the Vedic pantheon and recalls Ahura Mazda of the Avesta or Semitic deities. No proof of foreign influence is forthcoming, but the opinion of some scholars that the figure of Varuṇa somehow reflects Semitic

[1] In some passages of the Upanishads he is identified with the âtman (*e.g.* Kaushîtaki Up. III. 8), but then all persons, whether divine or human, are really the âtman if they only knew it.

[2] A.V. IV. 16. 2.

ideas is plausible. It has been suggested that he was originally a lunar deity, which explains his association with Mitra (the Persian Mithra) who was a sun god, and that the group of deities called Âdityas and including Mitra and Varuṇa were the sun, moon and the five planets known to the ancients. This resembles the Babylonian worship of the heavenly bodies and, though there is no record whatever of how such ideas reached the Aryans, it is not difficult to imagine that they may have come from Babylonia either to India[1] or to the country where Indians and Iranians dwelt together. There is a Semitic flavour too in the Indian legend of the Churning of the Ocean[2]. The Gods and Asuras effect this by using a huge serpent as a rope to whirl round a mountain and from the turmoil there arise various marvellous personages and substances including the moon. This resembles in tone if not in detail the Babylonian creation myths, telling of a primæval abyss of waters and a great serpent which is slain by the Gods who use its body as the material for making the heavens and the earth[3].

Yet Varuṇa is not the centre of a monotheistic religion any more than Indra, and in later times he becomes a water god of no marked importance. The Aryans and Semites, while both dissatisfied with polytheism and seeking the one among the many, moved along different paths and did not reach exactly the same goal. Semitic deities were representations of the forces of nature in human form but their character was stereotyped by images, at any rate in Assyria and Babylonia, and by the ritual of particular places with which they were identified. Semitic polytheism is mainly due to the number of tribes and localities possessing separate deities, not to the number of deities worshipped by each place and tribe. As villages and small towns were subordinate to great towns, so the deities of minor localities were subordinate to those of the greater. Hence the Semitic god was often thought of as a king who might be surrounded by a court and then became the head of a pantheon of inferior deities, but also might be thought of as tolerating no rivals. This latter conception when combined with moral earnestness

[1] The Indian alphabets are admittedly Semitic in origin.

[2] See Mahâbhâr. I. xvii–xviii and other accounts in the Râmâyaṇa and Purâṇas.

[3] It has also been conjectured that Sk. Asura = Ashur, the God of Assyria, and that Sumeru or Sineru (Meru) = Sumer or Shinar, see *J.R.A.S.* 1916, pp. 364–5.

gives us Jehovah, who resembles Varuṇa, except that Varuṇa is neither jealous nor national. Indian polytheism also originated in the personification of various phenomena, the sun, thunder, fire, rivers, and so forth, but these deities unlike the Semitic gods had little to do with special tribes or localities and the philosophic Indian easily traced a connection between them. It is not difficult to see that sun, fire and lightning have something in common. The gods are frequently thought of as joined in couples, triads or larger companies and early worship probably showed the beginnings of a feature which is prominent in the later ritual, namely, that a sacrifice is not an isolated oblation offered to one particular god but a series of oblations presented to a series of deities. There was thus little disposition to exalt one god and annihilate the others, but every disposition to identify the gods with one another and all of them with something else. Just as rivers, mountains and plains are dimly seen to be parts of a whole which later ages call nature, so are the gods seen to be parts of some divine whole which is greater than any of them. Even in the Rig Veda we find such sentiments as "The priests speak of the One Being in many ways: they call it Agni, Yama, Mâtariśvan[1]." Hence it is not surprising that when in the later Vedic period a tendency towards monotheism (but monotheism of a pantheistic type) appears, the supreme position is given to none of the old deities but to a new figure, Prajâpati. This word, meaning Lord of living creatures, occurs in the Rig Veda as an epithet of the sun and is also occasionally used as the name of the Being by whom all gods and worlds were generated and by whose power they continue to exist. In the Brâhmaṇas and later ritual literature he is definitely recognized as the supreme deity, the Creator, the first sacrificer and the sacrifice itself. It is perhaps owing to his close connection with ceremonial that enquiring and speculative minds felt Prajâpati not to be a final or satisfactory explanation of the universe. He is identified with Brahmâ, the active personal creator, and this later name gradually ousts the other but he does not, any more than Indra or Varuṇa, become the Âtman or supreme universal Being of the Upanishads.

The principal Vedic deities are male and the few goddesses that are mentioned such as Ushas, the Dawn, seem to owe their

[1] Ṛig V. I. 164. 46.

sex to purely dramatic reasons. Greece and Rome as well as India felt it appropriate to represent the daybreak as a radiant nymph. But though in later times such goddesses as Durgâ assumed in some sects a paramount position, and though the Veda is familiar with the idea of the world being born, there are few traces in it of a goddess corresponding to the Great Mother, Cybele or Astarte.

In an earlier period of Vedic studies many deities were identified with figures in the classical or Teutonic mythology chiefly on philological grounds but most of these identifications have now been abandoned. But a few names and figures seem to be found among both the Asiatic and European Aryans and to point to a common stock of ideas. Dyaus, the Sky God, is admittedly the same as Zeus and Jupiter. The Aśvins agree in character, though not in name, with the Dioscuri and other parallels are quoted from Lettish mythology. Bhaga, the bountiful giver, a somewhat obscure deity, is the same word as the Slavonic Bog, used in the general sense of God, and we find *deva* in Sanskrit, *deus* in Latin, and *devas* in Lithuanian. Ushas, the Dawn, is phonetically related to 'Hώς and Aurora who, however, are only half deities. Indra, if he cannot be scientifically identified with Thor, is a similar personage who must have grown out of the same stock of ideas. By a curious transference the Prophet Elias has in south-eastern Europe inherited the attributes of the thunder god and is even now in the imagination of the peasantry a jovial and riotous being who, like Indra, drives a noisy chariot across the sky.

The connection with ancient Persian mythology is closer. The Avestan religion was a reformation due to the genius of Zoroaster and therefore comparable with Buddhism rather than Hinduism, but the less systematic polytheism which preceded it contained much which reminds us of the Vedic hymns. It can hardly be doubted that the ancestors of the Indians and Iranians once practised almost identical forms of religion and had even a common ritual. The chief features of the fire cult and of the Soma or Haoma sacrifice appear in both. The sacrifice is called Yajña in the Veda, Yasna in the Avesta: the Hotri priest is Zaotar, Atharvan is Athravan, Mitra is Mithra. Vâyu and Âpaḥ (the divine waters) meet us in the Avesta in almost the same forms and Indra's epithet of Vritrahan (the slayer of Vritra) appears as Verethragna. Ahura Mazda seems to be a development of the deity who appears as Varuṇa in India though he has not the same name, and the main difference between Indian and Iranian religion lies in this, that the latter was systematized by a theistic reformer who exalted one deity above the others, whereas in India, where there was more religious vitality, polytheistic and pantheistic fancies flourished uncurbed and the greatest reformer, the Buddha, was not a theist.

One peculiarity of Indians in all ages is that they put more into religion than other races. It received most of the energy and talent which, elsewhere, went into art, politics and philosophy. Hence it became both intense and manifold, for deities and creeds were wanted for every stage of intelligence and variety of taste, and also very tolerant, for sects in India, though multitudinous, are not so sharply divided or mutually hostile as in Europe. Connected with the general interest which religion inspired is its strongly marked speculative character. The Rig Veda asks whether in the beginning there was being or not being, and the later Vedas and Brâhmaṇas are filled with discussions as to the meaning of ceremonies, which show that the most dreary formalism could not extinguish the innate propensity to seek for a reason. In the Upanishads we have the same spirit dealing with more promising material. And throughout the long history of Hinduism religion and philosophy are seldom separated: we rarely find detached metaphysicians: philosophers found new sects or support old ones: religion absorbs philosophy and translates it into theology or myths.

4

To the age of the Vedas succeeds that of the Brâhmaṇas or sacrificial treatises. The two periods are distinct and have each a well-marked tone, but they pass into one another, for the Yajur and Sâma Vedas pre-suppose the ritual of the Brâhmaṇas. These treatises introduce us to one feature of Indian religion mentioned above, namely the extraordinary elaboration of its ritual. To read them one would suppose that the one occupation of all India was the offering of sacrifices. The accounts are no doubt exaggerated and must often be treated as specimens of sacerdotal imagination, like the Biblical descriptions of the rites performed in the Tabernacle during the wanderings of the Israelites. But making all allowance for priestly enthusiasm, it still remains true that the intellect of India, so far as it is preserved in literature, was occupied during two centuries or so with the sacrificial art and that philosophy had difficulty in disentangling itself from ceremonies. One has only to compare Greek and Sanskrit literature to see how vast are the proportions assumed by ritual in India. Our information about the political institutions, the wars and chronology of ancient Greece is full, but of the details of Greek worship we hear little and probably there was not much to tell. But in India, where there are no histories and no dates, we know every prayer and gesture of the officiants throughout complicated sacrifices and possess a whole library describing their correct performance.

In most respects these sacrifices which absorbed so much intellect and energy belong to ancient history. They must not be confounded with the ceremonies performed in modern temples, which have a different origin and character. A great blow was struck at the sacrificial system by Buddhism. Not only did it withdraw the support of many kings and nobles (and the greater ceremonies being very costly depended largely on the patronage of the wealthy), but it popularized the idea that animal sacrifices are shocking and that attempts to win salvation by offerings are crude and unphilosophic. But though, after Buddhism had leavened India for a few centuries, we no longer find the religious world given over to sacrificing as it had been about 600 B.C., these rites did not die out. Even now they are occasionally performed in South India and the Deccan. There are still many Brahmans in these regions who, if they have not the means or learning to perform the greater Vedic ceremonies, at any rate sympathize with the mental attitude which they imply, and this attitude has many curious features.

The rite of sacrifice, which in the simple form of an offering supposed to be agreeable to the deity is the principal ceremony in the early stages of most religions, persists in their later stages but gives rise to clouds of theory and mystical interpretations. Thus in Christianity, the Jewish sacrifices are regarded as prototypes of the death of Christ and that death itself as a sacrifice to the Almighty, an offering of himself to himself, which in some way acts as an expiation for the sins of the world. And by a further development the sacrifice of the mass, that is, the offering of portions of bread and wine which are held to be miraculously transformed into the body and blood of Christ by the manipulations of a qualified priest, is believed to repeat every day the tragedy of Calvary. The prevalence of this view in Europe should make us chary of stigmatizing Hindu ideas about sacrifice as mental aberrations. They represent the fancies of acute intellects dealing with ancient ceremonies which they cannot abandon but which they transform into something more congenial to their own transitional mode of thought.

Though the Brâhmaṇas and Upanishads mix up ritual with physical and metaphysical theories in the most extraordinary fashion, their main motive deserves sympathy and respect. Their weakness lies in their inability to detach themselves (as the Buddha succeeded in doing) from a ritual which though elaborate was neither edifying nor artistic: they seem unable to see the great problems of existence except through the mists of altar smoke. Their merit is their evident conviction that this formalism is inadequate. Their wish is not to distort and cramp nature by bringing it within the limits of the ritual, but to enlarge and expand the ritual until it becomes cosmic. If they regard the whole universe as one long act of prayer and sacrifice, the idea is grandiose rather than pedantic, though the details may not always be to our taste[1]. And the Upanishads pass from ritual and theology to real speculation in a way unknown to Christian thought. To imagine a parallel, we must picture Spinoza beginning with an exposition of the Trinity and transubstantiation and proceeding to develop his own system without becoming unorthodox.

The conception of the sacrifice set forth in the Brâhmaṇas is that it is a scientific method of acquiring immortality as well as temporal blessings. Though originally a mere offering in the *do ut des* principle, it has assumed a higher and more mysterious position[2]. We are told that the gods obtained immortality and

[1] For instance chap. III. of the Châmdogya Upanishad, which compares the solar system to a beehive in which the bees are Vedic hymns, is little less than stupendous, though singular and hard for European thought to follow.

[2] I presume that the strong opinion expressed in Caland and Henri's *Agnishṭoma* p. 484 that the sacrifice is merely a *do ut des* operation refers only to the earliest Vedic period and not to the time of the Brâhmaṇas.

heaven by sacrifice, that they created the universe by sacrifice, that Prajâpati, the creator, *is* the sacrifice. Although some writers are disposed to distinguish magic sharply from religion, the two are not separated in the Vedas. Sacrifice is not merely a means of pleasing the gods: it is a system of authorized magic or sacred science controlling all worlds, if properly understood. It is a mysterious cosmic force like electricity which can be utilized by a properly trained priest but is dangerous in unskilful hands, for the rites, if wrongly performed, bring disaster or even death on bunglers. Though the Vedic sacrifices fell more and more out of general use, this notion of the power of rites and formulæ did not fade with them but has deeply infected modern Hinduism and even Buddhism, in both of which the lore of spells and gestures assumes monstrous proportions. The Vedic and modern tantric rituals are different but they are based on the same supposition that the universe (including the gods which are part of it) is regulated by some permeating principle, and that this principle can be apprehended by sacred science and controlled by the use of proper methods[1]. So far as these systems express the idea that the human mind can grasp the universe by knowledge, they offer an example of the bold sweep of the Hindu intellect, but the methods prescribed are often fatuous.

The belief in the potency of words and formulæ, though amplified and embellished by the Hindus, is not an Indian invention but a common aspect of early thought which was less emphasized in other countries. It is found in Persia and among the tribes of Central and Northern Asia and of Northern Europe, and attained a high development in Finland where *runot* or magical songs are credited with very practical efficacy. Thus the Kalevala relates how Wäinämöinen was building a boat by means of songs when the process came to a sudden stop because he had forgotten three words. This is exactly the sort of thing that might happen in the legends of a Vedic sacrifice if the priest had forgotten the texts he ought to recite.

[1] Thus both the Vedas and the Tantras devote considerable space to rites which have for object the formation of a new body for the sacrificer. Compare for instance the Aitareya Brâhmaṇa (I. 18–21: II. 35–38: III. 2 and VI. 27–31) with Avalon's account of Nyâsa, in his introduction to the Mahânirvâṇa Tantra pages cvii–cxi.

The external features of Vedic rites are remarkable and unlike what we know of those performed by other nations of antiquity. The sacrifice is not as a rule a gift presented to a single god to win his favour. Oblations are made to most members of the pantheon in the course of a prolonged ceremony, but the time, manner and recipients of these oblations are fixed rather by the mysteries of sacrificial science, than by the sacrificer's need to propitiate a particular deity. Also the sacrifice is not offered in a temple and it would appear that in pre-Buddhist times there were no religious edifices. It is not even associated with sacred spots, such as groves or fountains haunted by a deity. The scene of operations requires long and careful preparation, but it is merely an enclosure with certain sheds, fireplaces and mounds. It has no architectural pretensions and is not a centre round which shrines can grow for it requires reconsecration for each ceremony, and in many cases must not be used twice. There is little that is national, tribal or communal about these rites. Some of them, such as the Aśvamedha or horse sacrifice and the Râjasuya, or consecration of a king, may be attended by games and sports, but that is because they are connected with secular events. In their essence sacrifices are not popular festivals or holidays but private services, performed for the benefit of the sacrificer, that is, the person who pays the fees of the priests. Usually they have a definite object and, though ceremonies for the attainment of material blessings are not wanting, this object is most frequently supramundane, such as the fabrication of a body in the heavenly world. It is in keeping with these characteristics that there should be no pomp or spectacular effect: the rites resemble some complicated culinary operation or scientific experiment, and the sacrificial enclosure has the appearance of a laboratory rather than a place of worship.

Vedic ritual includes the sacrifice of animals, and there are indications of the former prevalence of human sacrifice. At the time when the Brâhmaṇas were composed the human victims were released alive, but afterwards the practice of real sacrifice was revived, probably owing to the continual incorporation into the Hindu community of semi-barbarous tribes and their savage deities. Human victims were offered to Mahâdevî the spouse of Siva until the last century, and would doubtless be offered now, were legal restrictions removed. But though the sporadic survival of an old custom in its most primitive and barbarous form is characteristic of Hinduism, the whole tendency of thought and practice since the rise of Buddhism has been adverse to religious bloodshed, even of animals. The doctrine of substitution and atonement, of offering the victim on behalf of the sacrificer, though not absent, plays a smaller part than in the religions of Western Asia.

Evidently it was not congenial: the Hindu has always been inclined to think that the individual earns his future in another world by his own thoughts and acts. Even the value of the victim is less important than the correct performance of the ceremony. The teaching of the Brâhmaṇas is not so much that a good heart is better than lavish alms as that the ritually correct sacrifice of a cake is better than a hecatomb not offered according to rule.

The offerings required by the Vedic ritual are very varied. The simplest are cakes and libations of melted butter poured on the fire from two wooden spoons held one over the other while Vedic verses are recited. Besides these there was the animal sacrifice, and still more important the Soma[1] sacrifice. This ceremony is very ancient and goes back to the time when the Hindus and Iranians were not divided. In India the sacrifice lasted at least five days and, even in its simpler forms, was far more complicated than any ceremony known to the Greeks, Romans or Jews. Only professional priests could perform it and as a rule a priest did not attempt to master more than one branch and to be for instance either a reciter (Hotṛi) or singer (Udgâtṛi). But the five-day sacrifices are little more than the rudiments of the sacrificial art and lead on to the Ahînas or sacrifices comprising from two to twelve days of Soma pressing which last not more than a month. The Ahinas again can be com-

[1] There is considerable doubt as to what was the plant originally known as Soma. That described in the Vedas and Brâhmaṇas is said to grow on the mountains and to have a yellow juice of a strong smell, fiery taste and intoxicating properties. The plants used as Haom (Hum) by the modern Parsis of Yezd and Kermaṅ are said to be members of the family Asclepiadaceæ (perhaps of the genus Sarcostemma) with fleshy stalks and milky juice, and the Soma tested by Dr Haug at Poona was probably made from another species of the same or an allied genus. He found it extremely nasty, though it had some intoxicating effect. (See his *Aitareya Brâhmaṇa* II. p. 489.)

bined into sacrificial sessions lasting a year or more[1], and it would seem that rites of this length were really performed, though when we read of such sessions extending over a hundred years, we may hope that they are creations of a fancy like that of the hymn-writer who celebrated the state

> Where congregations ne'er break up
> And Sabbaths never end.

The ritual literature of India is enormous and much of it has been edited and translated by European scholars with a care that merited a better object. It is a mine of information respecting curious beliefs and practices of considerable historical interest, but it does not represent the main current of religious ideas in post-Buddhist times. The Brahmans indeed never ceased to give the sacrificial system their theoretical and, when possible, their practical approval, for it embodies a principle most dear to them, namely, that the other castes can obtain success and heaven only under the guidance of Brahmans and by rites which only Brahmans can perform. But for this very reason it incurred the hostility not only of philosophers and morally earnest men, but of the military caste and it never really recovered from the blow dealt it by Buddhism, the religion of that caste. But with every Brahmanic revival it came to the front and the performance of the Aśvamedha or horse sacrifice[2] was long the culminating glory of an orthodox king.

[1] An ordinary sacrifice was offered for a private person who had to be initiated and the priests were merely officiants acting on his behalf. In a Sattra the priests were regarded as the sacrificers and were initiated. It had some analogy to Buddhist and Christian monastic foundations for reading sûtras and saying masses.

[2] The political importance of the Aśvamedha lay in the fact that the victim had to be let loose to roam freely for a year, so that only a king whose territories were sufficiently extensive to allow of its being followed and guarded during its wanderings could hope to sacrifice it at the end.

CHAPTER V

ASCETICISM AND KNOWLEDGE

1

As sacrifice and ceremonial are the material accompaniments of prayer, so are asceticism and discipline those of thought. This is less conspicuous in other countries, but in India it is habitually assumed that the study of what we call metaphysics or theology needs some kind of physical discipline and it will be well to elucidate this point before describing the beginnings of speculation.

Tapas, that is asceticism or self-mortification, holds in the religious thought and practice of India as large a place as sacrifice. We hear of it as early, for it is mentioned in the Rig Veda[1], and it lasts longer, for it is a part of contemporary Hinduism just as much as prayer or worship. It appears even in creeds which disavow it theoretically, *e.g.* in Buddhism, and evidently has its root in a deep-seated and persistent instinct.

Tapas is often translated penance but the idea of mortification as an expiation for sins committed, though not unknown in India, is certainly not that which underlies the austerities of most ascetics. The word means literally heat, hence pain or toil, and some think that its origin should be sought in practices which produced fever, or tended to concentrate heat in the body. One object of Tapas is to obtain abnormal powers by the suppression of desires or the endurance of voluntary tortures. There is an element of truth in this aspiration. Temperance, chastity and mental concentration are great aids for increasing the force of thought and will. The Hindu believes that intensity and perseverance in this road of abstinence and rapture will yield correspondingly increased results. The many singular phenomena connected with Indian asceticism have been imperfectly investigated but a psychological examination would probably find that subjective results (such as visions and the feeling of flying through the air) are really produced by the

[1] R.V. x. 136 and x. 190.

discipline recommended and there may be elements of much greater value in the various systems of meditation. But this is only the beginning of Tapas. To the idea that the soul when freed from earthly desires is best able to comprehend the divine is superadded another idea, namely that self-mortification is a process of productive labour akin to intellectual toil. Just as the whole world is supposed to be permeated by a mysterious principle which can be known and subdued by the science of the sacrificing priests, so the ascetic is able to control gods and nature by the force of his austerities. The creative deities are said to have produced the world by Tapas, just as they are said to have produced it by sacrifice and Hindu mythology abounds in stories of ascetics who became so mighty that the very gods were alarmed. For instance Râvaṇa, the Demon ruler of Lanka who carried off Sîtâ, had acquired his power by austerities which enabled him to extort a boon from Brahmâ. Thus there need be nothing moral in the object of asceticism or in the use of the power obtained. The epics and dramas frequently portray ascetics as choleric and unamiable characters and modern Yogis maintain the tradition.

Though asceticism resembles the sacrifice in being a means by which man can obtain his wishes whether religious or profane, it differs in being comparatively easy. Irksome as it may be, it demands merely strength of will and not a scientific training in ritual and Vedic texts. Hence in this sphere the supremacy of the Brahman could be challenged by other castes and an instructive legend relates how Râma slew a Śûdra whom he surprised in the act of performing austerities. The lowest castes can by this process acquire a position which makes them equal to the highest[1].

Of the non-Brahmanic sects, the Jains set the highest value on Tapas, but chiefly as a purification of the soul and a means of obtaining an unearthly state of pure knowledge[2]. In theory the Buddha rejected it; he taught a middle way, rejecting alike self-indulgence and self-mortification. But even Pali Buddhism

[1] Even the Upanishads (*e.g.* Chând. III. 17, Mahânâr. 64) admit that a good life which includes *tapas* is the equivalent of sacrifice. But this of course is teaching for the elect only. The Brih.-Âran. Up. (v. ii) contains the remarkable doctrine that sickness and pain, if regarded by the sufferer as *tapas*, bring the same reward.

[2] So too in the Taittirîya Upanishad *tapas* is described as the means of attaining the knowledge of Brahman (III. 1–5).

admits such practices as the Dhûtângas and the more extravagant sects, for instance in Tibet, allow monks to entomb themselves in dark cells. According to our standards even the ordinary religious life of both Hindus and Buddhists is severely ascetic. It is assumed as a *sine qua non* that strict chastity must be observed, nourishment be taken only to support life and not for pleasure, that all gratification coming from the senses must be avoided and the mind kept under rigid discipline. This discipline receives systematic treatment in the Yoga school of philosophy but it is really common to all varieties of Hinduism and Buddhism; all agree that the body must be subdued by physical training before the mind can apprehend the higher truths. The only question is how far asceticism is directly instrumental in giving higher knowledge. If some texts speak slightingly of it, we must remember that the life of a hermit dwelling in the woods without possessions or desires might not be regarded by a Hindu as *tapas* though we should certainly regard it as asceticism. It is also agreed that supernatural powers can be acquired by special forms of asceticism. These powers are sometimes treated as mere magic and spiritually worthless but their reality is not questioned.

2

We have now said something of two aspects of Indian religion—ritual and asceticism—and must pass on to the third, namely, knowledge or philosophy. Its importance was recognized by the severest ritualists. They admitted it as a supplement and crown to the life of ceremonial observances and in the public estimation it came to be reputed an alternative or superior road to salvation. Respect and desire for knowledge are even more intimately a part of Hindu mentality than a proclivity to asceticism or ritual. The sacrifice itself must be understood as well as offered. He who *knows* the meaning of this or that observance obtains his desires[1].

Nor did the Brahmans resent criticism and discussion. India has always loved theological argument: it is the national passion. The early Upanishads relate without disapproval how

[1] Any ritual without knowledge may be worse than useless. See Chând. Up. I. 10. 11.

kings such as Ajâtaśatru of Kâśi, Pravâhaṇa Jaivali and Aśvapati Kaikeya imparted to learned Brahmans philosophical and theological knowledge previously unknown to them[1] and even women like Gârgî and Maitreyî took part in theological discussions. Obviously knowledge in the sense of philosophical speculation commended itself to religiously disposed persons in the non-sacerdotal castes for the same reason as asceticism. Whatever difficulties it might offer, it was more accessible than the learning which could be acquired only under a Brahman teacher, although the Brahmans in the interests of the sacerdotal caste maintained that philosophy like ritual was a secret to be imparted, not a result to be won by independent thought.

Again and again the Upanishads insist that the more profound doctrines must not be communicated to any but a son or an accredited pupil and also that no one can think them out for himself[2], yet the older ones admit in such stories as those mentioned that the impulse towards speculation came in early periods, as it did in the time of the Buddha, largely from outside the priestly clans and was adopted rather than initiated by them. But in justice to the Brahmans we must admit that they have rarely—or at any rate much less frequently than other sacerdotal corporations—shown hostility to new ideas and then chiefly when such ideas (like those of Buddhism) implied that the rites by which they gained their living were worthless. Otherwise they showed great pliancy and receptivity, for they combined Vedic rites and mythology with such systems as the Sânkhya and Advaita philosophies, both of which really render superfluous everything which is usually called religion since, though their language is decorous, they teach that he who *knows* the truth about the universe is thereby saved.

The best opinion of India has always felt that the way of knowledge or Jñâna was the true way. The favourite thesis of the Brahmans was that a man should devote his youth to study, his maturity to the duties and ceremonies of a householder,

[1] See the various narratives in the Chândogya, Br.-Âran. and Kaushîtaki Upanishads. The seventh chapter of the Chândogya relating how Nârada, the learned sage, was instructed by Sanatkumâra or Skanda, the god of war, seems to hint that the active military class may know the great truths of religion better than deeply read priests who may be hampered and blinded by their learning. For Skanda and Nârada in this connection see Bhagavad-gîtâ x. 24, 26.

[2] For the necessity of a teacher see Kâth. Up. II. 8.

and his age to more sublime speculations. But at all periods the idea that it was possible to know God and the universe was allied to the idea that all ceremonies as well as all worldly effort and indeed all active morality are superfluous[1]. All alike are unessential and trivial, and merit the attention only of those who know nothing higher. Human feelings and interests qualified and contradicted this negative and unearthly view of religion, but still popular sentiment as well as philosophic thought during the whole period of which we know something of them in India tended to regard the highest life as consisting in rapt contemplation or insight accompanied by the suppression of desire and by disengagement from mundane ties and interests. But knowledge in Indian theology implies more intensity than we attach to the word and even some admixture of volition. The knowledge of Brahman is not an understanding of pantheistic doctrines such as may be obtained by reading *The Sacred Books of the East* in an easy chair but a realization (in all senses) of personal identity with the universal spirit, in the light of which all material attachments and fetters fall away.

The earlier philosophical speculations of the Brahmans are chiefly found in the treatises called Upanishads. The teaching contained in these works is habitually presented as something secret[2] or esoteric and does not, like Buddhism or Jainism, profess to be a gospel for all. Also the teaching is not systematized and has never been unified by a personality like the Buddha. It grew up in the various *parishads*, or communities of learned Brahmans, and perhaps flourished most in north western India[3]. There is of course a common substratum of ideas but they appear in different versions: we have the teaching of Yâjñavalkya, of Uddâlaka Âruṇi and other masters and each teaching has some individuality. They are merely reported as words of the wise without an attempt to harmonize them. There are many apparent inconsistencies due to the use of divergent metaphors to indicate different aspects of the indescribable, and some real inconsistencies due to the existence of

[1] See especially the bold passage at the end of Taitt. Upan. II. "He who knows the bliss of Brahman...fears nothing. He does not torment himself by asking what good have I left undone, what evil have I done?"

[2] The word Upanishad probably means sitting down at the feet of a teacher to receive secret instruction: hence a secret conversation or doctrine.

[3] Some allusions in the older Upanishads point to this district rather than the Ganges Valley as the centre of Brahmanic philosophy. Thus the Bṛihad-Âraṇyaka speaks familiarly of Gândhâra.

different schools. Hence, attempts whether Indian or European to give a harmonious summary of this ancient doctrine are likely to be erroneous.

There are a great number of Upanishads, composed at various dates and not all equally revered. They represent different orders of ideas and some of the later are distinctly sectarian. Collections of 45, 52 and 60 are mentioned, and the Muktikâ Upanishad gives a list of 108. This is the number currently accepted in India at the present day. But Schrader[1] describes many Upanishads existing in MS. in addition to this list and points out that though they may be modern there is no ground for calling them spurious. According to Indian ideas there is no *a priori* objection to the appearance now or in the future of new Upanishads[2]. All revelation is eternal and self-existent but it can manifest itself at its own good time.

Many of the more modern Upanishads appear to be the compositions of single authors and may be called tracts or poems in the ordinary European sense. But the older ones, unless they are very short, are clearly not the attempts of an individual to express his creed but collections of such philosophical sayings and narratives as a particular school thought fit to include in its version of the scriptures. There was so to speak a body of philosophic folk-lore portions of which each school selected and elaborated as it thought best. Thus an apologue proving that the breath is the essential vital constituent of a human being is found in five ancient Upanishads[3]. The Chândogya and Bṛihad-Âraṇyaka both contain an almost identical narrative of how the priest Âruṇi was puzzled and instructed by a king and a similar story is found at the beginning of the Kaushîtaki[4]. The two Upanishads last mentioned also

[1] Cat. Adyar Library. The Ṛig and Sâma Vedas have two Upanishads each, the Yajur Veda seven. All the others are described as belonging to the Atharva Veda. They have no real connection with it, but it was possible to add to the literature of the Atharva whereas it was hardly possible to make similar additions to the older Vedas.

[2] Debendranath Tagore composed a work which he called the Brâhmî Upanishad in 1848. See Autobiography, p. 170. The sectarian Upanishads are of doubtful date, but many were written between 400 and 1200 A.D. and were due to the desire of new sects to connect their worship with the Veda. Several are Śaktist (e.g. Kaula, Tripurâ, Devî) and many others show Śaktist influence. They usually advocate the worship of a special deity such as Gaṇeśa, Sûrya, Râma, Nṛi Siṃha.

[3] Br.-Âran. VI. 1, Ait. Âran. II. 4, Kaush. III. 3, Praśna, II. 3, Chând. V. 1. The apologue is curiously like in form to the classical fable of the belly and members.

[4] Br.-Âran. VI. 2, Chând. V. 3

contain two dialogues in which king Ajâtaśatru explains the fate of the soul after death and which differ in little except that one is rather fuller than the other[1]. So too several well-known stanzas and also quotations from the Veda used with special applications are found in more than one Upanishad[2].

The older Upanishads[3] are connected with the other parts of the Vedic canon and sometimes form an appendix to a Brâhmaṇa so that the topics discussed change gradually from ritual to philosophy[4]. It would be excessive to say that this arrangement gives the genesis of speculation in ancient India, for some hymns of the Rig Veda are purely philosophic, but it illustrates a lengthy phase of Brahmanic thought in which speculation could not disengage itself from ritual and was also hampered by physical ideas. The Upanishads often receive such epithets as transcendental and idealistic but in many passages—perhaps in the majority—they labour with imperfect success to separate the spiritual and material. The self or spirit is sometimes identified in man with the breath, in nature with air, ether or space. At other times it is described as dwelling in the heart and about the size of the thumb but capable of becoming smaller, travelling through the veins and showing itself in the pupil: capable also of becoming infinitely large and one with the world soul. But when thought finds its wings and soars above these material fancies, the teaching of the Upanishads shares with Buddhism the glory of being the finest product of the Indian intellect.

In India the religious life has always been regarded as a journey and a search after truth. Even the most orthodox and priestly programme admits this. There comes a time when

[1] Br.-Âran. II. 1, Kaush. IV. 2.

[2] The composite structure of these works is illustrated very clearly by the Bṛihad-Âraṇyaka. It consists of three sections each concluding with a list of teachers, namely (*a*) adhyâyas 1 and 2, (*b*) adh. 3 and 4, (*c*) adh. 5 and 6. The lists are not quite the same, which indicates some slight difference between the sub-schools which composed the three parts, and a lengthy passage occurs twice in an almost identical form. The Upanishad is clearly composed of two separate collections with the addition of a third which still bears the title of *Khila* or supplement. The whole work exists in two recensions.

[3] The Eleven translated in the *Sacred Books of the East*, vols. I and XV, include the oldest and most important.

[4] Thus the Aitareya Brâhmaṇa is followed by the Aitareya Âraṇyaka and that by the Aitareya-Âraṇyaka-Upanishad.

observances are felt to be vain and the soul demands knowledge of the essence of things. And though later dogmatism asserts that this knowledge is given by revelation, yet a note of genuine enquiry and speculation is struck in the Vedas and is never entirely silenced throughout the long procession of Indian writers. In well-known words the Vedas ask[1] "Who is the God to whom we shall offer our sacrifice?...Who is he who is the Creator and sustainer of the Universe...whose shadow is immortality, whose shadow is death?" or, in even more daring phrases[2], "The Gods were subsequent to the creation of this universe. Who then knows whence it sprang? He who in the highest heaven is the overseer of this universe, he knows or even he does not know." These profound enquiries, which have probably no parallel in the contemporary literature of other nations, are as time goes on supplemented though perhaps not enlarged by many others, nor does confidence fail that there is an answer—the Truth, which when known is the goal of life. A European is inclined to ask what use can be made of the truth, but for the Hindus divine knowledge is an end and a state, not a means. It is not thought of as something which may be used to improve the world or for any other purpose whatever. For use and purpose imply that the thing utilized is subservient and inferior to an end, whereas divine knowledge is the culmination and meaning of the universe, or, from another point of view, the annihilation of both the external world and individuality. Hence the Hindu does not expect of his saints philanthropy or activity of any sort.

As already indicated, the characteristic (though not the only) answer of India to these questionings is that nothing really exists except God or, better, except Brahman. The soul is identical with Brahman. The external world which we perceive is not real in the same sense: it is in some way or other an evolution of Brahman or even mere illusion. This doctrine is not universal: it is for instance severely criticized and rejected by the older forms of Buddhism but its hold on the Indian temperament is seen by its reappearance in later Buddhism where by an astounding transformation the Buddha is identified

[1] R.V. x. 121. The verses are also found in the Atharva Veda, the Vâjasaneyi, Taittirîya, Maitrâyaṇî, and Kâṭhaka Saṃhitâs and elsewhere.

[2] R.V. x. 129.

with the universal spirit. Though the form in which I have quoted the doctrine above is an epitome of the Vedânta, it is hardly correct historically to give it as an epitome of the older Upanishads. Their teaching is less complete and uncompromising, more veiled, tentative and allusive, and sometimes cumbered by material notions. But it is obviously the precursor of the Vedânta and the devout Vedântist can justify his system from it.

3

Instead of attempting to summarize the Upanishads it may be well to quote one or two celebrated passages. One is from the Bṛihad-Âraṇyaka[1] and relates how Yâjñavalkya, when about to retire to the forest as an ascetic, wished to divide his property between his two wives, Kâtyâyanî "who possessed only such knowledge as women possess" and Maitreyî "who was conversant with Brahman." The latter asked her husband whether she would be immortal if she owned the whole world. "No," he replied, "like the life of the rich would be thy life but there is no hope of immortality." Maitreyî said that she had no need of what would not make her immortal. Yâjñavalkya proceeded to explain to her his doctrine of the Âtman, the self or essence, the spirit present in man as well as in the universe. "Not for the husband's sake is the husband dear but for the sake of the Âtman. Not for the wife's sake is the wife dear but for the sake of the Âtman. Not for their own sake are sons, wealth, Brahmans, warriors, worlds, gods, Vedas and all things dear, but for the sake of the Âtman. The Âtman is to be seen, to be heard, to be perceived, to be marked: by him who has seen and known the Âtman all the universe is known.... He who looks for Brahmans, warriors, worlds, gods or Vedas anywhere but in the Âtman, loses them all...."

"As all waters have their meeting place in the sea, all touch in the skin, all tastes in the tongue, all odours in the nose, all colours in the eye, all sounds in the ear, all percepts in the mind, all knowledge in the heart, all actions in the hands....As a lump of salt has no inside nor outside and is nothing but taste, so has this Âtman neither inside nor outside and is nothing but

[1] IV. 5. 5 and repeated almost verbally II. 4. 5 with some omissions. My quotation is somewhat abbreviated and repetitions are omitted.

knowledge. Having risen from out these elements it (the human soul) vanishes with them. When it has departed (after death) there is no more consciousness." Here Maitreyî professes herself bewildered but Yâjñavalkya continues "I say nothing bewildering. Verily, beloved, that Âtman is imperishable and indestructible. When there is as it were duality, then one sees the other, one tastes the other, one salutes the other, one hears the other, one touches the other, one knows the other. But when the Âtman only is all this, how should we see, taste, hear, touch or know another? How can we know him by whose power we know all this? That Âtman is to be described by no, no (neti, neti). He is incomprehensible for he cannot be comprehended, indestructible for he cannot be destroyed, unattached for he does not attach himself: he knows no bonds, no suffering, no decay. How, O beloved, can one know the knower?" And having so spoken, Yâjñavalkya went away into the forest. In another verse of the same work it is declared that "This great unborn Âtman (or Self) undecaying, undying, immortal, fearless, is indeed Brahman."

It is interesting that this doctrine, evidently regarded as the quintessence of Yâjñavalkya's knowledge, should be imparted to a woman. It is not easy to translate. Âtman, of course, means self and is so rendered by Max Müller in this passage, but it seems to me that this rendering jars on the English ear for it inevitably suggests the individual self and selfishness, whereas Âtman means the universal spirit which is Self, because it is the highest (or only) Reality and Being, not definable in terms of anything else. Nothing, says Yâjñavalkya, has any value, meaning, or indeed reality except in relation to this Self[1]. The whole world including the Vedas and religion is an emanation from him. The passage at which Maitreyî expresses her bewilderment is obscure, but the reply is more definite. The Self is indestructible but still it is incorrect to speak of the soul having knowledge and perception after death, for knowledge and perception imply duality, a subject and an object. But when the human soul and the universal Âtman are one, there is no duality and no human expression can be

[1] The sentiment is perhaps the same as that underlying the words attributed to Florence Nightingale: "I must strive to see only God in my friends and God in my cats."

correctly used about the Âtman. Whatever you say of it, the answer must be *neti, neti*, it is not like that[1]; that is to say, the ordinary language used about the individual soul is not applicable to the Âtman or to the human soul when regarded as identical with it.

This identity is stated more precisely in another passage[2] where first occurs the celebrated formula Tat tvam asi, That art Thou, or Thou art It[3], *i.e.* the human soul is the Âtman and hence there is no real distinction between souls. Like Yâjñavalkya's teaching, the statement of this doctrine takes the form of an intimate conversation, this time between a Brahman, Uddâlaka Âruṇi, and his son Śvètaketu who is twenty-four years of age and having just finished his studentship is very well satisfied with himself. His father remarks on his conceit and says "Have you ever asked your teachers for that instruction by which the unheard becomes heard, the unperceived perceived and the unknown known?" Śvetaketu enquires what this instruction is and his father replies, "As by one lump of clay all that is made of clay is known, and the change[4] is a mere matter of words, nothing but a name, the truth being that all is clay, and as by one piece of copper or by one pair of nail-scissors all that is made of copper or iron can be known, so is that instruction." That is to say, it would seem, the reality is One: all diversity and multiplicity is secondary and superficial, merely a matter of words. "In the beginning," continues the father, "there was only that which is, one without a second. Others say in the beginning there was that only which is not (non-existence), one without a second, and from that which is not, that which is was born. But how could that which is be born of that which is not[5]? No, only that which is was in the beginning, one only without a second. It thought, may I be many: may I have

[1] It will be observed that he had said previously that the Âtman must be seen, heard, perceived and known. This is an inconsistent use of language.

[2] Chândogya Upanishad vi.

[3] In the language of the Upanishads the Âtman is often called simply Tat or it.

[4] *I.e.* the difference between clay and pots, etc. made of clay.

[5] Yet the contrary proposition is maintained in this same Upanishad (iii. 19. 1), in the Taittirîya Upanishad (ii. 8) and elsewhere. The reason of these divergent statements is of course the difficulty of distinguishing pure Being without attributes from not Being.

offspring. It sent forth fire." Here follows a cosmogony and an explanation of the constitution of animate beings, and then the father continues—"All creatures have their root in the Real, dwell in the Real and rest in the Real. That subtle being by which this universe subsists, it is the Real, it is the Âtman, and thou, Śvetaketu, art It." Many illustrations of the relations of the Âtman and the universe follow. For instance, if the life (sap) leaves a tree, it withers and dies. So "this body withers and dies when the life has left it: the life dies not." In the fruit of the Banyan (fig-tree) are minute seeds innumerable. But the imperceptible subtle essence in each seed is the whole Banyan. Each example adduced concludes with the same formula, Thou art that subtle essence, and as in the Bṛihad-Âraṇyaka salt is used as a metaphor. "'Place this salt in water and then come to me in the morning.' The son did so and in the morning the father said 'Bring me the salt.' The son looked for it but found it not, for of course it was melted. The father said, 'Taste from the surface of the water. How is it?' The son replied, 'It is salt.' 'Taste from the middle. How is it?' 'It is salt.' 'Taste from the bottom, how is it?' 'It is salt.'... The father said, 'Here also in this body you do not perceive the Real, but there it is. That subtle being by which this universe subsists, it is the Real, it is the Âtman and thou, Śvetaketu, art It.'"

The writers of these passages have not quite reached Śankara's point of view, that the Âtman is all and the whole universe mere illusion or Mâyâ. Their thought still tends to regard the universe as something drawn forth from the Âtman and then pervaded by it. But still the main features of the later Advaita, or philosophy of no duality, are there. All the universe has grown forth from the Âtman: there is no real difference in things, just as all gold is gold whatever it is made into. The soul is identical with this Âtman and after death may be one with it in a union excluding all duality even of perceiver and perceived.

A similar union occurs in sleep. This idea is important for it is closely connected with another belief which has had far-reaching consequences on thought and practice in India, the belief namely that the soul can attain without death and as the result of mental discipline to union[1] with Brahman. This idea

[1] The word union is a convenient but not wholly accurate term which covers several theories. The Upanishads sometimes speak of the union of the soul with

is common in Hinduism and though Buddhism rejects the notion of union with the supreme spirit yet it attaches importance to meditation and makes Samâdhi or rapture the crown of the perfect life. In this, as in other matters, the teaching of the Upanishads is manifold and unsystematic compared with later doctrines. The older passages ascribe to the soul three states corresponding to the bodily conditions of waking, dream-sleep, and deep dreamless sleep, and the Bṛihad-Âraṇyaka affirms of the last (IV. 3. 32): "This is the Brahma world. This is his highest world, this is his highest bliss. All other creatures live on a small portion of that bliss." But even in some Upanishads of the second stratum (Mâṇḍukya, Maitrâyaṇa) we find added a fourth state, Caturtha or more commonly Turîya, in which the bliss attainable in deep sleep is accompanied by consciousness[1]. This theory and various practices founded on it develop rapidly.

4

The explanation of dreamless sleep as supreme bliss and Yâjñavalkya's statement that the soul after death cannot be said to know or feel, may suggest that union with Brahman is another name for annihilation. But that is not the doctrine of the Upanishads though a European perhaps might say that the consciousness contemplated is so different from ordinary human consciousness that it should not bear the same name. In another passage[2] Yâjñavalkya himself explains "when he does not know, yet he is knowing though he does not know. For knowing is inseparable from the knower, because it cannot perish. But there is no second, nothing else different from him that he could know." A common formula for Brahman in the later philosophy

Brahman or its absorption in Brahman (*e.g.* Maitr. Up. VI. 22, *Sâyujyatvam* and *aśabde nidhanam eti*) but the soul is more frequently stated to be Brahman or a part of Brahman and its task is not to effect any act of union but simply to *know* its own nature. This knowledge is in itself emancipation. The well-known simile which compares the soul to a river flowing into the sea is found in the Upanishads (Chând. VI. 10. 1, Mund. III. 2, Praśna, VI. 5) but Śankara (on Brahma S. I. iv. 21–22) evidently feels uneasy about it. From his point of view the soul is not so much a river as a bay which *is* the sea, if the landscape can be seen properly.

[1] The Mâṇḍukya Up. calls the fourth state *ekâtmapratyayasâra*, founded solely on the certainty of its own self and Gauḍapâda says that in it there awakes the eternal which neither dreams nor sleeps. (Kâr. I. 15. See also III. 34 and 36.

[2] Bṛ.-Âraṇyaka, IV. 3. 33.

is Saccidânanda, Being, Thought and Joy[1]. This is a just summary of the earlier teaching. We have already seen how the Âtman is recognized as the only Reality. Its intellectual character is equally clearly affirmed. Thus the Bṛihad-Âraṇyaka (III. 7. 23) says: "There is no seer beside him, no hearer beside him, no perceiver beside him, no knower beside him. This is thy Self, the ruler within, the immortal. Everything distinct from him is subject to pain." This idea that pain and fear exist only as far as a man makes a distinction between his own self and the real Self is eloquently developed in the division of the Taittirîya Upanishad called the Chapter of Bliss. "He who knows Brahman" it declares, "which exists, which is conscious, which is without end, as hidden in the depth of the heart, and in farthest space, he enjoys all blessings, in communion with the omniscient Brahman.... He who knows the bliss (ânandam) of that Brahman from which all speech and mind turn away unable to reach it, he never fears[2]."

Bliss is obtainable by union with Brahman, and the road to such union is knowledge of Brahman. That knowledge is often represented as acquired by tapas or asceticism, but this, though repeatedly enjoined as necessary, seems to be regarded (in the nobler expositions at least) as an indispensable schooling rather than as efficacious by its own virtue. Sometimes the topic is treated in an almost Buddhist spirit of reasonableness and depreciation of self-mortification for its own sake. Thus Yâjñavalkya says to Gârgî[3]: "Whoever without knowing the imperishable one offers oblations in this world, sacrifices, and practises asceticism even for a thousand years, his work will perish." And in a remarkable scene described in the Chândogya Upanishad, the three sacred fires decide to instruct a student who is exhausted by austerities, and tell him that Brahman is life, bliss and space[4].

Analogous to the conception of Brahman as bliss, is the description of him as light or "light of lights." A beautiful

[1] Cf. Bradley, *Appearance and Reality*, p. 244. "The perfect...means the identity of idea and existence, attended also by pleasure."

[2] Tait. Up. II. 1–9. See too ib. III. 6.

[3] Bṛ.-Âran. III. 8. 10. See too VI. 2. 15, speaking of those who in the forest worship the truth with faith.

[4] Chândog. Up. IV. 10. 5.

passage[1] says: "To the wise who perceive him (Brahman) within their own self, belongs eternal peace, not to others. They feel that highest, unspeakable bliss saying, this is that. How then can I understand it? Has it its own light or does it reflect light? No sun shines there, nor moon nor stars, nor these lightnings, much less this fire. When he shines everything shines after him: by his light all the world is lighted."

In most of the texts which we have examined the words Brahman and Âtman are so impersonal that they cannot be replaced by God. In other passages the conception of the deity is more personal. The universe is often said to have been emitted or breathed forth by Brahman. By emphasizing the origin and result of this process separately, we reach the idea of the Maker and Master of the Universe, commonly expressed by the word Îśvara, Lord. But even when using this expression, Hindu thought tends in its subtler moments to regard both the creator and the creature as illusions. In the same sense as the world exists there also exists its creator who is an aspect of Brahman, but the deeper truth is that neither is real: there is but One who neither makes nor is made[2]. In a land of such multiform theology it would be hazardous to say that Monotheism has always arisen out of Pantheism, but in the speculative schools where the Upanishads were composed, this was often its genesis. The older idea is that a subtle essence pervades all nature and the deities who rule nature: this is spiritualized into the doctrine of Brahman attributed to Yâjñavalkya and it is only by a secondary process that this Brahman is personified and sometimes identified with a particular god such as Siva. The doctrine of the personal Îśvara is elaborated in the Śvetâśvatara Upanishad of uncertain date[3]. It celebrates him in hymns of almost Mohammedan monotheism. "Let us know that great Lord of Lords, the highest God of Gods, the Master of Masters, the highest above, as God, as Lord of the world, who is to be glorified[4]." But this monotheistic fervour does

[1] It occurs Kaṭha. Up. II. v. 13. 15, also in the Śvetâśvatara and Muṇḍaka Upanishads and there are similar words in the Bhagavad-gîtâ. "This is that" means that the individual soul is the same as Brahman.

[2] The Nṛisiṃhottaratapanîya Up. I. says that Îśvara is swallowed up in the Turîya.

[3] But still ancient and perhaps anterior to the Christian era.

[4] Śvet. Up. VI. 7.

not last long without relapsing into the familiar pantheistic strain. "Thou art woman," says the same Upanishad[1], "and Thou art man: Thou art youth and maiden: Thou as an old man totterest along on thy staff: Thou art born with thy face turned everywhere. Thou art the dark-blue bee: Thou the green parrot with the red eyes. Thou art the thunder cloud, the seasons and the seas. Thou art without beginning because Thou art infinite, Thou, from whom all worlds are born."

[1] Śvet. Up. IV. 3. Max Müller's translation. The commentary attributed to Śankara explains nîlaḥ pataṅgaḥ as bhramaraḥ but Deussen seems to think it means a bird.

CHAPTER VI

RELIGIOUS LIFE IN PRE-BUDDHIST INDIA

1

In reading the Brâhmaṇas and older Upanishads we often wish we knew more of the writers and their lives. Rarely can so many representative men have bequeathed so much literature and yet left so dim a sketch of their times. Thought was their real life: of that they have given a full record, imperfect only in chronology, for though their speculations are often set forth in a narrative form, we hear surprisingly little about contemporary events.

The territory familiar to these works is the western part of the modern United Provinces with the neighbouring districts of the Panjab, the lands of the Kurus, Pancâlas, and Matsyas, all in the region of Agra and Delhi, and further east Kâśi (Benares) with Videha or Tirhut. Gândhâra was known[1] but Magadha and Bengal are not mentioned. Even in the Buddha's lifetime they were still imperfectly brahmanized.

What we know of the period 800 to 600 B.C. is mostly due to the Brahmans, and many Indianists have accepted their view, that they were then socially the highest class and the repository of religion and culture. But it is clear from Buddhist writings (which, however, are somewhat later) that this pre-eminence was not unchallenged[2], and many admissions in the Brâhmaṇas and Upanishads indicate that some centuries before the Buddha the Kshatriyas held socially the first rank and shared intellectual honours with the Brahmans. Janaka, king of Videha[3], and Yâjñavalkya, the Brahman, meet on terms of mutual respect and other Kshatriyas, such as Ajâtaśatru of

[1] Chând. Up. VI. 14. 1. Śat. Brâh. VIII. 1. 4. 10.

[2] The Brahmans are even called low-born as compared with Kshatriyas and in the Ambattha Sutta (Dig. Nik. III.) the Buddha demonstrates to a Brahman who boasts of his caste that the usages of Hindu society prove that "the Kshatriyas are higher and the Brahmans lower," seeing that the child of a mixed union between the castes is accepted by the Brahmans as one of themselves but not by the Kshatriyas, because he is not of pure descent.

[3] He had learnt the Veda and Upanishads. Bṛih.-Âr. IV. 2. 1.

Kâśi and Pravâhaṇa Jaivali are represented as instructing Brahmans, and the latter in doing so says "this knowledge did not go to any Brahman before but belonged to the Kshatriyas alone[1]." But as a profession theology, both practical and speculative, was left to the Brahmans.

The proper relation between the nobles and Brahmans finds expression in the office of Purohita[2] or domestic chaplain, which is as old as the Vedas and has lasted to the present day. In early times he was not merely a spiritual guide but also a councillor expected to advise the king as to his enterprises and secure their success by appropriate rites. By king we should understand a tribal chief, entrusted with considerable powers in the not infrequent times of war, but in peace obliged to consult the clan, or at least the aristocratic part of it, on all matters of importance. A Purohita might attain a very high position, like Devabhaga, priest of both the Kurus and Srinjayas[3]. The Brahmans did not attempt to become kings, but the sacred books insist that though a Brahman can do without a king, yet a king cannot do without a Brahman. The two castes are compared to the deities Mitra and Varuṇa, typifying intelligence and will. When they are united deeds can be done[4]. But "the Gods do not eat the food of a king who is without a Purohita." Other castes can offer sacrifices only by the mediation of Brahmans, and it does not appear that kings disputed this, though they claimed the right to think for themselves and may have denied the utility of sacrifice[5]. Apart from kings the duties and claims of the Brahman extend to the people at large. He has four virtues, "birth, deportment, fame and the perfecting of the people," and in return the people owe him respect, liberality, security against oppression and against capital punishment.

Towns in this period must have been few and those few essentially forts, not collections of palaces and temples. We

[1] Chând. Up. v. 3. 7, Kaush. Up. IV., Bṛih.-Âr. Up. II. 1. The Kshatriyas seem to have regarded the doctrine of the two paths which can be taken by the soul after death (*devayâna* and *pitriyâna*, the latter involving return to earth and transmigration) as their special property.

[2] Literally set in front, præfectus.

[3] Śat. Brâh. II. 4. 4. 5.

[4] Śat. Brâh. IV. 1. 4. 1–6.

[5] The legends of Vena, Paraśurâma and others indicate the prevalence of considerable hostility between Brahmans and Kshatriyas at some period.

hear of Kâśi (Benares) but the name may signify a district. People are said to go to the Kurus or Pancâlas, not to Mithilâ or any other city. It was in village life—which is still the life of the greater part of India—that Brahmanism grew up. Probably then as now Brahman families occupied separate villages, or at least quarters, and were allowed to hold the land rent free as a reward for rendering religious services to the king. They followed various professions but the life which was most respected, and also most lucrative, was that devoted to the study and practice of sacred science, that is the learning and recitation of sacred texts, performance of ceremonies, and theological discussion. The later law books divide a Brahman's life into four stages or âśramas in which he was successively a student, a householder, a hermit and an ascetic[1]. The third and fourth stages are not very clearly distinguished. A hermit is supposed to renounce family life and live in the forest, but still to perform sacrifices, whereas the Sannyâsi or perfect ascetic, in many ways the ideal of India, subsists on alms, freed alike from duties and passions and absorbed in meditation. In the older Upanishads three stages are indicated as part of contemporary practice[2]. For a period of from nine to thirty-six years, a Brahman dwelt with a teacher. While his state of pupilage lasted he lived on alms and was bound by the severest vows of obedience and chastity. The instruction given consisted in imparting sacred texts which could be acquired only by hearing them recited, for writing, though it may have been known in India as early as the seventh century B.C., was not used for literature. The Śatapatha Brâhmaṇa recommends the study not only of the four Vedas but of the precepts (perhaps grammar, etymology, etc.), the sciences (perhaps philosophy), dialogues (no doubt such as those found in the Upanishads), traditions and ancient legends, stanzas and tales of heroes[3], showing that, besides the scriptures, more popular compositions

[1] Brahmacârin, Grihastha, Vanaprastha, Sannyâsin.

[2] Thus in the Bṛih.-Âraṇ. Yâjñavalkya retires to the forest. But even the theory of three stages was at this time only in the making, for the last section of the Chândogya Up. expressly authorizes a religious man to spend all his life as a householder after completing his studentship and the account given of the stages in Chând. II. 21 is not very clear.

[3] Śat. Brâh. XI. 5. 6. 8. Cf. the lists in the Chândogya Upanishad VII. secs. 1, 2 and 7.

which doubtless contained the germs of the later Epics and Puranas were held in esteem.

On terminating his apprenticeship the young Brahman became a householder and married, moderate polygamy being usual. To some extent he followed the occupations of an ordinary man of business and father of a family, but the most important point in establishing a home of his own was the kindling of his own sacred fire[1], and the householder's life was regarded as a series of rites, such as the daily offering of milk, the new and full moon ceremonies, seasonal sacrifices every four months and the Soma sacrifice once a year, besides oblations to ancestors and other domestic observances. The third stage of life should begin when a householder sees that his hair is turning grey and a grandson has been born. He should then abandon his home and live in the forest. The tradition that it is justifiable and even commendable for men and women to abandon their families and take to the religious life has at all times been strong in India and public opinion has never considered that the deserted party had a grievance. No doubt comfortable householders were in no hurry to take to the woods and many must always have shirked the duty. But on the other hand, the very pious, of whom India has always produced a superabundance, were not willing to bear the cares of domestic life and renounced the world before the prescribed time. On the whole Brahmanic (as opposed to Buddhist) literature is occupied in insisting not so much that the devout should abandon the world as that they must perform the ritual observances prescribed for householders before doing so.

The Brahman's existence as drawn in the law-books is a description of what the writers thought ought to be done rather than of the general practice. Still it cannot be dismissed as imaginary, for the Nambutiri[2] Brahmans of Travancore have not yet abandoned a mode of life which is in essentials that prescribed by Manu and probably that led by Brahmans in the seventh century B.C. or earlier[3].

[1] In southern India at the present day it is the custom for Brahmans to live as Agnihotris and maintain the sacred fire for a few days after their marriage.

[2] See Thurston, *Castes and Tribes of Southern India*, vol. V. s.v.

[3] The Emperor Jehangir writing about 1616 implies that the Aśramas, which he describes, were observed by the Brahmans of that time. See his *Memoirs*, edited by Beveridge, pp. 357–359.

They are for the most part landowners dwelling in large houses built to accommodate a patriarchal family and erected in spacious compounds. In youth they spend about eight years in learning the Veda, and in mature life religious ceremonies, including such observances as bathing and the preparation of meals, occupy about six hours of the day. As a profession, the performance of religious rites for others is most esteemed. In food, drink and pleasures, the Nambutiris are almost ascetics: their rectitude, punctiliousness and dignity still command exaggerated respect. But they seem unproductive and petrified, even in such matters as literature and scholarship, and their inability to adapt themselves to changing conditions threatens them with impoverishment and deterioration.

Yet the ideal Brahmanic life, which by no means excludes intellectual activity, is laid out in severe and noble lines and though on its good side somewhat beyond the reach of human endeavour and on its bad side overloaded with pedantry and superstition, it combines in a rare degree self-abnegation and independence. It differs from the ideal set up by Buddhism and by many forms of Hinduism which preach the renunciation of family ties, for it clearly lays down that it is a man's duty to continue his family and help his fellow men just as much as to engage in religious exercises. Thus, the Śatapatha Brâhmaṇa[1] teaches that man is born owing four debts, one to the gods, one to the Rishis or the sages to whom the Vedic hymns were revealed, one to his ancestors and one to men. To discharge these obligations he must offer sacrifices, study the Veda, beget a son and practise hospitality.

The tranquil isolation of village life in ancient India has left its mark on literature. Though the names of teachers are handed down and their opinions cited with pious care, yet for many centuries after the Vedic age we find no books attributed to human authors. There was an indifference to literary fame among these early philosophers and a curious selflessness. Doctors disputed as elsewhere, yet they were at no pains to couple their names with theories or sects. Like the Jewish Rabbis they were content to go down to posterity as the authors of a few sayings, and these are mostly contributions to a common stock with no pretension to be systems of philosophy. The

[1] Śat. Brâh. I. 7. 2. 1. Cf. Tait. Brâh. VI. 3. 10. 5.

Upanishads leave an impression of a society which, if reposeful, was also mentally alert and tolerant to an unusual degree. Much was absent that occupied the intelligence of other countries. Painting, sculpture and architecture can have attained but modest proportions and the purview of religion included neither temples nor images. India was untroubled by foreign invasions and all classes seem to have been content to let the Kshatriyas look after such internal politics as there were. Trade too was on a small scale. Doubtless the Indian was then, as now, a good man of business and the western coast may have been affected by its relations with the Persian Gulf, but Brahmanic civilization was a thing of the Midland and drew no inspiration from abroad. The best minds were occupied with the leisurely elaboration and discussion of speculative ideas and self-effacement was both practised and preached.

But movement and circulation prevented this calm rustic world from becoming stagnant. Though roads were few and dangerous, a habit of travel was conspicuous among the religious and intellectual classes. The Indian is by nature a pilgrim rather than a stationary monk, and we often hear of Brahmans travelling in quest of knowledge alone or in companies, and stopping in rest houses[1]. In the Śatapatha Brâhmaṇa[2], Uddâlaka Âruṇi is represented as driving about and offering a piece of gold as a prize to those who could defeat him in argument. Great sacrifices were often made the occasion of these discussions. We must not think of them as mere religious ceremonies, as a sort of high mass extending over several days. The fact that they lasted so long and involved operations like building sheds and altars made them unlike our church services and gave opportunities for debate and criticism of what was done. Such competition and publicity were good for the wits. The man who cut the best figure in argument was in greatest demand as a sacrificer and obtained the highest fees. But these stories of prizes and fees emphasize a feature which has characterized the Brahmans from Vedic times to the present day, namely, their shameless love of money. The severest critic cannot deny them a disinterested taste for intellectual, religious and spiritual things, but their own books often use language

[1] Such as those built by Jânaśruti Pautrâyaṇa. See Chând. Up. IV. 1.

[2] Śat. Brâh. XI. 4. 1. 1.

which shows them as professional men merely anxious to make a fortune by the altar. "The sacrifice is twofold," says the Śatapatha Brâhmaṇa, "oblations to the gods and gifts to the priests. With oblations men gratify the gods and with gifts the human gods. These two kinds of gods when gratified convey the worshipper to the heavenly world[1]." Without a fee the sacrifice is as dead as the victim. It is the fee which makes it living and successful[2].

Tradition has preserved the names of many of these acute, argumentative, fee-loving priests, but of few can we form any clear picture. The most distinguished is Yâjñavalkya who, though seen through a mist of myths and trivial stories about the minutiæ of ritual, appears as a personality with certain traits that are probably historical. Many remarks attributed to him are abrupt and scornful and the legend indicates dimly that he was once thought a dangerous innovator. But, as has happened so often since, this early heretic became the corner stone of later orthodoxy. He belonged to the school of the Yajur Veda and was apparently the main author of the new or White recension in which the prayers and directions are more or less separate, whereas in the old or Black recension they are mixed together. According to the legend he vomited forth the texts which he had learnt, calling his fellow pupils "miserable and inefficient Brahmans," and then received a new revelation from the Sun[3]. The quarrel was probably violent for the Śatapatha Brâhmaṇa mentions that he was cursed by priests of the other party. Nor does this work, while recognizing him as the principal teacher, endorse all his sayings. Thus it forbids the eating of beef but adds the curious remark "Nevertheless Yâjñavalkya said, I for one eat it, provided it is tender[4]." Remarkable, too, is his answer to the question what would happen if all the ordinary materials for sacrifices were absent, "Then indeed nothing would be offered here, but there would be offered the truth in faith[5]." It is probable that the Black Yajur Veda represents the more western schools and that the

[1] Śat. Brâh. II. 2. 2. 6 and IV. 3. 4. 4.

[2] Śat. Brâh. IV. 3. 4. 2.

[3] Vishnu Pur. III. 5.

[4] Śat. Brâh. III. 8. 2. 24. Yâjñavalkya is the principal authority cited in books I–V and X–XIV of this Brâhmaṇa, but not in books VI–IX, which perhaps represent an earlier treatise incorporated in the text.

[5] Or "in confidence." Śat. Brâh. XI. 3. 1. 4.

native land of the White recension and of Yâjñavalkya lay further east, perhaps in Videha. But his chief interest for us is not the reforms in text and ritual which he may have made, but his philosophic doctrines of which I have already spoken. Our principal authority for them is the Bṛihad-Âraṇyaka Upanishad of which he is the protagonist, much as Socrates is of the Platonic dialogues. Unfortunately the striking picture which it gives of Yâjñavalkya cannot be accepted as historical. He is a prominent figure in the Śatapatha Brâhmaṇa which is older than the Upanishad and represents an earlier stage of speculation. The sketch of his doctrines which it contains is clearly a preliminary study elaborated and amplified in the Upanishad. But if a personage is introduced in early works as expounding a rudimentary form of certain doctrines and in later works is credited with a matured philosophy, there can be little doubt that he has become a great name whose authority is invoked by later thought, much as Solomon was made the author of the Proverbs and Ecclesiastes and the Song which bears his name.

Yâjñavalkya appears in the Bṛihad-Âraṇyaka as the respected friend but apparently not the chaplain of King Janaka. This monarch celebrated a great sacrifice and offered a thousand cows with a present of money to him who should prove himself wisest. Yâjñavalkya rather arrogantly bade his pupil drive off the beasts. But his claim was challenged: seven Brahmans and one woman, Gârgî Vâcaknavî, disputed with him at length but had to admit his superiority. A point of special interest is raised by the question what happens after death. Yâjñavalkya said to his questioner, "'Take my hand, my friend. We two alone shall know of this. Let this question of ours not be discussed in public.' Then these two went out and argued, and what they said was Karma and what they praised was Karma[1]." The doctrine that a man's deeds cause his future existence and determine its character was apparently not popular among the priesthood who claimed that by their rites they could manufacture heavenly bodies for their clients.

2

This imperfect and sketchy picture of religious life in India so far as it can be gathered from the older Brahmanic books

[1] Bṛih.-Âr. III. 2. 13.

has reference mainly to the kingdoms of the Kuru-Pancâlas and Videha in 800–600 B.C. Another picture, somewhat fuller, is found in the ancient literature of the Buddhists and Jains, which depicts the kingdoms of Magadha (Bihar) and Kosala (Oudh) in the time of the Buddha and Mahâvîra, the founder of Jainism, that is, about 500 B.C. or rather earlier. It is probable that the picture is substantially true for this period or even for a period considerably earlier, for Mahâvîra was supposed to have revived with modifications the doctrines of Parśvanâtha and some of the Buddhas mentioned as preceding Gotama were probably historical personages. But the Brahmanic and Buddhist accounts do not give two successive phases of thought in the same people, for the locality is not quite the same. Both pictures include the territory of Kâśi and Videha, but the Brahmanic landscape lies mainly to the west and the Buddhist mainly to the east of this region. In the Buddhist sphere it is clear that in the youth of Gotama Brahmanic doctrines and ritual were well known but not predominant. It is hardly demonstrable from literature, but still probable, that the ideas and usages which found expression in Jainism and Buddhism existed in the western districts, though less powerful there than in the east[1].

A striking feature of the world in which Jainism and Buddhism arose was the prevalence of confraternities or religious orders. They were the recognized form of expression not only for piety but for the germs of theology, metaphysics and science. The ordinary man of the world kept on good terms with such gods as came his way, but those who craved for some higher interest often separated themselves from the body of citizens and followed some special rule of life. In one sense the Brahmans were the greatest of such communities, but they were a hereditary corporation and though they were not averse to new ideas, their special stock in trade was an acquaintance with traditional formulæ and rites. They were also, in the main, sedentary and householders. Somewhat opposed to them were other companies, described collectively as Paribbâjakas or Samanas[2]. These, though offering many differences among

[1] In the Pali Pitaka the Buddha is represented as preaching in the land of the Kurus.

[2] These are the Pali forms. The Sanskrit equivalents are Parivrâjaka and Śramaṇa.

themselves, were clearly distinguished from the Brahmans, and it is probable that they usually belonged to the warrior caste. But they did not maintain that religious knowledge was the exclusive privilege of any caste: they were not householders but wanderers and celibates. Often they were ascetics and addicted to extreme forms of self-mortification. They did not study the Vedas or perform sacrifices, and their speculations were often revolutionary, and as a rule not theistic. It is not easy to find any English word which describes these people or the Buddhist Bhikkhus. Monk is perhaps the best, though inadequate. Pilgrim and friar give the idea of wandering, but otherwise suggest wrong associations. But in calling them monks, we must remember that though celibates, and to some extent recluses (for they mixed with the world only in a limited degree), they were not confined in cloisters. The more stationary lived in woods, either in huts or the open air, but many spent the greater part of the year in wandering.

The practice of adopting a wandering religious life was frequent among the upper classes, and must have been a characteristic feature of society. No blame attached to the man who abruptly left his family, though well-to-do people are represented as dissuading their children from the step. The interest in philosophical and theological questions was perhaps even greater than among the Brahmans, and they were recognized not as parerga to a life of business or amusement, but as occupations in themselves. Material civilization had not kept pace with the growth of thought and speculation. Thus restless and inquisitive minds found little to satisfy them in villages or small towns, and the wanderer, instead of being a useless rolling stone, was likely not only to have a more interesting life but to meet with sympathy and respect. Ideas and discussion were plentiful but there were no books and hardly any centres of learning. Yet there was even more movement than among the travelling priests of the Kurus and Pancâlas, a coming and going, a trafficking in ideas. Knowledge was to be picked up in the market-places and highways. Up and down the main roads circulated crowds of highly intelligent men. They lived upon alms, that is to say, they were fed by the citizens who favoured their opinions or by those good souls who gave indiscriminately to all holy men—and in the larger places rest houses were erected for their comfort. It was natural that the more commanding and original spirits should collect others round them and form bands, for though there was public discussion, writing was not used for religious purposes and he who would study any doctrine had to become the pupil of a master. The doctrine too involved a discipline, or mode of life best led in common. Hence these bands easily grew into communities which we may call orders or sects, if we recognize that their constitution was more fluid and less formal than is implied by those words. It is not easy to say how much organization such communities possessed before the time of the Buddha. His Sangha was the most successful of them all and doubtless surpassed the others in this as in other respects. Yet it was modelled on existing institutions and the Vinaya Pitaka[1] itself represents him as prescribing the observance of times and seasons, not so much because he thought it necessary as because the laity suggested that he would do well to follow the practice of the Titthiya schools. By this phrase we are to understand the adherents of Makkhali Gosâla, Sâñjaya Belaṭṭhiputta and others. We know less about these sects than we could wish, but two lists of schools or theories are preserved, one in the Brahmajâla Sutta[2] where the Buddha himself criticises 62 erroneous views and another in Jain literature[3], which enumerates no fewer than 363.

Both catalogues are somewhat artificial, and it is clear that many views are mentioned not because they represent the tenets of real schools but from a desire to condemn all possible errors. But the list of topics discussed is interesting. From the Brahmajâla Sutta we learn that the problems which agitated ancient Magadha were such as the following:—is the world eternal or not: is it infinite or finite: is there a cause for the origin of things or is it without cause: does the soul exist after death: if so, is its existence conscious or unconscious: is it eternal or does it cease to exist, not necessarily at the end of its present life but after a certain number of lives: can it enjoy perfect bliss here or elsewhere? Theories on these and other points are commonly

[1] See for instance Mahâv. II. 1 and III. 1.

[2] Dig. Nik. 1.

[3] See O. Schrader, *Stand der indischen Philosophie zur Zeit Mahâvîras und Buddhas*, 1902.

See also Ang. Nik. vol. III. p. 276 and Rhys Davids' *Dialogues of the Buddha*, I. pp. 220 ff. But these passages give one an impression of the multitude of ascetic confraternities rather than a clear idea of their different views.

called vâda or talk, and those who hold them vâdins. Thus there is the Kâla-vâda[1] which makes Time the origin and principle of the universe, and the Svabhâva-vâda which teaches that things come into being of their own accord. This seems crude when stated with archaic frankness but becomes plausible if paraphrased in modern language as "discontinuous variation and the spontaneous origin of definite species." There were also the Niyati-vâdins, or fatalists, who believed that all that happens is the result of Niyati or fixed order, and the Yadricchâ-vâdins who, on the contrary, ascribed everything to chance and apparently denied causation, because the same result follows from different antecedents. It is noticeable that none of these views imply theism or pantheism but the Buddha directed so persistent a polemic against the doctrine of the Âtman that it must have been known in Magadha. The fundamental principles of the Sânkhya were also known, though perhaps not by that name. It is probably correct to say not that the Buddha borrowed from the Sânkhya but that both he and the Sânkhya accepted and elaborated in different ways certain current views.

The Pali Suttas[2] mention six agnostic or materialist teachers and give a brief but perhaps not very just compendium of their doctrines. One of them was the founder of the Jains who, as a sect that has lasted to the present day with a considerable record in art and literature, merit a separate chapter. Of the remaining five, one, Sâñjaya of the Belaṭṭha clan, was an agnostic, similar to the people described elsewhere[3] as eel-wrigglers, who in answer to such questions as, is there a result of good and bad actions, decline to say either (*a*) there is, (*b*) there is not, (*c*) there both is and is not, (*d*) there neither is nor is not. This form of argument has been adopted by Buddhism for some important questions but Sâñjaya and his

[1] It finds expression in two hymns of the Atharva Veda, XIX. 53 and 54. Cf. too Gauḍap. Kâr. 8. Kâlât prasûtim bhutânâm manyante kâlacintakâḥ.

[2] Dîgha Nikâya II. The opinions of the six teachers are quoted as being answers to a question put to them by King Ajâtasattu, namely, What is gained by renouncing the world? Judged as such, they are irrelevant but they probably represent current statements as to the doctrine of each sect. The six teachers are also mentioned in several other passages of the Dîgha and Maj. Nikâyas and also in the Sutta-Nipâta. It is clear that at a very early period the list of their names had become the usual formula for summarizing the teaching prevalent in the time of Gotama which was neither Brahmanic nor Buddhist.

[3] Dig. Nik. I. 23–28.

disciples appear to have applied it indiscriminately and to have concluded that positive assertion is impossible.

The other four were in many respects what we should call fatalists and materialists[1], or in the language of their time Akriya-vâdins, denying, that is, free will, responsibility and the merit or demerit of good or bad actions. They nevertheless believed in metempsychosis and practised asceticism. Apparently they held that beings are born again and again according to a natural law, but not according to their deeds: and that though asceticism cannot accelerate the soul's journey, yet at a certain stage it is a fore-ordained and indispensable preliminary to emancipation. The doctrines attributed to all four are crude and startling. Perhaps they are exaggerated by the Buddhist narrator, but they also reflect the irreverent exuberance of young thought. Pûraṇa Kassapa denies that there is any merit in virtue or harm in murder. Another ascetic called Ajita of the garment of hair teaches that nothing exists but the four elements, and that "fools and wise alike are annihilated on the dissolution of the body and after death they are not." Then why, one asks, was he an ascetic? Similarly Pakudha Kaccâyana states that "when a sharp sword cleaves a head in twain" the soul and pain play a part similar to that played by the component elements of the sword and head. The most important of these teachers was Makkhali Gosâla. His doctrine comprises a denial of causation and free will and an assertion that fools and wise alike will make an end of pain after wandering through eighty-four hundred thousand births. The followers of this teacher were called Âjîvikas: they were a distinct body in the time of Asoka, and the name[2] occurs as late as the thirteenth century in South Indian inscriptions. Several accounts[3] of the founder are extant, but all were compiled by bitter opponents, for he was hated by Jains and Buddhists alike. His doctrine was closely allied to Jainism, especially the Digambara sect, but was probably more extravagant and anti-social. He appears

[1] A rather defiant materialism preaching, "Let us eat and drink for to-morrow we die," crops up in India in various ages though never very prominent.

[2] But possibly the ascetics described by it were only Digambara Jains.

[3] See especially the article Âjîvikas by Hoernle, in Hastings' *Dictionary of Religion*. Also Hoernle, *Uvâsagadasao*, appendix, pp. 1–29. Rockhill, *Life of the Buddha*, pp. 249 ff. Schrader, *Stand der indischen Philosophie zur Zeit Mahâvîras und Buddhas*, p. 32. Sûtrakritânga II. 6.

to have objected to confraternities[1], to have enjoined a solitary life, absolute nudity and extreme forms of self-mortification, such as eating filth. The Jains accused his followers of immorality and perhaps they were ancient prototypes of the lower class of religious mendicants who have brought discredit on Hinduism.

3

None of the phases of religious life described above can be called popular. The religion of the Brahmans was the thought and science of a class. The various un-Brahmanic confraternities usually required their members to be wandering ascetics. They had little to say to village householders who must have constituted the great majority of the population. Also there are signs that priests and nobles, however much they quarrelled, combined to keep the lower castes in subjection[2]. Yet we can hardly doubt that then as now all classes were profoundly religious, and that just as to-day village deities unknown to the Vedas, or even to the Puranas, receive the worship of millions, so then there were gods and rites that did not lack popular attention though unnoticed in the scriptures of Brahmans and Buddhists.

We know little of this popular religion by direct description before or even during the Buddhist period, but we have fragmentary indications of its character. Firstly several incongruous observances have obtruded themselves into the Brahmanic ritual. Thus in the course of the Mahâvrata ceremony[3] the Hotri priest sits in a swing and maidens, carrying pitchers of water on their heads and singing, dance round an altar while drums are beaten. Parallels to this may be found to-day. The image of Krishna, or even a priest who represents Krishna, is swung to and fro in many temples, the use of drums in worship is distressingly common, and during the Pongol festivities in southern India young people dance round or leap over a fire.

[1] Makkhali lived some time with Mahâvîra, but they quarrelled. But his followers, though they may not have been a united body so much as other sects, had definite characteristics.

[2] *E.g.* Śat. Brâh. v. 4. 4. 13. "He thus encloses the Vaiśya and Śûdra on both sides by the priesthood and nobility and makes them submissive."

[3] See Śânkhâyana Âraṇyaka. Trans. Keith, pp. viii–xi, 78–85. Also Aitareya Âraṇ. book v.

Other remarkable features in the Mahâvrata are the shooting of arrows into a target of skin, the use of obscene language (such as is still used at the Holi festival) and even obscene acts[1]. We must not assume that popular religion in ancient India was specially indecent, but it probably included ceremonies analogous to the Lupercalia and Thesmophoria, in which licence in words and deeds was supposed to promote fertility and prosperity.

We are also justified in supposing that offerings to ancestors and many ceremonies mentioned in the Gṛihya-sûtras or handbooks of domestic ritual were performed by far larger classes of the population than the greater sacrifices, but we have no safe criteria for distinguishing between priestly injunctions and the real practice of ancient times.

Secondly, in the spells and charms of the Atharva[2], which received the Brahmanic imprimatur later than the other three Vedas, we find an outlook differing from that of the other Vedas and resembling the popular religion of China. Mankind are persecuted by a host of evil spirits and protect themselves by charms addressed directly to their tormentors or by invoking the aid of beneficent powers. All nature is animated by good and evil spirits, to be dealt with like other natural advantages or difficulties, but not thought of as moral or spiritual guides. It is true that the Atharva often rises above this phase, for it consists not of simple folk-lore, but of folk-lore modified under sacerdotal influence. The protecting powers invoked are often the gods of the Rig Veda[3], but prayers and incantations are also addressed directly to diseases[4] and demons[5] or, on the other hand, to healing plants and amulets[6]. We can hardly be wrong in supposing that in such invocations the Atharva reflects the

[1] Cf. the ritual for the Horse sacrifice. Śat. Brâh. XIII. 2. 8, and Hillebrandt, *Vedische Opfer.*, p. 152.

[2] Supplemented by the Kauśika Sûtra, which, whatever its age may be, has preserved a record of very ancient usages.

[3] *E.g.* I. 10. This hymn, like many others, seems to combine several moral and intellectual stages, the level at which the combination was possible not being very high. On the one hand Varuṇa is the Lord of Law and of Truth who punishes moral offences with dropsy. On the other, the sorcerer "releases" the patient from Varuṇa by charms, without imposing any moral penance, and offers the god a thousand other men, provided that this particular victim is released.

[4] *E.g.* VII. 116, VI. 105, VI. 83.

[5] *E.g.* V. 7, XI. 9.

[6] *E.g.* V. 4, XIX. 39, IV. 37, II. 8, XIX. 34, VIII. 7.

popular practice of its time, but it prefers the invocation of counteracting forces, whether Vedic deities or magical plants, to the propitiation of malignant spirits, such as the worship of the goddesses presiding over smallpox and cholera which is still prevalent in India. In this there is probably a contrast between the ideas of the Aryan and non-Aryan races. The latter propitiate the demon or disease; the Aryans invoke a beneficent and healing power. But though on the whole the Atharva is inclined to banish the black spectres of popular demonology with the help of luminous Aryan gods, still we find invoked in it and in its subsidiary literature a multitude of spirits, good and bad, known by little except their names which, however, often suffice to indicate their functions. Such are Âśâpati (Lord of the region), Kshetrapati (Lord of the field), both invoked in ceremonies for destroying locusts and other noxious insects, Śakambhara and Apvâ, deities of diarrhoea, and Arâti, the goddess of avarice and grudge. In one hymn[1] the poet invokes, together with many Vedic deities, all manner of nature spirits, demons, animals, healing plants, seasons and ghosts. A similar collection of queer and vague personalities is found in the popular pantheon of China to-day[2].

Thirdly, various deities who are evidently considered to be well known, play some part in the Pali Pitakas. Those most frequently mentioned are Mahâbrahmâ or Brahmâ Sahampati, and Sakka or Indra, but not quite the same as the Vedic Indra and less in need of libations of Soma. In two curious suttas[3] deputations of deities, clearly intended to include all the important gods worshipped at the time, are represented as visiting the Buddha. In both lists a prominent position is given to the Four Great Kings, or Ruling Spirits of the Four Quarters, accompanied by retinues called Gandhabbas, Kumbhandas, Nâgas, and Yakkhas respectively, and similar to the Nats of Burma. The Gandhabbas (or Gandharvas) are heavenly musicians and mostly benevolent, but are mentioned in the Brâhmaṇas as taking possession of women who then deliver oracles. The Nâgas are serpents, sometimes represented as cobras with one or more heads and sometimes as half human:

[1] A.V. XI. 6.

[2] See, for instance, Du Bose, *The Dragon, Image and Demon*, 1887, pp. 320–344.

[3] Aṭânâṭiya and Mahâsamaya. Dig. Nik. XX. and XXXII.

sometimes they live in palaces under the water or in the depths of the earth and sometimes they are the tutelary deities of trees. Serpent worship has undoubtedly been prevalent in India in all ages: indications of it are found in the earliest Buddhist sculptures and it still survives[1]. The Yakkhas (or Yakshas) though hardly demons (as their name is often rendered) are mostly ill disposed to the human race, sometimes man-eaters and often of unedifying conduct. The Mahâsamaya-sutta also mentions mountain spirits from the Himalaya, Satagiri, and Mount Vepulla. Of the Devas or chiefs of the Yakkhas in this catalogue only a few are known to Brahmanic works, such as Soma, Varuṇa, Veṇhu (Vishnu), the Yamas, Pajâpati, Inda (Indra), Sanan-kumâra. All these deities are enumerated together with little regard to the positions they occupy in the sacerdotal pantheon. The enquirer finds a similar difficulty when he tries in the twentieth century to identify rural deities, or even the tutelaries of many great temples, with any personages recognized by the canonical literature.

In several discourses attributed to the Buddha[2] is incorporated a tract called the Sîla-vagga, giving a list of practices of which he disapproved, such as divination and the use of spells and drugs. Among special observances censured, the following are of interest. (*a*) Burnt offerings, and offerings of blood drawn from the right knee. (*b*) The worship of the Sun, of Siri, the goddess of Luck, and of the Great One, meaning perhaps the Earth. (*c*) Oracles obtained from a mirror, or from a girl possessed by a spirit or from a god.

We also find allusions in Buddhist and Jain works as well as in the inscriptions of Asoka to popular festivals or fairs called Samajjas[3] which were held on the tops of hills and seem to have included music, recitations, dancing and perhaps dramatic performances. These meetings were probably like the modern *mela*, half religion and half entertainment, and it was in such surroundings that the legends and mythology which the great Epics show in full bloom first grew and budded.

Thus we have evidence of the existence in pre-Buddhist

[1] See Crooke's *Popular Religion of Northern India*, vol. II. chap. ii.

[2] In the Brahma-Jala and subsequent suttas of the Dîgha Nikâya.

[3] See Rhys Davids' *Dialogues of the Buddha*, vol. I. p. 7, note 4, and authorities there quoted.

India of rites and beliefs—the latter chiefly of the kind called animistic—disowned for the most part by the Buddhists and only tolerated by the Brahmans. No elaborate explanation of this popular religion or of its relation to more intellectual and sacerdotal cults is necessary, for the same thing exists at the present day and the best commentary on the Sîla-vagga is Crooke's *Popular Religion and Folk-lore of Northern India.*

In themselves such popular superstitions may seem despicable and repulsive (as the Buddha found them), but when they are numerous and vigorous, as in India, they have a real importance for they provide a matrix and nursery in which the beginnings of great religions may be reared. Śâktism and the worship of Râma and Krishna, together with many less conspicuous cults, all entered Brahmanism in this way. Whenever a popular cult grew important or whenever Brahmanic influence spread to a new district possessing such a cult, the popular cult was recognized and brahmanized. This policy can be abundantly illustrated for the last four or five centuries (for instance in Assam), and it was in operation two and a half millenniums ago or earlier. It explains the low and magical character of the residue of popular religion, every ceremony and deity of importance being put under Brahmanic patronage, and it also explains the sudden appearance of new deities. We can safely assert that in the time of the Buddha, and *a fortiori* in the time of the older Upanishads[1] and Brâhmaṇas, Krishna and Râma were not prominent as deities in Hindustan, but it may well be that they had a considerable position as heroes whose exploits were recited at popular festivals and that Krishna was growing into a god in other regions which have left no literature.

[1] Krishna is perhaps mentioned in the Chând. Up. III. 17. 6, but in any case not as a deity.

CHAPTER VII

THE JAINS[1]

1

BEFORE leaving pre-Buddhist India, it may be well to say something of the Jains. Many of their doctrines, especially their disregard not only of priests but of gods, which seems to us so strange in any system which can be called a religion, are closely analogous to Buddhism and from one point of view Jainism is part of the Buddhist movement. But more accurately it may be called an early specialized form of the general movement which culminated in Buddhism. Its founder, Mahâvîra, was an earlier contemporary of the Buddha and not a pupil or imitator[2]. Even had its independent appearance been later, we might still say that it represents an earlier stage of thought. Its kinship to the theories mentioned in the last chapter is clear. It does not indeed deny responsibility and free will, but its advocacy of extreme asceticism and death by starvation has a touch of the same extravagance and its list of elements in which physical substances and ideas are mixed together is curiously crude.

Jainism is atheistic, and this atheism is as a rule neither apologetic nor polemical but is accepted as a natural religious attitude. By atheism, of course, a denial of the existence of Devas is not meant; the Jains surpass, if possible, the exuberant

[1] See, besides the translations mentioned below, Bühler, *Ueber die indische Secte der Jainas* 1887; Hoernle, *Metaphysics and Ethics of the Jainas* 1908; and Guérinot, *Essai de Bibliographie Jaina* and *Répertoire d'Épigraphie Jaina*; Jagmanderlal Jaini, *Outlines of Jainism*; Jacobi's article Jainism in *E.R.E.* Much information may also be found in Mrs Stevenson's *Heart of Jainism.* Winternitz, *Geschichte d. Indischen Literatur*, vol. II. part II. (1920) treats of Jain literature but I have not been able to see it.

[2] In *J.R.A.S.* 1917, pp. 122–130 s.v. Venkateśvara argues that Vardhamâna died about 437 B.C. and that the Nigaṇṭhas of the Piṭakas were followers of Parśva. His arguments deserve consideration but he seems not to lay sufficient emphasis on the facts that (*a*) according to the Buddhist scriptures the Buddha and Gosâla were contemporaries, while according to the Jain scriptures Gosâla and Vardhamâna were contemporaries, (*b*) in the Buddhist scriptures Nâtaputta is the representative of the Nigaṇṭhas, while according to the Jain scriptures Vardhamâna was of the Ñata clan.

fancy of the Brahmans and Buddhists in designing imaginary worlds and peopling them with angelic or diabolical inhabitants, but, as in Buddhism, these beings are like mankind subject to transmigration and decay and are not the masters, still less the creators, of the universe. There were two principal world theories in ancient India. One, which was systematized as the Vedânta, teaches in its extreme form that the soul and the universal spirit are identical and the external world an illusion. The other, systematized as the Sânkhya, is dualistic and teaches that primordial matter and separate individual souls are both of them uncreated and indestructible. Both lines of thought look for salvation in the liberation of the soul to be attained by the suppression of the passions and the acquisition of true knowledge.

Jainism belongs to the second of these classes. It teaches that the world is eternal, self-existent and composed of six constituent substances: souls, dharma, adharma, space, time, and particles of matter[1]. Dharma and adharma are defined by modern Jains as subtle substances analogous to space which make it possible for things to move or rest, but Jacobi is probably right in supposing that in primitive speculation the words had their natural meaning and denoted subtle fluids which cause merit and demerit. In any case the enumeration places in singular juxtaposition substances and activities, the material and the immaterial. The process of salvation and liberation is not distinguished from physical processes and we see how other sects may have drawn the conclusion, which apparently the Jains did not draw, that human action is necessitated and that there is no such thing as free will. For Jainism individual souls are free, separate existences, whose essence is pure intelligence. But they have a tendency towards action and passion and are misled by false beliefs. For this reason, in the existence which we know they are chained to bodies and are found not only in Devas and in human beings but in animals, plants and inanimate matter. The habitation of the soul depends on the merit or demerit which it acquires

[1] The atoms are either simple or compound and from their combinations are produced the four elements, earth, wind, fire and water, and the whole material universe. For a clear statement of the modern Jain doctrine about *dharma* and *adharma*, see Jagmanderlal Jaini, l.c. pp. 22 ff.

and merit and demerit have respectively greater or less influence during immensely long periods called Utsarpinî and Avasarpinî, ascending and descending, in which human stature and the duration of life increase or decrease by a regular law. Merit secures birth among the gods or good men. Sin sends the soul to baser births, even in inanimate substances. On this downward path, the intelligence is gradually dimmed till at last motion and consciousness are lost, which is not however regarded as equivalent to annihilation.

Another dogmatic exposition of the Jain creed is based on seven principles, called soul, non-soul, influx, imprisonment, exclusion, dissipation, release[1]. Karma, which in the ordinary language of Indian philosophy means deeds and their effect on the soul, is here regarded as a peculiarly subtle form of matter[2] which enters the soul and by this influx (or âsrava, a term well-known in Buddhism) defiles and weighs it down. As food is transformed into flesh, so the Karma forms a subtle body which invests the soul and prevents it from being wholly isolated from matter at death. The upward path and liberation of the soul are effected by stopping the entrance of Karma, that is by not performing actions which give occasion to the influx, and by expelling it. The most effective means to this end is self-mortification, which not only prevents the entrance of new Karma but annihilates what has accumulated.

Like most Indian sects, Jainism considers the world of transmigration as a bondage or journey which the wise long to terminate. But joyless as is its immediate outlook, its ultimate ideas are not pessimistic. Even in the body the soul can attain a beatific state of perfect knowledge[3] and above the highest

[1] Jîva, ajîva, âsrava, bandha, saṃvara, nirjarâ, moksha. The principles are sometimes made nine by the addition of *puṇya*, merit, and *pâpa*, sin.

[2] Paudgalikam karma. It would seem that all these ideas about Karma should be taken in a literal and material sense. Karma, which is a specially subtle form of matter able to enter, stain and weigh down the soul, is of eight kinds (1 and 2) jñâna- and darśana-varanîya impede knowledge and faith, which the soul naturally possesses; (3) mohanîya causes delusion; (4) vedanîya brings pleasure and pain; (5) ayushka fixes the length of life; (6) nâma furnishes individual characteristics, and (7) gotra generic; (8) antarâya hinders the development of good qualities.

[3] Kevalam also called Jñâna, moksha, nirvâṇa. The nirvâṇa of the Jains is clearly not incompatible with the continuance of intelligence and knowledge.

heaven (where the greatest gods live in bliss for immense periods though ultimately subject to transmigration) is the paradise of blessed souls, freed from transmigration. They have no visible form but consist of life throughout, and enjoy happiness beyond compare. With a materialism characteristic of Jain theology, the treatise from which this account is taken[1] adds that the dimensions of a perfected soul are two-thirds of the height possessed in its last existence.

How is this paradise to be reached? By right faith, right knowledge and right conduct, called the three jewels, a phrase familiar to Buddhism. The right faith is complete confidence in Mahâvîra and his teaching. Right knowledge is correct theology as outlined above. Knowledge is of five degrees of which the highest is called Kevalam or omniscience. This sounds ambitious, but the special method of reasoning favoured by the Jains is the modest Syâdvâda[2] or doctrine of may-be, which holds that you can (1) affirm the existence of a thing from one point of view, (2) deny it from another, and (3) affirm both existence and non-existence with reference to it at different times. If (4) you should think of affirming existence and non-existence at the same time and from the same point of view, you must say that the thing cannot be spoken of. The essence of the doctrine, so far as one can disentangle it from scholastic terminology, seems just, for it amounts to this, that as to matters of experience it is impossible to formulate the whole and complete truth, and as to matters which transcend experience language is inadequate: also that Being is associated with production, continuation and destruction. This doctrine is called *anekânta-vâda*, meaning that Being is not one and absolute as the Upanishads assert: matter is permanent, but changes its shape, and its other accidents. Thus in many points the Jains adopt the common sense and *primâ facie* point of view. But the doctrines of metempsychosis and Karma are also admitted as obvious propositions, and though the fortunes and struggles of the embodied soul are described in materialistic terms, happiness is never placed in material well-being but in liberation from the material universe.

We cannot be sure that the existing Jain scriptures present

[1] Uttarâdhyâyana XXXVI. 64–68 in *S.B.E.* XLV. pp. 212–213.

[2] *S.B.E.* XLV. p. xxvii. Bhandarkar Report for 1883–4, pp. 95 ff.

these doctrines in their original form, but the full acceptance of metempsychosis, the animistic belief that plants, particles of earth and water have souls and the materialistic phraseology (from which the widely different speculations of the Upanishads are by no means free) agree with what we know of Indian thought about 550 B.C. Jainism like Buddhism ignores the efficacy of ceremonies and the powers of priests, but it bears even fewer signs than Buddhism of being in its origin a protestant or hostile movement. The intellectual atmosphere seems other than that of the Upanishads, but it is very nearly that of the Sânkhya philosophy, which also recognizes an infinity of individual souls radically distinct from matter and capable of attaining bliss only by isolation from matter. Of the origin of that important school we know nothing, but it differs from Jainism chiefly in the greater elaboration of its psychological and evolutionary theories and in the elimination of some materialistic ideas. Possibly the same region and climate of opinion gave birth to two doctrines, one simple and practical, inasmuch as it found its principal expression in a religious order, the other more intellectual and scholastic and, at least in the form in which we read it, later[1].

Right conduct is based on the five vows taken by every Jain ascetic, (1) not to kill, (2) not to speak untruth, (3) to take nothing that is not given, (4) to observe chastity, (5) to renounce all pleasure in external objects. These vows receive an extensive and strict interpretation by means of five explanatory clauses applicable to each and to be construed with reference to deed, word, and thought, to acting, commanding and consenting. Thus the vow not to kill forbids not only the destruction of the smallest insect but also all speech or thought which could bring about a quarrel, and the doing, causing or permitting of any action which could even inadvertently injure living beings, such as carelessness in walking. Naturally such rules can be kept only by an ascetic, and in addition to them asceticism is expressly enjoined. It is either internal or external. The former takes such forms as repentance, humility, meditation

[1] Somewhat similar seems to be the relation of Jainism to the Vaiśeshika philosophy. It accepted an early form of the atomic theory and this theory was subsequently elaborated in the philosophy whose founder Kaṇâda was according to the Jains a pupil of a Jain ascetic.

and the suppression of all desires: the latter comprises various forms of self-denial, culminating in death by starvation. This form of religious suicide is prescribed for those who have undergone twelve years' penance and are ripe for Nirvana[1] but it is wrong if adopted as a means of shortening austerities. Numerous inscriptions record such deaths and the head-teachers of the Digambaras are said still to leave the world in this way.

Important but not peculiar to Jainism is the doctrine of the periodical appearance of great teachers who from time to time restore the true faith[2]. The same idea meets us in the fourteen Manus, the incarnations of Vishnu, and the series of Buddhas who preceded Gotama. The Jain saints are sometimes designated as Buddha, Kevalin, Siddha, Tathâgata and Arhat (all Buddhist titles) but their special appellation is Jina or conqueror which is, however, also used by Buddhists[3]. It was clearly a common notion in India that great teachers appear at regular intervals and that one might reasonably be expected in the sixth century B.C. The Jains gave preference or prominence to the titles Jina or Tîrthankara: the Buddhists to Buddha or Tathâgata.

2

According to the Jain scriptures all Jinas are born in the warrior caste, never among Brahmans. The first called Rishabha, who was born an almost inexpressibly[4] long time ago and lived 8,400,000 years, was the son of a king of Ayodhyâ. But as ages elapsed, the lives of his successors and the intervals which separated them became shorter. Parśva, the twenty-third Jina, must have some historical basis[5]. We are told that he lived 250 years before Mahâvîra, that his followers still existed in the time of the latter: that he permitted the use of

[1] *E.g.* see Acarânga S. I. 7. 6.

[2] They seem to have authority to formulate it in a form suitable to the needs of the age. Thus we are told that Parśva enjoined four vows but Mahâvîra five.

[3] When Gotama after attaining Buddhahood was on his way to Benares he met Upaka, a naked ascetic, to whom he declared that he was the Supreme Buddha. Then, said Upaka, you profess to be the Jina, and Gotama replied that he did, "Tasmâ 'ham Upakâ jinoti." (Mahâvag. I. 6. 10.)

[4] The exact period is 100 billion sâgaras of years. A sâgara is 100,000,000,000 palyas. A palya is the period in which a well a mile deep filled with fine hairs can be emptied if one hair is withdrawn every hundred years.

[5] See M. Bloomfield, *Life and Stories of Pârçvanâtha* (1919).

clothes and taught that four and not five vows were necessary[1]. Both Jain and Buddhist scriptures support the idea that Mahâvîra was a reviver and reformer rather than an originator. The former do not emphasize the novelty of his revelation and the latter treat Jainism as a well-known form of error without indicating that it was either new or attributable to one individual.

Mahâvîra, or the great hero, is the common designation of the twenty-fourth Jina but his personal name was Vardhamâna. He was a contemporary of the Buddha but somewhat older and belonged to a Kshatriya clan, variously called Jñâta, Ñâta, or Ñâya. His parents lived in a suburb of Vaiśâlî and were followers of Parśva. When he was in his thirty-first year they decided to die by voluntary starvation and after their death he renounced the world and started to wander naked in western Bengal, enduring some persecution as well as self-inflicted penances. After thirteen years of this life, he believed that he had attained enlightenment and appeared as the Jina, the head of a religious order called Nirgaṇṭhas (or Nigaṇṭhas). This word, which means unfettered or free from bonds, is the name by which the Jains are generally known in Buddhist literature and it occurs in their own scriptures, though it gradually fell out of use. Possibly it was the designation of an order claiming to have been founded by Parśva and accepted by Mahâvîra.

The meagre accounts of his life relate that he continued to travel for nearly thirty years and had eleven principal disciples. He apparently influenced much the same region as the Buddha and came in contact with the same personalities, such as kings Bimbisâra and Ajâtasattu. He had relations with Makkhali Gosâla and his disciples disputed with the Buddhists[2] but it does not appear that he himself ever met Gotama. He died at the age of seventy-two at Pâvâ near Râjagaha. Only one of his principal disciples, Sudharman, survived him and a schism broke out immediately after his death. There had already been

[1] See the discussions between followers of Parśva and Mahâvîra given in Uttarâdhyâyana XXIV. and Sûtrakritânga II. 7.

[2] There are many references to the Nigaṇṭhas in the Buddhist scriptures and the Buddha, while by no means accepting their views, treats them with tolerance. Thus he bade Siha, General of the Licchavis, who became his disciple after being an adherent of Nâtaputta to continue to give alms as before to Nigaṇṭha ascetics (Mahâvag. VI. 32).

one in the fifteenth year of his teaching brought about by his son-in-law.

3

We have no information about the differences on which these schisms turned, but Jainism is still split into two sects which, though following in most respects identical doctrines and customs, refuse to intermarry or eat together. Their sacred literature is not the same and the evidence of inscriptions indicates that they were distinct at the beginning of the Christian era and perhaps much earlier.

The Digambara sect, or those who are clothed in air, maintain that absolute nudity is a necessary condition of saintship: the other division or Śvetâmbaras, those who are dressed in white, admit that Mahâvîra went about naked, but hold that the use of clothes does not impede the highest sanctity, and also that such sanctity can be attained by women, which the Digambaras deny. Nudity as a part of asceticism was practised by several sects in the time of Mahâvîra[1] but it was also reprobated by others (including all Buddhists) who felt it to be barbarous and unedifying. It is therefore probable that both Digambaras and Śvetâmbaras existed in the infancy of Jainism, and the latter may represent the older sect reformed or exaggerated by Mahâvîra. Thus we are told[2] that "the law taught by Vardhamâna forbids clothes but that of the great sage Parśva allows an under and an upper garment." But it was not until considerably later that the schism was completed by the constitution of two different canons[3]. At the present day most Digambaras wear the ordinary costume of their district and only the higher ascetics attempt to observe the rule of nudity. When they go about they wrap themselves in a large cloth, but lay it aside when eating. The Digambaras are divided into four principal sects and the Śvetâmbaras into no less than eighty-four, which are said to date from the tenth century A.D.

Apart from these divisions, all Jain communities are differen-

[1] Especially among the Âjîvikas. Their leader Gosâla had a personal quarrel with Mahâvîra but his teaching was almost identical except that he was a fatalist.

[2] Uttarâdhyâyana XXIII. 29.

[3] According to Śvetâmbara tradition there was a great schism 609 years after Mahâvîra's death. The canon was not fixed until 904 (? 454 A.D.) of the same era. The Digambara traditions are different but appear to be later.

tiated into laymen and members of the order or Yatis, literally strivers. It is recognized that laymen cannot observe the five vows. Killing, lying, and stealing are forbidden to them only in their obvious and gross forms: chastity is replaced by conjugal fidelity and self-denial by the prohibition of covetousness. They can also acquire merit by observing seven other miscellaneous vows (whence we hear of the twelvefold law) comprising rules as to residence, trade, etc. Agriculture is forbidden since it involves tearing up the ground and the death of insects.

Mahâvîra was succeeded by a long line of teachers sometimes called Patriarchs and it would seem that their names have been correctly preserved though the accounts of their doings are meagre. Various notices in Buddhist literature confirm the idea that the Jains were active in the districts corresponding to Oudh, Tirhut and Bihar in the period following Mahâvîra's death, and we hear of them in Ceylon before our era. Further historical evidence is afforded by inscriptions[1]. The earliest in which the Jains are mentioned are the edicts of Asoka. He directed the officials called "superintendents of religion" to concern themselves with the Nigaṇṭhas[2]: and when[3] he describes how he has provided medicine, useful plants and wells for both men and animals, we are reminded of the hospitals for animals which are still maintained by the Jains. According to Jain tradition (which however has not yet been verified by other evidence) Samprati, the grandson of Asoka, was a devout patron of the faith. More certain is the patronage accorded to it by King Khâravela of Orissa about 157 B.C. which is attested by inscriptions. Many dedicatory inscriptions prove that the Jains were a flourishing community at Muttra in the reigns of Kanishka, Huvishka and Vasudeva and one inscription from the same locality seems as old as 150 B.C. We learn from these records that the sect comprised a great number of schools and subdivisions. We need not suppose that the different teachers were necessarily hostile to one another but their existence testifies to an activity and freedom of interpretation which have left traces in the multitude of modern subsects.

[1] See especially Guérinot, *Répertoire d'Épigraphie Jaina*

[2] So Bühler, Pillar Edict no. VIII. Senart Inscrip. de Piyadasi II. 97 translates somewhat differently, but the reference to the Jains is not disputed.

[3] Rock Edict VI.

Jainism also spread in the south of India and before our era it had a strong hold in Tamil lands, but our knowledge of its early progress is defective. According to Jain tradition there was a severe famine in northern India about 200 years after Mahâvîra's death and the patriarch Bhadrabâhu led a band of the faithful to the south[1]. In the seventh century A.D. we know from various records of the reign of Harsha and from the Chinese pilgrim Hsüan Chuang that it was flourishing in Vaiśâlî and Bengal and also as far south as Conjeevaram. It also made considerable progress in the southern Maratha country under the Câlukya dynasty of Vatapi, in the modern district of Bijapur (500–750) and under the Râshṭrakûta sovereigns of the Deccan. Amoghavarsha of this line (815–877) patronized the Digambaras and in his old age abdicated and became an ascetic. The names of notable Digambara leaders like Jinasena and Guṇabhadra dating from this period are preserved and Jainism must in some districts have become the dominant religion. Bijjala who usurped the Câlukya throne (1156–1167) was a Jain and the Hoysala kings of Mysore, though themselves Vaishnavas, protected the religion. Inscriptions[2] appear to attest the presence of Jainism at Girnar in the first century A.D. and subsequently Gujarat became a model Jain state after the conversion of King Kumârapâla about 1160.

Such success naturally incurred the enmity of the Brahmans and there is more evidence of systematic persecution directed against the Jains than against the Buddhists. The Cola kings who ruled in the south-east of the Madras Presidency were jealous worshippers of Siva and the Jains suffered severely at their hands in the eleventh century and also under the Pândya kings of the extreme south. King Sundara of the latter dynasty is said to have impaled 8000 of them and pictures on the walls of the great temple at Madura represent their tortures. A little later (1174) Ajayadeva, a Saiva king of Gujarat, is said to have raged against them with equal fury. The rise of the Lingâyats

[1] Rice (*Mysore and Coorg from the Inscriptions*, 1909, p. 310) thinks that certain inscriptions at Sravana Belgola in Mysore establish that this tradition is true and also that the expedition was accompanied by King Candragupta who had abdicated and become a Jain ascetic. But this interpretation has been much criticised. It is probably true that a migration occurred and increased the differences which ultimately led to the division into Śvetâmbaras and Digambaras.

[2] Guérinot, *Épig. Jaina*, no. 11.

in the Deccan must also have had an unfavourable effect on their numbers. But in the fourteenth century greater tolerance prevailed, perhaps in consequence of the common danger from Islam. Inscriptions found at Sravana Belgola and other places[1] narrate an interesting event which occurred in 1368. The Jains appealed to the king of Vijayanagar for protection from persecution and he effected a public reconciliation between them and the Vaishnavas, holding the hands of both leaders in his own and declaring that equal protection would be given to both sects. Another inscription records an amicable agreement regulating the worship of a lingam in a Jain temple at Halebid. Many others, chiefly recording grants of land, testify to the prosperity of Jainism in the Hindu kingdom of Vijayanagar and in the region of Mt Abu in the sixteenth and seventeenth centuries[2]. The great Emperor Akbar himself came under the influence of Jainism and received instruction from three Jain teachers from 1578 to 1597.

Persecution and still more the steady pressure and absorptive power of Hinduism have reduced the proportions of the sect, and the last census estimated it at one million and a third. It is probable, however, that many Jains returned themselves as Hindus, and that their numbers are really greater. More than two-fifths of them are found in Bombay, Rajputana, and Central India. Elsewhere they are generally distributed but only in small numbers. They observe caste, at least in some districts, and generally belong to the Baniyas. They include many wealthy merchants who expend large sums on the construction and maintenance of temples, houses for wandering ascetics and homes for cattle. Their respect and care for animal life are remarkable. Wherever Jains gain influence beasts are not slaughtered or sacrificed, and when old or injured are often kept in hospitals or asylums, as, for instance, at Ahmadabad[3]. Their ascetics take stringent precautions to avoid killing the smallest creature: they strain their drinking water, sweep the ground before them with a broom as they walk and wear a veil

[1] Rice, *Mysore and Coorg from the Inscriptions*, 1909, pp. 113–114, 207–208.

[2] Similar tolerance is attested by inscriptions (*e.g.* Guérinot, nos. 522 and 5776) recording donations to both Jain and Saiva temples.

[3] They also make a regular practice of collecting and rearing young animals which the owners throw away or wish to kill.

over their mouths. Even in the shops of the laity lamps are carefully screened to prevent insects from burning themselves.

The principal divisions are the Digambara and Śvetâmbara as above described and an offshoot of the latter called Dhundia[1] who refuse to use images in worship and are remarkable even among Jains for their aversion to taking life. In Central India the Digambaras are about half the total number; in Baroda and Bombay the Śvetâmbaras are stronger. In Central India the Jains are said to be sharply distinguished from Hindus but in other parts they intermarry with Vaishnavas and while respecting their own ascetics as religious teachers, employ the services of Brahmans in their ceremonies.

4

The Jains have a copious and in part ancient literature. The oldest works are found in the canon (or Siddhânta) of the Śvetâmbaras, which is not accepted by the Digambaras. In this canon the highest rank is given to eleven works[2] called Angas or limbs of the law but it also comprises many other esteemed treatises such as the Kalpasûtra ascribed to Bhadrabâhu. Fourteen older books called Puvvas (Sk. Pûrvas) and now lost are said to have together formed a twelfth anga. The language of the canon is a variety of Prakrit[3], fairly ancient though more modern than Pali, and remarkable for its habit of omitting or softening consonants coming between two vowels, *e.g.* sûyam for sûtram, loo for loko[4]. We cannot, however,

[1] Or Sthânakavâsi. See for them *Census of India*, 1911, I. p. 127 and *Baroda*, p. 93. The sect was founded about A.D. 1653.

[2] Their names are as follows in Jain Prakrit, the Sanskrit equivalent being given in brackets: 1. *Âyârângasuttam (Âcârânga). 2. *Sûyagadangam (Sûtrakṛitângam). 3. Thânangam (Sthâ.). 4. Samavâyangam. 5. Viyâhapaññatti (Vyâkhyâprajnâpti). This work is commonly known as the Bhagavatî. 6. Ñâyâdhammakahâo (Jñâtadharmakathâ). 7. *Uvâsagadasao (Upâsakadasâḥ). 8. *Antagadadasao (Antakritad.). 9. *Anuttarovavâidasâo (Anuttaraupapâtikad.). 10. Panhâvâgaranâim (Prasnavyakaraṇâni). 11. Vivâgasuyam (Vipâkasrutam).

The books marked with an asterisk have been translated by Jacobi (*S.B.E.* vols. XXII. and XIV.), Hoernle and Barnett. See too Weber, *Indische Studien*, Bd. XVI. pp. 211–479 and Bd. XVIII. pp. 1–90.

[3] It is called Ârsha or Ardha-Mâgadhî and is the literary form of the vernacular of Berar in the early centuries of the Christian era. See H. Jacobi, Ausgewählte Erzählungen in *Maharashtri*, and introduction to edition of *Ayarânga-sutta*.

[4] The titles given in note 2 illustrate some of its peculiarities.

conclude that it is the language in which the books were composed, for it is probable that the early Jains, rejecting Brahmanical notions of a revealed text, handed down their religious teaching in the vernacular and allowed its grammar and phonetics to follow the changes brought about by time. According to a tradition which probably contains elements of truth the first collection of sacred works was made about 200 years after Mahâvîra's death by a council which sat at Pataliputra. Just about the same time came the famine already mentioned and many Jains migrated to the south. When they returned they found that their co-religionists had abandoned the obligation of nakedness and they consequently refused to recognize their sacred books. The Śvetâmbara canon was subsequently revised and written down by a council held at Valabhi in Gujarat in the middle of the fifth century A.D. This is the edition which is still extant. The canon of the Digambaras, which is less well known, is said to be chiefly in Sanskrit and according to tradition was codified by Pushpadanta in the second century A.D. but appears to be really posterior to the Śvetâmbara scriptures[1]. It is divided into four sections called Vedas and treating respectively of history, cosmology, philosophy and rules of life[2].

Though the books of the Jain canon contain ancient matter, yet they seem, as compositions, considerably later than the older parts of the Buddhist Tripitaka. They do not claim to record recent events and teaching but are attempts at synthesis which assume that Jainism is well known and respected. In style they offer some resemblance to the Pitakas: there is the same inordinate love of repetition and in the more emotional passages great similarity of tone and metaphor[3].

Besides the two canons, the Jains have a considerable literature consisting both of commentaries and secular works. The most eminent of their authors is Hemacandra, born in 1088, who though a monk was an ornament of the court and rendered

[1] When I visited Sravana Belgola in 1910, the head of the Jains there, who professed to be a Digambara, though dressed in purple raiment, informed me that their sacred works were partly in Sanskrit and partly in Prakrit. He showed me a book called Trilokasâra.

[2] But see Jagmanderlal Jaini, l.c. appendix v.

[3] Compare for instance Uttarâdyâyana X., XXIII. and XXV. with the Sutta-Nipâta and Dhammapada.

an important service to his sect by converting Kumârapâla, King of Gujarat. He composed numerous and valuable works on grammar, lexicography, poetics and ecclesiastical biography. Such subjects were congenial to the later Jain writers and they not only cultivated both Sanskrit and Prakrit but also had a vivifying effect on the vernaculars of southern India. Kanarese, Tamil, and Telugu in their literary form owe much to the labours of Jain monks, and the Jain works composed in these languages, such as the Jîvakacintâmaṇi in Tamil, if not of world-wide importance, at least greatly influenced Dravidian civilization.

Though the Jains thus occupy an honourable, and even distinguished place in the history of letters it must be confessed that it is hard to praise their older religious books. This literature is of considerable scientific interest for it contains many data about ancient India as yet unsifted but it is tedious in style and rarely elevated in sentiment. It has an arid extravagance, which merely piles one above the other interminable lists of names and computations of immensity in time and space. Even more than in the Buddhist suttas there is a tendency to repetition which offends our sense of proportion and though the main idea, to free the soul from the trammels of passion and matter, is not inferior to any of the religious themes of India, the treatment is not adequate to the subject and the counsels of perfection are smothered under a mass of minute precepts about the most unsavoury details of life and culminate in the recommendation of death by voluntary starvation.

5

But observation of Jainism as it exists to-day produces a quite different impression. The Jains are well-to-do, industrious and practical: their schools and religious establishments are well ordered: their temples have a beauty, cleanliness, and cheerfulness unusual in India and due to the large use made of white marble and brilliant colours. The tenderness for animal life may degenerate into superstition (though surely it is a fault on the right side) and some observances of the ascetics (such as pulling out the hair instead of shaving the head) are severe, but as a community the Jains lead sane and serious lives, hardly practising and certainly not parading the extravagances of self-torture which they theoretically commend. Mahâvîra is said to have taught that place, time and occasion should be taken into consideration and his successors adapted their precepts to the age in which they lived. Such monks as I have met[1] maintained that extreme forms of *tapas* were good for the nerves of ancient saints but not for the weaker natures of to-day. But in avoiding rigorous severity, they have not fallen into sloth or luxury.

The beauty of Jainism finds its best expression in architecture. This reached its zenith both in style and quantity during the eleventh and twelfth centuries which accords with what we know of the growth of the sect. After this period the Mohammedan invasions were unfavourable to all forms of Hindu architecture. But the taste for building remained and somewhat later pious Jains again began to construct large edifices which are generally less degenerate than modern Hindu temples, though they often show traces of Mohammedan influence. Hathi Singh's temple at Ahmadabad completed in 1848 is a fine example of this modern style.

There is a considerable difference between Jain and Buddhist architecture both in intention and effect. Jain monks did not live together in large communities and there was no worship of relics. Hence the vihâra and the stûpa—the two principal types of Buddhist buildings—are both absent. Yet there is some resemblance between Jain temples (for instance those at Palitâna) and the larger Burmese sanctuaries, such as the Shwe Dagon Pagoda. It is partly due to the same conviction, namely that the most meritorious work which a layman can perform is to multiply shrines and images. In both localities the general plan is similar. On the top of a hill or mound is a central building round which are grouped a multitude of other shrines. The repetition of chapels and images is very remarkable: in Burma they all represent Gotama, in Jain temples the figures of Tîrthankaras are nominally different personalities but so alike in presentment that the laity rarely know them apart. In both styles of art white and jewelled images are common as well as groups of four sitting figures set back to back and facing the

[1] I have only visited establishments in towns. Possibly Yatis who follow a severer rule may be found in the country, especially among Digambaras.

four quarters[1]: in both we meet with veritable cities of temples, on the hill tops of Gujarat and in the plain of Pagan on the banks of the Irawaddy. As some features of Burmese art are undoubtedly borrowed from India[2], the above characteristics may be due to imitation of Jain methods. It might be argued that the architectural style of late Indian Buddhism survives among the Jains but there is no proof that the multiplication of temples and images was a feature of this style. But in some points it is clear that the Jains have followed the artistic conventions of the Buddhists. Thus Pârśvanâtha is sheltered by a cobra's hood, like Gotama, and though the Bo-tree plays no part in the legend of the Tîrthankaras, they are represented as sitting under such trees and a living tree is venerated at Palitâna.

As single edifices illustrating the beauty of Jain art both in grace of design and patient elaboration of workmanship may be mentioned the Towers of Fame and Victory at Chitore, and the temples of Mt Abu. Some differences of style are visible in north and south India. In the former the essential features are a shrine with a portico attached and surmounted by a conical tower, the whole placed in a quadrangular court round which are a series of cells or chapels containing images seated on thrones. These are the Tîrthankaras, almost exactly alike and of white marble, though some of the later saints are represented as black. The Śvetâmbaras represent their Tîrthankaras as clothed but in the temples of the Digambaras the images are naked.

In the south are found religious monuments of two kinds known as Bastis and Bettus. The Bastis consist of pillared vestibules leading to a shrine over which rises a dome constructed in three or four stages. The Bettus are not temples in the ordinary sense but courtyards surrounding gigantic images of a saint named Gommateśvara who is said to have been the son of the first Tîrthankara[3]. The largest of these colossi is at

[1] In Gujarat they are called Cho-mukhji and it is said that when a Tîrthankara preached in the midst of his audience each side saw him facing them. In Burma the four figures are generally said to be the last four Buddhas.

[2] This seems clear from the presence in Burma of the curvilinear sikra and even of copies of Indian temples, *e.g.* of Bodh-Gaya at Pagan. Burmese pilgrims to Gaya might easily have visited Mt Parasnath on their way.

[3] I have this information from the Jain Guru at Sravana Belgola. He said that Gomateśvara (who seems unknown to the Śvetâmbaras) was a Kevalin but not a Tîrthankara.

Sravana Belgola. It is seventy feet in height and carved out of a mass of granite standing on the top of a hill and represents a sage so sunk in meditation that anthills and creepers have grown round his feet without breaking his trance. An inscription states that it was erected about 983 A.D. by the minister of a king of the Ganga dynasty[1].

But even more remarkable than these gigantic statues are the collections of temples found on several eminences, such as Girnar and Satrunjaya[2], mountain masses which rise abruptly to a height of three or four thousand feet out of level plains. On the summit of Satrunjaya are innumerable shrines, arranged in marble courts or along well-paved streets. In each enclosure is a central temple surrounded by others at the sides, and all are dominated by one which in the proportions of its spire and courtyard surpasses the rest. Only a few Yatis are allowed to pass the night in the sacred precincts and it is a strange experience to enter the gates at dawn and wander through the interminable succession of white marble courts tenanted only by flocks of sacred pigeons. On every side sculptured chapels gorgeous in gold and colour stand silent and open: within are saints sitting grave and passionless behind the lights that burn on their altars. The multitude of calm stone faces, the strange silence and emptiness, unaccompanied by any sign of neglect or decay, the bewildering repetition of shrines and deities in this aerial castle, suggest nothing built with human purpose but some petrified spirit world.

Soon after dawn a string of devotees daily ascends the hill. Most are laymen, but there is a considerable sprinkling of ascetics, especially nuns. After joining the order both sexes wear yellowish white robes and carry long sticks. They spend much of their time in visiting holy places and usually do not stop at one rest house for more than two months. The worship

[1] Two others, rather smaller, are known, one at Karkâl (dated 1431) and one at Yannur. These images are honoured at occasional festivals (one was held at Sravana Belgola in 1910) attended by a considerable concourse of Jains. The type of the statues is not Buddhist. They are nude and represent sages meditating in a standing position whereas Buddhists prescribe a sitting posture for meditation.

[2] The mountain of Satrunjaya rises above Palitâna, the capital of a native state in Gujarat. Other collections of temples are found on the hill of Parasnath in Bengal, at Sonâgir near Datiâ, and Muktagiri near Gâwîlgarh. There are also a good many on the hills above Rajgîr.

performed in the temples consists of simple offerings of flowers, incense and lights made with little ceremony. Pilgrims go their rounds in small bands and kneeling together before the images sing the praises of the Jinas.

6

It is remarkable that Jainism is still a living sect, whereas the Buddhists have disappeared from India. Its strength and persistence are centred in its power of enlisting the interest of the laity and of forming them into a corporation. In theory the position of the Jain and Buddhist layman is the same. Both revere and support a religious order for which they have not a vocation, and are bound by minor vows less stringent than those of the monks. But among the Buddhists the members of the order came to be regarded more and more as the true church[1] and the laity tended to become (what they actually have become in China and Japan) pious persons who revere that order as something extraneous to themselves and very often only as one among several religious organizations. Hence when in India monasteries decayed or were destroyed, little active Buddhism was left outside them. But the wandering ascetics of the Jains never concentrated the strength of the religion in themselves to the same extent; the severity of their rule limited their numbers: the laity were wealthy and practically formed a caste; persecution acted as a tonic. As a result we have a sect analogous in some ways to the Jews, Parsis, and Quakers[2], among all of whom we find the same features, namely a wealthy laity, little or no sacerdotalism and endurance of persecution.

Another question of some interest is how far Jainism should be regarded as separate from Buddhism. Historically the position seems clear. Both are offshoots of a movement which was active in India in the sixth century B.C. in certain districts and especially among the aristocracy. Of these offshoots—the survivors among many which hardly outlived their birth—

[1] The strength of Buddhism in Burma and Siam is no doubt largely due to the fact that custom obliges every one to spend part of his life—if only a few days—as a member of the order.

[2] One might perhaps add to this list the Skoptsy of Russia and the Armenian colonies in many European and Asiatic towns.

Jainism was a trifle the earlier, but Buddhism was superior and more satisfying to the intellect and moral sense alike. Out of the theory and practice of religious life current in their time Gotama fashioned a beautiful vase, Mahâvîra a homely but still durable pot. The resemblances between the two systems are not merely obvious but fundamental. Both had their origin outside the priestly class and owed much of their success to the protection of princes. Both preach a road to salvation open to man's unaided strength and needing neither sacrifice nor revealed lore. Both are universal, for though Buddhism set about its world mission with more knowledge and grasp of the task, the Jain sûtras are addressed "to Aryans and non-Aryans" and it is said that in modern times Mohammedans have been received into the Jain Church. Neither is theistic. Both believe in some form of reincarnation, in karma and in the periodical appearance of beings possessed of superhuman knowledge and called indifferently Jinas or Buddhas. The historian may therefore be disposed to regard the two religions as not differing much more than the varieties of Protestant Dissenters to be found in Great Britain. But the theologian will perceive real differences. One of the most important doctrines of Buddhism—perhaps in the Buddha's own esteem the central doctrine—is the non-existence of the soul as a permanent entity: in Jainism on the contrary not only the human body but the whole world including inanimate matter is inhabited by individual souls who can also exist apart from matter in individual blessedness. The Jain theory of fivefold knowledge is unknown to the Buddhists, as is their theory of the Skandhas to the Jains. Secondly as to practice Jainism teaches (with some concessions in modern times) that salvation is obtainable by self-mortification but this is the method which the Buddha condemned after prolonged trial. It is clear that in his own opinion and that of his contemporaries the rule and ideal of life which he prescribed differed widely from those of the Jains, Âjîvikas and other wandering ascetics.

BOOK III

PALI BUDDHISM

BOOK III

In the previous book I have treated chiefly the general characteristics of Indian religion. They persist in its later phases but great changes and additions are made. In the present book I propose to speak about the life and teaching of the Buddha which even hostile critics must admit to be a turning point in the history of Indian thought and institutions, and about the earliest forms of Buddhism. For twelve centuries or more after the death of this great genius Indian religion flows in two parallel streams, Buddhist and Brahmanic, which subsequently unite, Buddhism colouring the whole river but ceasing within India itself to have any important manifestations distinct from Brahmanism.

In a general survey it is hardly possible to follow the order of strict chronology until comparatively modern times. We cannot, for instance, give a sketch of Indian thought in the first century B.C., simply because our data do not permit us to assign certain sects and books to that period rather than to the hundred years which preceded or followed it. But we can follow with moderate accuracy the two streams of thought in their respective courses. I have wondered if I should not take Hinduism first. Its development from ancient Brahmanism is continuous and Buddhism is merely an episode in it, though a lengthy one. But many as are the lacunæ in the history of Buddhism, it offers more data and documents than the history of Hinduism. We know more about the views of Asoka for instance than about those of Candragupta Maurya. I shall therefore deal first with Buddhism and then with Hinduism, while regretting that a parallel and synoptic treatment is impracticable.

The eight chapters of this book deal mainly with Pali Buddhism[1]—a convenient and non-controversial term—and not with the Mahayana, though they note the tendencies which

[1] Throughout this book I have not hesitated to make use of the many excellent translations of Pali works which have been published. Students of Indian religion need hardly be reminded how much our knowledge of Pali writings and of early Buddhism owes to the labours of Professor and Mrs Rhys Davids.

found expression in it. In the first chapter I treat of the Buddha's life: in the second I venture to compare him with other great religious teachers: in the third I consider his doctrine as expounded in the Pali Tripitaka and in the fourth the order of mendicants which he founded. The nature and value of the Pali Canon form the subject of the fifth chapter and the sixth is occupied with the great Emperor Asoka whose name is the clearest landmark in the early history of Buddhism, and indeed of India.

The seventh and eighth chapters discuss topics which belong to Hinduism as well as to Buddhism, namely, meditation and mythology. The latter is anterior to Buddhism and it is only in a special sense that it can be called an addition or accretion. Indian thought makes clearings in the jungle of mythology, which become obliterated or diminished as the jungle grows over them again. Buddhism was the most thorough of such clearings, yet it was invaded more rapidly and completely than any other. The Vedânta and Sânkhya are really, if less obviously, similar clearings. They raise no objection to popular divinities but such divinities do not come within the scope of religious philosophy as they understand it.

CHAPTER VIII

LIFE OF THE BUDDHA

1

We have hitherto been occupied with obscure and shadowy personalities. The authors of the Upanishads are nameless and even Mahâvîra is unknown outside India. But we now come to the career of one who must be ranked among the greatest leaders of thought that the world has seen, the Indian prince generally known as Gotama or the Buddha. His historical character has been called in question, but at the present day probably few, if any, competent judges doubt that he was a real person whose date can be fixed and whose life can be sketched at least in outline.

We have seen that apart from the personality of Gotama, ancient India was familiar with the idea of a Buddha and had even classified the attributes he should possess. Two styles of biography are therefore possible: an account of what Gotama actually was and did and an account of what a Buddha is expected to be and do. This second style prevails in later Buddhist works: they contain descriptions of the deeds and teaching of a Buddha, adapted to such facts in Gotama's life as seemed suitable for such treatment or could not be ignored. Rhys Davids has well compared them to *Paradise Regained*, but the supernatural element is, after the Indian fashion, more ornate.

The reader will perhaps ask what are the documents describing Gotama's sayings and doings and what warrant we have for trusting them. I will treat of this question in more detail in a later chapter and here will merely say that the Pali works called Vinaya or monastic rules and Suttas[1] or sermons recount the circumstances in which each rule was laid down

[1] Sanskrit Sûtra, Pali Sutta. But the use of the words is not quite the same in Buddhist and Brahmanic literature. A Buddhist sutta or sûtra is a discourse, whether in Pali or in Sanskrit; a Brahmanic sûtra is an aphorism. But the 227 divisions of the Pâtimokkha are called Suttas, so that the word may have been originally used in Pali to denote short statements of a single point. The longer Suttas are often called Suttanta.

and each sermon preached. Some narrative passages, such as the Sutta which relates the close of the Buddha's life and the portion of the Vinaya which tells how he obtained enlightenment and made his first converts, are of considerable length. Though these narratives are compilations which accepted new matter during several centuries, I see no reason to doubt that the oldest stratum contains the recollections of those who had seen and heard the master.

In basing the following account on the Pali Canon, I do not mean to discredit Sanskrit texts merely because they are written in that language or to deny that many Pali texts contain miraculous and unhistorical narratives[1]. But the principal Sanskrit Sûtras such as the Lotus and the Diamond Cutter are purely doctrinal and those texts which profess to contain historical matter, such as the Vinayas translated from Sanskrit into Chinese, are as yet hardly accessible to European scholars. So far as they are known, they add incidents to the career of the Buddha without altering its main lines, and when the accounts of such incidents are not in themselves improbable they merit consideration. On the whole these Sanskrit texts are later and more embellished than their Pali counterparts, but it is necessary not to forget the existence of this vast storehouse of traditions, which may contain many surprises[2].

Though the Pali texts do not give the story of the Buddha's life in a connected form, they do give us details about many important events in it and they offer a picture of the world in which he moved. The idea of biography was unknown to the older Indian literature. The Brâhmaṇas and Upanishads tell us of the beliefs and practices of their sages, the doctrines they taught and the sacrifices they offered, but they rarely give even an outline of their lives. And whenever the Hindus write about a man of religion or a philosopher, their weak historical sense and their strong feeling for the importance of the teaching lead them to neglect the figure of the teacher and present a portrait which seems to us dim and impersonal. Indian saints are distinguished by what they said, not by what they did and it is a strong testimony to Gotama's individuality and force of character, that in spite of the centuries

[1] *E.g.* Maj. Nik. 123 about the marvels attending the birth of a Buddha.

[2] See some further remarks on this subject at the end of chap. XIII. (on the Canon).

which separate us from him and the misty unreal atmosphere which in later times hangs round his name, his personality is more distinct and lifelike than that of many later teachers.

Most of the stories of his youth and childhood have a mythical air and make their first appearance in works composed long after his death, but there is no reason to distrust the traditional accounts of his lineage. He was the son of Suddhodana of the Kshatriya clan known as Sâkya or Sâkiya[1]. In later literature his father is usually described as a king but this statement needs qualification. The Sâkyas were a small aristocratic republic. At the time of the Buddha's birth they recognized the suzerainty of the neighbouring kingdom of Kosala or Oudh and they were subsequently annexed by it, but, so long as they were independent, all that we know of their government leads us to suppose that they were not a monarchy like Kosala and Magadha. The political and administrative business of the clan was transacted by an assembly which met in a council hall[2] at Kapilavatthu. Its president was styled Râjâ but we do not know how he was selected nor for how long he held office. The Buddha's father is sometimes spoken of as Râjâ, sometimes as if he were a simple citizen. Some scholars think the position was temporary and elective[3]. But in any case it seems clear that he was not a Mahârâja like Ajâtasattu and other monarchs of the period. He was a prominent member of a wealthy and aristocratic family rather than a despot. In some passages[4] Brahmans are represented as discussing the Buddha's claims to respect. It is said that he is of a noble and wealthy family but not that he is the son of a king or heir to the throne, though the statement, if true, would be so obvious and appropriate that its omission is sufficient to disprove it. The point is of psychological importance, for the later literature in its desire to emphasize the sacrifice made by

[1] Also Sakya or Sakka. The Sanskrit form is Śâkya.

[2] See among other passages the Ambaṭṭha Sutta of the Dîgha Nikâya in which Ambattha relates how he saw the Sâkyas, old and young, sitting on grand seats in this hall.

[3] But in Cullavagga VII. 1 Bhaddiya, a cousin of the Buddha who is described as being the Râjâ at that time, says when thinking of renouncing the world "Wait whilst I hand over the kingdom to my sons and my brothers," which seems to imply that the kingdom was a family possession. Rajja perhaps means Consulship in the Roman sense rather than kingdom.

[4] *E.g.* the Sonadaṇḍa and Kûṭadanta Suttas of the Dîgha Nikâya.

the Buddha exaggerates the splendour and luxury by which he was surrounded in youth and produces the impression that his temperament was something like that reflected in the book of Ecclesiastes, the weary calm, bred of satiety and disenchantment, of one who has possessed everything and found everything to be but vanity. But this is not the dominant note of the Buddha's discourses as we have them. He condemns the pleasures and ambitions of the world as unsatisfying, but he stands before us as one who has resisted and vanquished temptation rather than as a disillusioned pleasure-seeker. The tone of these sermons accords perfectly with the supposition, supported by whatever historical data we possess, that he belonged to a fighting aristocracy, active in war and debate, wealthy according to the standard of the times and yielding imperfect obedience to the authority of kings and priests. The Pitakas allude several times to the pride of the Sâkyas, and in spite of the gentleness and courtesy of the Buddha this family trait is often apparent in his attitude, in the independence of his views, his calm disregard of Brahmanic pretensions and the authority that marks his utterances.

The territory of the Sâkyas lay about the frontier which now divides Nepal from the United Provinces, between the upper Rapti and the Gandak rivers, a hundred miles or so to the north of Benares. The capital was called Kapilavatthu[1], and the mention of several other towns in the oldest texts indicates that the country was populous. Its wealth was derived chiefly from rice-fields and cattle. The uncultivated parts were covered with forest and often infested by robbers. The spot where the Buddha was born was known as the Lumbini Park and the site, or at least what was supposed to be the site in Asoka's time, is marked by a pillar erected by that monarch at a place now called Rummindei[2]. His mother was named Mâyâ and was also of the Sâkya clan. Tradition states that she

[1] Sanskrit Kapilavastu: red place or red earth.

[2] Tradition is unanimous that he died in his eightieth year and hitherto it has been generally supposed that this was about 487 B.C., so that he would have been born a little before 560. But Vincent Smith now thinks that he died about 543 B.C. See *J.R.A.S.* 1918, p. 547. He was certainly contemporary with kings Bimbisâra and Ajâtasattu, dying in the reign of the latter. His date therefore depends on the chronology of the Śaisunâga and Nanda dynasties, for which new data are now available.

died seven days after his birth and that he was brought up by her sister, Mahâprajâpatî, who was also a wife of Suddhodana. The names of other relatives are preserved, but otherwise the older documents tell us nothing of his childhood and the copious legends of the later church seem to be poetical embellishments. The Sutta-Nipâta contains the story of an aged seer named Asita who came to see the child and, much like Simeon, prophesied his future greatness but wept that he himself must die before hearing the new gospel.

The personal name of the Buddha was Siddhârtha in Sanskrit or Siddhattha in Pali, meaning he who has achieved his object, but it is rarely used. Persons who are introduced in the Pitakas as addressing him directly either employ a title or call him Gotama (Sanskrit Gautama). This was the name of his *gotra* or gens and roughly corresponds to a surname, being less comprehensive than the clan name Sâkya. The name Gotama is applied in the Pitakas to other Sâkyas such as the Buddha's father and his cousin Ânanda. It is said to be still in use in India and has been borne by many distinguished Hindus. But since it seemed somewhat irreverent to speak of the Buddha merely by his surname, it became the custom to describe him by titles. The most celebrated of these is the word Buddha[1] itself, the awakened or wise one. But in Pali works he is described just as frequently by the name of Bhagavâ or the Lord. The titles of Śâkya-Muni and Śâkya-Siṃha have also passed into common use and the former is his usual designation in the Sanskrit sûtras. The word Tathâgata, of somewhat obscure signification[2], is frequently found as an equivalent of Buddha and is put into the mouth of Gotama himself as a substitute for the first personal pronoun.

We can only guess what was the religious and moral atmosphere in which the child grew up. There were certainly Brahmans in the Sâkya territory: everyone had heard of their

[1] It was some time before the word came to mean definitely the Buddha. In Udâna I. 5, which is not a very early work, a number of disciples including Devadatta are described as being all *Buddhâ*.

[2] The Chinese translators render this word by Ju-lai (he who has come thus). As they were in touch with the best Indian tradition, this translation seems to prove that Tathâgata is equivalent to Tathâ-âgata not to Tathâ-gata and the meaning must be, he who has come in the proper manner: a holy man who conforms to a type and is one in a series of Buddhas or Jinas.

Vedic lore, their ceremonies and their claims to superiority. But it is probable that their influence was less complete here than further west[1] and that even before this time they encountered a good deal of scepticism and independent religious sentiment. This may have been in part military impatience of priestly pedantry, but if the Sâkyas were not submissive sheep, their waywardness was not due to want of interest in religion. A frequent phrase in the Buddha's discourses speaks of the "highest goal of the holy life for the sake of which clansmen leave their homes and go forth into homelessness." The religious mendicant seemed the proper incarnation of this ideal to which Kshatriyas as well as Brahmans aspired, and we are justified in supposing that the future Buddha's thoughts would naturally turn towards the wandering life. The legend represents him as carefully secluded from all disquieting sights and as learning the existence of old age, sickness and death only by chance encounters which left a profound impression. The older texts do not emphasize this view of his mental development, though they do not preclude it. It is stated incidentally that his parents regretted his abandonment of worldly life and it is natural to suppose that they may have tried to turn his mind to secular interests and pleasures[2]. His son, Râhula, is mentioned several times in the Pitakas but his wife only once and then not by name but as "the princess who was the mother of Râhula[3]." His separation from her becomes in the later legend the theme of an affecting tale but the scanty allusions to his family found in the Pitakas are devoid of sentimental touches. A remarkable passage is preserved in the Anguttara Nikâya[4] describing his feelings as a young man and may be the origin of the story[5] about the four visions of old age, sickness, death and of peace in the religious life. After describing the wealth and comfort in which he lived[6], he says that he reflected how people feel

[1] See the article on the neighbouring country of Magadha in Macdonell and Keith's *Vedic Index*.

[2] Cf. the Ratthapâla-sutta.

[3] Mahâv. I. 54. 1.

[4] Devadûtavagga. Ang. Nik. III. 35.

[5] But the story is found in the Mahâpadâna-sutta. See also Winternitz, *J.R.A.S.* 1911, p. 1146.

[6] He mentions that he had three palaces or houses, for the hot, cold and rainy seasons respectively, but this is not necessarily regal for the same words are used of Yasa, the son of a Treasurer (Mahâv. 1. 7. 1) and Anuruddha, a Sâkyan noble (Cullav. VII. 1. 1).

repulsion and disgust at the sight of old age, sickness and death. But is this right? "I also" he thought "am subject to decay and am not free from the power of old age, sickness and death. Is it right that I should feel horror, repulsion and disgust when I see another in such plight? And when I reflected thus, my disciples, all the joy of life which there is in life died within me."

No connected account of his renunciation of the world has been found in the Pitakas but[1] people are represented as saying that in spite of his parents' grief he "went out from the household life into the homeless state" while still a young man. Accepted tradition, confirmed by the Mahâparinibbâna Sutta, says that he retired from worldly life when he was twenty-nine years old. The event is also commemorated in a poem of the Sutta-Nipâta[2] which reads like a very ancient ballad.

It relates how Bimbisâra, King of Magadha, looking out from his palace, saw an unknown ascetic, and feeling he was no ordinary person went himself to visit him. It would appear from this that Gotama on leaving his family went down to the plains and visited Râjagaha, the capital of Magadha, now Rajgîr to the south of Patna. The teachers of the Ganges valley had probably a greater reputation for learning and sanctity than the rough wits of the Sâkya land and this may have attracted Gotama. At any rate he applied himself diligently to acquire what knowledge could be learned from contemporary teachers of religion. We have an account put into his own mouth[3] of his experiences as the pupil of Alâra Kâlâma and Uddaka Râmaputta but it gives few details of his studies. It would appear however that they both had a fixed system (dhamma) to impart and that their students lived in religious discipline (vinaya) as members of an Order. They were therefore doing exactly what the Buddha himself did later on a larger scale and with more conspicuous success. The instruction, we gather, was oral. Gotama assimilated it thoroughly and rapidly but was dissatisfied because he found that it did not conduce to perfect knowledge and salvation[4]. He evidently

[1] In the Sonadaṇḍa-sutta and elsewhere.

[2] The Pabbajjâ-sutta.

[3] Maj. Nik. Ariyapariyesana-sutta. It is found in substantially the same form in the Mahâsaccaka-sutta and the Bodhirâjakumâra-sutta.

[4] The teaching of Alâra Kâlâma led to rebirth in the sphere called akiñcaññâyatanam or the sphere in which nothing at all is specially present to the mind

accepted his teachers' general ideas about belief and conduct—a dhamma, a vinaya, and the practice of meditation—but rejected the content of their teaching as inadequate. So he went away.

The European mystic knows the dangers of Quietism[1]. When Molinos and other quietists praise the Interior Silence in which the soul neither speaks nor desires nor thinks, they suggest that the suspension of all mental activity is good in itself. But more robust seekers hold that this "orison of quiet" is merely a state of preparation, not the end of the quest, and valuable merely because the soul recuperates therein and is ready for further action. Some doctrine akin to that of the quietists seems to underlie the mysterious old phrases in which the Buddha's two teachers tried to explain their trances, and he left them for much the same reasons as led the Church to condemn Quietism. He did not say that the trances are bad; indeed he represented them as productive of happiness[2] in a sense which Europeans can hardly follow. But he clearly refused to admit that they were the proper end of the religious life. He felt there was something better and he set out to find it.

The interval between his abandonment of the world and his enlightenment is traditionally estimated at seven years and this accords with our other data. But we are not told how long he remained with his two teachers nor where they lived. He says however that after leaving them he wandered up and down the land of Magadha, so that their residence was probably in or near that district[3]. He settled at a place called Uruvelâ. "There" he says "I thought to myself, truly this is a pleasant spot and a beautiful forest. Clear flows the river and pleasant are the bathing places: all around are meadows and villages." Here he determined to devote himself to the severest forms of asceticism. The place is in the neighbourhood of Bodh-Gaya, near the river now called Phalgu or Lilañja but formerly

and that of Uddaka Râmaputta to rebirth in the sphere where neither any idea nor the absence of any idea is specially present to the mind. These expressions occur elsewhere (*e.g.* in the Mahâparinibbâṇa-sutta) as names of stages in meditation or of incorporeal worlds (arûpabrahmâloka) where those states prevail. Some mysterious utterances of Uddaka are preserved in Sam. Nik. xxxv. 103.

[1] Underhill, *Introd. to Mysticism*, p. 387.

[2] Sam. Nik. xxxvi. 19.

[3] The Lalita Vistara says Alâra lived at Vesâlî and Uddaka in Magadha.

Nerañjara. The fertile fields and gardens, the flights of steps and temples are modern additions but the trees and the river still give the sense of repose and inspiration which Gotama felt, an influence alike calming to the senses and stimulating to the mind. Buddhism, though in theory setting no value on the pleasures of the eye, is not in practice disdainful of beauty, as witness the many allusions to the Buddha's personal appearance, the persistent love of art, and the equally persistent love of nature which is found in such early poems as the Theragâthâ and still inspires those who select the sites of monasteries throughout the Buddhist world from Burma to Japan. The example of the Buddha, if we may believe the story, shows that he felt the importance of scenery and climate in the struggle before him and his followers still hold that a holy life is led most easily in beautiful and peaceful landscapes.

2

Hitherto we have found allusions to the events of the Buddha's life rather than consecutive statements and narratives but for the next period, comprising his struggle for enlightenment, its attainment and the commencement of his career as a teacher, we have several accounts, both discourses put into his own mouth and narratives in the third person like the beginning of the Mahâvagga. It evidently was felt that this was the most interesting and critical period of his life and for it, as for the period immediately preceding his death, the Piṭakas provide the elements of a biography. The accounts vary as to the amount of detail and supernatural events which they contain, but though the simplest is perhaps the oldest, it does not follow that events consistent with it but only found in other versions are untrue. One cannot argue that anyone recounting his spiritual experiences is bound to give a biographically complete picture. He may recount only what is relevant to the purpose of his discourse.

Gotama's ascetic life at Uruvelâ is known as the wrestling or struggle for truth. The story, as he tells it in the Piṭakas, gives no dates, but is impressive in its intensity and insistent iteration[1]. Fire, he thought to himself, cannot be produced

[1] The following account is based on Maj. Nik. suttas 85 and 26. Compare the beginning of the Mahâvagga of the Vinaya.

from damp wood by friction, but it can from dry wood. Even so must the body be purged of its humours to make it a fit receptacle for illumination and knowledge. So he began a series of terrible fasts and sat "with set teeth and tongue pressed against the palate" until in this spiritual wrestling the sweat poured down from his arm pits. Then he applied himself to meditation accompanied by complete cessation of breathing, and, as he persevered and went from stage to stage of this painful exercise, he heard the blood rushing in his head and felt as if his skull was being split, as if his belly were being cut open with a butcher's knife, and finally as if he were thrown into a pit of burning coals. Elsewhere[1] he gives further details of the horrible penances which he inflicted on himself. He gradually reduced his food to a grain of rice each day. He lived on seeds and grass, and for one period literally on dung. He wore haircloth or other irritating clothes: he plucked out his hair and beard: he stood continuously: he lay upon thorns. He let the dust and dirt accumulate till his body looked like an old tree. He frequented a cemetery—that is a place where corpses were thrown to decay or be eaten by birds and beasts—and lay among the rotting bodies.

But no enlightenment, no glimpse into the riddle of the world came of all this, so, although he was nearly at death's door, he determined to abstain from food altogether. But spirits appeared and dissuaded him, saying that if he attempted thus to kill himself they would nourish him by infusing a celestial elixir through his skin and he reflected that he might as well take a little food[2]. So he took a palmful or two of bean soup. He was worn almost to a shadow, he says. "When I touched my belly, I felt my backbone through it and when I touched my back, I felt my belly—so near had my back and my belly come together through this fasting. And when I rubbed my limbs to refresh them the hair fell off[3]." Then he

[1] Maj. Nik. 12. See too Dig. Nik. 8.

[2] If this discourse is regarded as giving in substance Gotama's own version of his experiences, it need not be supposed to mean much more than that his good angel (in European language) bade him not take his own life. But the argument represented as appealing to him was that if spirits sustained him with supernatural nourishment, entire abstinence from food would be a useless pretence.

[3] The remarkable figures known as "fasting Buddhas" in Lahore Museum and elsewhere represent Gotama in this condition and show very plainly the falling in of the belly.

reflected that he had reached the limit of self-mortification and yet attained no enlightenment. There must be another way to knowledge. And he remembered how once in his youth he had sat in the shade of a rose apple tree and entered into the stage of contemplation known as the first rapture. That, he now thought, must be the way to enlightenment: why be afraid of such bliss? But to attain it, he must have more strength and to get strength he must eat. So he ate some rice porridge. There were five monks living near him, hoping that when he found the Truth he would tell it to them. But when they saw that he had begun to take food, their faith failed and they went away.

The Buddha then relates how, having taken food, he began to meditate and passed through four stages of contemplation, culminating in pure self-possession and equanimity, free alike from all feeling of pain or ease. Such meditation was nothing miraculous but supposed to be within the power of any trained ascetic. Then there arose before him a vision of his previous births, the hundreds of thousands of existences with all their details of name, family and caste through which he had passed. This was succeeded by a second and wider vision in which he saw the whole universe as a system of karma and reincarnation, composed of beings noble or mean, happy or unhappy, continually "passing away according to their deeds," leaving one form of existence and taking shape in another. Finally, he understood the nature of error[1] and of suffering, the cessation of suffering and the path that leads to the cessation of suffering. "In me thus set free the knowledge of freedom arose and I knew 'Rebirth has been destroyed, the higher life has been led; what had to be done has been done, I have no more to do with this world[2].' This third knowledge came to me in the last watch of the night: ignorance was destroyed, knowledge had arisen, darkness was destroyed, light had arisen, as I sat there earnest, strenuous, resolute[3]."

[1] Âsava. The word appears to mean literally an intoxicating essence. See *e.g.* Vinaya, vol. IV. p. 110 (Rhys Davids and Oldenburg's ed.). Cf. the use of the word in Sanskrit.

[2] Nâparam itthattâyâti. Itthattam is a substantive formed from ittham thus. It was at this time too that he thought out the chain of causation.

[3] Tradition states that it was on this occasion that he uttered the well-known stanzas now found in the Dhammapada 154–5 (cf. Theragâthâ 183) in which he

On attaining enlightenment he at first despaired of preaching the truth to others. He reflected that his doctrine was abstruse and that mankind are given over to their desires. How can such men understand the chain of cause and effect or teaching about Nirvana and the annihilation of desire? So he determined to remain quiet and not to preach. Then the deity Brahmâ Sahampati appeared before him and besought him to preach the Truth, pleading that some men could understand. The Buddha surveyed the world with his mind's eye and saw the different natures of mankind. "As in a pool of lotuses, blue, red or white, some lotuses born in the water, grown up in the water, do not rise above the water but thrive hidden under the water and other lotuses, blue, red or white, born in the water, grown up in the water, reach to the surface: and other lotuses, blue, red or white, born in the water, grown up in the water, stand up out of the water and the water does not touch them." Thus did he perceive the world to be and he said to Brahmâ "The doors of immortality are open. Let them that have ears to hear, show faith."

Then he began to wonder to whom he should first preach his doctrine, and he thought of his former teachers. But a spirit warned him that they had recently died. Then he thought of the five monks who had tended him during his austerities but left him when he ceased to fast. By his superhuman power of vision he perceived that they were living at Benares in the deer park, Isipatana. So, after remaining awhile at Uruvelâ he started to find them and on the way met a naked ascetic, in answer to whose enquiries he proclaimed himself as the Buddha; "I am the Holy One in this world, I am the highest teacher, I alone am the perfect supreme Buddha, I have gained calm and nirvana, I go to Benares to set moving the wheels of righteousness[1]. I will beat the drum of immortality in the darkness of this world." But the ascetic replied. "It may be

exults in having, after long search in repeated births, found the maker of the house. "Now, O maker of the house thou art seen: no more shalt thou make a house." The lines which follow are hard to translate. The ridge-pole of the house has been destroyed (visankhitaṃ more literally de-com-posed) and so the mind passes beyond the sankhâras (visankhâragataṃ). The play of words in visankhitaṃ and visankhâra can hardly be rendered in English.

[1] As Rhys Davids observes, this expression means "to found the Kingdom of Righteousness" but the metaphor is to make the wheels of the chariot of righteous ness move unopposed over all the Earth.

so, friend," shook his head, took another road and went away, with the honour of being the first sceptic.

When the Buddha reached the deer park[1], a wood where ascetics were allowed to dwell and animals might not be killed, the five monks saw him coming and determined not to salute him since he had given up his exertions, and turned to a luxurious life. But as he drew near they were overawed and in spite of their resolution advanced to meet him, and brought water to wash his feet. While showing him this honour they called him Friend Gotama but he replied that it was not proper to address the Tathâgata[2] thus. He had become a Buddha and was ready to teach them the Truth but the monks demurred saying that if he had been unable to win enlightenment while practising austerities, he was not likely to have found it now that he was living a life of ease. But he overcame their doubts and proceeded to instruct them, apparently during some days, for we are told that they went out to beg alms.

Can this account be regarded as in any sense historical, as being not perhaps the Buddha's own words but the reminiscences of some one who had heard him describe the crisis of his life? Like so much of the Pitakas the narrative has an air of patchwork. Many striking passages, such as the descriptions of the raptures through which he passed, occur in other connections but the formulæ are ancient and their use here may be as early and legitimate as elsewhere. In its main outlines the account is simple, unpretentious and human. Gotama seeks to obtain enlightenment by self-mortification: finds that this is the wrong way: tries a more natural method and succeeds: debates whether he shall become a teacher and at first hesitates. These are not features which the average Indian hagiographer, anxious to prove his hero omnipotent and omniscient, would invent or emphasize. Towards the end of the narrative the language is more majestic and the compiler introduces several stanzas, but though it is hardly likely that Gotama would have used these stanzas in telling his own story, they may be ancient and in substance authentic. The supernatural intervention recorded is not really great. It amounts to this, that in mental crises the Buddha received warnings somewhat similar to those

[1] At the modern Sarnath.

[2] It is from this point that he begins to use this title in speaking of himself.

delivered by the dæmon of Socrates[1]. The appearance of Brahmâ Sahampati is related with more detail and largely in verse, which suggests that the compiler may have inserted some legend which he found ready to hand, but on the whole I am inclined to believe that in this narrative we have a tradition not separated from the Buddha by many generations and going back to those who had themselves heard him describe his wrestling to obtain the Truth and his victory.

Other versions of the enlightenment give other incidents which are not rendered less credible by their omission from the narrative quoted, for it is clearly an epitome put together for a special didactic purpose. But still the story as related at the beginning of the Mahâvagga of the Vinaya has a stronger smack of mythology than the passages quoted from the Sutta-Pitaka. In these last the Bodhi-tree[2] is mentioned only incidentally, which is natural, for it is a detail which would impress later piety rather than the Buddha himself. But there is no reason to be sceptical as to the part it has played in Buddhist history. Even if we had not been told that he sat under a tree, we might surmise that he did so, for to sit under a tree or in a cave was the only alternative for a homeless ascetic. The Mahâvagga states that after attaining Buddhahood he sat crosslegged at the foot of the tree for seven days uninterruptedly, enjoying the bliss of emancipation, and while there thought out the chain of causation which is only alluded to in the suttas quoted above. He also sat under three other trees, seven days under each. Heavy rain came on but Mucalinda, the king of the serpents, "came out of his abode and seven times encircled the body of the Lord with his windings and spread his great hood over the Lord's head." Here we are in the domain of mythology: this is not a vignette from the old religious life on the banks of the Nerañjara but a work of sacred art: the Holy Supreme Buddha sitting immovable and imperturbable in the midst of a storm sheltered by the folds of some pious monster that the artist's fancy has created.

[1] Similar heavenly messages were often received by Christian mystics and were probably true as subjective experiences. Thus Suso was visited one Whitsunday by a heavenly messenger who bade him cease his mortifications.

[2] It is the Pipal tree or Ficus religiosa, as is mentioned in the Dîgha Nikâya, XIV. 30, not the Banyan. Its leaves have long points and tremble continually. Popular fancy says this is in memory of the tremendous struggle which they witnessed.

The narrative quoted from the Majjhima-Nikâya does not mention that the Buddha during his struggle for enlightenment was assailed or tempted by Mâra, the personification of evil and of transitory pleasures but also of death. But that such an encounter—in some respects analogous to the temptation of Christ by the Devil—formed part of the old tradition is indicated by several passages in the Pitakas[1] and not merely by the later literature where it assumes a prominent and picturesque form. This struggle is psychologically probable enough but the origin of the story, which is exhaustively discussed in Windisch's *Buddha und Mâra*, seems to lie not so much in any account which the Buddha may have given of his mental struggles as in amplifications of old legends and in dramatizations of metaphors which he may have used about conquering death.

The Bodhi-tree is still shown at Bodh-Gaya. It stands on a low terrace behind the temple, the whole lying in a hollow, below the level of the surrounding modern buildings, and still attracts many pilgrims from all Buddhist lands though perhaps not so many as the tree at Anuradhapura in Ceylon, which is said to be sprung from one of its branches transplanted thither. Whatever title it may have to the reverence of the faithful rests on lineage rather than identity, for the growth which we see at Bodh-Gaya now cannot claim to be the branches under which the Buddha sat or even the trunk which Asoka tended. At best it is a modern stem sprung from the seeds of the old tree, and this descent is rendered disputable by legends of its destruction and miraculous restoration. Even during the time that Sir A. Cunningham knew the locality from 1862 to 1880 it would seem that the old trunk decayed and was replaced by scions grown from seed.

The texts quoted above leave the Buddha occupied in teaching the five monks in the Deer Park and the Mahâvagga gives us the text of the sermon[2] with which he opened his instruction. It is entitled Turning the Wheel of Righteousness, and is also known as The Sermon at Benares. It is a very early statement of the main doctrines of primitive Buddhism and I see no reason to doubt that it contains the ideas and phrases

[1] Such are the Padhâna-sutta of the Sutta-Nipâta which has an air of antiquity and the tales in the Mahâvagga of the Saṃyutta-Nikâya. The Mahâvagga of the Vinaya (I. 11 and 13) mentions such an encounter but places it considerably later after the conversion of the five monks and of Yasa.

[2] The text is also found in the Saṃyutta-Nikâya.

of the Buddha. The gist of the sermon is extremely simple. He first says that those who wish to lead a religious life should avoid the two extremes of self-indulgence and self-torture and follow a middle way. Then he enunciates what he calls the four truths[1] about evil or suffering and the way to make an end of it. He opens very practically, and it may be noticed that abstruse as are many of his discourses they generally go straight to the heart of some contemporary interest. Here he says that self-indulgence is low and self-mortification crazy: that both are profitless and neither is the religious life. That consists in walking in the middle path, or noble eightfold path defined in a celebrated formula as right views, right aspirations, right speech, right conduct, right livelihood, right effort, right mindfulness, right rapture. He then enunciates the four truths. The first declares that all clinging to existence involves suffering. I shall have occasion to examine later the pessimism which is often said to characterize Buddhism and Indian thought generally. Here let it suffice to say that the first truth must be taken in conjunction with the others. The teaching of the Buddha is a teaching not so much of pessimism as of emancipation: but emancipation implies the existence of evil from which men must be freed: a happy world would not need it. Buddhism recognizes the evil of the world but it is not on that account a religion of despair: the essence of it is that it provides a remedy and an escape.

The second and third truths must be taken together and in connection with the formula known as the chain of causation (paṭiccasamuppâda). Everything has a cause and produces an effect. If this is, that is: if this is not, then that is not. This simple principle of uniform causation is applied to the whole universe, gods and men, heaven, earth and hell. Indian thought has always loved wide applications of fundamental principles and here a law of the universe is propounded in a form both simple and abstract. Everything exists in virtue of a cause and does not exist if that cause is absent. Suffering has a cause and if that cause can be detected and eliminated, suffering itself will be eliminated. This cause of evil is Tanhâ, the thirst or craving for existence, pleasure and success. And the cure is to remove it. It may seem to the European that this is a

[1] Concisely stated as suffering, the cause of suffering, the suppression of suffering and the method of effecting that suppression.

proposal to cure the evils of life by removing life itself but when in the fourth truth we come to the course to be followed by the seeker after salvation—the eightfold path—we find it neither extravagant nor morbid. We may imagine that an Indian of that time asking different schools of thinkers for the way to salvation would have been told by Brahmans (if indeed they had been willing to impart knowledge to any but an accredited pupil) that he who performs a certain ceremony goes to the abode of the gods: other teachers would have insisted on a course of fasting and self-torture: others again like Sâñjaya and Makkhali would have given argumentative and unpractical answers. The Buddha's answer is simple and practical: seven-eighths of it would be accepted in every civilized country as a description of the good life. It is not merely external, for it insists on right thought and right aspiration: the motive and temper are as important as the act. It does not neglect will-power and activity, for right action, right livelihood and right effort are necessary—a point to be remembered when Buddhism is called a dreamy unpractical religion. But no doubt the last stage of the path, right rapture or right meditation, is meant to be its crown and fulfilment. It takes the place of prayer and communion with the deity and the Buddha promises the beatific vision in this life to those who persevere. The negative features of the Path are also important. It contains no mention of ceremonial, austerities, gods, many or one, nor of the Buddha himself. He is the discoverer and teacher of the truth; beyond that his personality plays no part.

But we are here treating of his life rather than of his doctrine and must now return to the events which are said to have followed the first sermon.

The first converts had, even before embracing the Buddha's teaching, been followers of a religious life but the next batch of recruits came from the wealthy mercantile families of Benares. The first was a youth named Yasa who joined the order, while his father, mother and former wife became lay believers. Then came first four and subsequently fifty friends of Yasa and joined the order. "At that time" says the Mahâvagga "there were sixty-one Arhats[1] in the world," so that at

[1] Writers on Buddhism use this word in various forms, arhat, arahat and arahant. Perhaps it is best to use the Sanskrit form arhat just as karma and nirvana are commonly used instead of the Pali equivalents.

first arhatship seems to have followed immediately on ordination. Arhat, it may be mentioned, is the commonest word in early Buddhist literature (more common than any phrase about nirvana) for describing sanctity and spiritual perfection. The arhat is one who has broken the fetters of the senses and passions, for whom there will be no new birth or death, and who lives in this world like the Buddha, detached but happy and beneficent.

The Buddha then addressed his followers and said—"Monks, I am delivered from all fetters, human and divine, and so are you. Go now and wander for the gain of many, for the welfare of many, out of compassion for the world, for the good, for the gain and for the welfare of gods and men. Let not two of you go the same way. Preach the doctrine which is glorious in the beginning, glorious in the middle and glorious in the end, in the spirit and in the letter; proclaim a consummate, perfect and pure life of holiness." The monks then went forth and returned bringing candidates to be formally ordained by the Buddha. But seeing that these journeys caused fatigue and trouble, he authorized the ordained monks to confer ordination without reference to himself. He then returned to Uruvelâ, where he had dwelt before attaining Buddhahood, and converted a thousand Jaṭilas, that is to say Brahmans living the life of hermits, which involved the abandonment of household life but not of sacrifices. The admission of these hermits to the order is probably historical and explains the presence among the Buddha's disciples of a tendency towards self-mortification of which he himself did not wholly approve. The Mahâvagga[1] contains a series of short legends about these occurrences, one of them in two versions. The narratives are miraculous but have an ancient tone and probably represent the type of popular story current about the Buddha shortly after or even during his life. One of them is a not uncommon subject in Buddhist art. It relates how the chamber in which a Brahman called Kassapa kept his sacred fire was haunted by a fire-breathing magical serpent. The Buddha however spent the night in this chamber and after a contest in which both emitted flames succeeded in conquering the beast. After converting the Jaṭilas he preached to them the celebrated Fire Sermon, said to

[1] I. 15–20.

have been delivered on the eminence now called Brahma Yoen[1] near Gaya and possibly inspired by the spectacle of grass fires which at some seasons may be seen creeping over every hill-side in an Indian night. "Everything, Monks, is burning and how is it burning? The eye is burning: what the eye sees is burning: thoughts based on the eye are burning: the contact of the eye (with visible things) is burning and the sensation produced by that contact, whether pleasant, painful or indifferent is also burning. With what fire is it burning? It is burning with the fire of lust, the fire of anger, with the fire of ignorance; it is burning with the sorrows of birth, decay, death, grief, lamentation, suffering, dejection and despair."

The Buddha now went on with his converts to Râjagaha. He stopped in a bamboo grove outside the town and here the king, Bimbisâra, waited on him and with every sign of respect asked him to take food in his palace. It was on this occasion that we first hear of him accepting an invitation to dinner[2], which he did frequently during the rest of his career. After the repast the king presented a pleasure garden just outside the town "to the fraternity of monks with the Buddha at their head." At that time another celebrated teacher named Sâñjaya was stopping at Râjagaha with a train of two hundred and fifty disciples. Two of them, Sâriputta and Moggallâna, joined the Buddha's order and took with them the whole body of their companions.

The Mahâvagga proceeds to relate that many of the young nobility joined the order and that the people began to murmur saying "The Monk Gotama causes fathers to beget no sons and families to become extinct." And again "The Great Monk has come to Giribbaja of the Magadha people, leading with him all the followers of Sâñjaya. Whom will he lead off next?" When this was told to the Buddha he replied that the excitement would only last seven days and bade his followers answer with the following verse "It is by the true doctrine that the great heroes, the Buddhas, lead men. Who will murmur at the wise who lead men by the power of truth?" It is possible, as Oldenburg suggests, that we have here two popular couplets which were really bandied between the friends and enemies of the Buddha.

[1] Brahmayoni. I make this suggestion about grass fires because I have myself watched them from this point.

[2] This meal, the only solid one in the day, was taken a little before midday.

3

It now becomes difficult to give dates but the Mahâvagga[1] relates that the Buddha stopped some time at Râjagaha and then revisited his native town, Kapilavatthu. That he should have done so is natural enough but there is little trace of sentiment in the narrative of the Vinaya. Its object is to state the occasion on which the Buddha laid down the rules of the order. Irrelevant incidents are ignored and those which are noticed are regarded simply as the circumstances which led to the formulation of certain regulations. "The Lord dwelt in the Sakka country near Kapilavatthu in the Banyan Grove. And in the forenoon having put on his robes and taken his alms bowl he went to the home of the Sakka Suddhodana[2] and sat down on a seat prepared for him. Then the princess who was the mother of Râhula[3] said to him 'This is your father, Râhula, go and ask him for your inheritance.' Then young Râhula went to the place where the Lord was, and standing before him said 'Your shadow, Monk, is a place of bliss.' Then the Lord rose from his seat and went away but Râhula followed him saying 'Give me my inheritance, Monk.' Then the Lord said to Sâriputta (who had already become his chief disciple) 'Well, Sâriputta, confer the preliminary ordination on young Râhula.' Sâriputta asked how he should do so and the Buddha explained the forms.

"Then the Sakka Suddhodana went to the place where the Lord was and after respectfully saluting him asked for a boon. 'Lord, when the Blessed One gave up the world, it was great pain to me and so it was when Nanda[4] did the same. Great too was my pain when Râhula did it. The love for a son, Lord, cuts into the skin, the flesh, the bones, and reaches the marrow. Let not the preliminary ordination be conferred on a son without his parents' permission.' The Buddha assented. Three or four years later Suddhodana died."

From Kapilavatthu the Buddha is said to have gone to Sâvatthî, the capital of Kosala where Pasenadi was king, but now we lose the chronological thread and do not find it again

[1] I. 53–54.
[2] His father.
[3] *I.e.* the Buddha's former wife.
[4] Half brother of the Buddha and Suddhodana's son by Mahâprajâpatî.

until the last years of his life. Few of the numerous incidents recorded in the Pitakas can be dated. The narrators resemble those Indian artists who when carving a story in relief place all the principal figures in one panel without attempting to mark the sequence of the incidents which are represented simultaneously. For the connection of events with the Buddha's teaching the compilers of the Pitakas had an eye; for their connection with his life none at all. And though this attitude is disquieting to the historic sense it is not unjustifiable. The object and the achievement of the Buddha was to preach a certain doctrine and to found an order. All the rest—years and countries, pains and pleasures—was of no importance. And it would appear that we have not lost much: we should have a greater sense of security if we had an orderly account of his wanderings and his relations with the kings of his time, but after he had once entered on his ministry the events which broke the peaceful tenour of his long life were few and we probably know most of them though we cannot date them. For about forty-five years he moved about Kosala, Magadha and Anga visiting the two capitals Sâvatthî and Râjagaha and going as far west as the country of the Kurus. He took little part in politics or worldly life, though a hazy but not improbable story[1] represents him as pacifying the Sâkyas and Koliyas, who were on the point of fighting about the water of the Rohini which irrigated the lands of both clans. He uniformly enjoyed the respect and attention of kings and the wealthy classes. Doubtless he was not popular with the Brahmans or with those good people who disliked seeing fine young men made into monks. But it does not appear that his teaching provoked any serious tumults or that he was troubled by anything but schism within the order. We have, if not a history, at least a picture of a life which though peaceful was active and benevolent but aloof, majestic and authoritative.

We are told[2] that at first his disciples wandered about at all seasons but it was not long before he bade them observe the already established routine for itinerant monks of travelling on foot during the greater part of the year but of resting for three months during the rainy season known as Vassa and beginning some time in June. When moving about he appears to have

[1] Jâtaka, 356.

[2] Mahâvag. III. 1.

walked from five to ten miles a day, regulating his movements so as to reach inhabited places in time to collect food for the midday meal. The afternoon he devoted to meditation and in the evening gave instruction. He usually halted in woods or gardens on the outskirts of villages and cities, and often on the bank of a river or tank, for shade and water would be the first requisites for a wandering monk. On these journeys he was accompanied by a considerable following of disciples: five hundred or twelve hundred and fifty are often mentioned and though the numbers may be exaggerated there is no reason to doubt that the band was large. The suttas generally commence with a picture of the surroundings in which the discourse recorded was delivered. The Buddha is walking along the high road from Râjagaha to Nâlanda with a great company of disciples. Or he is journeying through Kosala and halting in a mango-grove on the banks of the Aciravatî river. Or he is stopping in a wood outside a Brahman village and the people go out to him. The principal Brahmans, taking their siesta on the upper terraces of their houses, see the crowd and ask their doorkeepers what it means. On hearing the cause they debate whether they or the Buddha should pay the first call and ultimately visit him. Or he is halting on the shore of the Gaggarâ Lake at Campâ in Western Bengal, sitting under the fragrant white flowers of a campaka tree. Or he visits the hills overlooking Râjagaha haunted by peacocks and by wandering monks. Often he stops in buildings described as halls, which were sometimes merely rest houses for travellers. But it became more and more the custom for the devout to erect such buildings for his special use and even in his lifetime they assumed the proportions of monasteries[1]. The people of Vesâlî built one in a wood to the north of their city known as the Gabled Hall. It was a storied house having on the ground floor a large room surrounded by pillars and above it the private apartments of the Buddha. Such private rooms (especially those which he occupied at Sâvatthî), were called Gandhakûṭî or the perfumed chamber. At Kapilavatthu[2] the Sâkyas erected a new building known as Santhagâra. The Buddha was asked to inaugurate it

[1] Thus we hear how Dasama of Atthakam (Maj. Nik. 52) built one for fifteen hundred monks, and Ghotamukha another in Pataliputta, which bore his name.

[2] Maj. Nik. 53.

and did so by a discourse lasting late into the night which he delivered sitting with his back against a pillar. At last he said his back was tired and lay down, leaving Ânanda to continue the edification of the congregation who were apparently less exhausted than the preacher.

But perhaps the residence most frequently mentioned is that in the garden called Jetavana at Sâvatthî. Anâthapiṇḍika, a rich merchant of that town, was converted by the Buddha when staying at Râjagaha and invited him to spend the next rainy season at Sâvatthî[1]. On returning to his native town to look for a suitable place, he decided that the garden of the Prince Jeta best satisfied his requirements. He obtained it only after much negotiation for a sum sufficient to cover the whole ground with coins. When all except a small space close to the gateway had been thus covered Jeta asked to be allowed to share in the gift and on receiving permission erected on the vacant spot a gateway with a room over it. "And Anâthapiṇḍika the householder built dwelling rooms and retiring rooms and storerooms and halls with fireplaces, and outside storehouses and closets and cloisters and halls attached to the bath rooms and ponds and roofed open sheds[2]."

Buddhaghosa has given an account[3] of the way in which the Buddha was wont to spend his days when stopping in some such resting-place, and his description is confirmed by the numerous details given in the Pitakas. He rose before dawn and would often retire and meditate until it was time to set out on the round for alms but not unfrequently he is represented as thinking that it was too early to start and that he might first visit some monk of the neighbourhood. Then he went round the town or village with his disciples, carrying his almsbowl and accepting everything put into it. Sometimes he talked to his disciples while walking[4]. Frequently, instead of begging for alms, he accepted an invitation to dine with some pious person who asked the whole band of disciples and made strenuous culinary efforts. Such invitations were given at the conclusion of a visit paid to the Buddha on the previous day and were

[1] Cullavag. VI. 4.

[2] Probably sheds consisting of a roof set on posts, but without walls.

[3] Translated by Rhys Davids, *American Lectures*, pp. 108 ff.

[4] *E.g.* Maj. Nik. 62.

accepted by him with silence which signified consent. On the morning of the next day the host announced in person or through a messenger that the meal was ready and the Buddha taking his mantle and bowl went to the house. The host waited on the guests with his own hands, putting the food which he had prepared into their bowls. After the repast the Buddha delivered a discourse or catechized the company. He did the same with his own disciples when he collected food himself and returned home to eat it. He took but one meal a day[1], between eleven and twelve, and did not refuse meat when given to him, provided that he did not know the animals had been slaughtered expressly for his food. When he had given instruction after the meal he usually retired to his chamber or to a quiet spot under trees for repose and meditation. On one occasion[2] he took his son Râhula with him into a wood at this hour to impart some of the deepest truths to him, but as a rule he gave no further instruction until the late afternoon.

The Pitakas represent all believers as treating the Buddha with the greatest respect but the salutations and titles which they employ hardly exceed those ordinarily used in speaking to eminent persons[3]. Kings were at this time addressed as Deva, whereas the Buddha's usual title is Bhagavâ or Bhante, Lord. A religious solemnity and deliberation prevails in the interviews which he grants but no extravagance of adoration is recorded. Visitors salute him by bowing with joined hands, sit respectfully on one side while he instructs them and in departing are careful to leave him on their right hand. He accepts such gifts as food, clothes, gardens and houses but rejects all ceremonial honours. Thus Prince Bodhi[4] when receiving him carpeted his mansion with white cloths but the Buddha would not walk on them and remained standing at the entrance till they were taken up.

The introduction to the Ariyapariyesana-Sutta gives a fairly complete picture of a day in his life at Sâvatthî. It relates how

[1] But in Maj. Nik. II. 5 he says he is not bound by rules as to eating.

[2] Maj. Nik. 147.

[3] In an exceedingly curious passage (Dig. Nik. IV.) the Brahman Sonadaṇḍa, while accepting the Buddha's teaching, asks to be excused from showing the Buddha such extreme marks of respect as rising from his seat or dismounting from his chariot, on the ground that his reputation would suffer. He proposes and apparently is allowed to substitute less demonstrative salutations.

[4] Cullavagga V. 21 and Maj. Nik. 85.

in the morning he took his bowl and mantle and went to the town to collect food. While he was away, some monks told his personal attendant Ânanda that they wished to hear a discourse from him, as it was long since they had had the privilege. Ânanda suggested that they had better go to the hermitage of the Brahman Rammaka near the town. The Buddha returned, ate his meal and then said "Come, Ânanda, let us go to the terrace of Migâra's mother[1] and stay there till evening." They went there and spent the day in meditation. Towards evening the Buddha rose and said "Let us go to the old bath to refresh our limbs." After they had bathed, Ânanda suggested that they should go to Rammaka's hermitage: the Buddha assented by his silence and they went together. Within the hermitage were many monks engaged in instructive conversation, so the Buddha waited at the door till there was a pause in the talk. Then he coughed and knocked. The monks opened the door, and offered him a seat. After a short conversation, he recounted to them how he had striven for and obtained Buddhahood.

These congregations were often prolonged late into the night. We hear for instance how he sat on the terrace belonging to Migâra's mother[2] in the midst of an assembly of monks waiting for his words, still and silent in the light of the full moon; how a monk would rise, adjusting his robe so as to leave one shoulder bare, bow with his hands joined and raised to his forehead and ask permission to put a question and the Lord would reply, Be seated, monk, ask what you will. But sometimes in these nightly congregations the silence was unbroken. When King Ajâtasattu went to visit him[3] in the mango grove of Jîvaka he was seized with sudden fear at the unearthly stillness of the place and suspected an ambush. "Fear not, O King," said Jîvaka, "I am playing you no tricks. Go straight on. There in the pavilion hall the lamps are burning...and there is the Blessed One sitting against the middle pillar, facing the east with the brethren round him." And when the king beheld the assembly seated in perfect silence, calm as a clear lake, he

[1] Visâkhâ, a lady of noted piety. It was probably a raised garden planted with trees.

[2] Maj. Nik. 110.

[3] Dig. Nik. No. 2. Compare Jâtaka 150, which shows how much variation was permitted in the words ascribed to the Buddha.

exclaimed "Would that my son might have such calm as this assembly now has."

The major part of the Buddha's activity was concerned with the instruction of his disciples and the organization of the Sangha or order. Though he was ready to hear and teach all, the portrait presented to us is not that of a popular preacher who collects and frequents crowds but rather that of a master, occupied with the instruction of his pupils, a large band indeed but well prepared and able to appreciate and learn by heart teaching which, though freely offered to the whole world, was somewhat hard to untrained ears. In one passage[1] an enquirer asks him why he shows more zeal in teaching some than others. The answer is, if a landowner had three fields, one excellent, one middling and one of poor soil, would he not first sow the good field, then the middling field, and last of all the bad field, thinking to himself; it will just produce fodder for the cattle? So the Buddha preaches first to his own monks, then to lay-believers, and then, like the landowner who sows the bad field last, to Brahmans, ascetics and wandering monks of other sects, thinking if they only understand one word, it will do them good for a long while. It was to such congregations of disciples or to enquirers belonging to other religious orders that he addressed his most important discourses, iterating in grave numbered periods the truths concerning the reality of sorrow and the equal reality of salvation, as he sat under a clump of bamboos or in the shade of a banyan, in sight perhaps of a tank where the lotuses red, white and blue, submerged or rising from the water, typified the various classes of mankind.

He did not start by laying down any constitution for his order. Its rules were formed entirely by case law. Each incident and difficulty was referred to him as it arose and his decision was accepted as the law on that point. During his last illness he showed a noble anxiety not to hamper his followers by the prestige of his name but to leave behind him a body of free men, able to be a light and a help to themselves. But a curious passage[2] represents an old monk as saying immediately after his

[1] Sam. Nik. XLII. 7.

[2] Mahâparinib-sutta, 6. 20. The monk Subhadda, in whose mouth these words are put, was apparently not the person of the same name who was the last convert made by the Buddha when dying.

death "Weep not, brethren; we are well rid of the Great Monk. We used to be annoyed by being told, 'This beseems you and this does not beseem you. But now we shall be able to do what we like and not have to do what we don't like.'" Clearly the laxer disciples felt the Master's hand to be somewhat heavy and we might have guessed as much. For though Gotama had a breadth of view rare in that or in any age, though he refused to multiply observances or to dogmatize, every sutta indicates that he was a man of exceptional authority and decision; what he has laid down he has laid down; there is no compulsion or punishment, no vow of obedience or *sacrificium intellectus*; but it is equally clear that there is no place in the order for those who in great or small think differently from the master.

In shepherding his flock he had the assistance of his senior disciples. Of these the most important were Sâriputta and Moggallâna, both of them Brahmans who left their original teacher Sâñjaya to join him at the outset of his ministry. Sâriputta[1] enjoyed his confidence so fully that he acted as his representative and gave authoritative expositions of doctrine. The Buddha even compared him to the eldest son of an Emperor who assists his father in the government. But both he and Moggallâna died before their master and thus did not labour independently. Another important disciple Upâli survived him and probably contributed materially to the codification of the Vinaya. Anuruddha and Ânanda, both of them Sâkyas, are also frequently mentioned, especially the latter who became his personal attendant[2] and figures in the account of his illness and death as the beloved disciple to whom his last instructions were committed. These two together with four other young Sâkya nobles and Upâli joined the order twenty-five years before Gotama's death and perhaps formed an inner circle of trusted relatives, though we have no reason to think there was any friction between them and Brahmans like Sâriputta. Upâli is said to have been barber of the Sâkyas. It is not easy to say what his social status may have been, but it probably did not preclude intimacy.

The Buddha was frequently occupied with maintaining peace and order among his disciples. Though the profession of a monk

[1] His personal name was Upatissa.

[2] This position was also held, previously no doubt, by Sagata.

excluded worldly advancement, it was held in great esteem and was hence adopted by ambitious and quarrelsome men who had no true vocation. The troubles which arose in the Sangha are often ascribed in the Vinaya to the Chabbaggiyas, six brethren who became celebrated in tradition as spirits of mischief and who are evidently made the peg on which these old monkish anecdotes are hung. As a rule the intervention of the Buddha was sufficient to restore peace, but one passage[1] indicates resistance to his authority. The brethren quarrelled so often that the people said it was a public scandal. The Buddha endeavoured to calm the disputants, but one of them replied, "Lord, let the Blessed One quietly enjoy the bliss which he has obtained in this life. The responsibility for these quarrels will rest with us alone." This seems a clear hint that the Blessed One had better mind his own business. Renewed injunctions and parables met with no better result. "And the Blessed One thought" says the narrative "'truly these fools are infatuated,' and he rose from his seat and went away."

Other troubles are mentioned but by far the most serious was the schism of Devadatta, represented as occurring in the old age of Gotama when he was about seventy-two. The story as told in the Cullavagga[2] is embellished with supernatural incidents and seems not to observe the natural sequence of events but perhaps three features are historical: namely that Devadatta wished to supersede the Buddha as head of the order, that he was the friend of Ajâtasattu, Crown Prince and afterwards King of Magadha[3], and that he advocated a stricter rule of life than the Buddha chose to enforce. This combination of piety and ambition is perhaps not unnatural. He was a cousin of the Buddha and entered the order at the same time as Ânanda and other young Sâkya nobles. Sprung from that quarrelsome breed he possessed in a distorted form some of Gotama's own ability. He is represented as publicly urging the Master to retire and dwell at ease but met with an absolute

[1] Mahâvag. x. 2. Compare the singular anecdote in vi. 22 where the Buddha quite unjustifiably suspects a Doctor of making an indelicate joke. The story seems to admit that the Buddha might be wrong and also that he was sometimes treated with want of respect.

[2] vii. 2 ff.

[3] The introductions to Jâtakas 26 and 150 say that Ajâtasattu built a great monastery for him at Gayâsîsa.

refusal. Sâriputta was directed to "proclaim" him in Râjagaha, the proclamation being to the effect that his nature had changed and that all his words and deeds were disowned by the order. Then Devadatta incited the Crown Prince to murder his father, Bimbisâra. The plot was prevented by the ministers but the king told Ajâtasattu that if he wanted the kingdom he could have it and abdicated. But his unnatural son put him to death all the same[1] by starving him slowly in confinement. With the assistance of Ajâtasattu, Devadatta then tried to compass the death of the Buddha. First he hired assassins, but they were converted as soon as they approached the sacred presence. Then he rolled down a rock from the Vulture's peak with the intention of crushing the Buddha, but the mountain itself interfered to stop the sacrilege and only a splinter scratched the Lord's foot. Then he arranged for a mad elephant to be let loose in the road at the time of collecting alms, but the Buddha calmed the furious beast. It is perhaps by some error of arrangement that after committing such unpardonable crimes Devadatta is represented as still a member of the order and endeavouring to provoke a schism by asking for stricter rules. The attempt failed and according to later legends he died on the spot, but the Vinaya merely says that hot blood gushed from his mouth.

That there are historical elements in this story is shown by the narrative of Fa Hsien, the Chinese pilgrim who travelled in India about 400 A.D. He tells us that the followers of Devadatta still existed in Kosala and revered the three previous Buddhas but refused to recognize Gotama. This is interesting, for it seems to show that it was possible to accept Gotama's doctrine, or the greater part of it, as something independent of his personality and an inheritance from earlier teachers.

The Udâna and Jâtaka relate another plot without specifying the year. Some heretics induced a nun called Sundarî to pretend she was the Buddha's concubine and hired assassins to murder her. They then accused the Bhikkhus of killing her to conceal their master's sin, but the real assassins got drunk with the money they had received and revealed the conspiracy in their cups.

But these are isolated cases. As a whole the Buddha's long

[1] The Buddha says so himself (Dig. Nik. II.) but does not mention the method.

career was marked by a peace and friendliness which are surprising if we consider what innovations his teaching contained. Though in contending that priestly ceremonies were useless he refrained from neither direct condemnation nor satire, yet he is not represented as actively attacking[1] them and we may doubt if he forbade his lay disciples to take part in rites and sacrifices as a modern missionary might do. We find him sitting by the sacred fire of a Brahman[2] and discoursing, but not denouncing the worship carried on in the place. When he converted Siha[3], the general of the Licchavis, who had been a Jain, he bade him continue to give food and gifts as before to the Jain monks who frequented his house—an instance of toleration in a proselytizing teacher which is perhaps without parallel. Similarly in the Sîgâlovâda-sutta it is laid down that a good man ministers to monks and to Brahmans. If it is true that Ajâtasattu countenanced Devadatta's attempts to murder him, he ignored such disagreeable details with a sublime indifference, for he continued to frequent Râjagaha, received the king, and preached to him one of his finest sermons without alluding to the past. He stands before us in the suttas as a man of amazing power of will, inaccessible to fear, promises and, one may add, to argument but yet in comparison with other religious leaders singularly gentle in taking the offensive against error. Often he simply ignored it as irrelevant: "Never mind" he said on his deathbed to his last convert "Never mind, whether other teachers are right or wrong. Listen to me, I will teach you the truth." And when he is controversial his method is often to retain old words in honourable use with new meanings. The Brahmans are not denounced like the Pharisees in the New Testament but the real Brahman is a man of uprightness and wisdom: the real sacrifice is to abstain from sin and follow the Truth.

Women played a considerable part in the entourage of Gotama. They were not secluded in India at that time and he admitted that they were capable of attaining saintship. The work of ministering to the order, of supplying it with food and raiment, naturally fell largely to pious matrons, and their

[1] The Dhamma-saṅgaṇi defines courtesy as being of two kinds: hospitality and considerateness in matters of doctrine.

[2] Maj. Nik. 75.

[3] Mahâv. VI. 31. 11.

attentive forethought delighted to provide for the monks those comforts which might be accepted but not asked for. Prominent among such donors was Visâkhâ, who married the son of a wealthy merchant at Sâvatthî and converted her husband's family from Jainism to the true doctrine. The Vinaya recounts how after entertaining the Buddha and his disciples she asked eight boons which proved to be the privileges of supplying various classes of monks with food, clothing and medicine and of providing the nuns with bathing dresses, for, said she, it shocked her sense of propriety to see them bathing naked. But the anecdotes respecting the Buddha and women, whether his wife or others, are not touched with sentiment, not even so much as is found in the conversation between Yâjñavalkya and Maitreyî in the Upanishad. To women as a class he gave their due and perhaps in his own opinion more than their due, but if he felt any interest in them as individuals, the sacred texts have obliterated the record. In the last year of his life he dined with the courtezan Ambapâlî and the incident has attracted attention on account of its supposed analogy to the narrative about Christ and "the woman which was a sinner." But the resemblance is small. There is no sign that the Buddha, then eighty years of age, felt any personal interest in Ambapâlî. Whatever her morals may have been, she was a benefactress of the order and he simply gave her the same opportunity as others of receiving instruction. When the Licchavi princes tried to induce him to dine with them instead of with her, he refused to break his promise. The invitations of princes had no attraction for him, and he was a prince himself. A fragment of conversation introduced irrelevantly into his deathbed discourses[1] is significant—"How, Lord, are we to conduct ourselves with regard to womankind? Don't see them, Ânanda. But if we see them, what are we to do? Abstain from speech. But if they should speak to us what are we to do? Keep wide awake."

This spirit is even more evident in the account of the admission of Nuns to the order. When the Buddha was visiting his native town his aunt and foster mother, Mahâprajâpatî, thrice begged him to grant this privilege to women but was thrice refused and went away in tears. Then she followed him to Vesâlî and stood in the entrance of the Kûṭagâra Hall "with

[1] Cullavag. x. 1. 3.

swollen feet and covered with dust, and sorrowful." Ânanda, who had a tender heart, interviewed her and, going in to the Buddha, submitted her request but received a triple refusal. But he was nôt to be denied and urged that the Buddha admitted women to be capable of attaining saintship and that it was unjust to refuse the blessings of religion to one who had suckled him. At last Gotama yielded—perhaps the only instance in which he is represented as convinced by argument—but he added "If, Ânanda, women had not received permission to enter the Order, the pure religion would have lasted long, the good law would have stood fast a thousand years. But since they had received that permission, it will now stand fast for only five hundred years[1]."

He maintained and approved the same hard detached attitude in other domestic relations. His son Râhula received special instruction but is not represented as enjoying his confidence like Ânanda. A remarkable narrative relates how, when the monk Sangâmaji was sitting beneath a tree absorbed in meditation, his former wife (whom he had left on abandoning the world) laid his child before him and said "Here, monk, is your little son, nourish me and nourish him." But Sangâmaji took no notice and the woman went away. The Buddha who observed what happened said "He feels no pleasure when she comes, no sorrow when she goes: him I call a true Brahman released from passion[2]." This narrative is repulsive to European sentiment, particularly as the chronicler cannot spare the easy charity of a miracle to provide for the wife and child, but in taking it as an index of the character of Gotama, we must bear in mind such sayings of Christ as "If any man come to me and hate not his father and mother and wife and children and brethren and sisters, yea and his own life also, he cannot be my disciple[3]."

[1] Mahâparinib. v. 23. Perhaps the Buddha was supposed to be giving Ânanda last warnings about his besetting weakness.

[2] Udâna 1. 8.

[3] Compare too the language of Angela of Foligno (1248–1309) "By God's will there died my mother who was a great hindrance unto me in following the way of God: my husband died likewise and all my children. And because I had commenced to follow the aforesaid way and had prayed God that he would rid me of them, I had great consolation of their deaths, although I did also feel some grief." Beatae Angelae de Fulginio Visionum et Instructionum Liber. Cap. IX.

4

Political changes, in which however he took no part, occurred in the last years of the Buddha's life. In Magadha Ajâtasattu had come to the throne. If, as the Vinaya represents, he at first supported the schism of Devadatta, he subsequently became a patron of the Buddha. He was an ambitious prince and fortified Pâṭaligâma (afterwards Pâṭaliputra) against the Vajjian confederation, which he destroyed a few years after the Buddha's death. This confederation was an alliance of small oligarchi like the Licchavis and Videhans. It would appear that this form of constitution was on the wane in northern India and that the monarchical states were annexing the decaying commonwealths. In Kosala, Viḍûḍabha conquered Kapilavatthu a year or two before the Buddha's death, and is said to have perpetrated a great massacre of the Sâkya clan[1]. Possibly in consequence of these events the Buddha avoided Kosala and the former Sâkya territory. At any rate the record of his last days opens at Râjagaha, the capital of Magadha.

This record is contained in the Mahâparinibbâna Sutta, the longest of the suttas and evidently a compilation. The style is provokingly uneven. It often promises to give a simple and natural narrative but such passages are interrupted by more recent and less relevant matter. No general estimate of its historical value can be given but each incident must be apprized separately. Nearly all the events and discourses recorded in it are found elsewhere in the canon in the same words[2] and it contains explanatory matter of a suspiciously apologetic nature. Also the supernatural element is freely introduced. But together with all this it contains plain pathetic pictures of an old man's fatigue and sufferings which would not have been inserted by a later hand, had they not been found ready in tradition.

[1] No account of this event has yet been found in the earliest texts but it is no doubt historical. The versions found in the Jâtaka and Commentaries trace it back to a quarrel about a marriage, but the story is not very clear or consistent and the real motive was probably that indicated above.

[2] See Rhys Davids, *Dialogues*, II. p. 70 and Przyluski's articles (in *J.A.* 1918 ff.) Le Parinirvana et les funérailles du Bouddha where the Pali texts are compared with the Mûlasarvâstivâdin Vinaya and with other accounts.

And though events and sermonettes are strung together in a way which is not artistic, there is nothing improbable in the idea that the Buddha when he felt his end approaching should have admonished his disciples about all that he thought most important.

The story opens at Râjagaha about six months before the Buddha's death. The King sends his minister to ask whether he will be successful in attacking the Vajjians. The Buddha replies that as long as they act in concord, behave honourably, and respect the Faith, so long may they be expected not to decline but prosper. The compiler may perhaps have felt this narrative to be an appropriate parallel to the Buddha's advice to his disciples to live in peace and order. He summoned and addressed the brethren living in Râjagaha and visited various spots in the neighbourhood. In these last utterances one phrase occurs with special frequency, "Great is the fruit, great the advantage of meditation accompanied by upright conduct: great is the advantage of intelligence accompanied by meditation. The mind which has such intelligence is freed from intoxications, from the desires of the senses, from love of life, from delusion and from ignorance."

He then set forth accompanied by Ânanda and several disciples. Judging from the route adopted his intention was to go ultimately to Sâvatthî. This was one of the towns where he resided from time to time, but we cannot tell what may have been his special motives for visiting it on the present occasion, for if the King of Kosala had recently massacred the Sâkyas his presence there would have been strange. The road was not direct but ran up northwards and then followed the base of the mountains, thus enabling travellers to cross rivers near their sources where they were still easy to ford. The stopping-places from Râjagaha onwards were Nâlanda, Pâṭaliputra, Vesâlî, Bhandagâma, Pâvâ, Kusinârâ, Kapilavatthu, Setavya, Sâvatthî. On his last journey the Buddha is represented as following this route but he died at the seventh stopping-place, Kusinârâ. When at Pâṭaligâma, he prophesied that it would become a great emporium[1]. He was honourably entertained by the officers of the King who decided that the

[1] This was probably written after Pâṭaliputra had become a great city but we do not know when its rise commenced.

gate and ferry by which he left should be called Gotama's gate and Gotama's ferry. The gate received the name, but when he came to the Ganges he vanished miraculously and appeared standing on the further bank. He then went on to Vesâlî, passing with indifference and immunity from the dominions of the King of Magadha into those of his enemies, and halted in the grove of the courtezan Ambapâlî[1]. She came to salute him and he accepted her invitation to dine with her on the morrow, in spite of the protests of the Licchavi princes.

The rainy season was now commencing and the Buddha remained near Vesâlî in the village of Beluva, where he fell seriously ill. One day after his recovery he was sitting in the shade with Ânanda, who said that during the illness his comfort had been the thought that the Buddha would not pass away without leaving final instructions to the Order. The reply was a remarkable address which is surely, at least, in parts the Buddha's own words.

"What does the order expect of me, Ânanda? I have preached the truth without any distinction of esoteric or exoteric, for in respect of the truth, there is no clenched hand in the teaching of the Tathâgata. If there is anyone who thinks 'it is I who will lead the brotherhood' or 'the order is dependent on me,' it is he who should give instructions. But the Tathâgata does not think that he should lead the order or that the order is dependent on him. Why then should he leave instructions? I am an old man now, and full of years, my pilgrimage is finished, I have reached my sum of days, I am turning eighty years; and just as a worn-out cart can only be made to move along with much additional care, so can the body of the Tathâgata be kept going only with much additional care. It is only when the Tathâgata, ceasing to attend to any outward thing becomes plunged in meditation, it is only then that the body of the Tathâgata is at ease. Therefore, Ânanda, be a lamp and a refuge to yourselves. Seek no other refuge. Let the Truth be your lamp and refuge; seek no refuge elsewhere.

"And they, Ânanda, who now or when I am dead shall be a lamp and a refuge to themselves, seeking no other refuge but

[1] She was a noted character in Vesâlî. In Mahâvag. VIII. 1, people are represented as saying that it was through her the place was so flourishing and that it would be a good thing if there were some one like her in Râjagaha.

taking the Truth as their lamp and refuge, these shall be my foremost disciples—these who are anxious to learn."

This discourse is succeeded by a less convincing episode, in which the Buddha tells Ânanda that he can prolong his life to the end of a world-period if he desires it. But though the hint was thrice repeated, the heedless disciple did not ask the Master to remain in the world. When he had gone, Mâra, the Evil one, appeared and urged on the Buddha that it was time for him to pass away. He replied that he would die in three months but not before he had completely established the true religion. Thus he deliberately rejected his allotted span of life and an earthquake occurred. He explained the cause of it to Ânanda, who saw his mistake too late. "Enough, Ânanda, the time for making such a request is past[1]."

The narrative becomes more human when it relates how one afternoon he looked at the town and said, "This will be the last time that the Tathâgata will behold Vesâlî. Come, Ânanda, let us go to Bhandagâma." After three halts he arrived at Pâvâ and stopped in the mango grove of Cunda, a smith, who invited him to dinner and served sweet rice, cakes, and a dish which has been variously interpreted as dried boar's flesh or a kind of truffle. The Buddha asked to be served with this dish and bade him give the sweet rice and cakes to the brethren. After eating some of it he ordered the rest to be buried, saying that no one in heaven or earth except a Buddha could digest it, a strange remark to chronicle since it was this meal which killed him[2]. But before he died he sent word to Cunda that he had no need to feel remorse and that the two most meritorious offerings in the world are the first meal given to a Buddha after he has obtained enlightenment and the last one given him before his death. On leaving Cunda's house he was attacked by dysentery and violent pains but bore them patiently and started for Kusinârâ with his disciples. In going thither he crossed the river Kakutthâ[3], and some verses inserted into the

[1] The whole passage is interesting as displaying even in the Pali Canon the germs of the idea that the Buddha is an eternal spirit only partially manifested in the limits of human life. In the Mahâparinib.-sutta Gotama is only voluntarily subject to natural death.

[2] The phrase occurs again in the Sutta-Nipâta. Its meaning is not clear to me.

[3] The text seems to represent him as crossing first a streamlet and then the river.

text, which sound like a very old ballad, relate how he bathed in it and then, weary and worn out, lay down on his cloak. A curious incident occurs here. A young Mallian, named Pukkusa, after some conversation with the Buddha, presents him with a robe of cloth of gold, but when it is put on it seems to lose its splendour, so exceedingly clear and bright is his skin. Gotama explains that there are two occasions when the skin of a Buddha glows like this—the night of his enlightenment and the night before his death. The transfiguration of Christ suggests itself as a parallel and is also associated with an allusion to his coming death. Most people have seen a face so light up under the influence of emotion that this popular metaphor seemed to express physical truth and it is perhaps not excessive to suppose that in men of exceptional gifts this illumination may have been so bright as to leave traces in tradition.

Then they went on[1] to a grove at Kusinârâ, and he lay down on a couch spread between two Sâla trees. These trees were in full bloom, though it was not the season for their flowering; heavenly strains and odours filled the air and spirits unseen crowded round the bed. But Ânanda, we are told, went into the Vihâra, which was apparently also in the grove, and stood leaning against the lintel weeping at the thought that he was to lose so kind a master. The Buddha sent for him and said, "Do not weep. Have I not told you before that it is the very nature of things most near and dear to us that we must part from them, leave them, sever ourselves from them? All that is born, brought into being and put together carries within itself the necessity of dissolution. How then is it possible that such a being should not be dissolved? No such condition is possible. For a long time, Ânanda, you have been very near me by words of love, kind and good, that never varies and is beyond all measure. You have done well, Ânanda. Be earnest in effort and you too shall soon be free from the great evils—from sensuality, from individuality, from delusion and from ignorance."

The Indians have a strong feeling that persons of distinction

[1] It is not said how much time elapsed between the meal at Cunda's and the arrival at Kusinârâ but since it was his last meal, he probably arrived the same afternoon.

should die in a suitable place[1], and now comes a passage in which Ânanda begs the Buddha not to die "in this little wattle and daub town in the midst of the jungle" but rather in some great city. The Buddha told him that Kusinârâ had once been the capital of King Mahâsudassana and a scene of great splendour in former ages. This narrative is repeated in an amplified form in the Sutta and Jâtaka[2] called Mahâsudassana, in which the Buddha is said to have been that king in a previous birth.

Kusinârâ was at that time one of the capitals of the Mallas, who were an aristocratic republic like the Sâkyas and Vajjians. At the Buddha's command Ânanda went to the Council hall and summoned the people. "Give no occasion to reproach yourself hereafter saying, The Tathâgata died in our own village and we neglected to visit him in his last hours." So the Mallas came and Ânanda presented them by families to the dying Buddha as he lay between the flowering trees, saying "Lord, a Malla of such and such a name with his children, his wives, his retinue and his friends humbly bows down at the feet of the Blessed One."

A monk called Subhadda, who was not a believer, also came and Ânanda tried to turn him away but the Buddha overhearing said "Do not keep out Subhadda. Whatever he may ask of me he will ask from a desire for knowledge and not to annoy me and he will quickly understand my replies." He was the last disciple whom the Buddha converted, and he straightway became an Arhat.

Now comes the last watch of the night. "It may be, Ânanda," said the Buddha, "that some of you may think, the word of the Master is ended. We have no more a teacher. But you should not think thus. The truths and the rules which I have declared and laid down for you all, let them be the teacher for you after I am gone.

"When I am gone address not one another as hitherto, saying 'Friend.' An elder brother may address a younger brother by his name or family-name or as friend, but a younger brother should say to an elder, Sir, or Lord.

[1] Cf. Lyall's poem, on a Rajput Chief of the Old School, who when nearing his end has to leave his pleasure garden in order that he may die in the ancestral castle.

[2] Dig. Nik. 17 and Jâtaka 95.

"When I am gone let the order, if it should so wish, abolish all the lesser and minor precepts."

Thus in his last address the dying Buddha disclaims, as he had disclaimed before in talking to Ânanda, all idea of dictating to the order: his memory is not to become a paralyzing tradition. What he had to teach, he has taught freely, holding back nothing in "a clenched fist." The truths are indeed essential and immutable. But they must become a living part of the believer, until he is no longer a follower but a light unto himself. The rest does not matter: the order can change all the minor rules if expedient. But in everyday life discipline and forms must be observed: hitherto all have been equal compared with the teacher, but now the young must show more respect for the older. And in the same spirit of solicitude for the order he continues:

"When I am gone, the highest penalty should be imposed on Channa." "What is that, Lord?" "Let him say what he likes, but the brethren should not speak to him or exhort him or admonish him[1]."

The end approaches. "It may be, that there is some doubt or misgiving in the mind of some as to the Buddha, or the truth, or the path, or the way. Enquire freely. Do not have to reproach yourselves afterwards with the thought, 'Our teacher was face to face with us and we could not bring ourselves to enquire when we were face to face with him.'" All were silent. A second and third time he put the same question and there was silence still. "It may be, that you put no questions out of awe for the teacher. Let one friend communicate to another." There was still silence, till Ânanda said "How wonderful, Lord, and how marvellous. In this whole assembly there is no one who has any doubt or misgiving as to the Buddha, the truth, the path and the way." "Out of the fulness of faith hast thou spoken Ânanda, but the Tathâgata knows for certain that it is so. Even the most backward of all these five hundred brethren has become converted and is no longer liable to be born in a state of suffering and is assured of final salvation."

"Behold, I exhort you saying, The elements of being are

[1] It is said that this discipline was efficacious and that Channa became an Arhat.

transitory[1]. Strive earnestly. These were the last words of the Tathâgata." Then he passed through a series of trances (no less than twenty stages are enumerated) and expired.

An earthquake and thunder, as one might have predicted, occurred at the moment of his death but comparatively little stress is laid on these prodigies. Anuruddha seems to have taken the lead among the brethren and bade Ânanda announce the death to the Mallas. They heard it with cries of grief: "Too soon has the Blessed One passed away. Too soon has the light gone out of the world."

No less than six days were passed in preparation for the obsequies[2]. On the seventh they decided to carry the body to the south of the city and there burn it. But when they endeavoured to lift it, they found it immoveable. Anuruddha explained that spirits who were watching the ceremony wished it to be carried not outside the city but through it. When this was done the corpse moved easily and the heaven rained flowers. The meaning of this legend is that the Mallas considered a corpse would have defiled the city and therefore proposed to carry it outside. By letting it pass through the city they showed that it was not the ordinary relics of impure humanity.

Again, when they tried to light the funeral pile it would not catch fire. Anuruddha explained that this delay also was due to the intervention of spirits who wished that Mahâkassapa, the same whom the Buddha had converted at Uruvelâ and then on his way to pay his last respects, should arrive before the cremation. When he came attended by five hundred monks the pile caught fire of itself and the body was consumed completely,

[1] It is difficult to find a translation of these words which is both accurate and natural in the mouth of a dying man. The Pali text *vayadhammâ saṅkhârâ* (transitory-by-nature are the Saṅkhâras) is brief and simple but any correct and adequate rendering sounds metaphysical and is dramatically inappropriate. Perhaps the rendering "All compound things must decompose" expresses the Buddha's meaning best. But the verbal antithesis between compound and decomposing is not in the original and though saṅkhâra is etymologically the equivalent of confection or synthesis it hardly means what we call a compound thing as opposed to a simple thing.

[2] The Buddha before his death had explained that the corpse of a Buddha should be treated like the corpse of a universal monarch. It should be wrapped in layers of new cloth and laid in an iron vessel of oil. Then it should be burnt and a Dagoba should be erected at four cross roads.

leaving only the bones. Streams of rain extinguished the flames and the Mallas took the bones to their council hall. There they set round them a hedge of spears and a fence of bows and honoured them with dance and song and offerings of garlands and perfumes.

Whatever may be thought of this story, the veneration of the Buddha's relics, which is attested by the Piprava vase, is a proof that we have to do with a man rather than a legend. The relics may all be false, but the fact that they were venerated some 250 years after his death shows that the people of India thought of him not as an ancient semi-divine figure like Rama or Krishna but as something human and concrete.

Seven persons or communities sent requests for a portion of the relics, saying that they would erect a stupa over them and hold a feast. They were King Ajâtasattu of Magadha, the Licchavis of Vesâlî, the Sâkyas of Kapilavatthu, the Bulis of Allakappa, the Koḷiyas of Râmagâma, the Mallas of Pâvâ[1] and the Brahman of Veṭhadîpa. All except the last were Kshatriyas and based their claim on the ground that they like the Buddha belonged to the warrior caste. The Mallas at first refused, but a Brahman called Doṇa bade them not quarrel over the remains of him who taught forbearance. So he divided the relics into eight parts, one for Kusinârâ and one for each of the other seven claimants. At this juncture the Moriyas of Pipphalivana sent in a claim for a share but had to be content with the embers of the pyre since all the bones had been distributed. Then eight stupas were built for the relics in the towns mentioned and one over the embers and one by Doṇa the Brahman over the iron vessel in which the body had been burnt.

5

Thus ended the career of a man who was undoubtedly one of the greatest intellectual and moral forces that the world has yet seen, but it is hard to arrive at any certain opinion as to the details of his character and abilities, for in the later accounts he is deified and in the Pitakas though veneration has not gone so far as this, he is ecclesiasticized and the human side is neglected. The narrative moves like some stately ceremonial in

[1] The Mallas had two capitals, Kusinârâ and Pâvâ, corresponding to two subdivisions of the tribe.

which emotion and incident would be out of place until it reaches the strange deathbed, spread between the flowering trees, and Ânanda introduces with the formality of a court chamberlain the Malla householders who have come to pay their last respects and bow down at the feet of the dying teacher. The scenes described are like stained glass windows; the Lord preaching in the centre, sinners repenting and saints listening, all in harmonious colours and studied postures. But the central figure remains somewhat aloof; when once he had begun his ministry he laboured uninterruptedly and with continual success, but the foundation of the kingdom of Righteousness seems less like the triumphant issue of a struggle than the passage through the world of some compassionate angel. This is in great part due to the fact that the Pitakas are works of edification. True, they set before us the teacher as well as his teaching but they speak of his doings and historical surroundings only in order to provide a proper frame for the law which he preached. A less devout and more observant historian would have arranged the picture differently and even in the narratives that have come down to us there are touches of human interest which seem authentic.

When the Buddha was dying Ânanda wept because he was about to lose so kind a master and the Buddha's own language to him is even more affectionate. He cared not only for the organization of the order but for its individual members. He is frequently represented as feeling that some disciple needed a particular form of instruction and giving it. Nor did he fail to provide for the comfort of the sick and weary. For instance a ballad[1] relates how Panthaka driven from his home took refuge at the door of the monastery garden. "Then came the Lord and stroked my head and taking me by the arm led me into the garden of the monastery and out of kindness he gave me a towel for my feet." A striking anecdote[2] relates how he once found a monk who suffered from a disagreeable disease lying on the ground in a filthy state. So with Ânanda's assistance he washed him and lifting him up with his own hands laid him on his bed. Then he summoned the brethren and told

[1] Theragâthâ 557 ff. Water to refresh tired and dusty feet is commonly offered to anyone who comes from a distance.

[2] Mahâvag. VIII. 26.

them that if a sick brother had no special attendant the whole order should wait on him. "You, monks, have no mothers or fathers to care for you. If you do not wait one on the other, who is there who will wait on you? Whosoever would wait on me, he should wait on the sick." This last recalls Christ's words, "Inasmuch as ye have done it unto the least of these brethren, ye have done it unto me." And, if his approval of monks being deaf to the claims of family affection seems unfeeling, it should also be mentioned that in the book called *Songs of the Nuns*[1] women relate how they were crazy at the loss of their children but found complete comfort and peace in his teaching. Sometimes we are told that when persons whom he wished to convert proved refractory he "suffused them with the feeling of his love" until they yielded to his influence[2]. We can hardly doubt that this somewhat cumbrous phrase preserves a tradition of his personal charm and power.

The beauty of his appearance and the pleasant quality of his voice are often mentioned but in somewhat conventional terms which inspire no confidence that they are based on personal reminiscence, nor have the most ancient images which we possess any claim to represent his features, for the earliest of them are based on Greek models and it was not the custom to represent him by a figure until some centuries after his death. I can imagine that the truest idea of his person is to be obtained not from the abundant effigies which show him as a somewhat sanctimonious ascetic, but from statues of him as a young man, such as that found at Sarnath, which may possibly preserve not indeed the physiognomy of Gotama but the general physique of a young Nepalese prince, with powerful limbs and features and a determined mouth. For there is truth at the bottom of the saying that Gotama was born to be either a Buddha or a universal monarch: he would have made a good general, if he had not become a monk.

We are perhaps on firmer ground when we find speakers in the Pitakas[3] commenting on his calm and bright expression and

[1] *E.g.* Therîgâthâ 133 ff. It should also be remembered that orientals, particularly Chinese and Japanese, find Christ's behaviour to his mother as related in the gospels very strange.

[2] *E.g.* Roja, the Malla, in Mahâvag. VI. 36 and the account of the interview with the Five Monks in the Nidânakathâ (Rhys Davids, *Budd. Birth Stories*, p. 112).

[3] *E.g.* Maj. Nik. 36.

his unruffled courtesy in discussion. Of his eloquence it is hard to judge. The Suttas may preserve his teaching and some of his words but they are probably rearrangements made for recitation. Still it is impossible to prove that he did not himself adopt this style, particularly when age and iteration had made the use of certain formulæ familiar to him. But though these repetitions and subdivisions of arrangement are often wearisome, there are not wanting traces of another manner, which suggest a terse and racy preacher going straight to the point and driving home his meaning with homely instances.

Humour often peeps through the Buddha's preaching. It pervades the Jâtaka stories, and more than once he is said to have smiled when remembering some previous birth. Some suttas, such as the tales of the Great King of Glory, and of King Mahâ Vijita's sacrifice[1], are simply Jâtakas in another form—interesting stories full of edification for those who can understand but not to be taken as a narrative of facts. At other times he simply states the ultimate facts of a case and leaves them in their droll incongruity. Thus when King Ajâtasattu was moved and illuminated by his teaching, he observed to his disciples that His Majesty had all the makings of a saint in him, if only he had not killed that excellent man his own father. Somewhat similar is his judgment[2] on two naked ascetics, who imitated in all things the ways of a dog and a cow respectively, in the hope of thus obtaining salvation. When pressed to say what their next birth would be, he opined that if their penance was successful they would be reborn as dogs and cows, if unsuccessful, in hell. Irony and modesty are combined in his rejection of extravagant praise. "Such faith have I, Lord[3]" said Sâriputta, "that methinks there never has been nor will be nor is now any other greater or wiser than the Blessed One." "Of course, Sâriputta" is the reply, "you have known all the Buddhas of the past." "No, Lord." "Well then, you know those of the future." "No, Lord." "Then at least you know me and have penetrated my mind thoroughly." "Not even that, Lord." "Then why, Sâriputta, are your words so grand and bold."

There is much that is human in these passages yet we should

[1] Dig. Nik. XVII. and V.

[2] Maj. Nik. 57.

[3] Mahâparib. Sutta, I. 61.

be making a fancy portrait did we allow ourselves to emphasize them too much and neglect the general tone of the Pitakas. These scriptures are the product of a school; but that school grew up under the Buddha's personal influence and more than that is rooted in the very influences and tendencies which produced the Buddha himself. The passionless, intellectual aloofness; the elemental simplicity with which the facts of life are stated and explained without any concession to sentiment, the rigour of the prescription for salvation, that all sensual desire and attachment must be cut off, are too marked and consistent for us to suppose them due merely to monkish inability to understand the more human side of his character. The Buddha began his career as an Indian Muni, one supposed to be free from all emotions and intent only on seeking deliverance from every tie connecting him with the world. This was expected of him and had he done no more it would have secured him universal respect . The fact that he did a great deal more, that he devoted his life to active preaching, that he offered to all happiness and escape from sorrow, that he personally aided with advice and encouragement all who came to him, caused both his contemporaries and future generations to regard him as a saviour. His character and the substance of his teaching were admirably suited to the needs of the religious world of India in his day. Judged by the needs of other temperaments, which are entitled to neither more nor less consideration, they seem too severe, too philosophic and the later varieties of Buddhism have endeavoured to make them congenial to less strenuous natures.

Before leaving the personality of the Buddha, we must say a word about the more legendary portions of his biography, for though of little importance for history they have furnished the chief subjects of Buddhist art and influenced the minds of his followers as much as or more than the authentic incidents of his career[1]. The later legend has not distorted the old narrative. It is possible that all its incidents may be founded on stories

[1] The earliest sources for these legends are the Mahâvastu, the Sanskrit Vinayas (preserved in Chinese translations), the Lalita Vistara, the Introduction to the Jâtaka and the Buddha-carita. For Burmese, Sinhalese, Tibetan and Chinese lives of the Buddha, see the works of Bigandet, Hardy, Rockhill and Schiefner, Wieger and Beal. See also Foucher, *Liste indienne des actes du Buddha* and Hackin, *Scènes de la Vie du Buddha d'après des peintures tibétaines*.

known to the compilers of the Pitakas, though this is not at present demonstrable, but they are embellished by an unstinted use of the supernatural and of the hyperbole usual in Indian poetry. The youthful Buddha moves through showers of flowers and an atmosphere crowded with attendant deities. He cannot even go to school without an escort of ten thousand children and a hundred thousand maidens and astonishes the good man who proposes to teach him the alphabet by suggesting sixty-four systems of writing.

The principal scenes in this legend are as follows. The Bodhisattva, that is the Buddha to-be, resides in the Tusita Heaven and selects his birth-place and parentage. He then enters the womb of his mother Mâyâ in the shape of a white elephant, which event she sees in a dream. Brahmans are summoned and interpret the vision to mean that her son will be a Universal Monarch or a Buddha. When near her confinement Mâyâ goes to visit her parents but on the way brings forth her son in the Lumbini grove. As she stands upright holding the bough of a tree, he issues from her side without pain to her and is received by deities, but on touching the ground, takes seven steps and says, "I am the foremost in the world." On the same day are born several persons who play a part in his life—his wife, his horse, Ânanda, Bimbisâra and others. Asita does homage to him, as does also his father, and it is predicted that he will become a Buddha and renounce the world. His father in his desire to prevent this secludes him in the enjoyment of all luxury. At the ploughing festival he falls into a trance under a tree and the shadow stands still to protect him and does not change. Again his father does him homage. He is of herculean strength and surpasses all as an archer. He marries his cousin Yasodharâ, when sixteen years old. Then come the four visions, which are among the scenes most frequently depicted in modern sacred art. As he is driving in the palace grounds the gods show him an old man, a sick man, a corpse and a monk of happy countenance. His charioteer explains what they are and he determines to abandon the world. It was at this time that his son was born and on hearing the news he said that a new fetter now bound him to worldly life but still decided to execute his resolve. That night he could take no pleasure in the music of the singing women who were wont to play to him and they fell asleep. As he looked at their sleeping forms he felt disgust and ordered Channa, his charioteer, to saddle Kaṇṭhaka, a gigantic white horse, eighteen cubits long from head to tail. Meanwhile he went to his wife's room and took a last but silent look as she lay sleeping with her child.

Then he started on horseback attended by Channa and a host of heavenly beings who opened the city gates. Here he was assailed by Mâra the Tempter who offered him universal empire but in vain. After jumping the river Anomâ on his steed, he cut off his long hair with his sword and flinging it up into the air wished it might stay there if he was really to become a Buddha. It remained suspended; admiring gods placed it in a heavenly shrine and presented Gotama with the robes of a monk.

Not much is added to the account of his wanderings and austerities as given in the Pitakas, but the attainment of Buddhahood naturally stimulates the devout imagination. At daybreak Gotama sits at the foot of a tree, lighting up the landscape with the golden rays which issue from his person. Sujârâ a noble maiden and her servant Pûrṇâ offer him rice and milk in a golden vessel and he takes no more food for seven weeks. He throws the vessel into the river, wishing that if he is to become a Buddha it may ascend the stream against the current. It does so and then sinks to the abode of the Nâgas. Towards evening he walks to the Bodhi-tree and meets a grass-cutter who offers him grass to make a seat. This he accepts and taking his seat vows that rather than rise before attaining Buddhahood, he will let his blood dry up and his body decay. Then comes the great assault of the Tempter. Mâra attacks him in vain both with an army of terrible demons and with bands of seductive nymphs. During the conflict Mâra asked him who is witness to his ever having performed good deeds or bestowed alms? He called on the earth to bear witness. Earthquakes and thunders responded to the appeal and the goddess of the Earth herself rose and bore testimony. The rout of Mâra is supposed to have taken place in the late evening. The full moon[1] came out and in the three watches of the night he attained enlightenment.

The Pali and early Sanskrit texts place the most striking

[1] It was the full moon of the month Vaiśâkha.

legendary scenes in the first part of the Buddha's life just as scribes give freest rein to their artistic imagination in tracing the first letter and word of a chapter. In the later version, the whole text is coloured and gilded with a splendour that exceeds the hues of ordinary life but no incidents of capital importance are added after the Enlightenment[1]. Historical names still occur and the Buddha is still a wandering teacher with a band of disciples, but his miracles continually convulse the universe: he preaches to mankind from the sky and retires for three months to the Tusita Heaven in order to instruct his mother, who had died before she could hear the truth from her son's lips, and often the whole scene passes into a vision where the ordinary limits of space, time and number cease to have any meaning.

[1] The best known of the later biographies of the Buddha, such as the Lalita Vistara and the Buddha-carita of Aśvaghosha stop short after the Enlightenment.

CHAPTER IX

THE BUDDHA COMPARED WITH OTHER RELIGIOUS TEACHERS

THE personality of the Buddha invites comparison with the founders of the other world-religions, Christ and Mohammed. We are tempted to ask too if there is any resemblance between him and Confucius, a contemporary Asiatic whose influence has been equally lasting, but here there is little common ground. For Confucius's interest was mainly in social and ethical problems, not in religion. He laid stress on those ties of kinship and society, respecting which the Indian monk (like Christ) sometimes spoke harshly, although there is a strong likeness between the moral code of the Buddhist layman and Confucianism: he was full of humility and respect for antiquity, whereas Gotama had a good share of that self-confidence which is necessary for all who propound to the world a new religion[1].

But with Mohammed comparison, or rather contrast, is easier. Both were seekers after truth: both found what they believed to be the truth only when of mature years, Gotama when about thirty-six, Mohammed when forty or more: both lived to be elderly men and possessed great authority. But there the analogy ends. Perhaps no single human being has had so great an effect on the world as Mohammed. His achievements are personal and, had he never lived, it is not clear that the circumstances of the age would have caused some one else to play approximately the same part. He more than Cæsar or Alexander was individually the author of a movement which transformed part of three continents. No one else has been able to fuse the two noble instincts of religion and empire in so perfect a manner, perfect because the two do not conflict or jar, as do the teachings of Christ and the pretensions of his Church to temporal power.

[1] There are some curious coincidences of detail between the Buddha and Confucius. Both disliked talking about prodigies (Analects. VII. 20) Confucius concealed nothing from his disciples (ib. 23), just as the Buddha had no "closed fist," but he would not discuss the condition of the dead (Anal. XI. 11), just as the Buddha held it unprofitable to discuss the fate of the saint after death. Neither had any great opinion of the spirits worshipped in their respective countries.

But it is precisely this fusion of religion and politics which disqualifies Islam as a universal religion and prevents it from satisfying the intellectual and spiritual wants of that part of humanity which is most intellectual and most spiritual. Law and religion are inextricably mixed in it and a Moslim, more than the most superstitious of Buddhists or Christians, is bound by a vast number of ties and observances which have nothing to do with religion. It is in avoiding these trammels that the superior religious instinct of Gotama shows itself. He was aided in this by the temper of his times. Though he was of the warrior caste and naturally brought into association with princes, he was not on that account tempted to play a part in politics, for to the Hindus, then as now, renunciation of the world was indispensable for serious religion and there is no instance of a teacher obtaining a hearing among them without such renunciation as a preliminary. According to Indian popular ideas a genius might become either an Emperor or a Buddha but not like Mohammed a mixture of the two. But the danger which beset Gotama, and which he consistently and consciously avoided, though Mohammed could not, was to give authoritative decisions on unessential points as to both doctrine and practice. There was clearly a party which wished to make the rule of his order more severe and, had he consented, the religious world of his day would have approved. But by so doing he would have made Buddhism an Indian sect like Jainism, incapable of flourishing in lands with other institutions. If Buddhism has had little influence outside Asia, that is because there are differences of temperament in the world, not because it sanctions anachronisms or prescribes observances of a purely local and temporary value. In all his teaching Gotama insists on what is essential only and will not lend his name and authority to what is merely accessory. He will not for instance direct or even recommend his disciples to be hermits. "Whoever wishes may dwell in a wood and whoever wishes may dwell near a village." And in his last days he bade them be a light unto themselves and gave them authority to change all the lesser precepts. It is true that the order decided to make no use of this permission, but the spirit which dictated it has shaped the destinies of the faith.

Akin to this contrast is another—that between the tolerance of Gotama and the persecuting spirit of Islam. Mohammed and his followers never got rid of the idea that any other form of religion is an insult to the Almighty: that infidels should if possible be converted by compulsion, or, if that were impossible, allowed to exist only on sufferance and in an inferior position. Such ideas were unknown to Gotama. He laboured not for his own or his Creator's glory but simply and solely to benefit mankind. Conversion by force had no meaning for him, for what he desired was not a profession of allegiance but a change of disposition and amid many transformations his Church has not lost this temper.

When we come to compare Gotama and Christ we are struck by many resemblances of thought but also by great differences of circumstances and career. Both were truly spiritual teachers who rose above forms and codes: both accepted the current ideals of their time and strove to become the one a Buddha, the other Messiah. But at the age when Christ was executed Gotama was still in quest of truth and still on the wrong track. He lived nearly fifty years longer and had ample opportunity of putting his ideas into practice. So far as our meagre traditions allow us to trace the development of the two, the differences are even more fundamental. Peaceful as was the latter part of Gotama's life, the beginning was a period of struggle and disillusion. He broke away from worldly life to study philosophy: he broke away from philosophy to wear out his body with the severest mortification; that again he found to be vanity and only then did he attain to enlightenment. And though he offers salvation to all without distinction, he repeatedly says that it is difficult: with hard wrestling has he won the truth and it is hard for ordinary men to understand.

Troubled as was the life of Christ, it contains no struggle of this sort. As a youth he grew up in a poor family where the disenchantment of satiety was unknown: his genius first found expression in sermons delivered in the synagogue—the ordinary routine of Jewish ritual: his appearance as a public teacher and his ultimate conviction that he was the Messiah were a natural enlargement of his sphere, not a change of method: the temptation, though it offers analogies to Gotama's mental struggle and particularly to the legends about Mâra, was not an internal revolution in which old beliefs were seen to be false and new knowledge arose from their ashes. So far as we know, his inner life was continuous and undisturbed, and its final expression is emotional rather than intellectual. He gives no explanations and leaves no feeling that they are necessary. He is free in his use of metaphor and chary of definition. The teaching of the Buddha on the other hand is essentially intellectual. The nature and tastes of his audience were a sufficient justification for his style, but it indicates a temper far removed from the unquestioning and childlike faith of Christ. We can hardly conceive him using such a phrase as Our Father, but we may be sure that if he had done so he would have explained why and how and to what extent such words can be properly used of the Deity.

The most sceptical critics of the miracles recorded in the Gospels can hardly doubt that Christ possessed some special power of calming and healing nervous maladies and perhaps others. Sick people naturally turned to him: they were brought to him when he arrived in a town. Though the Buddha was occasionally kind to the sick, no such picture is drawn of the company about him and persons afflicted with certain diseases could not enter the order. When the merchant Anâthapiṇḍika is seriously ill, he sends a messenger with instructions to inform the Buddha and Sâriputta of his illness and to add in speaking to Sâriputta that he begs him to visit him out of compassion[1]. He does not presume to address the same request to the Buddha. Christ teaches that the world is evil or, perhaps we should say, spoiled, but wishes to remove the evil and found the Kingdom of Heaven: the Buddha teaches that birth, sickness and death are necessary conditions of existence and that disease, which like everything else has its origin in Karma, can be destroyed only when the cause is destroyed[2]. Nor do we find ascribed to him that love of children and tenderness towards the weak and erring which are beautiful features in the portrait of Christ[3]. He had no prejudices: he turned robust villains like Angulimâla, the brigand, into saints and dined with prostitutes but one

[1] Maj. Nik. 143.

[2] The miraculous cure of Suppiyâ (Mahâvag. VI. 23) is no exception. She was ill not because of the effects of Karma but because, according to the legend, she had cut off a piece of her flesh to cure a sick monk who required meat broth. The Buddha healed her.

[3] The most human and kindly portrait of the Buddha is that furnished by the Commentary on the Thera- and Therî-gâthâ. See Thera-gâthâ XXX, XXXI and Mrs Rhys Davids' trans. of *Therî-gâthâ*, pp. 71, 79.

cannot associate him with simple friendly intercourse. When he accepted invitations he did not so much join in the life of the family which he visited as convert the entertainment offered to him into an edifying religious service. Yet in propaganda and controversy he was gracious and humane beyond the measure of all other teachers. He did not call the priests of his time a generation of vipers, though he laughed at their ceremonies and their pretensions to superior birth.

Though the Buddha passed through intellectual crises such as the biographies of Christ do not hint at, yet in other matters it is he rather than Christ who offers a picture and example of peace. Christ enjoyed with a little band of friends an intimacy which the Hindu gave to none, but from the very commencement of his mission he is at enmity with what he calls the world. The world is evil and a great event is coming of double import, for it will bring disaster on the wicked as well as happiness for the good. "Repent ye, for the Kingdom of Heaven is at hand." He is angry with the world because it will not hear him. He declares that it hates him and the gospel according to St John even makes him say, "I pray not for the world, but for them which thou hast given me[1]." The little towns of Galilee are worse in his eyes than the wicked cities of antiquity because they are not impressed by his miracles and Jerusalem which has slighted all the prophets and finally himself is to receive signal punishment. The shadow of impending death fell over the last period of his ministry and he felt that he was to be offered as a sacrifice. The Jews even seem to have thought at one time that he was unreasonably alarmed[2].

But the Buddha was not angry with the world. He thought of it as unsatisfactory and transitory rather than wicked, as ignorant rather than rebellious. He troubled little about people who would not listen. The calm and confidence which so many narratives attribute to him rarely failed to meet with the respect which they anticipated. In his life there is no idea of sacrifice, no element of the tragic, no nervous irritability. When Devadatta meditated his assassination, he is represented as telling his disciples that they need not be uneasy because it was physically impossible to kill a Buddha. The saying is perhaps not historical but it illustrates Indian sentiment. In his previous

[1] John xvii. 9. But he prayed for his executioners.

[2] John vii. 19–20.

existences, when preparing for Buddhahood, he had frequently given his life for others, not because it was any particular good to them but in order to perfect his character for his own great career and bring about the selflessness which is essential to a Buddha. When once he had attained enlightenment any idea of sacrifice, such as the shepherd laying down his life for the sheep, had no meaning. It would be simply the destruction of the more valuable for the less valuable. Even the modern developments of Buddhism which represent the Buddha Amida as a saviour do not contain the idea that he gives up his life for his followers.

Gotama instituted a religious order and lived long enough to see it grow out of infancy, but its organization was gradual and for a year or two it was simply a band of disciples not more bound by rules than the seventy whom Christ sent forth to preach. Would Christ, had he lived longer, have created something analogous to the Buddhist *sangha*, a community not conflicting with national and social institutions but independent of them? The question is vain and to Europeans Christ's sketch of the Christian life will appear more satisfactory than the finished portrait of the Bhikkhu. But though his maxims are the perfect expression of courtesy and good feeling with an occasional spice of paradox, such as the command to love one's enemies, yet the experience of nearly twenty centuries has shown that this morality is not for the citizens of the world. The churches which give themselves his name preach with rare exceptions that soldiering, financing and the business of government—things about which he cared as little as do the birds and the lilies of the field—are the proper concern of Christian men and one wonders whether he would not, had his life been prolonged, have seen that many of his precepts, such as turning the other cheek and not resisting evil, are incompatible with ordinary institutions and have followed the example of the great Indian by founding a society in which they could be kept. The monastic orders of the Roman and Eastern Churches show that such a need was felt.

There are many resemblances between the Gospels and the teaching of the Buddha but the bases of the two doctrines are different and, if the results are sometimes similar, this shows that the same destination can be reached by more than one road. It is perhaps the privilege of genius to see the goal by intuition: the road and the vehicle are subsidiary and may be varied to suit the minds of different nations. Christ, being a Jew, took for his basis a refined form of the old Jewish theism. He purged Jehovah of his jealousy and prejudices and made him a spirit of pure benevolence who behaves to men as a loving father and bids them behave to one another as loving brethren. Such ideas lie outside the sphere of Gotama's thought and he would probably have asked why on this hypothesis there is any evil in the world. That is a question which the Gospels are chary of discussing but they seem to indicate that the disobedience and sinfulness of mankind are the root of evil. A godly world would be a happy world. But the Buddha would have said that though the world would be very much happier if all its inhabitants were moral and religious, yet the evils inherent in individual existence would still remain; it would still be impermanent and unsatisfactory.

Yet the Buddha and Christ are alike in points which are of considerable human interest, though they are not those emphasized by the Churches. Neither appears to have had much taste for theology or metaphysics. Christ ignored them: the Buddha said categorically that such speculations are vain. Indeed it is probably a general law in religions that the theological phase does not begin until the second generation, when the successors of the founder try to interpret and harmonize his words. He himself sees clearly and says plainly what mankind ought to do. Neither the Buddha, nor Christ, nor Mohammed cared for much beyond this, and such of their sayings as have reference to the whence, the whither and the why of the universe are obscure precisely because these questions do not fall within the field of religious genius and receive no illumination from its light. Argumentative as the Buddhist suttas are, their aim is strictly practical, even when their language appears scholastic, and the burden of all their ratiocination is the same and very simple. Men are unhappy because of their foolish desires: to become happy they must make themselves a new heart and will and, perhaps the Buddha would have added, new eyes.

Neither the Buddha nor Christ thought it worth while to write anything and both of them ignored ceremonial and sacerdotal codes in a way which must have astounded their contemporaries. The law-books and sacrifices to which Brahmans and Pharisees devoted time and study are simply left on one side. The former are replaced by injunctions to cultivate a good habit of mind, such as is exemplified in the Eightfold Path and the Beatitudes, the latter by some observances of extreme simplicity, such as the Pâtimokkha and the Lord's Prayer. In both cases subsequent generations felt that the provision made by the Founders was inadequate and the Buddhist and Christian Churches have multiplied ceremonies which, though not altogether unedifying, would certainly have astonished Gotama and Christ.

For Christ the greatest commandments were that a man should love God and his neighbours. This summary is not in the manner of Gotama and though love (mettâ) has an important place in his teaching, it is rather an inseparable adjunct of a holy life than the force which creates and animates it. In other words the Buddha teaches that a saint must love his fellow men rather than that he who loves his fellow men is a saint. But the passages extolling *mettâ* are numerous and striking, and European writers have, I think, shown too great a disposition to maintain that *mettâ* is something less than Christian love and little more than benevolent equanimity. The love of the New Testament is not ἔρως but ἀγάπη, a new word first used by Jewish and Christian writers and nearly the exact equivalent of *mettâ*. For both words love is rather too strong a rendering and charity too weak. Nor is it just to say that the Buddha as compared with Christ preaches inaction. The Christian nations of Europe are more inclined to action than the Buddhist nations of Asia, yet the Beatitudes do not indicate that the strenuous life is the road to happiness. Those declared blessed are the poor, the mourners, the meek, the hungry, the pure and the persecuted. Such men have just the virtues of the patient Bhikkhu and like Christ the Buddha praised the merciful and the peacemakers. And similarly Christ's phrase about rendering unto Cæsar the things that are Cæsar's seems to dissociate his true followers (like the Bhikkhus) from political life. Money and taxes are the affair of those who put their heads on coins; God and the things which concern him have quite another sphere.

CHAPTER X

THE TEACHING OF THE BUDDHA

1

WHEN the Buddha preached his first sermon[1] to the five monks at Benares the topics he selected were the following. First comes an introduction about avoiding extremes of either self-indulgence or self-mortification. This was specially appropriate to his hearers who were ascetics and disposed to over-rate the value of austerities. Next he defines the middle way or eightfold path. Then he enunciates the four truths of the nature of suffering, its origin, its cessation, and the method of bringing about that cessation. This method is no other than the eightfold path. Then his hearers understood that whatever has a beginning must have an end. This knowledge is described as the pure and spotless Eye of Truth. The Buddha then formally admitted them as the first members of the Sangha. He then explained to them that there is no such thing as self. We are not told that they received any further instruction before they were sent forth to be teachers and missionaries: they were, it would seem, sufficiently equipped. When the Buddha instructs his sixth convert, Yasa, the introduction is slightly different, doubtless because he was a layman. It treats of "almsgiving, of moral duties, of heaven, of the evil, vanity and sinfulness of desires, of the blessings which come from abandoning desires." Then when his catechumen's mind was prepared, he preached to him "the chief doctrine of the Buddhas, namely suffering, its cause, its cessation and the Path." And when Yasa understood this he obtained the Eye of Truth.

It is clear, therefore, that the Buddha regarded practice as the foundation of his system. He wished to create a temper and a habit of life. Mere acquiescence in dogma, such as a Christian creed, is not sufficient as a basis of religion and test of membership. It is only in the second stage that he enunciates

[1] See chap. VIII. of this book.

the four great theorems of his system (of which one, the Path, is a matter of practice rather than doctrine) and only later still that he expounds conceptions which are logically fundamental, such as his view of personality. "Just as the great ocean has only one taste, the taste of salt, so has this doctrine and discipline only one taste, the taste of emancipation[1]." This practical aim has affected the form given to much of the Buddha's teaching, for instance the theory of the Skandhas and the chain of causation. When examined at leisure by a student of to-day, the dogmas seem formulated with imperfect logic and the results trite and obvious. But such doctrines as that evil must have a cause which can be discovered and removed by natural methods: that a bad unhappy mind can be turned into a good, happy mind by suppressing evil thoughts and cultivating good thoughts, are not commonplaces even now, if they receive a practical application, and in 500 B.C. they were not commonplaces in any sense.

And yet no one can read Buddhist books or associate with Buddhist monks without feeling that the intellectual element is preponderant, not the emotional. The ultimate cause of suffering is ignorance. The Buddha has won the truth by understanding the universe. Conversion is usually described by some such phrase as acquiring the Eye of Truth, rather than by words expressing belief or devotion. The major part of the ideal life, set forth in a recurring passage of the Dîgha Nikâya, consists in the creation of intellectual states, and though the Buddha disavowed all speculative philosophy his discourses are full, if not of metaphysics, at least of psychology. And this knowledge is essential. It is not sufficient to affirm one's belief in it; it must be assimilated and taken into the life of every true Buddhist. All cannot do this: most of the unconverted are blinded by lust and passion, but some are incapacitated by want of mental power. They must practise virtue and in a happier birth their minds will be enlarged.

The reader who has perused the previous chapters will have some idea of the tone and subject matter of the Buddha's preaching. We will now examine his doctrine as a system and will begin with the theory of existence, premising that it disclaims all idea of doing more than analyze our experience.

[1] Cullavag. IX. I. IV.

With speculations or assertions as to the origin, significance and purpose of the Universe, the Buddha has nothing to do. Such questions do not affect his scheme of salvation. What views—if any—he may have held or implied about them we shall gather as we go on. But it is dangerous to formulate what he did not formulate himself, and not always easy to understand what he did formulate. For his words, though often plain and striking, are, like the utterances of other great teachers, apt to provoke discordant explanations. They meet our thoughts half way, but no interpretation exhausts their meaning. When we read into them the ideas of modern philosophy and combine them into a system logical and plausible after the standard of this age, we often feel that the result is an anachronism: but if we treat them as ancient simple discourses by one who wished to make men live an austere and moral life, we still find that there are uncomfortably profound sayings which will not harmonize with this theory.

The Buddha's aversion to speculation did not prevent him from insisting on the importance of a correct knowledge of our mental constitution, the chain of causation and other abstruse matters; nor does it really take the form of neglecting metaphysics: rather of defining them in a manner so authoritative as to imply a reserve of unimparted knowledge. Again and again questions about the fundamental mysteries of existence are put to him and he will not give an answer. It would not conduce to knowledge, peace, or freedom from passion, we are told, and, therefore, the Lord has not declared it. *Therefore*: not, it would seem, because he did not know, but because the discussion was not profitable. And the modern investigator, who is not so submissive as the Buddha's disciples, asks why not? Can it be that the teacher knew of things transcendental not to be formulated in words? Once[1] he compared the truths he had taught his disciples to a bunch of leaves which he held in his hand and the other truths which he knew but had not taught to the leaves of the whole forest in which they were walking. And the story of the blind men and the elephant[2] seems to

[1] Sam. Nik. LVI. 31.

[2] Udâna VI. 4. The story is that a king bade a number of blind men examine an elephant and describe its shape. Some touched the legs, some the tusks, some the tail and so on and gave descriptions accordingly, but none had any idea of the general shape.

hint that Buddhas, those rare beings who are not blind, can see the constitution of the universe. May we then in chance phrases get a glimpse of ideas which he would not develop? It may be so, but the quest is temerarious. "What I have revealed[1] hold as revealed, and what I have not revealed, hold as not revealed." The gracious but authoritative figure of the Master gives no further reply when we endeavour to restate his teaching in some completer form which admits of comparison with the ancient and modern philosophies of Europe.

The best introduction to his theory of existence is perhaps the instruction given to the five monks after his first sermon. The body[2] is not the self, he says, for if it were, it would not be subject to disease and we should be able to say, let my body be or not be such and such. As the denial of the existence of the self or ego (Attâ in Pali, Âtman in Sanskrit) is one of the fundamental and original tenets of Gotama, we must remember that this self whose existence is denied is something not subject to decay, and possessing perfect free will with power to exercise it. The Brahmanic Âtman is such a self but it is found nowhere in the world of our experience[3]. For the body or form is not the self, neither is sensation or feeling (*vedanâ*) for they are not free and eternal. Neither is perception (*saññâ*)[4] the self. Neither, the Buddha goes on to say, are the *Sankhâras* the self, and for the same reason.

Here we find ourselves sailing on the high seas of dogmatic terminology and must investigate the meaning of this important and untranslateable word. It is equivalent to the Sanskrit *saṃskâra*, which is akin to the word Sanskrit itself, and means compounding, making anything artificial and elaborate. It may be literally translated as synthesis or confection, and is often used in the general sense of phenomena since all phenomena are

[1] Or "determined."

[2] Or form: *rûpa*.

[3] The word Jîva, sometimes translated *soul*, is not equivalent to *âtman*. It seems to be a general expression for all the immaterial side of a human being. It is laid down (Dig. Nik. VI. and VII.) that it is fruitless to speculate whether the Jîva is distinct from the body or not.

[4] Saññâ like many technical Buddhist terms is difficult to render adequately, because it does not cover the same ground as any one English word. Its essential meaning is recognition by a mark. When we perceive a blue thing we recognize it as blue and as like other blue things that we have marked. See Mrs Rhys Davids, Dhamma-Saṅgaṇi, p. 8.

compound[1]. Occasionally[2] we hear of three Sankhâras, body or deed, word and thought. But in later literature the Sankhâras become a category with fifty-two divisions and these are mostly mental or at least subjective states. The list opens with contact (phasso) and then follow sensation, perception, thought, reflection, memory and a series of dispositions or states such as attention, effort, joy, torpor, stupidity, fear, doubt, lightness of body or mind, pity, envy, worry, pride. As European thought does not class all these items under one heading or, in other words, has no idea equivalent to Sankhâra, it is not surprising that no adequate rendering has been found, especially as Buddhism regards everything as mere becoming, not fixed existence, and hence does not distinguish sharply between a process and a result—between the act of preparing and a preparation. Conformations, confections, syntheses, co-efficients, tendencies, potentialities have all been used as equivalents but I propose to use the Pali word as a rule. In some passages the word phenomena is an adequate literary equivalent, if it is remembered that phenomena are not thought of apart from a perceiving subject: in others some word like predispositions or tendencies is a more luminous rendering, because the Sankhâras are the potentialities for good and evil action existing in the mind as a result of Karma[3].

The Buddha has now enumerated four categories which are not the self. The fifth and last is Viññâṇa, frequently rendered by consciousness. But this word is unsuitable in so far as it suggests in English some unified and continuous mental state. Viññâṇa sometimes corresponds to thought and sometimes is hardly distinguished from perception, for it means awareness[4] of what is pleasant or painful, sweet or sour and so on. But the Pitakas continually insist[5] that it is not a unity and that its varieties come into being only when they receive proper nourishment or, as we should say, an adequate stimulus. Thus visual consciousness depends on the sight and on visible objects,

[1] The Saṃyutta-Nikâya xxii. 79. 8 states that the Sankhâras are so-called because they compose what is compound (sankhatam). [2] Maj. Nik. 44.

[3] In this sense Sankhâra has also some affinity to the Sanskrit use of Saṃskâra to mean a sacramental rite. It is the essential nature of such a rite to produce a special effect. So too the Sankhâras present in one existence inevitably produce their effect in the next existence. For Sankhâra see also the long note by S. Z. Aung at the end of the *Compendium of Philosophy* (P.T.S. 1910).

[4] The use of this word for Viññâṇa is, I believe, due to Mrs Rhys Davids.

[5] See especially Maj. Nik. 38.

auditory consciousness on the hearing and on sounds. Viññâṇa is divided into eighty-nine classes according as it is good, bad or indifferent, but none of these classes, nor all of them together, can be called the self.

These five groups—body, feeling, perception, the saṇkhâras, thought—are generally known as the Skandhas[1] signifying in Sanskrit collections or aggregates. The classification adopted is not completely logical, for feeling and perception are both included in the Sankhâras and also counted separately. But the object of the Buddha was not so much to analyze the physical and mental constitution of a human being as to show that this constitution contains no element which can be justly called self or soul. For this reason all possible states of mind are catalogued, sometimes under more than one head. They are none of them the self and no self, ego, or soul in the sense defined above is discernible, only aggregates of states and properties which come together and fall apart again. When we investigate ourselves we find nothing but psychical states: we do not find a psyche. The mind is even less permanent than the body[2], for the body may last a hundred years or so "but that which is called mind, thought or consciousness, day and night keeps perishing as one thing and springing up as another." So in the Saṃyutta-Nikâya, Mâra the Tempter asks the nun Vajirâ by whom this being, that is the human body, is made. Her answer is "Here is a mere heap of *sankhâras*: there is no 'being.' As when various parts are united, the word 'chariot[3]' is used (to describe the whole), so when the *skandhas* are present, the word 'being' is commonly used. But it is suffering only that comes into existence and passes away." And Buddhaghosa[4] says:

"Misery only doth exist, none miserable;
No doer is there, naught but the deed is found;
Nirvana is, but not the man that seeks it;
The path exists but not the traveller on it."

[1] Pali, Khanda. But it has become the custom to use the Sanskrit term. Cf. Karma, nirvâṇa.

[2] See Sam. Nik. XII. 62. For parallels to this view in modern times see William James, *Text Book of Psychology*, especially pp. 203, 215, 216.

[3] Cf. Milinda Panha II. 1. 1 and also the dialogue between the king of Sauvîra and the Brahman in Vishnu Pur. II. XIII.

[4] Vis. Mag. chap. XVI. quoted by Warren, *Buddhism in Translations*, p. 146. Also it is admitted that viññâṇa cannot be disentangled and sharply distinguished from feeling and sensation. See passages quoted in Mrs Rhys Davids, *Buddhist Psychology*, pp. 52–54.

Thus the Buddha and his disciples rejected such ideas as soul, being and personality. But their language does not always conform to this ideal of negative precision, for the vocabulary of Pali (and still more of English) is inadequate for the task of discussing what form conduct and belief should take unless such words are used. Also the Attâ (Âtman), which the Buddha denies, means more than is implied by our words self and personality. The word commonly used to signify an individual is puggalo. Thus in one sutta[1] the Buddha preaches of the burden, the bearer of the burden, taking it up and laying it down. The burden is the five skandhas and the bearer is the individual or puggalo. This, if pressed, implies that there is a personality apart from the skandhas which has to bear them. But probably it should not be pressed and we should regard the utterance as merely a popular sermon using language which is, strictly speaking, metaphorical.

2

The doctrine of Anattâ—the doctrine that there is no such thing as a soul or self—is justly emphasized as a most important part of the Buddha's teaching and Buddhist ethics might be summarized as the selfless life. Yet there is a danger that Europeans may exaggerate and misunderstand the doctrine by taking it as equivalent to a denial of the soul's immortality or of free will or to an affirmation that mind is a function of the body. The universality of the proposition really diminishes its apparent violence and nihilism. To say that some beings have a soul and others have not is a formidable proposition, but to say that absolutely no existing person or thing contains anything which can be called a self or soul is less revolutionary than it sounds. It clearly does not deny that men exist for decades and mountains for millenniums: neither does it deny that before birth or after death there may be other existences similar to human life. It merely states that in all the world, organic and inorganic, there is nothing which is simple, self-existent, self-determined, and permanent: everything is compound, relative and transitory. The obvious fact that infancy, youth and age form a series is not denied: the series may be

[1] Sam. Nik. XXII. 22. 1.

called a personality and death need not end it. The error to be avoided is the doctrine of the Brahmans that through this series there runs a changeless self, which assumes new phases like one who puts on new garments.

The co-ordination and apparent unity observable in our mental constitution is due to *mano* which is commonly translated mind but is really for Buddhism, as for the Upanishads, a *sensus communis*. Whereas the five senses have different spheres or fields which are independent and do not overlap, *mano* has a share in all these spheres. It receives and cognizes all sense impressions.

The philosophy of early Buddhism deals with psychology rather than with metaphysics. It holds it profitable to analyze and discuss man's mental constitution, because such knowledge leads to the destruction of false ideals and the pursuit of peace and insight. Enquiry into the origin and nature of the external world is not equally profitable: in fact it is a vain intellectual pastime. Still in treating of such matters as sensation, perception and consciousness, it is impossible to ignore the question of external objects or to avoid propounding, at least by implication, some theory about them. In this connection we often come upon the important word Dhamma (Sanskrit, Dharma). It means a law, and more especially the law of the Buddha, or, in a wider sense, justice, righteousness or religion[1]. But outside the moral and religious sphere it is commonly used in the plural as equivalent to phenomena, considered as involving states of consciousness. The Dhamma-saṅgaṇi[2] divides phenomena into those which exist for the subject and those which exist for other individuals and ignores the possibility of things existing apart from a knowing subject. This hints at idealism and other statements seem more precise. Thus the Saṃyutta-Nikâya declares: "Verily, within this mortal body, some six feet high, but conscious and endowed with mind, is the world, and its origin, and its passing away[3]." And similarly[4] the problem is posed, "Where do the four elements pass away and leave no trace behind." Neither gods nor men can answer

[1] With reference to a teacher dhamma is the doctrine which he preaches. With reference to a disciple, it may often be equivalent to duty. Cf. the Sanskrit expressions: sva-dharma, one's own duty; para-dharma, the duty of another person or caste.

[2] Dhamma-s. 1044–5. [3] II. 3. 8. [4] Dig. Nik. XI. 85.

it, and when it is referred to the Buddha, his decision is that the question is wrongly put and therefore admits of no solution. "Instead of asking where the four elements pass away without trace, you should have asked:

> Where do earth, water, fire and wind,
> And long and short and fine and coarse,
> Pure and impure no footing find?
> Where is it that both name and form[1]
> Die out and leave no trace behind?"

To that the answer is: In the mind of the Saint.

Yet it is certain that such passages should not be interpreted as equivalent to the later Yogâcâra doctrine that only thought really exists or to any form of the doctrine that the world is Mâyâ or illusion. The Pitakas leave no doubt on this point, for they elaborate with clearness and consistency the theory that sensation and consciousness depend on contact, that is contact between sense organs and sense objects. "Man is conceived as a compound of instruments, receptive and reacting[2]" and the Saṃyutta-Nikâya puts into the Buddha's mouth the following dogmatic statement[3]. "Consciousness arises because of duality. What is that duality? Visual[4] consciousness arises because of sight and because of visible objects. Sight is transitory and mutable: it is its very nature to change. Visible objects are the same. So this duality is both in movement and transitory."

The question of the reality of the external world did not present itself to the early Buddhists. Had it been posed we may surmise that the Buddha would have replied, as in similar cases, that the question was not properly put. He would not, we may imagine, have admitted that the human mind has the creative power which idealism postulates, for such power seems to imply the existence of something like a self or âtman. But still though the Pitakas emphasize the empirical duality of sense-organs and sense-objects, they also supply a basis for the doctrines of Nâgârjuna and Asanga, which like much late Buddhist metaphysics insist on using logic in regions where the master would not use it. When it is said that the genesis of the world and its

[1] Name and form is the Buddhist equivalent for subject and object or mind and body.

[2] Mrs Rhys Davids, *Buddhist Psychology*, p. 39.

[3] Sam. Nik. XXXV. 93.

[4] The same formula is repeated for the other senses.

passing away are within this mortal frame, the meaning probably is that the world as we experience it with its pains and pleasures depends on the senses and that with the modification or cessation of the senses it is changed or comes to an end. In other words (for this doctrine like most of the Buddha's doctrines is at bottom ethical rather than metaphysical) the saint can make or unmake his own world and triumph over pain. But the theory of sensation may be treated not ethically but metaphysically. Sensation implies a duality and on the one side the Buddha's teaching argues that there is no permanent sentient self but merely different kinds of consciousness arising in response to different stimuli. It is admitted too that visible objects are changing and transitory like sight itself and thus there is no reason to regard the external world, which is one half of the duality, as more permanent, self-existent and continuous than the other half. When we apply to it the destructive analysis which the Buddha applied only to mental states, we easily arrive at the nihilism or idealism of the later Buddhists. Of this I will treat later. For the present we have only to note that early Buddhism holds that sensation depends on contact, that is on a duality. It does not investigate the external part of this duality and it is clear that such investigation leads to the very speculations which the Buddha declared to be unprofitable, such as arguments about the eternity and infinity of the universe.

The doctrine of Anattâ is counterbalanced by the doctrine of causation. Without this latter the Buddha might seem to teach that life is a chaos of shadows. But on the contrary he teaches the universality of law, in this life and in all lives. For Hindus of most schools of thought, metempsychosis means the doctrine that the immortal soul passes from one bodily tenement to another, and is reborn again and again: karma is the law which determines the occurrence and the character of these births. In Buddhism, though the Pitakas speak continually of rebirth, metempsychosis is an incorrect expression since there is no soul to transmigrate and there is strictly speaking nothing but karma. This word, signifying literally action or act, is the name of the force which finds expression in the fact that every event is the result of causes and also is itself a cause which produces effects; further in the fact (for Indians regard it as one) that when a life, whether of a god, man or lower creature, comes to an end, the sum of its actions (which is in many connections equivalent to personal character) takes effect as a whole and determines the character of another aggregation of skandhas—in popular language, another being—representing the net result of the life which has come to an end. Karma is also used in the more concrete sense of the merit or demerit acquired by various acts. Thus we hear of karma which manifests itself in this life, and of karma which only manifests itself in another. No explanation whatever is given of the origin of karma, of its reason, method or aims and it would not be consistent with the principles of the Buddha to give such an explanation. Indeed, though it is justifiable to speak of karma as a force which calls into being the world as we know it, such a phrase goes beyond the habitual language of early Buddhism which merely states that everything has a cause and that every one's nature and circumstances are the result of previous actions in this or other existences. Karma is not so much invoked as a metaphysical explanation of the universe as accorded the consideration which it merits as an ultimate moral fact.

It has often been pointed out that the Buddha did not originate or even first popularize the ideas of reincarnation and karma: they are Indian, not specifically Buddhist. In fact, of all Indian systems of thought, Buddhism is the one which has the greatest difficulty in expressing these ideas in intelligible and consistent language, because it denies the existence of the ego. Some writers have gone so far as to suggest that the whole doctrine formed no part of the Buddha's original teaching and was an accretion, or at most a concession of the master to the beliefs of his time. But I cannot think this view is correct. The idea is woven into the texture of the Buddha's discourses. When in words which have as strong a claim as any in the Pitakas to be regarded as old and genuine he describes the stages by which he acquired enlightenment and promises the same experiences to those who observe his discipline[1], he says that he first followed the thread of his own previous existences through past æons, plumbing the unfathomed depths of time: next, the whole of existence was spread out before him, like a view seen from above, and he saw beings passing away from

[1] See Maj. Nik. 36 for his own experiences and Dig. Nik. 2. 93–96.

one body and taking shape in another, according to their deeds. Only when he understood both the perpetual transformation of the universe and also the line and sequence in which that transformation occurs, only then did he see the four truths as they really are.

It is unfortunate for us that the doctrine of reincarnation met with almost universal assent in India[1]. If some one were to found a new Christian sect, he would probably not be asked to prove the immortality of the soul: it is assumed as part of the common religious belief. Similarly, no one asked the Buddha to prove the doctrine of rebirth. If we permit our fancy to picture an interview between him and someone holding the ordinary ideas of an educated European about the soul, we may imagine that he would have some difficulty in understanding what is the alternative to rebirth. His interlocutor might reply that there are two types of theory among Europeans. Some think that the soul comes into existence with the body at birth but continues to exist everlasting and immortal after the death of the body. Others, commonly called materialists, while agreeing that the soul comes into existence with the birth of the body, hold that it ceases to exist with the death of the body. To the first theory the Buddha would probably have replied that there is one law without exception, namely that whatever has a beginning has also an end. The whole universe offers no analogy or parallel to the soul which has a beginning but no end, and not the smallest logical need is shown for believing a doctrine so contrary to the nature of things. And as for materialism he would probably say that it is a statement of the processes of the world as perceived but no explanation of the mental or even of the physical world. The materialists forget that objects as known cannot be isolated from the knowing subject. Sensation implies contact and duality but it

[1] In Dig. Nik. XXIII. Pâyâsi maintains the thesis, regarded as most unusual (sec. 5), that there is no world but this and no such things as rebirth and karma. He is confuted not by the Buddha but by Kassapa. His arguments are that dead friends whom he has asked to bring him news of the next world have not done so and that experiments performed on criminals do not support the idea that a soul leaves the body at death. Kassapa's reply is chiefly based on analogies of doubtful value but also on the affirmation that those who have cultivated their spiritual faculties have intuitive knowledge of rebirth and other worlds. But Pâyâsi did not draw any distinction between rebirth and immortality as understood in Europe. He was a simple materialist.

is no real explanation to say that mental phenomena are caused by physical phenomena. The Buddha reckoned among vain speculations not only such problems as the eternity and infinity of the world but also the question, Is the principle of life (Jîva) identical with the body or not identical. That question, he said, is not properly put, which is tantamount to condemning as inadequate all theories which derive life and thought from purely material antecedents[1]. Other ideas of modern Europe, such as that the body is an instrument on which the soul works, or the expression of the soul, seem to imply, or at least to be compatible with, the pre-existence of the soul.

It is probable too that the Buddha would have said, and a modern Buddhist would certainly say, that the fact of rebirth can easily be proved by testimony and experience, because those who will make the effort can recall their previous births. For his hearers the difficulty must have been not to explain why they believed in rebirth but to harmonize the belief with the rest of the master's system, for what is reborn and how? We detect a tendency to say that it is Viññâṇa, or consciousness, and the expression paṭisandhiviññâṇam or rebirth-consciousness occurs[2]. The question is treated in an important dialogue in the Majjhima-Nikâya[3], where a monk called Sâti maintains that, according to the Buddha's teaching, consciousness transmigrates unchanged. The Buddha summoned Sâti and rebuked his error in language of unusual severity, for it was evidently capital and fatal if persisted in. The Buddha does not state what transmigrates, as the European reader would wish him to do, and would no doubt have replied to that question that it is improperly framed and does not admit of an answer.

His argument is directed not so much against the idea that consciousness in one existence can have some connection with consciousness in the next, as against the idea that this consciousness is a unity and permanent. He maintains that it is a complex process due to many causes, each producing its own effect. Yet the Pitakas seem to admit that the processes which constitute

[1] The more mythological parts of the Pitakas make it plain that the early Buddhists were not materialists in the modern sense. It is also said that there are formless worlds in which there is thought, but no form or matter.

[2] See too the story of Godhika's death. Sam. Nik. I. iv. 3 and Buddhaghosa on Dhammap. 57.

[3] No. 38 called the Mahâtaṇhâsankhaya-suttam.

consciousness in one life, can also produce their effect in another life, for the character of future lives may be determined by the wishes which we form in this life. Existence is really a succession of states of consciousness following one another irrespective of bodies. If *ABC* and *abc* are two successive lives, *ABC* is not more of a reality or unity than *BCa*. No personality passes over at death from *ABC* to *abc* but then *ABC* is itself not a unity: it is merely a continuous process of change[1].

The discourse seems to say that taṇhâ, the thirst for life, is the connecting link between different births, but it does not use this expression. In one part of his address the Buddha exhorts his disciples not to enquire what they were or what they will be or what is the nature of their present existence, but rather to master and think out for themselves the universal law of causation, that every state has a cause for coming into being and a cause for passing away. No doubt his main object is as usual practical, to incite to self-control rather than to speculation. But may he not also have been under the influence of the idea that time is merely a form of human thought? For the ordinary mind which cannot conceive of events except as following one another in time, the succession of births is as true as everything else. The higher kinds of knowledge, such as are repeatedly indicated in the Buddha's discourse, though they are not described because language is incapable of describing them, may not be bound in this way by the idea of time and may see that the essential truth is not so much a series of births in which something persists and passes from existence to existence, as the timeless fact that life depends upon taṇhâ, the desire for life. Death, that is the breaking up of such constituents of human life as the body, states of consciousness, etc., does not affect taṇhâ. If taṇhâ has not been deliberately suppressed, it collects skandhas again. The result is called a new individual. But the essential truth is the persistence of the taṇhâ until it is destroyed.

Still there is no doubt that the earliest Buddhist texts and the discourse ascribed to the Buddha himself speak, when using ordinary untechnical language, of rebirth and of a man dying

[1] See too Dig. Nik. II. 63, "If Viññâṇa did not descend into the womb, would body and mind be constituted there?" and Sam. Nik. XII. 12. 3, "Viññâṇa food is the condition for bringing about rebirth in the future."

and being born[1] in such and such a state. Only we must not suppose that the man's self is continued or transferred in this operation. There is no entity that can be called soul and strictly speaking no entity that can be called body, only a variable aggregation of skandhas, constantly changing. At death this collocation disperses but a new one reassembles under the influence of taṇhâ, the desire of life, and by the law of karma which prescribes that every act must have its result. The illustration that comes most naturally is that of water. Waves pass across the surface of the sea and successive waves are not the same, nor is what we call the same wave really the same at two different points in its progress, and yet one wave causes another wave and transmits its form and movement. So are beings travelling through the world (saṃsâra) not the same at any two points in a single life and still less the same in two consecutive lives: yet it is the impetus and form of the previous lives, the desire that urges them and the form that it takes, which determine the character of the succeeding lives.

But Buddhist writers more commonly illustrate rebirth by fire than by water and this simile is used with others in the Questions of Milinda. We cannot assume that this book reflects the views of the Buddha or his immediate followers, but it is the work of an Indian in touch with good tradition who lived a few centuries later and expressed his opinions with lucidity. It denies the existence of transmigration and of the soul and then proceeds to illustrate by metaphors and analogies how two successive lives can be the same and yet not the same. For instance, suppose a man carelessly allows his lamp to set his thatch on fire with the result that a whole village is burnt down. He is held responsible for the loss but when brought before the judge argues that the flame of his lamp was not the same as the flame that burnt down the village. Will such a plea be allowed? Certainly not. Or to take another metaphor. Suppose a man were to choose a young girl in marriage and after making a contract with her parents were to go away, waiting for her to grow up. Meanwhile another man comes and marries her. If the two men appeal to the King and the later suitor says to the earlier, The little child whom you chose and paid for is one and the full grown girl whom I paid for and

[1] Uppajjati is the usual word.

married is another, no one would listen to his argument, for clearly the young woman has grown out of the girl and in ordinary language they are the same person. Or again suppose that one man left a jar of milk with another and the milk turned to curds. Would it be reasonable for the first man to accuse the second of theft because the milk has disappeared?

The caterpillar and butterfly might supply another illustration. It is unfortunate that the higher intelligences offer no example of such metamorphosis in which consciousness is apparently interrupted between the two stages. Would an intelligent caterpillar take an interest in his future welfare as a butterfly and stigmatize as vices indulgences pleasant to his caterpillar senses and harmful only to the coming butterfly, between whom and the caterpillar there is perhaps no continuity of consciousness? We can imagine how strongly butterflies would insist that the foundation of morality is that caterpillars should realize that the butterflies' interests and their own are the same.

3

When the Buddha contemplated the saṃsâra, the world of change and transmigration in which there is nothing permanent, nothing satisfying, nothing that can be called a self, he formulated his chief conclusions, theoretical and practical, in four propositions known as the four noble[1] truths, concerning suffering, the cause of suffering, the extinction of suffering, and the path to the extinction of suffering[2]. These truths are always represented as the essential and indispensable part of Buddhism. Without them, says the Buddha more than once, there can be no emancipation, and agreeably to this we find them represented as having formed part of the teaching of previous Buddhas[3] and consequently as being rediscovered rather than invented by Gotama. He even compares himself to one who has found

[1] Ariyasaccâni. Rhys Davids translates the phrase as Aryan truths and the word Ariya in old Pali appears not to have lost its national or tribal sense, *e.g.* Dig. Nik. II. 87 Ariyam âyatanam the Aryan sphere (of influence). But was a religious teacher preaching a doctrine of salvation open to all men likely to describe its most fundamental and universal truths by an adjective implying pride of race?

[2] In Maj. Nik. 44 the word dukkha is replaced by sakkâya, individuality, which is apparently regarded as equivalent in meaning. So for instance the Noble Eightfold path is described as sakkâya-nirodha-gâminî patipadâ.

[3] Theragâthâ 487–493, and Puggala Pañ. IV. 1.

in the jungle the site of an ancient city and caused it to be restored. It would therefore not be surprising if they were found in pre-Buddhist writings, and it has been pointed out that they are practically identical with the four divisions of the Hindu science of medicine: roga, disease; rogahetu, the cause of disease; arogya, absence of disease; bhaisajya, medicine. A similar parallel between the language of medicine and moral science can be found in the Yoga philosophy, and if the fourfold division of medicine can be shown to be anterior to Buddhism[1], it may well have suggested the mould in which the four truths were cast. The comparison of life and passion to disease is frequent in Buddhist writings and the Buddha is sometimes hailed as the King of Physicians. It is a just compendium of his doctrine—so far as an illustration can be a compendium—to say that human life is like a diseased body which requires to be cured by a proper regimen. But the Buddha's claim to originality is not thereby affected, for it rests upon just this, that he was able to regard life and religion in this spirit and to put aside the systems of ritual, speculation and self-mortification which were being preached all round him.

The first truth is that existence involves suffering. It receives emotional expression in a discourse in the Saṃyutta-Nikâya[2]. "The world of transmigration, my disciples, has its beginning in eternity. No origin can be perceived, from which beings start, and hampered by ignorance, fettered by craving, stray and wander. Which think you are more—the tears which you have shed as you strayed and wandered on this long journey, grieving and weeping because you were bound to what you hated and separated from what you loved—which are more, these tears, or the waters in the four oceans? A mother's death, a son's death, a daughter's death, loss of kinsmen, loss of property, sickness, all these have you endured through long ages—and while you felt these losses and strayed and wandered on this long journey, grieving and weeping because you were bound to what you hated and separated from what you loved, the tears that you shed are more than the water in the four oceans."

It is remarkable that such statements aroused no contradiction. The Buddha was not an isolated and discontented philosopher, like Schopenhauer in his hotel, but the leader of

[1] But it has not been proved so far as I know.

[2] Sam. Nik. xv. 3.

an exceptionally successful religious movement in touch and sympathy with popular ideas. On many points his assertions called forth discussion and contradiction but when he said that all existence involves suffering no one disputed the dictum: no one talked of the pleasures of life or used those arguments which come so copiously to the healthy-minded modern essayist when he devotes a page or two to disproving pessimism[1]. On this point the views and temperament of the Buddha were clearly those of educated India. The existence of this conviction and temperament in a large body of intellectual men is as important as the belief in the value of life and the love of activity for its own sake which is common among Europeans. Both tempers must be taken into account by every theory which is not merely personal but endeavours to ascertain what the human race think and feel about existence.

The sombre and meditative cast of Indian thought is not due to physical degeneration or a depressing climate. Many authors speak as if the Hindus lived in a damp relaxing heat in which physical and moral stamina alike decay. I myself think that as to climate India is preferable to Europe, and without arguing about what must be largely a question of personal taste, one may point to the long record of physical and intellectual labour performed even by Europeans in India. Neither can it be maintained that in practice Buddhism destroys the joy and vigour of life. The Burmese are among the most cheerful people in the world and the Japanese among the most vigorous, and the latter are at least as much Buddhists as Europeans are Christians. It might be plausibly maintained that Europeans' love of activity is mainly due to the intolerable climate and uncomfortable institutions of their continent, which involve a continual struggle with the weather and continual discussion forbidding any calm and comprehensive view of things. The Indian being less troubled by these evils is able to judge what is the value of life in itself, as an experience for the individual, not as part of a universal struggle, which is the common view of seriously minded Europeans, though as to this

[1] Buddhist works sometimes insist on the impurity of human physical life in a way which seems morbid and disagreeable. But this view is not exclusively Buddhist or Asiatic. It is found in Marcus Aurelius and perhaps finds its strongest expression in the De Contemptu Mundi of Pope Innocent III (in Pat. Lat. CCXVII. cols. 701–746).

struggle they have but hazy ideas of the antagonists, the cause and the result.

The Buddhist doctrine does not mean that life is something trifling and unimportant, to be lived anyhow. On the contrary, birth as a human being is an opportunity of inestimable value. He who is so born has at least a chance of hearing the truth and acquiring merit. "Hard is it to be born as a man, hard to come to hear the true law" and when the chance comes, the good fortune of the being who has attained to human form and the critical issues which depend on his using it rightly are dwelt on with an earnestness not surpassed in Christian homiletics. He who acts ill as a man may fall back into the dreary cycles of inferior births, among beasts and blind aimless beings who cannot understand the truth, even if they hear it. From this point of view human life is happiness, only like every form of existence it is not satisfying or permanent.

Dukkha is commonly rendered in English by pain or suffering, but an adequate literary equivalent which can be used consistently in translating is not forthcoming. The opposite state, sukha, is fairly rendered by well-being, satisfaction and happiness. Dukkha is the contrary of this: uneasiness, discomfort, difficulty. Pain or suffering are too strong as renderings, but no better are to hand. When the Buddha enlarges on the evils of the world it will be found that the point most emphasized as vitiating life is its transitoriness.

"Is that which is impermanent sorrow or joy?" he asks of his disciples. "Sorrow, Lord," is the answer, and this oft-repeated proposition is always accepted as self-evident. The evils most frequently mentioned are the great incurable weaknesses of humanity, old age, sickness and death, and also the weariness of being tied to what we hate, the sadness of parting from what we love. Another obvious evil is that we cannot get what we want or achieve our ambitions. Thus the temper which prompts the Buddha's utterances is not that of Ecclesiastes—the melancholy of satiety which, having enjoyed all, finds that all is vanity—but rather the regretful verdict of one who while sympathizing with the nobler passions—love, ambition, the quest of knowledge—is forced to pronounce them unsatisfactory. The human mind craves after something which is permanent, something of which it can say This is mine. It longs to be something or to produce something which is not transitory and which has an absolute value in and for itself. But neither in this world nor in any other world are such states and actions possible. Only in Nirvana do we find a state which rises above the transitory because it rises above desire. Not merely human life but all possible existences in all imaginable heavens must be unsatisfactory, for such existences are merely human life under favourable conditions. Some great evils, such as sickness, may be absent but life in heaven must come to an end: it is not eternal, it is not even permanent, it does not, any more than this life, contain anything that god or man can call his own. And it may be observed that when Christian writers attempt to describe the joys of a heaven which is eternally satisfying, they have mostly to fall back on negative phrases such as "Eye hath not seen nor ear heard."

The European view of life differs from the Asiatic chiefly in attributing a value to actions in themselves, and in not being disturbed by the fact that their results are impermanent. It is, in fact, the theoretical side of the will to live, which can find expression in a treatise on metaphysics as well as in an act of procreation. An Englishman according to his capacity and mental culture is satisfied with some such rule of existence as having a good time, or playing the game, or doing his duty, or working for some cause. The majority of intelligent men are prepared to devote their lives to the service of the British Empire: the fact that it must pass away as certainly as the Empire of Babylon and that they are labouring for what is impermanent does not disturb them and is hardly ever present to their minds. Those Europeans who share with Asiatics some feeling of dissatisfaction with the impermanent try to escape it by an unselfish morality and by holding that life, which is unsatisfactory if regarded as a pursuit of happiness, acquires a new and real value if lived for others. And from this point of view the European moralist is apt to criticize the Buddhist truths of suffering and the release from suffering as selfish. But Buddhism is as full as or fuller than Christianity of love, self-sacrifice and thought for others. It says that it is a fine thing to be a man and have the power of helping others: that the best life is that which is entirely unselfish and a continual sacrifice. But looking at existence as a whole, and accepting the theory that the happiest and best life is a life of self-sacrifice, it declines to consider as satisfactory the world in which this principle holds good. Many of the best Europeans would probably say that their ideal is not continual personal enjoyment but activity which makes the world better. But this ideal implies a background of evil just as much as does the Buddha's teaching. If evil vanished, the ideal would vanish too.

There is one important negative aspect of the truth of suffering and indeed of all the four truths. A view of human life which is common in Christian and Mohammedan countries represents man as put in the world by God, and human life as a service to be rendered to God. Whether it is pleasant, worth living or not are hardly questions for God's servants. There is no trace of such a view in the Buddha's teaching. It is throughout assumed that man in judging human life by human standards is not presumptuous or blind to higher issues. Life involves unhappiness: that is a fact, a cardinal truth. That this unhappiness may be ordered for disciplinary or other mysterious motives by what is vaguely called One above, that it would disappear or be explained if we could contemplate our world as forming part of a larger universe, that "there is some far off divine event," some unexpected solution in the fifth act of this complicated tragedy, which could justify the creator of this *dukkhakkhandha*, this mass of unhappiness—for all such ideas the doctrine of the Blessed One has nothing but silence, the courteous and charitable silence which will not speak contemptuously. The world of transmigration has neither beginning nor end nor meaning: to those who wish to escape from it the Buddha can show the way: of obligation to stop in it there can be no question[1].

Buddhism is often described as pessimistic, but is the epithet just? What does it mean? The dictionary defines pessimism as the doctrine which teaches that the world is as bad as it can be and that everything naturally tends towards evil. That is

[1] As a general rule suicide is strictly forbidden (see the third Pârâjika and Milinda, IV. 13 and 14) for in most cases it is not a passionless renunciation of the world but rather a passionate and irritable protest against difficulties which simply lays up bad karma in the next life. Yet cases such as that of Godhika (see Buddhaghosa on the Dhammapada, 57) seem to imply that it is unobjectionable if performed not out of irritation but by one who having already obtained mental release is troubled by disease.

emphatically not Buddhist teaching. The higher forms of religion have their basis and origin in the existence of evil, but their justification and value depend on their power to remove it. A religion, therefore, can never be pessimistic, just as a doctor who should simply pronounce diseases to be incurable would never be successful as a practitioner. The Buddha states with the utmost frankness that religion is dependent on the existence of evil. "If three things did not exist, the Buddha would not appear in the world and his law and doctrine would not shine. What are the three? Birth, old age and death." This is true. If there were people leading perfectly happy, untroubled lives, it is not likely that any thought of religion would enter their minds, and their irreligious attitude would be reasonable, for the most that any deity is asked to give is perfect happiness, and that these imaginary folk are supposed to have already. But according to Buddhism no form of existence can be perfectly happy or permanent. Gods and angels may be happier than men but they are not free from the tyranny of desire and ultimately they must fall from their high estate and pass away.

4

The second Truth declares the origin of suffering. "It is," says the Buddha, "the thirst which causes rebirth, which is accompanied by pleasure and lust and takes delight now here, now there; namely, the thirst for pleasure, the thirst for another life, the thirst for success." This Thirst (Taṇhâ) is the craving for life in the widest sense: the craving for pleasure which propagates life, the craving for existence in the dying man which brings about another birth, the craving for wealth, for power, for pre-eminence within the limits of the present life. What is the nature of this craving and of its action? Before attempting to answer we must consider what is known as the chain of causation[1], one of the oldest, most celebrated, and most obscure formulæ of Buddhism. It is stated that the Buddha knew it before attaining enlightenment[2], but it is second in importance only to the four truths, and in the opening sections of the Mahâvagga, he is represented as meditating on it under the Bo-tree, both in its positive and negative form. It runs as follows: "From ignorance come the sankhâras, from the sank-

[1] Pali Paṭicca-samuppâda. Sanskrit Pratîtya-samutpâda. [2] Sam. Nik. XII. 10.

hâras comes consciousness, from consciousness come name-and-form, from name-and-form come the six provinces (of the senses), from the six provinces comes contact, from contact comes sensation, from sensation comes craving, from craving comes clinging, from clinging comes existence, from existence comes birth, from birth come old age and death, pain and lamentation, suffering, sorrow, and despair. This is the origin of this whole mass of suffering. But by the destruction of ignorance, effected by the complete absence of lust, the sankhâras are destroyed, by the destruction of the sankhâras, consciousness is destroyed" and so on through the whole chain backwards.

The chain is also known as the twelve Nidânas or causes. It is clearly in its positive and negative forms an amplification of the second and third truths respectively, or perhaps they are a luminous compendium of it.

Besides the full form quoted above there are shorter versions. Sometimes there are only nine links[1] or there are five links combined in an endless chain[2]. So we must not attach too much importance to the number or order of links. The chain is not a genealogy but a statement respecting the interdependence of certain stages and aspects of human nature. And though the importance of cause (hetu) is often emphasized, the causal relation is understood in a wider sense than is usual in our idiom. If there were no birth, there would be no death, but though birth and death are interdependent we should hardly say that birth is the cause of death.

In whatever way we take the Chain of Causation, it seems to bring a being into existence twice, and this is the view of Buddhaghosa who says that the first two links (ignorance and the sankhâras) belong to past time and explain the present existence: the next eight (consciousness to existence) analyse the present existence: and the last two (birth and old age) belong to future time, representing the results in another existence of desire felt in this existence. And that is perhaps what the constructor of the formula meant. It is clearest if taken backwards. Suppose, the Buddha once said to Ânanda[3], there were no birth,

[1] Dig. Nik. xv.

[2] "Contact comes from consciousness: sensation from contact: craving from sensation: the sankhâras from craving: consciousness from the sankhâras: contact from consciousness" and so on *ad infinitum*. See Mil. Pan. 51.

[3] Dig. Nik. xv.

would there then be any old age or death? Clearly not. That is the meaning of saying that old age and death depend on birth: if birth were annihilated, they too would be annihilated. Similarly birth depends on Bhava which means becoming and does not imply anything self-existent and stationary: all the world is a continual process of coming into existence and passing away. It is on the universality of this process that birth (jâti) depends. But on what does the endless becoming itself depend? We seem here on the threshold of the deepest problems but the answer, though of wide consequences, brings us back to the strictly human and didactic sphere. Existence depends on Upâdâna. This word means literally grasping or clinging to and should be so translated here but it also means fuel and its use is coloured by this meaning, since Buddhist metaphor is fond of describing life as a flame. Existence cannot continue without the clinging to life, just as fire cannot continue without fuel[1].

The clinging in its turn depends on Taṇhâ, the thirst or craving for existence. The distinction between taṇhâ and upâdâna is not always observed, and it is often said taṇhâ is the cause of karma or of sorrow. But, strictly speaking, upâdâna is the grasping at life or pleasure: taṇhâ is the incessant, unsatisfied craving which causes it. It is compared to the birana, a weed which infests rice fields and sends its roots deep into the ground. So long as the smallest piece of root is left the weed springs up again and propagates itself with surprising rapidity, though the cultivator thought he had exterminated it. This metaphor is also used to illustrate how taṇhâ leads to a new birth. Death is like cutting down the plant: the root remains and sends up another growth.

We now seem to have reached an ultimate principle and basis, namely, the craving for life which transcends the limits of one existence and finds expression in birth after birth. Many passages in the Pitakas justify the idea that the force which constructs the universe of our experience is an impersonal appetite, analogous to the Will of Schopenhauer. The shorter

[1] Sam. Nik. XII. 53. Cf. too the previous sutta 51. In the Abhidhamma Pitaka and later scholastic works we find as a development of the law of causation the theory of relations (paccaya) or system of correlation (paṭṭhâna-nayo). According to this theory phenomena are not thought of merely in the simple relation of cause and effect. One phenomenon can be the assistant agency (upakâraka) of another phenomenon in 24 modes. See Mrs Rhys Davids' article Relations in *E.R.E.*

formula quoted above in which it is said that the sankhâras come from taṇhâ also admits of such an interpretation. But the longer chain does not, or at least it considers taṇhâ not as a cosmic force but simply as a state of the human mind. Suffering can be traced back to the fact that men have desire. To what is desire due? To sensation. With this reply we leave the great mysteries at which the previous links seemed to hint and begin one of those enquiries into the origin and meaning of human sensation which are dear to early Buddhism. Just as there could be no birth if there were no existence, so there could be no desire if there were no sensation. What then is the cause of sensation? Contact (phasso). This word plays a considerable part in Buddhist psychology and is described as producing not only sensation but perception and volition (cetanâ)[1]. Contact in its turn depends on the senses (that is the five senses as we know them, and mind as a sixth) and these depend on name-and-form. This expression, which occurs in the Upanishads as well as in Buddhist writings, denotes mental and corporeal life. In explaining it the commentators say that form means the four elements and shape derived from them and that name means the three skandhas of sensation, perception and the sankhâras. This use of the word nâma probably goes back to ancient superstitions which regarded a man's name as containing his true being but in Buddhist terminology it is merely a technical expression for mental states collectively. Buddhaghosa observes that name-and-form are like the playing of a lute which does not come from any store of sound and when it ceases does not go to form a store of sound elsewhere.

On what do name-and-form depend? On consciousness. This point is so important that in teaching Ânanda the Buddha adds further explanations. "Suppose," he says, "consciousness were not to descend into the womb, would name-and-form consolidate in the womb? No, Lord. Therefore, Ânanda, consciousness is the cause, the occasion, the origin of name-and-form." But consciousness according to the Buddha's teaching[2] is not a unity, a thinking soul, but mental activity produced

[1] Mrs Rhys Davids, Dhamma-sangaṇi, pref. p. lii. "The sensory process is analysed in each case into (*a*) an apparatus capable of reaching to an impact not itself: (*b*) an impinging form (rûpam): (*c*) contact between (*a*) and (*b*): (*d*) resultant modification of the mental continuum, viz. first, contact of a specific sort, then hedonistic result or intellectual result or presumably both."

[2] See *e.g.* Maj. Nik. 38.

by various appropriate causes. Hence it cannot be regarded as independent of name-and-form and as their generator. So the Buddha goes on to say that though name-and-form depend on consciousness it is equally true that consciousness depends on name-and-form. The two together make human life: everything that is born, and dies or is reborn in another existence[1], is name-and-form plus consciousness.

What we have learnt hitherto is that suffering depends on desire and desire on the senses. For didactic purposes this is much, but as philosophy the result is small: we have merely discovered that the world depends on name-and-form plus consciousness, that is on human beings. The first two links of the chain (the last in our examination) do not leave the previous point of view—the history of individual life and not an account of the world process—but they have at least that interest which attaches to the mysterious.

"Consciousness depends on the sankhâras." Here the sankhâras seem to mean the predispositions anterior to consciousness which accompany birth and hence are equivalent to one meaning of Karma, that is the good and bad qualities and tendencies which appear when rebirth takes place. Perhaps the best commentary on the statement that consciousness depends on the sankhâras is furnished by a Sutta called Rebirth according to the sankhâras[2]. The Buddha there says that if a monk possessed of the necessary good qualities cherishes a wish to be born after death as a noble, or in one of the many heavens, "then those predispositions (sankhâra) and mental conditions (vihâro) if repeated[3] conduce to rebirth" in the place he desires. Similarly when Citta is dying, the spirits of the wood come round his death-bed and bid him wish to be an Emperor in his next life. Thus a personality with certain predispositions and aptitudes may be due to the thought and wishes of a previous personality[4], and these predispositions, asserts the last article of the formula, depend upon ignorance. We might be tempted

[1] This does not mean that the same name-and-form plus consciousness which dies in one existence reappears in another.

[2] Maj. Nik. 120 Sankhâruppatti sutta.

[3] He should make it a continual mental exercise to think of the rebirth which he desires.

[4] So too in the Sânkhya philosophy the saṃskâras are said to pass from one human existence to another. They may also remain dormant for several existences and then become active.

to identify this ignorance with some cosmic creative force such as the Unconscious of Hartmann or the Mâyâ of Śankara. But though the idea that the world of phenomena is a delusion bred of ignorance is common in India, it does not enter into the formula which we are considering. Two explanations of the first link are given in the Pitakas, which are practically the same. One[1] states categorically that the ignorance which produces the sankhâras is not to know the four Truths. Elsewhere[2] the Buddha himself when asked what ignorance means replies that it is not to know that everything must have an origin and a cessation. The formula means that it is ignorance of the true nature of the world and the true interests of mankind that brings about the suffering which we see and feel. We were born into the world because of our ignorance in our last birth and of the desire for re-existence which was in us when we died.

Of the supreme importance attached to this doctrine of causation there can be no doubt. Perhaps the best instance is the story of Sâriputta's conversion. In the early days of the Buddha's mission he asked for a brief summary of the new teaching and in reply the essential points were formulated in the well-known verses which declare that all things have a cause and an end[3]. Such utterances sound like a scientific dictum about the uniformity of nature or cosmic law. But though the Pitakas imply some such idea, they seem to shrink from stating it clearly. They do not emphasize the orderly course of nature or exhort men to live in harmony with it. We are given to understand that the intelligence of those supermen who are called Buddhas sees that the four Truths are a consequence of the nature of the universe but subsequent instruction bids us attend to the truths themselves and not to their connection with the universal scheme. One reason for this is that Indians were little inclined to think of impersonal laws and forces[4].

[1] Maj. Nik. 9 Sammâdiṭṭhi sutta. [2] Sam. Nik. XXII. 126.

[3] Mahâvag. I. 23. 4 and 5:

Ye dhammâ hetuppabhavâ tesam hetum Tathâgato
Âha tesañca yo nirodho evamvâdî Mahâsamano ti.

The passage is remarkable because it insists that this is the principal and essential doctrine of Gotama. Compare too the definition of the Dhamma put in the Buddha's own mouth in Majjhima, 79: Dhammam te desessâmi: imasmim sati, idam hoti: imass'uppâdâ idaṃ upajjhati, etc.

[4] The Sânkhya might be described as teaching a law of evolution, but that is not the way it is described in its own manuals.

The law of karma and the periodic rhythm of growth and decay which the universe obeys are ideas common to Hinduism and Buddhism and not incompatible with the mythology and ritual to which the Buddha objected. And though the Pitakas insist on the universality of causation, they have no notion of the uniformity of nature in our sense[1]. The Buddhist doctrine of causation states that we cannot obtain emancipation and happiness unless we understand and remove the cause of our distress, but it does not discuss cosmic forces like karma and Mâyâ. Such discussion the Buddha considered unprofitable[2] and perhaps he may have felt that insistence on cosmic law came dangerously near to fatalism[3].

Though the number of the links may be varied the Buddha attached importance to the method of concatenation and the impersonal formulation of the whole and in one passage[4] he objects to the questions, what are old age and death and who is it that has old age and death. Though the chain of causation treats of a human life, it never speaks of a person being born or growing old and Buddhaghosa[5] observes that the Wheel of existence is without known beginning, without a personal cause or passive recipient and empty with a twelvefold emptiness. It has no external cause such as Brahmâ or any deity "and is also wanting in any ego passively recipient of happiness and misery."

The twelve Nidânas have passed into Buddhist art as the Wheel of Life. An ancient example of this has been discovered in the frescoes of Ajanta and modern diagrams, which represent the explanations current in mediæval India, are still to be found in Tibet and Japan[6]. In the nave of the wheel are three female figures signifying passion, hatred and folly and in the spaces between the spokes are scenes depicting the phases of human life: round the felly runs a series of pictures representing the twelve links of the chain. The first two links are represented

[1] Take among hundreds of instances the account of the Buddha's funeral.

[2] The Anguttara Nikâya, book IV. chap. 77, forbids speculation on four subjects as likely to bring madness and trouble. Two of the four are kamma-vipâko and loka-cintâ. An attempt to make the chain of causation into a cosmic law would involve just this sort of speculation.

[3] The Pitakas insist that causation applies to mental as well as physical phenomena.

[4] Sam. Nik. XII. 35.

[5] Vis. Mag. XVII. Warren, p. 175.

[6] See Waddell, *J.R.A.S.* 1894, pp. 367–384: Rhys Davids, *Amer. Lectures*, pp. 155–160.

by a blind man or blind camel and by a potter making pots. The third, or consciousness, is an ape. Some have thought that this figure represents the evolution of mind, which begins to show itself in animals and is perfected in man. It may however refer to a simile found in the Pitakas[1] where the restless, changeable mind is compared to a monkey jumping about in a tree.

5

We have now examined three of the four Truths, for the Chain of Causation in its positive form gives us the origin of suffering and in its negative form the facts as to the extinction of suffering: it teaches that as its links are broken suffering disappears. The fourth truth, or the way which leads to the extinction of suffering, gives practical directions to this effect. The way is the Noble Eightfold Path consisting of: right views, right aspirations, right speech, right conduct, right livelihood, right effort, right mindfulness, right rapture. This formula is comparable not with the Decalogue, to which correspond the precepts for monks and laymen, but rather with the Beatitudes. It contains no commands or prohibitions but in the simplest language indicates the spirit that leads to emancipation. It breathes an air of noble freedom. It says nothing about laws and rites: it simply states that the way to be happy is to have a good heart and mind, taking shape in good deeds and at last finding expression and fulfilment in the rapture of ecstasy. We may think the numerical subdivisions of the Path pedantic and find fault with its want of definition, for it does not define the word right (sammâ) which it uses so often, but in thus ignoring ceremonialism and legalism and making simple goodness in spirit and deed the basis of religion, Gotama rises above all his contemporaries and above all subsequent teachers except Christ. In detaching the perfect life from all connection with a deity or outside forces and in teaching man that the worst and best that can happen to him lie within his own power, he holds a unique position.

Indian thought has little sympathy with the question whether morality is utilitarian or intuitionist, whether we do good to benefit ourselves or whether certain acts and states are intrinsically good. The Buddha is a physician who prescribes

[1] Sam. Nik. XII. 61. See too Theragâthâ, verses 125 and 1111, and for other illustrative quotations Mrs Rhys Davids, *Buddhist Psychology*, pp. 34, 35.

a cure for a disease—the disease of suffering—and that cure is not a quack medicine which pretends to heal rapidly but a regime and treatment. If we ask whether the reason for following the regime is that it is good for us or that it is scientifically correct; or why we want to be well or whether health is really good: both the Buddha and the physician would reply that such questions are tiresome and irrelevant. With an appearance of profundity, they ask nothing worth answering. The eightfold path is the way and the only way of salvation. Its form depends on the fact that the knowledge of the Buddha, which embraces the whole universe, sees that it is a consequence of the nature of things. In that sense it may be described as an eternal law, but this is not the way in which the Pitakas usually speak of it and it is not represented as a divine revelation dictated by other than human motives. "Come, disciples," the Buddha was wont to say, "lead a holy life for the complete extinction of suffering." Holiness is simply the way out of misery into happiness. To ask why we should take that way, would seem to an Indian an unnecessary question, as it might seem to a Christian if he were asked why he wants to save his soul, but if the question is pressed, the answer must be at every point, for the Christian as much as for the Buddhist, to gain happiness[1]. Incidentally the happiness of others is fully cared for, since both religions make unselfishness the basis of morality and hold that the conscious and selfish pursuit of happiness is not the way to gain it, but if we choose to apply European methods of analysis to the Buddha's preaching, it is utilitarian. But the fact that he and his first disciples did not think such analysis and discussion necessary goes far to show that the temper created in his Order was not religiously utilitarian. It never occurred to them to look at things that way.

The eightfold path is the road to happiness but it is the way, not the destination, and the action of the Buddha and his disciples is something beyond it. They had obtained the goal, for they were all Arhats, and they might, if they had been inspired by that selfishness which some European authors find prominent in Buddhism, have entered into their rest. Yet the Buddha bade them go among men and preach "for the gain and welfare of many" and they continued their benevolent activity although it could add nothing to the reward which they had already won.

[1] But see Maj. Nik. 79, for the idea that there is something beyond happiness.

The Buddha often commented on the eightfold path, and we may follow one of the expositions attributed to him[1]. What, he asks, is meant by right views (*Sammâdiṭṭhi*)? Simply a knowledge of the four truths, and of such doctrines about personality and karma as are implied in them. But the negative aspects of this *Sammâdiṭṭhi* are more striking than the positive. It does not imply any philosophical or metaphysical system: the Buddha has shaken off all philosophical theories[2]. Secondly, it does not imply that any knowledge or belief is of efficacy in itself, as the lore of the Brahmans is supposed to be or those Christian creeds which save by faith. The Buddha has not a position such as the Church attributes to Christ, or later Buddhism to Amida. All that is required under the head of right belief is a knowledge of the general principles and programme of Buddhism.

The Buddha continues, What is right resolve? It is the resolve to renounce pleasures, to bear no malice and do no harm. What is right speech? To abstain from lying and slandering, harsh words and foolish chatter. What is right conduct? To abstain from taking life, from stealing, from immorality. What is right livelihood? To abandon wrong occupations and get one's living by a right occupation. This is elsewhere defined as one that does not bring hurt or danger to any living thing, and five bad occupations are enumerated, namely, those of a caravan-trader, slave-dealer, butcher, publican and poison seller. European critics of Buddhism have often found fault with its ethics as being a morality of renunciation, and in the explanation epitomized above each section of the path is interpreted in this way. But this negative form is not a peculiarity of Buddhism. Only two of the commandments in our Decalogue are positive precepts; the rest are prohibitions. The same is true of most early codes. The negative form is at once easier and more practical for it requires a mental effort to formulate any ideal of human life; it is comparatively easy to note the bad things people do, and say, don't. The pruning of the feelings, the cutting off of every tendril which can cling to the pleasures of sense, is an essential part of that mental cultivation in which the higher Buddhism consists. But the Pitakas say clearly that what is to be eliminated is only bad mental states. Desire for pleasure and striving after wealth are bad,

[1] Dig. Nik. 22.

[2] Sutta-Nipâta, 787.

but it does not follow that desire and striving are bad in themselves. Desire for what is good (Dhammachando as opposed to Kâmachando) is itself good, and the effort to obtain nirvana is often described as a struggle or wrestling[1]. Similarly though absolute indifference to pains and pleasures is the ideal for a Bhikkhu, this by no means implies, as is often assumed, a general insensibility and indifference, the harmless oyster-like life of one who hurts nobody and remains in his own shell. European criticisms on the selfishness and pessimism of Buddhism forget the cheerfulness and buoyancy which are the chief marks of its holy men. The Buddhist saint is essentially one who has freed himself. His first impulse is to rejoice in his freedom and share it with others, not to abuse the fetters he has cut away. Active benevolence and love[2] are enjoined as a duty and praised in language of no little beauty and earnestness. In the Itivuttaka[3] the following is put into the mouth of Buddha. "All good works whatever[4] are not worth one sixteenth part of love which sets free the heart. Love which sets free the heart comprises them: it shines, gives light and radiance. Just as the light of all the stars is not worth one sixteenth of the light of the moon: as in the last month of the rains in the season of autumn, when the sky is clear and cloudless the sun mounts up on high and overcomes darkness in the firmament: as in the last hour of the night when the dawn is breaking, the morning star shines and gives light and radiance: even so does love which sets free the soul and comprises all good works, shine and give light and radiance." So, too, the Sutta-Nipâta bids a man love not only his neighbour but all the world. "As a mother at the risk of her life watches over her own child, her only child, so let every one cultivate a boundless love towards all beings[5]." Nor are such precepts left vague and universal. If some of his acts and words seem wanting in family affection, the Buddha enjoined filial piety as emphatically as Moses or

[1] Padhânam. But in later Buddhism we also find the idea that nirvana is something which comes only when we do not struggle for it.

[2] Mettâ, corresponding exactly to the Greek ἀγάπη of the New Testament.

[3] III. 7. The translation is abbreviated.

[4] More literally, "All the occasions which can be used for doing good works."

[5] Sutta-Nipâta, 1–8, *S.B.E.* vol. x. p. 25 and see also Ang. Nik. IV. 190 which says that love leads to rebirth in the higher heavens and Sam. Nik. XX. 4 to the effect that a little love is better than great gifts. Also *Questions of Milinda*, 4. 4. 16.

Confucius. There are two beings, he says, namely Father and Mother, who can never be adequately repaid[1]. If a man were to carry his parents about on his shoulders for a hundred years or could give them all the kingdoms and treasures of the earth, he still would not discharge his debt of gratitude[2]. But whereas Confucius said that the good son does not deviate from the way of his father, the Buddha, who was by no means conservative in religious matters, said that the only way in which a son could repay his parents was by teaching them the True Law.

The Buddha defines the sixth section of the path more fully than those which precede. Right effort, he says, is when a monk makes an effort, and strives to prevent evil states of mind from arising: to suppress them if they have arisen: to produce good states of mind, and develop and perfect them. Hitherto we have been considering morality, indispensable but elementary. This section is the beginning of the specially Buddhist discipline of mental cultivation. The process is apt to seem too self-conscious: we wonder if a freer growth would not yield better fruits. But in a comparison with the similar programmes of other religions Buddhism has little to fear. Its methods are not morbid or introspective: it does not fetter the intellect with the bonds of authority. The disciple has simply to discriminate between good and bad thoughts, to develop the one and suppress the other. It is noticeable that under this heading of right effort, or right wrestling as it is sometimes called, both desire and striving for good ends are consecrated. Sloth and torpor are as harmful to spiritual progress as evil desires and as often reprimanded. Also the aim is not merely negative: it is partly creative. The disciple is not to suppress will and feeling, but he is to make all the good in him grow; he should foster, increase and perfect it.

What is right-mindfulness[3], the seventh section of the path? It is "When a monk lives as regards the body, observant of the body, strenuous, conscious, mindful and has rid himself of covetousness and melancholy": and similarly as regards the sensations, the mind and phenomena. The importance of this mindfulness is often insisted on. It amounts to complete self-

[1] Ang. Nik. 1. 2. 4.

[2] Cf. too Mahâvag. VIII. 22 where a monk is not blamed for giving the property of the order to his parents.

[3] Sati is the Sanskrit Smṛiti.

mastery by means of self-knowledge which allows nothing to be done heedlessly and mechanically and controls not merely recognized acts of volition but also those sense-impressions in which we are apt to regard the mind as merely receptive. "Self is the lord of self: who else should be the lord? With self well subdued, a man finds a lord such as few can find[1]."

Although the Buddha denies that there is any soul or self (attâ) apart from the skandhas, yet here his ethical system seems to assume that a ruling principle which may be called self does exist. Nor is the discrepancy fully explained by saying that the non-existence of self or soul is the correct dogma and that expressions like self being the lord of self are concessions to the exigencies of exposition. The evolution of the self-controlled saint out of the confused mental states of the ordinary man is a psychological difficulty. As we shall see, when the eightfold path has been followed to the end new powers arise in the mind, new lights stream into it. Yet if there is no self or soul, where do they arise, into what do they stream?

The doctrine of Gotama as expressed in his earliest utterance on the subject to the five monks at Benares is that neither the body, nor any mental faculty to which a name can be given, is what was called in Brahmanic theology âtman, that is to say an entity which is absolutely free, imperishable, changeless and not subject to pain. This of course does not exclude the possibility that there may be something which does not come under any of the above categories and which may be such an entity as described. Indeed Brahmanic works which teach the existence of the âtman often use language curiously like that of Buddhism. Thus the Bhagavad-gîtâ[2] says that actions are performed by the Guṇas and only he who is deluded by egoism thinks "I am the doer." And the Vishnu Purana objects to the use of personal pronouns. "When one soul is dispersed in all bodies, it is idle to ask who are you, who am I[3]?" The accounts of the Buddhist higher life would be easier to understand if we could suppose that there is such a self: that the

[1] Dhammap. 160. [2] Bhag-gîtâ, 3. 27.

[3] Vishnu Pur. II. 13. The ancient Egyptians also, though for quite different reasons, did not accept our ideas of personality. For them man was not an individual unity but a compound consisting of the body and of several immaterial parts called for want of a better word souls, the *ka*, the *ba*, the *sekhem*, etc., which after death continue to exist independently.

pilgrim who is walking in the paths gradually emancipates, develops and builds it up: that it becomes partly free in nirvana before death and wholly free after death. Schrader[1] has pointed out texts in the Pitakas which seem to imply that there is something which is absolute and therefore not touched by the doctrine of anattâ. In a remarkable passage[2] the Buddha says: Therefore my disciples get rid of what is not yours. To get rid of it will mean your health and happiness for a long time. Form, sensation, perception, etc., are not yours; get rid of them. If a man were to take away, or burn, or use for his needs, all the grass, and boughs, and branches and leaves in this Jeta wood, would it ever occur to you to say, the man is taking *us* away, burning *us*, or using *us* for his needs? Certainly not, Lord. And why not? Because, Lord, it is not our self or anything belonging to our self. Just in the same way, replies the Buddha, get rid of the skandhas. The natural sense of this seems to be that the skandhas have no more to do with the real being of man than have the trees of the forest where he happens to be[3]. This suggests that there is in man something real and permanent, to be contrasted with the transitory skandhas and when the Buddha asks whether anything which is perishable and changeable can be called the self, he seems to imply that there is somewhere such a self. But this point cannot be pressed, for it is perfectly logical to define first of all what you mean by a ghost and then to prove that such a thing does not exist. If we take the passages at present collected as a whole, and admit that they are somewhat inconsistent or imperfectly understood, the net result is hardly that the name of self can be given to some part of human nature which remains when the skandhas are set on one side.

But though the Buddha denied that there is in man anything permanent which can be called the self, this does not imply a denial that human nature can by mental training be changed into something different, something infinitely superior to the

[1] *Ueber den Stand der indischen Philosophie zur Zeit Mahâvîras und Buddhas*, 1902. And On the problem of Nirvana in *Journal of Pali Text Society*, 1905. See too Sam. Nik. XXII. 15–17.

[2] Maj. Nik. 22.

[3] Compare also the sermon on the burden and the bearer and Sam Nik. XXII. 15–17. It is admitted that Nirvana is not dukkha and not aniccam and it seems to be implied it is not anattam.

nature of the ordinary man, perhaps something other than the skandhas[1]. One of his principal objections to the doctrine of the permanent self was that, if it were true, emancipation and sanctity would be impossible[2], because human nature could not be changed. In India the doctrine of the âtman was really dangerous, because it led a religious man to suppose that to ensure happiness and emancipation it is only necessary to isolate the âtman by self-mortification and by suppressing discursive thought as well as passion. But this, the Buddha teaches, is a capital error. That which can make an end of suffering is not something lurking ready-made in human nature but something that must be built up: man must be reborn, not flayed and stripped of everything except some core of unchanging soul. As to the nature of this new being the Pitakas are reticent, but not absolutely silent, as we shall see below. Our loose use of language might possibly lead us to call the new being a soul, but it is decidedly not an âtman, for it is something which has been brought into being by deliberate effort. The collective name for these higher states of mind is *paññâ*[3], wisdom or knowledge. This word is the Pali equivalent of the Sanskrit *prajñâ* and is interesting as connecting early and later Buddhism, for *prajñâ* in the sense of transcendental or absolute knowledge plays a great part in Mahayanism and is even personified.

The Pitakas imply that Buddhas and Arhats can understand things which the ordinary human mind cannot grasp and human words cannot utter. Later Indian Buddhists had no scruples in formulating what the master left unformulated. They did not venture to use the words âtman or attâ but they said that the saint can rise above all difference and plurality, transcend the distinction between subject and object and that nirvana is the absolute (Bhûtatathatâ). The Buddha would doubtless have objected to this terminology as he objected to all attempts to express the ineffable but perhaps the thought which struggles for expression in such language is not far removed from his own thought.

One of the common Buddhist similes for human life is fire and it is the best simile for illuminating all Buddhist psychology.

[1] See the argument with Yamaka in Sam. Nik. XXII. 85.

[2] See Sam. Nik. III., XXII. 97.

[3] Also paññâkkhandha or vijjâ.

To insist on finding a soul is like describing flames as substances. Fire is often spoken of as an element but it is really a process which cannot be isolated or interrupted. A flame is not the same as its fuel and it can be distinguished from other flames. But though you can individualize it and propagate it indefinitely, you cannot isolate it from its fuel and keep it by itself. Even so in the human being there is not any soul which can be isolated and go on living eternally but the analogy of the flame still holds good. Unseizable though a flame may be, and undefinable as substance, it is not unreasonable to trim a fire and make a flame rise above its fuel, free from smoke, clear and pure. If it were a conscious flame, such might be its own ideal.

The eighth and last section of the path is sammâ-samâdhi, right concentration or rapture. Mental concentration is essential to samâdhi, which is the opposite of those wandering desires often blamed as seeking for pleasure here and there. But samâdhi is more than mere concentration or even meditation and may be rendered by rapture or ecstasy, though like so many technical Buddhist terms it does not correspond exactly to any European word. It takes in Buddhism the place occupied in other religions by prayer—prayer, that is, in the sense of ecstatic communion with the divine being. The sermon[1] which the Buddha preached to King Ajâtasattu on the fruits of the life of a recluse gives an eloquent account of the joys of samâdhi. He describes how a monk[2] seats himself in the shade of a tree or in some mountain glen and then "keeping his body erect and his intelligence alert and intent" purifies his mind from all lust, ill-temper, sloth, fretfulness and perplexity. When these are gone, he is like a man freed from jail or debt, gladness rises in his heart and he passes successively through four stages of meditation[3]. Then his whole mind and even his body is permeated with a feeling of purity and peace. He concentrates his thoughts and is able to apply them to such great matters as he may select. He may revel in the enjoyment of supernatural powers, for we cannot deny that the oldest documents which we possess credit the sage with miraculous gifts, though they attach little importance to them, or he may follow the train of thought which led the Buddha himself to enlightenment. He

[1] Dig. Nik. II. [2] These exercises are hardly possible for the laity.

[3] See chap. XIV. for details.

thinks of his previous births and remembers them as clearly as a man who has been a long walk remembers at the end of the day the villages through which he has passed. He thinks of the birth and deaths of other beings and sees them as plainly as a man on the top of a house sees the people moving in the streets below. He realizes the full significance of the four truths and he understands the origin and cessation of the three great evils, love of pleasure, love of existence and ignorance. And when he thus sees and knows, his heart is set free. "And in him thus set free there arises the knowledge of his freedom and he knows that rebirth has been destroyed, the higher life has been led, what had to be done has been done. He has no more to do with this life. Just as if in a mountain fastness there were a pool of water, clear, translucent and serene and a man standing on the bank and with eyes to see should perceive the mussels and the shells, the gravel and pebbles and the shoals of fish as they move about or lie within it."

Similar accounts occur in many other passages with variations in the number of stages described. We must not therefore insist on the details as essential. But in all cases the process is marked by mental activity. The meditations of Indian recluses are often described as self-hypnotism, and I shall say something on this point elsewhere, but it is clear that in giving the above account the Buddha did not contemplate any mental condition in which the mind ceases to be active or master of itself. When, at the beginning, the monk sits down to meditate it is "with intelligence alert and intent": in the last stage he has the sense of freedom, of duty done, and of knowledge immediate and unbounded, which sees the whole world spread below like a clear pool in which every fish and pebble is visible.

6

With this stage he attains Nirvâṇa[1], the best known word and the most difficult to explain in all the vocabulary of Buddhism.

It is perhaps used more by western students than by oriental believers and it belongs to the same department of religious language as the word saint. For most Christians there is something presumptuous in trying to be a saint or in defining the

[1] Sanskrit Nirvâṇa: Pali Nibbâna.

precise form of bliss enjoyed by saints in heaven and it is the same with nirvana. Yet no one denies that sanctity and nirvana are religious ideals. In a passage already quoted[1], Gotama described how in attaining Buddhahood he sought and arrived at the incomparable security of nirvana in which there is no birth, age, sickness, death, pain or defilement. This, confirmed by many other statements, shows that nirvana is a state attainable in this existence and compatible with a life of intellectual and physical exertion such as he himself led. The original meaning is the state of peace and happiness in which the fires of lust, hatred and stupidity are extinguished and the participle *nibbuto* apparently derived from the same root had passed into popular language in the sense of happy[2]. Two forms of nirvana are distinguished. The first is upâdi-sesa-nibbânam[3] or nirvana in which the skandhas remain, although passion is destroyed. This state is also called arhatship, the condition of an arhat, meaning originally a worthy or venerable man, and the person enjoying it is alive. The idea that the emancipated saint who has attained the goal still lingers in the world, though no longer of the world, and teaches others, is common to all Indian religions. With the death of an arhat comes the state known as an-upâdi-sesa-nibbânam in which no skandhas remain. It is also called Parinibbânam and this word and the participle parinibbuto are frequently used with special reference to the death of the Buddha[4]. The difference between the two forms of nirvana is important though the second is only the continuation of the first. Nirvana in this life

[1] Maj. Nik. 26.

[2] *E.g.* the words addressed to Buddha, nibbutâ nûna sâ narî yassâyam îdiso pati. Happy is the woman who has such a husband. In the Anguttara Nikâya, III. 55 the Brahman Jâṇussoṇi asks Buddha what is meant by Sanditthikam nibbâṇam, that is nirvâṇa which is visible or belongs to this world. The reply is that it is effected by the destruction of lust, hatred and stupidity and it is described as *akâlikam, ehipassikam opanayikam, paccattam veditabbam viññûhi*—difficult words which occur elsewhere as epithets of Dhamma and apparently mean immediate, inviting (it says "come and see"), leading to salvation, to be known by all who can understand. For some views as to the derivation of nibbana, nibbuto, etc. see *J.P.T.S.* 1919, pp. 53 ff. But the word nirvâṇa occurs frequently in the Mahâbhârata and was probably borrowed by the Buddhists from the Brahmans.

[3] Or sa-upâdi.

[4] But parinirvâṇa is not always rigidly distinguished from nirvâṇa, *e.g.* Sutta Nipâta, 358. And in Cullavag. VI. 4. 4 the Buddha describes himself as Brâhmaṇo parinibbuto. Parinibbuto is even used of a horse in Maj. Nik. 65 *ad fin.*

admits of approximate definition: it is the goal of the religious life, though only the elect can even enter the struggle. Nirvana after death is not a goal in the same sense. The correct doctrine is rather that death is indifferent to one who has obtained nirvana and the difficulty of defining his nature after death does not mean that he has been striving for something inexplicable and illusory.

Arhatship is the aim and sum of the Buddha's teaching: it is associated in many passages with love for others, with wisdom, and happiness and is a condition of perfection attainable in this life. The passages in the Pitakas which seem to be the oldest and the most historical suggest that the success of the Buddha was due to the fact that he substituted for the chilly ideal of the Indian Munis something more inspiring and more visibly fruitful, something akin to what Christ called the Kingdom of Heaven. Thus we are told in the Vinaya that Bhaddiya was found sitting at the foot of a tree and exclaiming ecstatically, O happiness, happiness. When asked the reason of these ejaculations, he replied that formerly when he was a raja he was anxious and full of fear but that now, even when alone in the forest, he had become tranquil and calm, "with mind as peaceful as an antelope's."

Nirvana is frequently described by such adjectives as deathless, endless and changeless. These epithets seem to apply to the quality, not to the duration of the arhat's existence (for they refer to the time before the death of the body) and to signify that in the state which he has attained death and change have no power over him. He may suffer in body but he does not suffer in mind, for he does not identify himself with the body or its feelings[1].

Numerous passages could be quoted from the poetical books of the Pali Canon to the effect that nirvana is happiness and the same is stated in the more dogmatic and logical portions. Thus we hear of the bliss of emancipation and of the happiness which is based on the religious life[2] and the words "Nirvana is the greatest happiness" are put into Gotama's own mouth[3].

[1] Sam. Nik. XXII. 1. 18.

[2] Vimuttisukham and brahmacariyogadham sukham.

[3] Maj. Nik. 139, cf. also Ang. Nik. II. 7 where various kinds of sukham or happiness are enumerated, and we hear of nekkhammasukham nirupadhis, upekkhâs, arûparamanam sukham, etc.

The middle way preached by him is declared to be free from all distress, and those who walk in it make an end of pain even in this life[1]. In one passage[2] Gotama is found meditating in a wood one winter night and is asked if he feels well and happy. The night is cold, his seat is hard, his clothes are light and the wind bitter. He replies emphatically that he is happy. Those who live in comfortable houses suffer from the evils of lust, hatred and stupidity but he has made an end of those evils and therefore is happy. Thus nirvana is freedom and joy: it is not extinction in the sense we give the word but light to them that sit in darkness, release to those in prison and torture. But though it is legitimately described in terms which imply positive happiness it transcends all human standards of good and evil, pleasure and pain. In describing the progress to it we all—whether Indians or Europeans—necessarily use such words as better, higher, happier, but in truth it is not to be expressed in terms of such values. In an interesting sutta[3] a Jain argues that happiness is the goal of life. But the Buddha states categorically first that perfect happiness is only attainable by abandoning the conscious pursuit of happiness and secondly that even absolute happiness when attained is not the highest goal: there is a better state beyond, and that state is certainly not annihilation or extinction of feeling, for it is described in terms of freedom and knowledge.

The Dhamma-saṅgaṇi speaks of Nirvana as the Uncompounded Element[4] and as a state not productive of good or evil. Numerous assertions[5] are made about it incidentally but, though we hear that it is perfected and supramundane, most of the epithets are negative and amount to little more than that it transcends, or is absolutely detached from, all human experience. Uncompounded (asankhato) may refer to the passing away of all sankhâras but what may be the meaning of dhâtu or element in this context, I do not presume to conjecture. But whatever else the word may mean, it clearly does not signify annihilation. Both here and in the Questions of Milinda an impression is produced in the mind of the reader, and perhaps was not absent

[1] *E.g.* Maj. Nik. 9 Ditthe dhamme dukkhass' antakaro hoti.

[2] Ang. Nik. v. xxxii.

[3] Maj. Nik. 79.

[4] Asankhatadhâtu, cf. the expression asankhâraparinibbâyî. Pugg. Pan. 1. 44.

[5] Tabulated in Mrs Rhys Davids' translation, pp. 367–9.

in the mind of the writer, that nirvana is a sphere or plane of existence resembling though excelling space or ether. It is true that the language when carefully examined proves to be cautious and to exclude material interpretations but clearly the expositor when trying to make plain the inexplicable leaned to that side of error rather than towards annihilation[1].

Somewhat similar is the language attributed to the Buddha in the Udâna[2]. "There is a state (âyatanam) where there is neither earth nor water, fire nor air, nor infinity either of space or of consciousness, nor nothingness, nor the absence of perception or non-perception[3], neither this world nor another, neither sun nor moon. That I call neither coming, going, nor standing, neither death nor birth. It is without stability, without movement, without basis: it is the end of sorrow, unborn, unoriginated, uncreated, uncompounded[4]." The statements about nirvana in the Questions of Milinda are definite and interesting. In this work[5], Nâgasena tells King Milinda that there are two things which are not the result of a cause, to wit space and Nirvana. Nirvana is unproduceable (which does not mean unattainable) without origin, not made of anything and uncompounded. He who orders his life aright passes beyond the transitory, and gains the Real, the highest fruit. And when he has gained that, he has realized Nirvana[6].

The parts of the Pitakas which seem oldest leave the impression that those who heard and understood the Buddha's teaching at once attained this blissful state, just as the Church regards the disciples of Christ as saints. But already in the

[1] Such a phrase as *Nibbâṇassa sacchikiriyâya* "for the attainment or realization of Nirvana" would be hardly possible if Nirvana were annihilation.

[2] Udâna VII. near beginning.

[3] These are the formless stages of meditation. In Nirvana there is neither any ordinary form of existence nor even the forms of existence with which we become acquainted in trances.

[4] This negative form of expression is very congenial to Hindus. Thus many centuries later Kabir sung "With God is no rainy season, no ocean, no sunshine, no shade: no creation and no destruction: no life nor death: no sorrow nor joy is felt....There is no water, wind, nor fire. The True Guru is there contained."

[5] IV. 7. 13 ff.

[6] See also Book VII. of the Milinda containing a long list of similes illustrating the qualities necessary for the attainment of arhatship. Thirty qualities of arhatship are mentioned in Book VI. of the same work. See also Mahâparinib. Sut. III. 65–60 and Rhys Davids' note.

Pitakas[1] we find the idea that the struggle to obtain nirvana extends over several births and that there are four routes leading to sanctification. These routes are described by the names of those who use them and are commonly defined in terms of release from the ten fetters binding man to the world[2]. The first is the Sotâpanno, he who has entered into the stream and is on his way to salvation. He has broken the first three fetters called belief in the existence of self, doubt, and trust in ceremonies or good works. He will be born again on earth or in some heaven but not more than seven times before he attains nirvana. He who enters on the next stage is called Sakadâgâmin or coming once, because he will be born once more in this world[3] and in that birth attain nirvana. He has broken the fetters mentioned and also reduced to a minimum the next two, lust and hate. The Anâgâmin, or he who does not return, has freed himself entirely from these five fetters and will not be reborn on earth or any sensuous heaven but in a Brahmâ world once only. The fourth route is that of the Arhat who has completed his release by breaking the bonds called love of life, pride, self-righteousness and ignorance and has made an end of all evil and impurity. He attains nirvana here and is no more subject to rebirth. This simple and direct route is the one contemplated in the older discourses but later doctrine and popular feeling came to regard it as more and more unusual, just as saints grow fewer as the centuries advance further from the Apostolic age. In the dearth of visible Arhats it was consoling to think that nirvana could be won in other worlds.

The nirvana hitherto considered is that attained by a being living in this or some other world. But all states of existence whatever come to an end. When one who has not attained nirvana dies, he is born again. But what happens when an Arhat or a Buddha dies? This question did not fail to arouse

[1] *E.g.* Dig. Nik. XVI. ii. 7, Cullavag. IX. 1. 4.

[2] *E.g.* Pugg. Pan. 1. 39. The ten fetters are (1) sakkâyadiṭṭhi, belief in the existence of the self, (2) vicikicchâ, doubt, (3) sîlabbataparamâso, trust in ceremonies of good works, (4) kâmarâgo, lust, (5) paṭigho, anger, (6) rûparâgo, desire for rebirth in worlds of form, (7) arûparâgo, desire for rebirth in formless worlds, (8) mano, pride, (9) uddhaccam, self-righteousness, (10) avijjâ, ignorance.

[3] There is some diversity of doctrine about the Sakadâgâmin. Some hold that he has two births, because he *comes back* to the world of men after having been born once meanwhile in a heaven, others that he has only one birth either on earth or in a devaloka.

interest during the Buddha's lifetime yet in the Pitakas the discussion, though it could not be stifled, is relegated to the background and brought forward only to be put aside as unpractical. The greatest teachers of religion—Christ as well as Buddha—have shown little disposition to speak of what follows on death. For them the centre of gravity is on this side of the grave not on the other: the all-important thing is to live a religious life, at the end of which death is met fearlessly as an incident of little moment. The Kingdom of Heaven, of which Christ speaks, begins on earth though it may end elsewhere. In the Gospels we hear something of the second coming of Christ and the Judgment: hardly anything of the place and character of the soul's eternal life. We only gather that a child of God who has done his best need have no apprehension in this or another world. Though expressed in very different phraseology, something like that is the gist of what the Buddha teaches about the dying Saint. But this reticent attitude did not satisfy ancient India any more than it satisfies modern Europe and we have the record of how he was questioned and what he said in reply. Within certain limits that reply is quite definite. The question, does the Tathâgata, that is the Buddha or perfected saint, exist after death, which is the phraseology usually employed by the Pitakas in formulating the problem, belongs to the class of questions called not declared or undetermined[1], because they do not admit of either an affirmative or a negative answer. Other problems belonging to this class are: Is the world eternal or not: Is the world infinite or not: Is the soul[2] the same as the body or different from it? It is categorically asserted that none of these questions admit of a reply: thus it is not right to say that (*a*) the saint exists after death, (*b*) or that he does not exist, (*c*) or that he both does and does not exist, (*d*) or that he neither exists nor does not exist. The Buddha's teaching about these problems is stated with great clearness in a Sutta named after Mâlunkyaputta[3], an enquirer who visits him and after enumerating them says frankly that he is dissatisfied because the Buddha will not

[1] Avyâkatâni. The Buddha, being omniscient, *sabaññu*, must have known the answer but did not declare it, perhaps because language was incapable of expressing it

[2] Jîva not attâ.

[3] Maj. Nik. 63.

answer them. "If the Lord answers them, I will lead a religious life under him, but if he does not answer them, I will give up religion and return to the world. But if the Lord does not know, then the straightforward thing is to say, I do not know." This is plain speaking, almost discourtesy. The Buddha's reply is equally plain, but unyielding. "Have I said to you, come and be my disciple and I will teach you whether the world is eternal or not, infinite or not: whether the soul is identical with the body, or separate, whether the saint exists after death or not?" "No, Lord." "Now suppose a man were wounded by a poisoned arrow and his friends called in a physician to dress his wound. What if the man were to say, I shall not have my wound treated until I know what was the caste, the family, the dwelling-place, the complexion and stature of the man who wounded me; nor shall I let the arrow be drawn out until I know what is the exact shape of the arrow and bow, and what were the animals and plants which supplied the feathers, leather, shaft and string. The man would never learn all that, because he would die first." "Therefore" is the conclusion, "hold what I have determined as determined and what I have not determined, as not determined."

This sutta may be taken in connection with passages asserting that the Buddha knows more than he tells his disciples. The result seems to be that there are certain questions which the human mind and human language had better leave alone because we are incapable of taking or expressing a view sufficiently large to be correct, but that the Buddha has a more than human knowledge which he does not impart because it is not profitable and overstrains the faculties, just as it is no part of a cure that the patient should make an exhaustive study of his disease.

With reference to the special question of the existence of the saint after death, the story of Yamaka[1] is important. He maintained that a monk in whom evil is destroyed (khînâsavo) is annihilated when he dies, and does not exist. This was considered a grave heresy and refuted by Sâriputta who argues that even in this life the nature of a saint passes understanding because he is neither all the skandhas taken together nor yet one or more of them.

[1] Sam. Nik. xvii. 85.

Yet it would seem that according to the psychology of the Pitakas an ordinary human being is an aggregate of the skandhas and nothing more. When such a being dies and in popular language is born again, the skandhas reconstitute themselves but it is expressly stated that when the saint dies this does not happen. The Chain of Causation says that consciousness and the sankhâras are interdependent. If there is no rebirth, it is because (as it would seem) there are in the dying saint no sankhâras. His nature cannot be formulated in the same terms as the nature of an ordinary man. It may be noted that karma is not equivalent to the effect produced on the world by a man's words and deeds, for if that were so, no one would have died leaving more karma behind him than the Buddha himself, yet according to Hindu doctrine, whether Buddhist or Brahmanic, no karma attaches to the deeds of a saint. His acts may affect others but there is nothing in them which tends to create a new existence.

In another dialogue[1] the Buddha replies to a wandering monk called Vaccha who questioned him about the undetermined problems and in answer to every solution suggested says that he does not hold that view. Vaccha asks what objection he has to these theories that he has not adopted any of them?

"Vaccha, the theory that the saint exists (or does not exist and so on) after death is a jungle, a desert, a puppet show, a writhing, an entanglement and brings with it sorrow, anger, wrangling and agony. It does not conduce to distaste for the world, to the absence of passion, to the cessation of evil, to peace, to knowledge, to perfect enlightenment, to nirvana. Perceiving this objection, I have not adopted any of these theories." "Then has Gotama any theory of his own?" "Vaccha, the Tathâgata has nothing to do with theories, but this is what he knows: the nature of form, how form arises, how form perishes: the nature of perception, how it arises and how it perishes (and so on with the other skandhas). Therefore I say that the Tathâgata is emancipated because he has completely and entirely abandoned all imaginations, agitations and false notions about the Ego and anything pertaining to the Ego." But, asks Vaccha, when one who has attained this

[1] Maj. Nik. 72.

emancipation of mind dies where is he reborn? "Vaccha, the word 'reborn' does not fit the case." "Then, Gotama, he is not reborn." "To say he is not reborn does not fit the case, nor is it any better to say he is both reborn and not reborn or that he is neither reborn nor not reborn." "Really, Gotama, I am completely bewildered and my faith in you is gone."

"Never mind your bewilderment. This doctrine is profound and difficult. Suppose there was a fire in front of you. You would see it burning and know that its burning depended on fuel. And if it went out (nibbâyeyya) you would know that it had gone out. But if some one were to ask you, to which quarter has it gone, East, West, North or South, what would you say?"

"The expression does not fit the case, Gotama. For the fire depended on fuel and when the fuel is gone it is said to be extinguished, being without nourishment."

"In just the same way, all form by which one could predicate the existence of the saint is abandoned and uprooted like a fan palm[1], so that it will never grow up in future. The saint who is released from what is styled form is deep, immeasurable, hard to fathom, like the great ocean. It does not fit the case to say either that he is reborn, not reborn, both reborn and not reborn, or neither reborn nor not reborn." Exactly the same statement is then repeated four times the words sensation, perception, sankhâras and consciousness being substituted successively for the word form. Vaccha, we are told, was satisfied.

To appreciate properly the Buddha's simile we must concentrate our attention on the fire. When we apply this metaphor to annihilation, we usually think of the fuel or receptacle and our mind dwells sadly on the heap of ashes or the extinguished lamp. But what has become of the fire? It is hardly correct to say that it has been destroyed. If a particular fire may be said to be annihilated in the sense that it is impossible to reconstitute it by repeating the same process of burning, the reason is not so much that we cannot get the same flames as that we cannot burn the same fuel twice. But so long as there is continuous combustion in the same fireplace or pile of fuel, we speak of the same fire although neither the flame nor the fuel remains

[1] Which is said not to grow up again.

the same. When combustion ceases, the fire goes out in popular language. To what quarter does it go? That question clearly does not "fit the case." But neither does it fit the case to say that the fire is annihilated[1].

Nirvana is the cessation of a process not the annihilation of an existence. If I take a walk, nothing is annihilated when the walk comes to an end: a particular form of action has ceased. Strictly speaking the case of a fire is the same: when it goes out a process ceases. For the ordinary man nirvana is annihilation in the sense that it is the absence of all the activities which he considers desirable. But for the arhat (who is the only person able to judge) nirvana after death, as compared with nirvana in life, may be quiescence and suspension of activity, only that such phrases seem to imply that activity is the right and normal condition, quiescence being negative and unnatural, whereas for an arhat these values are reversed.

We may use too the parallel metaphor of water. A wave cannot become an immortal personality. It may have an indefinitely long existence as it moves across the ocean, although both its shape and substance are constantly changing, and when it breaks against an obstacle the resultant motion may form new waves. And if a wave ceases to struggle for individual existence and differentiation from the surrounding sea, it cannot be said to exist any more as a wave. Yet neither the water which was its substance nor the motion which impelled it have been annihilated. It is not even quite correct to say that it has been merged in the sea. A drop of water added to a larger liquid mass is merged. The wave simply ceases to be active and differentiated.

In the Saṃyutta-Nikâya[2] the Buddha's statement that the saint after death is deep and immeasurable like the ocean is expanded by significant illustration of the mathematician's inability to number the sand or express the sea in terms of

[1] It may be that the Buddha had in his mind the idea that a flame which goes out returns to the primitive invisible state of fire. This view is advocated by Schrader (*Jour. Pali Text Soc.* 1905, p. 167). The passages which he cites seem to me to show that there was supposed to be such an invisible store from which fire is born but to be less conclusive as proving that fire which goes out is supposed to return to that store, though the quotation from the Maitreyi Up. points in this direction. For the metaphor of the flame see also Sutta-Nipâta, verses 1074–6.

[2] XLIV. 1.

liquid measure. It is in fact implied that if we cannot say *he is*, this is only because that word cannot properly be applied to the infinite, innumerable and immeasurable.

The point which is clearest in the Buddha's treatment of this question is that whatever his disciples may have thought, he did not himself consider it of importance for true religion. Speculation on such points may be interesting to the intellect but is not edifying. It is a jungle where the traveller wanders without advancing, and a puppet-show, a vain worldly amusement which wears a false appearance of religion because it is diverting itself with quasi-religious problems. What is the state of the saint after death, is not as people vainly suppose a question parallel to, am I going to heaven or hell, what shall I do to be saved? To those questions the Buddha gives but one answer in terms of human language and human thought, namely, attain to nirvana and arhatship on this side of death, if possible in your present existence; if not now, then in the future good existences which you can fashion for yourself. What lies beyond is impracticable as a goal, unprofitable as a subject of speculation. We shall probably not be transgressing the limits of Gotama's thought if we add that those who are not arhats are bound to approach the question with misconception and it is a necessary part of an Arhat's training to get rid of the idea "I am[1]." The state of a Saint after death cannot be legitimately described in language which suggests that it is a fuller and deeper mode of life[2]. Yet it is clear that nearly all who dispute about it wish to make out that it is a state they could somehow regard with active satisfaction. In technical language they are infected with arûparâgo, or desire for life in a formless world, and this is the seventh of the ten fetters, all of which must be broken before arhatship is attained. I imagine that those modern sects, such as the Zen in Japan, which hold that the deepest mysteries of the faith cannot be communicated in words but somehow grow clear in meditation are not far from the master's teaching, though to the best of my belief no passage has been produced from the Pitakas stating that an arahat has special knowledge about the avyâkatâni or undetermined questions.

[1] Maj. Nik. 9, *ad init.* Asmîti diṭṭhim ânânusayam samûhanitvâ.

[2] See especially Sutta-Nipâta, 1076 Atthan gatassa na pamâṇam atthi, etc.

Almost all who treat of nirvana after death try to make the Buddha say, is or is not. That is what he refused to do. We still want a plain answer to a plain question and insist that he really means either that the saint is annihilated or enters on an infinite existence. But the true analogues to this question are the other insoluble questions, for instance, is the world infinite or finite in space? This is in form a simple physical problem, yet it is impossible for the mind to conceive either an infinite world or a world stopping abruptly with not even space beyond. A common answer to this antinomy is that the mind is attempting to deal with a subject with which it is incompetent to deal, that the question is wrongly formulated and that every answer to it thus formulated must be wrong. The way of truth lies in first finding the true question. The real difficulty of the Buddha's teaching, though it does not stimulate curiosity so much as the question of life after death, is the nature and being of the saint in this life before death, raised in the argument with Yamaka[1].

Another reason for not pressing the Buddha's language in either direction is that, if he had wished to preach in the subtlest form either infinite life or annihilation, he would have found minds accustomed to the ideas and a vocabulary ready for his use. If he had wished to indicate any form of absorption into a universal soul, or the acquisition by the individual self of the knowledge that it is identical with the universal self, he could easily have done so. But he studiously avoided saying anything of the kind. He teaches that all existence involves suffering and he preaches escape from it. After that escape the words being and not being no longer apply, and the reason why some people adopt the false idea of annihilation is because they have commenced by adopting the false alternative of either annihilation or an eternal prolongation of this life. A man makes[2] himself miserable because he thinks he has lost something or that there is something which he cannot get. But if he does not think he has lost something or is deprived of something he might have, then he does not feel miserable. Similarly, a man holds the erroneous opinion, "This world is the self, or soul and I shall become it after death and be eternal, and unchanging." Then he hears the preaching of a Buddha and he thinks "I shall be annihilated, I shall not exist any more," and he feels

[1] Sam. Nik. XXII. 85.

[2] Maj. Nik. 22, Alagaddûpama-suttam.

miserable. But if a man does not hold this doctrine that the soul is identical with the universe and will exist eternally—which is just complete full-blown folly[1]—and then hears the preaching of a Buddha it does not occur to him to think that he will be annihilated and he is not miserable. Here the Buddha emphasizes the fact that his teaching is not a variety of the Brahmanic doctrine about the Âtman. Shortly afterwards in the same sutta he even more emphatically says that he does not teach annihilation. He teaches that the saint is already in this life inconceivable (*ananuvejjo*): "And when I teach and explain this some accuse me falsely and without the smallest ground[2] saying 'Gotama is an unbeliever; he preaches the annihilation, the destruction, the dying out of real being.' When they talk like this they accuse me of being what I am not, of saying what I do not say."

Though the Buddha seems to condemn by anticipation the form of the Vedanta known as the Advaita, this philosophy illustrates the difficulty of making any statement about the saint after his death. For it teaches that the saint knows that there is but one reality, namely Brahman, and that all individual existences are illusion: he is aware that he is Brahman and that he is not differentiated from the world around him. And when he dies, what happens? Metaphors about drops and rivers are not really to the point. It would be more correct to say that nothing at all has happened. His physical life, an illusion which did not exist for himself, has ceased to exist for others.

Perhaps he will be nearest to the Buddha's train of thought who attempts to consider, by reflection rather than by discussion in words, what is meant by annihilation. By thinking of the mystery of existence and realizing how difficult it is to explain how and why anything exists, we are apt to slip into thinking that it would be quite natural and intelligible if nothing existed or if existing things became nothing. Yet as a matter of fact our minds have no experience of this nothing of which we talk and it is inconceivable. When we try to think of nothingness we really think of space from which we try to remove all content, yet could we create an absolute vacuum within a vessel, the interior of the vessel would not be annihilated. The man who

[1] Later in the same Sutta: Kevalo paripûro bâladhammo.

[2] Four emphatic synonyms in the original.

has attained nirvana cannot be adequately defined or grasped even in this life: what binds him to being is cut[1] but it is inappropriate and inadequate to say that he has become nothing[2].

[1] Dig. Nik. I. 73 uccinna-bhava-nettiko.

[2] I recommend the reader to consider carefully the passage at the end of Book IV. of Schopenhauer's *Die Welt als Wille und Vorstellung* (Haldane and Kemp's translation, vol. I. pp. 529–530). Though he evidently misunderstood what he calls "the Nirvana of the Buddhists" yet his own thought throws much light on it.

CHAPTER XI

MONKS AND LAYMEN

1

THE great practical achievement of the Buddha was to found a religious order which has lasted to the present day. It is known as the Sangha and its members are called Bhikkhus[1]. It is chiefly to this institution that the permanence of his religion is due.

Corporations or confraternities formed for the purpose of leading a particular form of life are among the most widespread manifestations, if not of primitive worship, at any rate of that stage in which it passes into something which can be called personal religion and at least three causes contribute to their formation. First, early institutions were narrower and more personal than those of to-day. In politics as well as religion such relatively broad designations as Englishman or Frenchman, Buddhist or Christian, imply a slowly widening horizon gained by centuries of cooperation and thought. In the time of the Buddha such national and religious names did not exist. People belonged to a clan or served some local prince. Similarly in religious matters they followed some teacher or worshipped some god, and in either case if they were in earnest they tended to become members of a society. Societies such as the Pythagorean and Orphic brotherhoods were also common in Greece from the sixth century B.C. onwards but the result was small, for the genius of the Greeks turned towards politics and philosophy. But in India, where politics had strangely little attraction for the cultured classes, energy and intelligence found an outlet in the religious life and created a multitude of religious societies. Even to-day Hinduism has no one creed or code and those who take a serious interest in religion are not merely Hindus but follow some sect which, without damning

[1] Sk. *Bhikshu*, beggar or mendicant, because they live on alms. *Bhikshâcaryam* occurs in Brihad-Âr. Up. III. 5. I.

what it does not adopt, selects its own dogmas and observances. This is not sectarianism in the sense of schism. It is merely the desire to have for oneself some personal, intimate religious life. Even in so uncompromising and levelling a creed as Islam the devout often follow special *tariqs*, that is, roads or methods of the devotional life, and these *tariqs*, though differing more than the various orders of the Roman Catholic Church, are not regarded as sects distinct from ordinary orthodoxy. When Christ died, Christianity was not much more than such a *tariq*. It was an incipient religious order which had not yet broken with Judaism.

This idea of the private, even secret religious body is closely allied to another, namely, that family life and worldly business are incompatible with the quest for higher things. In early ages only priests and consecrated persons are expected to fast and practise chastity but when once the impression prevails that such observances not only achieve particular ends but produce wiser, happier, or more powerful lives, then they are likely to be followed by considerable numbers of the more intelligent, emotional and credulous sections of the population. The early Christian Church was influenced by the idea that the world is given over to Satan and that he who would save himself must disown it. The gentler Hindus were actuated by two motives. First, more than other races, they felt the worry and futility of worldly life. Secondly, they had a deep-rooted belief that miraculous powers could be acquired by self-mortification and the sensations experienced by those who practised fasting and trances confirmed this belief.

The third cause for the foundation and increase of religious orders is a perception of the influence which they can exercise. The disciples of a master or the priests of a god, if numerous and organized, clearly possess a power analogous to that of an army. To use such institutions for the service and protection of the true faith is an obvious expedient of the zealot: ecclesiastical statecraft and ambition soon make their appearance in most orders founded for the assistance of the Church militant. But of this spirit Buddhism has little to show; except in Tibet and Japan it is almost absent. The ideal of the Buddha lay within his order and was to be realized in the life of the members. They had no need to strive after any extraneous goal.

The Sangha, as this order was called, arose naturally out of the social conditions of India in the time of Gotama. It was considered proper that an earnest-minded man should renounce the world and become a wanderer. In doing this and in collecting round him a band of disciples who had a common mode of life Gotama created nothing new. He merely did with conspicuous success what every contemporary teacher was doing. The confraternity which he founded differed from others chiefly in being broader and more human, less prone to extravagances and better organized. As we read the accounts in the Pitakas, its growth seems so simple and spontaneous that no explanation is necessary. Disciples gather round the master and as their numbers increase he makes a few salutary regulations. It is almost with surprise that we find the result to be an organization which became one of the great forces of the world.

The Buddha said that he taught a middle path equally distant from luxury and from self-mortification, but Europeans are apt to be struck by his condemnation of pleasure and to be repelled by a system which suppresses so many harmless activities. But contemporary opinion in India criticized his discipline as easy-going and lax. We frequently hear in the Vinaya that the people murmured and said his disciples behaved like those who still enjoy the good things of the world. Some, we are told, tried to enter the order merely to secure a comfortable existence[1]. It is clear that he went to the extreme limits which public opinion allowed in dispensing with the rigours considered necessary to the religious life, and we shall best understand his spirit if we fix our attention not so much on the regime, to our way of thinking austere, which he prescribed—the single meal a day and so on—as on his insistence that what is necessary is emancipation of heart and mind and the cultivation of love and knowledge, all else being a matter of indifference. Thus he says to the ascetic Kassapa[2] that though a man perform all manner of penances, yet if he has not attained the bliss which comes of good conduct, a good heart and good mind, he is far from being a true monk. But when he has the heart of love that knows no anger nor ill-will, when he has destroyed lust and become emancipated even before death, then he deserves the name of monk. It is a

[1] Mahâvag. I. 49, cf. ib. I. 39.

[2] Dig. Nik. VIII.

common thing to say, he goes on, that it is hard to lead the life of a monk. But asceticism is comparatively easy; what is really hard is the conversion and emancipation of the heart.

In India, where the proclivity to asceticism and self-torture is endemic, it was only natural that penance should in very truth seem easier and more satisfactory than this spiritual discipline. It won more respect and doubtless seemed more tangible and definite, more like what the world expected from a holy man. Accordingly we find that efforts were made by Devadatta and others to induce the Buddha to increase the severity of his discipline. But he refused[1]. The more ascetic form of life, which he declined to make obligatory, is described in the rules known as Dhutângas, of which twelve or thirteen are enumerated. They are partly a stricter form of the ordinary rules about food and dress and partly refer to the life of a hermit who lives in the woods or in a cemetery.

In the Pitakas[2] Kassapa's disciples are described as *dhutavâdâ* and the advantages arising from the observance of the Dhutângas are enumerated in the Questions of Milinda. It is probable that the Buddha himself had little sympathy with them. He was at any rate anxious that they should not degenerate into excesses. Thus he forbade[3] his disciples to spend the season of the rains in a hollow tree, or in a place where dead bodies are kept, or to use an alms bowl made out of a skull. Now Kassapa had been a Brahman ascetic and it is probable that in tolerating the Dhutângas the Buddha merely intended to allow him and his followers to continue the practices to which they were accustomed. They were an influential body and he doubtless desired their adhesion, for he was sensitive to public opinion[4] and anxious to conform to it when conformity involved no sacrifice of principle. We hear repeatedly that the laity complained of some practice of his Bhikkhus and that when the complaint was brought to his ears he ordered the objectionable practice to cease. Once the king of Magadha asked the congregation to postpone the period of retreat during the rains until the next full moon day. They referred the matter to the Buddha: "I prescribe that you obey kings," was his reply.

[1] Cullavag. I. 1. 3.
[2] Sam. Nik. XIV. 15. 12, Ang. Nik. I. xiv. [3] Mahâvag. III. 12.
[4] Or the opinion of single persons, *e.g.* Visâkhâ in Mahâvag. III. 13.

One obvious distinction between the Buddha's disciples and other confraternities was that they were completely clad, whereas the Âjîvikas, Jains and others went about naked. The motive for this rule was no doubt decency and a similar thought made Gotama insist on the use of a begging bowl, whereas some sectaries collected scraps of food in their hands. Such extravagances led to abuses resembling the degradation of some modern fakirs. Even the Jain scriptures admit that pious householders were disgusted by the ascetics who asked for a lodging in their houses—naked, unwashed men, foul to smell and loathsome to behold[1]. This was the sort of life which the Buddha called anariyam, ignoble or barbaric. With such degradation of humanity he would have nothing to do. He forbade nakedness, as well as garments of hair and other uncomfortable costumes. The raiment which he prescribed consisted of three pieces of cloth of the colour called kâsâva. This was probably dull orange, selected as being unornamental. It would appear that in mediæval India the colour in use was reddish: at present a rather bright and not unpleasing yellow is worn in Burma, Ceylon, Siam and Camboja. Originally the robes were made of rags collected and sewed together but it soon became the practice for pious laymen to supply the Order with raiment.

2

In the Mahâ and Culla-vaggas of the Vinaya Pitaka we possess a large collection of regulations purporting to be issued by the Buddha for the guidance of the Order on such subjects as ceremonial, discipline, clothes, food, furniture and medicine. The arrangement is roughly chronological. Gotama starts as a new teacher, without either followers or a code. As disciples multiply the need for regulations and uniformity of life is felt. Each incident and difficulty that arises is reported to him and he defines the correct practice. One may suspect that many usages represented as originating in the injunctions of the master really grew up gradually. But the documents are ancient; they date from the generations immediately following the Buddha's death, and their account of his activity as an

[1] Acârângasut, II. 2. 2.

organizer is probably correct in substance. One of the first reasons which rendered regulations necessary was the popularity of the order and the respect which it enjoyed. King Bimbisâra of Magadha is represented as proclaiming that "It is not permitted to do anything to those who join the order of the Sakyaputtiya[1]." Hence robbers[2], debtors, slaves, soldiers anxious to escape service and others who wished for protection against the law or merely to lead an idle life, desired to avail themselves of these immunities. This resulted in the gradual elaboration of a code of discipline which did much to secure that only those actuated by proper motives could enter the order and only those who conducted themselves properly could stay within it.

We find traces of a distinction between those Bhikkhus who were hermits and lived solitary lives in the woods and those who moved about in bands, frequenting rest houses. In the time of the Buddha the wandering life was a reality but later most monks became residents in monasteries. Already in the Vinaya we seem to breathe the atmosphere of large conventual establishments where busy superintendents see to the lodging and discipline of crowds of monks, and to the distribution of the gifts made by pious laymen. But the Buddha himself knew the value of forests and plant life for calming and quickening the mind. "Here are trees," he would say to his disciples at the end of a lecture, "go and think it out[3]."

In the poetical books of the Tripitaka, especially the collections known as the Songs of the Monks and Nuns, this feeling is still stronger: we are among anchorites who pass their time in solitary meditation in the depths of forests or on mountain tops and have a sense of freedom and a joy in the life of wild things not found in cloisters. These old monkish poems are somewhat wearisome as continuous reading, but their monotonous enthusiasm about the conquest of desire is leavened by a sincere and observant love of nature. They sing of the scenes in which meditation is pleasant, the flowery banks of streams that flow through reeds and grasses of many colours as well as

[1] Mahâv. I. 42.

[2] But converted robbers were occasionally admitted, *e.g.* Angulimâla.

[3] Sam. Nik. IV. XXXV., Maj. Nik. 8 *ad fin.* On the value attached by mystics in all countries to trees and flowers, see Underhill, *Mysticism*, p. 231.

the mysterious midnight forest when the dew falls and wild beasts howl; they note the plumage of the blue peacock, the flight of the yellow crane and the gliding movements of the water snake. It does not appear that these amiable hermits arrogated any superiority to themselves or that there was any opposition between them and the rest of the brethren. They preferred a form of the religious life which the Buddha would not make compulsory, but it is older than Buddhism and not yet dead in India. The Sangha exercised no hierarchical authority over them and they accepted such simple symbols of union as the observance of Uposatha days.

The character of the Sangha has not materially changed since its constitution took definite shape towards the end of the master's life. It was and is simply a body of people who believe that the higher life cannot be lived in any existing form of society and therefore combine to form a confraternity where they are relieved of care for food and raiment, where they can really take no thought for the morrow and turn the cheek to the smiter. They were not a corporation of priests and they had no political aims. Any free man, unless his parents or the state had a claim on him and unless he suffered from certain diseases, was admitted; he took no vows of obedience and was at any time at liberty to return to the world.

Though the Sangha as founded by the Buddha did not claim, still less exact, anything from the laity, yet it was their duty, their most obvious and easy method of acquiring merit, to honour and support monks, to provide them with food, clothes and lodging and with everything which they might lawfully possess. Strictly speaking a monk does not beg for food nor thank for what he receives. He gives the layman a chance of doing a good deed and the donor, not the recipient, should be thankful.

At first the Buddha admitted converts to the order himself, but he subsequently prescribed two simple ceremonies for admission to the novitiate and to full privileges respectively. They are often described as ordinations but are rather applications from postulants which are granted by a Chapter consisting of at least ten members. The first, called pabbajjâ or going forth—that is leaving the world—is effected when the would-be novice, duly shorn and robed in yellow, recites the three refuges and the ten precepts[1]. Full membership is obtained by the further ceremony called upasampadâ. The postulant, who must be at least twenty years old, is examined in order to ascertain that he is *sui juris* and has no disqualifying disease or other impediment. Then he is introduced to the Chapter by "a learned and competent monk" who asks those who are in favour of his admission to signify the same by their silence and those who are not, to speak. If this formula is repeated three times without calling forth objection, the upasampadâ is complete. The newly admitted Bhikkhu must have an Upajjhâya or preceptor on whom he waits as a servant, seeing to his clothes, bath, bed, etc. In return the preceptor gives him spiritual instruction, supervises his conduct and tends him when sick.

The Chapter which had power to accept new monks and regulate discipline consisted of the monks inhabiting a parish or district, whose extent was fixed by the Sangha itself. Its reality as a corporate body was secured by stringent regulations that under no excuse must the Bhikkhus resident in a parish omit to assemble on Uposatha days[2]. The Vinaya[3] represents the initiative for these simple observances as coming not from the Buddha but from King Bimbisâra, who pointed out that the adherents of other schools met on fixed days and that it would be well if his disciples did the same. He assented and ordered that when they met they should recite a formula called Pâtimokkha which is still in use. It is a confessional service, in which a list of offences is read out and the brethren are asked three times after each item "Are you pure in this matter?" Silence indicates a good conscience. Only if a monk has anything to confess does he speak. It is then in the power of the assembly to prescribe some form of expiation. The offender may be rebuked, suspended or even expelled. But he must admit his guilt. Otherwise disciplinary measures are forbidden.

What has been said above[4] about the daily life of the Buddha applies equally to the life of his disciples. Like him

[1] They are abstinence from (1) destroying life, (2) stealing, (3) impurity, (4) lying, (5) intoxicants, (6) eating at forbidden times, (7) dancing, music and theatres, (8) garlands, perfumes, ornaments, (9) high or large beds, (10) accepting gold or silver.

[2] These are practically equivalent to Sundays, being the new moon, full moon and the eighth days from the new and full moon. In Tibet however the 14th, 15th, 29th and 30th of each month are observed.

[3] Mahâvag. II. 1–2.

[4] Chap. VIII. Sec. 3.

they rose early, journeyed or went to beg their only meal until about half-past eleven and spent the heat of the day in retirement and meditation. In the evening followed discussion and instruction. It was forbidden to accept gold and silver but the order might possess parks and monasteries and receive offerings of food and clothes. The personal possessions allowed to a monk were only the three robes, a girdle, an alms bowl, a razor, a needle and a water strainer[1]. Everything else which might be given to an individual had to be handed over to the confraternity and held in common and the Vinaya shows clearly how a band of wandering monks following their teacher from place to place speedily grew into an influential corporation possessing parks and monasteries near the principal cities. The life in these establishments attained a high level of comfort according to the standard of the times and the number of restrictive precepts suggests a tendency towards luxury. This was natural, for the laity were taught that their duty was to give and the Order had to decide how much it could properly receive from those pious souls who were only too happy to acquire merit. In the larger Vihâras, for instance at Sâvatthî, there were halls for exercise (that is walking up and down), halls with fires in them, warm baths and store rooms.

The year of the Bhikkhus was divided into two parts. During nine months they might wander about, live in the woods or reside in a monastery. During the remaining three months, known as Vassa[2] or rainy season, residence in a monastery was obligatory. This custom, as mentioned, existed in India before the Buddha's time and the Pitakas represent him as adopting it, chiefly out of deference to public opinion. He did not prescribe any special observances for the period of Vassa, but this was the time when people had most leisure, since it was hard to move about, and also when the monks were brought into continual contact with the inhabitants of a special locality. So it naturally became regarded as the appropriate season for giving instruction to the laity. The end of the rainy season was marked by a ceremony called Pavâraṇâ, at which the monks

[1] Required not so much to purify water as to prevent the accidental destruction of insects.

[2] It might begin either the day after the full moon of Asâlha (June–July) or a month later. In either case the period was three months. Mahâvag. III. 2.

asked one another to pardon any offences that might have been committed, and immediately after it came the Kathiṇa ceremony or distribution of robes. Kathiṇa signifies the store of raw cotton cloth presented by the laity and held as common property until distributed to individuals.

It would be tedious to give even an abstract of the regulations contained in the Vinaya. They are almost exclusively concerned with matters of daily life, dwellings, furniture, medicine and so forth, and if we compare them with the statutes of other religious orders, we are struck by the fact that the Buddha makes no provision for work, obedience or worship. In the western branches of the Christian Church—and to some extent, though less markedly, in the eastern—the theory prevails that "Satan finds some mischief still for idle hands to do" and manual labour is a recognized part of the monastic life. But in India conditions and ideals were different. The resident monk grew out of the wandering teacher or disputant, who was not likely to practise any trade; it was a maxim that religious persons lived on alms, and occupations which we consider harmless, such as agriculture, were held to be unsuitable because such acts as ploughing may destroy animal life. Probably the Buddha would not have admitted the value of manual labour as a distraction and defence against evil thoughts. No one was more earnestly bent on the conquest of such thoughts, but he wished to extirpate them, not merely to crowd them out. Energy and activity are insisted on again and again, and there is no attempt to discourage mental activity. Reading formed no part of the culture of the time, but a life of travel and new impressions, continual discussion and the war of wits, must have given the Bhikkhus a more stimulating training than was to be had in the contemporary Brahmanic schools.

The Buddha's regulations contain no vow of obedience or recognition of rank other than simple seniority or the relation of teacher to pupil. As time went on various hierarchical expedients were invented in different countries, since the management of large bodies of men necessitates authority in some form, but except in Lamaism this authority has rarely taken the form familiar to us in the Roman and Oriental Churches, where the Bishops and higher clergy assume the right to direct both the belief and conduct of others. In the Sangha, no monk could give orders to another: he who disobeyed the precepts of the order ceased to be a member of it either *ipso facto*, or if he refused to comply with the expiation prescribed. Also there was no compulsion, no suppression of discussion, no delegated power to explain or supplement the truth. Hence differences of opinion in the Buddhist Church have largely taken the shape of schools of thought rather than of separate and polemical sects. Dissension indeed has not been absent but of persecution, such as stains the annals of the Christian Church, there is hardly any record. The fact that the Sangha, though nearly five hundred years older than any Christian institution, is still vigorous shows that this noble freedom is not unsuccessful as a practical policy.

The absence of anything that can be called worship or cultus in Gotama's regulations is remarkable. He not merely sets aside the older religious rites, such as prayer and sacrifice; he does not prescribe anything whatever which is in ordinary language a religious act. For the Pâtimokkha, Pavâraṇâ, etc., are not religious ceremonies, but chapters of the order held with an ethical object, and the procedure (the proposal of a resolution and the request for an expression of opinion) is that adopted in modern public meetings, except that assent is signified by silence. It is true that the ceremonial of a religion is not likely to develop during the life of the founder, for pious recollection and recitation of his utterances in the form of scripture are as yet impossible. Still, if the Buddha had had any belief whatever in the edifying effect of ritual, he would not have failed to institute some ceremony, appealing if not to supernatural beings at least to human emotions. Even the few observances which he did prescribe seem to be the result of suggestion from others and the only inference to be drawn is that he regarded every form of religious observance as entirely superfluous.

At first the Sangha consisted exclusively of men. It was not until about five years after its establishment that the entreaties of the Buddha's fostermother, who had become a widow, and of Ânanda prevailed on him to throw it open to women as well[1] but it would seem that the permission was wrung from him against his judgment. His reluctance was not due to a low estimate of female ability, for he recognized and made use of

[1] Cullavag. x. 1.

the influence of women in social and domestic life and he admitted that they were as capable as men of attaining the highest stages of spiritual and intellectual progress. This is also attested by the Pitakas, for some of the most important and subtle arguments and expositions are put into the mouths of nuns[1]. Indeed the objections raised by the Buddha, though emphatic, are as arguments singularly vague and the eight rules for nuns which he laid down and compared to an embankment built to prevent a flood seem dictated not by the danger of immorality but by the fear that women might aspire to the management of the order and to be the equals or superiors of monks.

So far as we can tell, his fears were not realized. The female branch of the order showed little vigour after its first institution but it does not appear that it was a cause of weakness or corruption. Women were influential in the infancy of Buddhism, but we hear little of the nuns when this first ardour was over. We may surmise that it was partly due to personal devotion to Gotama and also that there was a growing tendency to curtail the independence allowed to women by earlier Aryan usage. The daughters of Asoka play some part in the narratives of the conversion of Ceylon and Nepal but after the early days of the Church female names are not prominent: subsequently the succession became interrupted and, as nuns can receive ordination only from other nuns and not from monks, it could not be restored. The so-called nuns of the present day are merely religious women corresponding to the sisters of Protestant Churches, but are not ordained members of an order. But the right of women to enjoy the same spiritual privileges as men is not denied in theory and in practice Buddhism has done nothing to support or commend the system of the harem or zenana. In some Buddhist countries such as Burma and Siam women enjoy almost the same independence as in Europe. In China and Japan their status is not so high, but one period when Buddhism was powerful in Japan (800–1100 A.D.) was marked by the number of female writers and among the Manchus and Tibetans women enjoy considerable freedom and authority.

[1] See the papers by Mrs Bode in *J.R.A.S.* 1893, pp. 517–66 and 763–98, and Mrs Rhys Davids in *Ninth Congress of Orientalists*, vol. I. p. 344.

3

Those who follow the law of the Buddha but are not members of the Sangha are called Upâsakas[1], that is worshippers or adherents. The word may be conveniently rendered by laymen although the distinction between clergy and laity, as understood in most parts of Europe, does not quite correspond to the distinction between Bhikkhus and Upâsakas. European clergy are often thought of as interpreters of the Deity, and whenever they have had the power they have usually claimed the right to supervise and control the moral or even the political administration of their country. Something similar may be found in Lamaism, but it forms no part of Gotama's original institution nor of the Buddhist Church as seen to-day in Burma, Siam and Ceylon. The members of the Sangha are not priests or mediators. They have joined a confraternity in order to lead a higher life for which ordinary society has no place. They will teach others, not as those whose duty it is to make the laity conform to their standard but as those who desire to make known the truth. And easy as is the transition from this attitude to the other, it must be admitted that Buddhism has rarely laid itself open to the charge of interfering in politics or of seeking temporal authority. Rather may it be accused of a tendency to indolence. In some cases elementary education is in the hands of the monks and their monasteries serve the purpose of village schools. Elsewhere they are harmless recluses whom the unsympathetic critic may pity as useless but can hardly condemn as ambitious or interfering. This is not however altogether true of Tibet and the Far East.

It is sometimes said that the only real Buddhists are the members of the Sangha and there is some truth in this, particularly in China, where one cannot count as a Buddhist every one who occasionally attends a Buddhist service. But on the other hand Gotama accorded to the laity a definite and honourable position and in the Pitakas they notify their conversion by a special formula. They cannot indeed lead the perfect life but they can ensure birth in happy states and a good layman may even attain nirvana on his death-bed. But though the pious householder "takes his refuge in the law and in the order of

[1] Feminine Upâsikâ.

monks" from whom he learns the law, yet these monks make no attempt to supervise or even to judge his life. The only punishment which the Order inflicts, to turn down the bowl and refuse to accept alms from guilty hands, is reserved for those who have tried to injure it and is not inflicted on notorious evil livers. It is the business of a monk to spread true knowledge and good feeling around him without enquiring into the thoughts and deeds of those who do not spontaneously seek his counsel. Indeed it may be said that in Burma it is the laity who supervise the monks rather than *vice versa*. Those Bhikkhus who fall short of the accepted standard, especially in chastity, are compelled by popular opinion to leave the monastery or village where they have misbehaved. This reminds us of the criticisms of laymen reported in the Vinaya and the deference which the Buddha paid to them.

The ethical character of Buddhism and its superiority to other Indian systems are shown in the precepts which it lays down for laymen. Ceremony and doctrine have hardly any place in this code, but it enjoins good conduct and morality: moderation in pleasures and consideration for others. Only five commandments are essential for a good life but they are perhaps more comprehensive and harder to keep than the Decalogue, for they prescribe abstinence from the five sins of taking life, drinking intoxicants, lying, stealing and unchastity. It is meritorious to observe in addition three other precepts, namely, to use no garlands or perfumes: to sleep on a mat spread on the ground and not to eat after midday. Pious laymen keep all these eight precepts, at least on Uposatha days, and often make a vow to observe them for some special period. The nearer a layman can approximate to the life of a monk the better for his spiritual health, but still the aims and ideals, and consequently the methods, of the lay and religious life are different. The Bhikkhu is not of this world, he has cut himself loose from its ties, pleasures and passions; he strives not for heaven but for arhatship. But the layman, though he may profitably think of nirvana and final happiness, may also rightly aspire to be born in some temporary heaven. The law merely bids him be a kind, temperate, prudent man of the world. It is only when he speaks to the monks that the Buddha really speaks to his own and gives his own thoughts: only for them are the high selfless aspirations, the austere counsels of perfection and the promises of bliss and something beyond bliss. But the lay morality is excellent in its own sphere—the good respectable life—and its teaching is most earnest and natural in those departments where the hard unsentimental precepts of the higher code jar on western minds. Whereas the monk severs all family ties and is fettered by no domestic affection, this is the field which the layman can cultivate with most profit. It was against his judgment that the Buddha admitted women to his order and in bidding his monks beware of them he said many hard things. But for women in the household life the Pitakas show an appreciation and respect which is illustrated by the position held by women in Buddhist countries from the devout and capable matron Visâkhâ down to the women of Burma in the present day. The Buddha even praised the ancients because they married for love and did not buy their wives[1].

The right life of a layman is described in several suttas[2] and in all of them, though almsgiving, religious conversation and hearing the law are commended, the main emphasis is on such social virtues as pleasant speech, kindness, temperance, consideration for others and affection. The most complete of these discourses, the Sigâlovâda-sutta[3], relates how the Buddha when starting one morning to beg alms in Râjagaha saw the householder Sigâla bowing down with clasped hands and saluting the four quarters, the nadir and the zenith. The object of the ceremony was to avert any evil which might come from these six points. The Buddha told him that this was not the right way to protect oneself: a man should regard his parents as the east, his teachers as the south, his wife and children as the west, his friends as the north, his servants as the nadir and monks and Brahmans as the zenith. By fulfilling his duty to these six classes a man protects himself from all evil which may come from the six points. Then he expounded in order the mutual duties of (1) parents and children, (2) pupils and teachers, (3) husband and wife, (4) friends, (5) master and servant, (6) laity and clergy. The precepts which follow show how much

[1] Sutta-Nipâta, 289.
[2] *E.g.* Mahâmangala and Dhammika-Sutta in Sut. Nip. II. 4 and 14.
[3] Dig. Nik. 31.

common sense and good feeling Gotama could bring to bear on the affairs of every-day life when he gave them his attention and the whole classification of reciprocal obligations recalls the five relationships of Chinese morality, three of which are identical with Gotama's divisions, namely parents and children, husband and wife, and friends. But national characteristics make themselves obvious in the differences. Gotama says nothing about politics or loyalty; the Chinese list, which opens with the mutual duties of sovereigns and subjects, is silent respecting the church and clergy.

The Sangha is an Indian institution and invites comparison with that remarkable feature of Indian social life, the Brahman caste. At first sight the two seem mutually opposed, for the one is a hereditary though intellectual aristocracy, claiming the possession of incommunicable knowledge and power, the other a corporation open to all who choose to renounce the world and lead a good life. And this antithesis contains historical truth: the Sangha, like the similar orders of the Jains and other Kshatriya sects, was in its origin a protest against the exclusiveness and ritualism of the Brahmans. Yet compared with anything to be found in other countries the two bodies have something in common. For instance it is a meritorious act to feed either Brahmans or Bhikkhus. Europeans are inclined to call both of them priests, but this is inaccurate for a Bhikkhu rarely deserves the title[1] and nowadays Brahmans are not necessarily priests nor priests Brahmans. But in India there is an old and widespread idea that he who devotes himself to a religious and intellectual life (and the two spheres, though they do not coincide, overlap more than in Europe) should be not only respected but supported by the rest of the world. He is not a professional man in the sense that lawyers, doctors and clergymen are, but rather an aristocrat. Though from the earliest times the nobles of India have had a full share of pride and self-confidence, the average Hindu has always believed in another kind of upper class, entered in some sects by birth, in others by merit, but in general a well-defined body, the conduct of whose members does not fail to command respect. The *do ut des* principle is certainly not wanting, but

[1] It may seem superfluous to insist on this, yet Warren in his *Buddhism in Translations* uniformly renders Bhikkhu by priest.

the holy man is honoured not so much because he will make an immediate return by imparting some instruction or performing some ceremony but because to honour him is a good act which, like other good acts, will sooner or later find its reward. The Buddha is not represented as blaming the respect paid to Brahmans but as saying that Brahmans must deserve it. Birth and plaited hair do not make a true Brahman any more than a shaven head makes a Bhikkhu, but he who has renounced the world, who is pure in thought, word and deed, who follows the eight-fold path, and perfects himself in knowledge, he is the true Brahman[1]. Men of such aspirations are commoner in India than elsewhere and more than elsewhere they form a class, which is defined by each sect for itself. But in all sects it is an essential part of piety to offer respect and gifts to this religious aristocracy.

[1] The same idea occurs in the Upanishads, *e.g.* Brih.-Âr. Up. IV. 4. 23, "he becomes a true Brahman."

CHAPTER XII

ASOKA

1

THE first period in the history of Buddhism extends from the death of the founder to the death of Asoka, that is to about 232 B.C. It had then not only become a great Indian religion but had begun to send forth missionaries to foreign countries. But this growth had not yet brought about the internal changes which are inevitable when a creed expands far beyond the boundaries within which it was a natural expression of local thought. An intellectual movement and growth is visible within the limits of the Pali Canon and is confirmed by what we hear of the existence of sects or schools, but it does not appear that in the time of Asoka the workings of speculation had led to any point of view materially different from that of Gotama.

Our knowledge of general Indian history before the reign of Asoka is scanty and the data which can be regarded as facts for Buddhist ecclesiastical history are scantier still. We hear of two (or including the Mahâsangîti three) meetings sometimes called Councils; scriptures, obviously containing various strata, were compiled, and eighteen sects or schools had time to arise and some of them to decay. Much doubt has been cast upon the councils[1] but to my mind this suspicion is unmerited, provided that too ecclesiastical a meaning is not given to the word. We must not suppose that the meetings held at Râjagaha and Vesâlî were similar to the Council of Nicaea or that they produced the works edited by the Pali Text Society. Such terms as canon, dogma and council, though indispensable, are misleading at this period. We want less formal equivalents for the same ideas. A number of men who were strangers to those conceptions

[1] Especially in R. O. Franke's article in the *J.P.T.S.* 1908. To demonstrate the "literary dependence" of chapters XI., XII. of the Cullavagga does not seem to me equivalent to demonstrating that the narratives contained in those chapters are "air-bubbles."

of a hierarchy and a Bible[1] which are so familiar to us met together to fix and record the opinions and injunctions of the Master or to remove misapprehensions and abuses. It would be better if we could avoid using even the word Buddhist at this period, for it implies a difference sharper than the divisions existing between the followers of Gotama and others. They were in the position of the followers of Christ before they received at Antioch the name of Christians and the meeting at Râjagaha was analogous to the conferences recorded in the first chapter of the Acts of the Apostles.

The record of this meeting and of the subsequent meeting at Vesâlî is contained in Chapters XI. and XII. of the Cullavagga, which must therefore be later than the second meeting and perhaps considerably later. Other accounts are found in the Dîpavaṃsa, Mahâ-Bodhi-Vaṃsa and Buddhaghosa's commentaries. The version given in the Cullavagga is abrupt and does not entirely agree with other narratives of what followed on the death of the Buddha[2]. It seems to be a combination of two documents, for it opens as a narrative by Kassapa, but it soon turns into a narrative about him. But the clumsiness in compilation and the errors of detail are hardly sufficient to discredit an event which is probable in itself and left an impression on tradition. The Buddha combined great personal authority with equally great liberality. While he was alive he decided all questions of dogma and discipline himself, but he left to the Order authority to abolish all the minor precepts. It seems inevitable that some sort of meeting should have been held to consider the position created by this wide permission. Brief and confused as the story in the Cullavagga is, there is nothing improbable in its outline—namely that a resolution was taken at Kusinârâ where he died to hold a synod during the next rains at Râjagaha, a more central place where alms and lodgings were plentiful, and there come to an agreement as to what should be accepted as the true doctrine and discipline. Accordingly five hundred monks met near this town and enquired into the authenticity of the various rules and suttas. They

[1] The mantras of the Brahmans were hardly a sacred book analogous to the Bible or Koran and, besides, the early Buddhists would not have wished to imitate them.

[2] *E.g.* Dig. Nik. XVI.

then went on to ask what the Buddha had meant by the lesser and minor precepts which might be abolished. Ânanda (who came in for a good deal of blame in the course of the proceedings) confessed that he had forgotten to ask the Master for an explanation and divergent opinions were expressed as to the extent of the discretion allowed. Kassapa finally proposed that the Sangha should adopt without alteration or addition the rules made by the Buddha. This was approved and the Dhamma and Vinaya as chanted by the assembled Bhikkhus were accepted. The Abhidhamma is not mentioned. The name usually given to these councils is Sangîti, which means singing or chanting together. An elder is said to have recited the text sentence by sentence and each phrase was intoned after him by the assembly as a sign of acceptance. Upâli was the principal authority for the Vinaya and Ânanda for the Dhamma but the limits of the authority claimed by the meeting are illustrated by an anecdote[1] which relates that after the chanting of the law had been completed Pûraṇa and his disciples arrived from the Southern Hills. The elders asked him to accept the version rehearsed by them. He replied, "The Dhamma and Vinaya have been well sung by the Theras, nevertheless as they have been received and heard by me from the mouth of the Lord, so will I hold them." In other words the council has put together a very good account of the Buddha's teaching but has no claim to impose it on those who have personal reminiscences of their own.

This want of a central authority, though less complete than in Brahmanism, marks the early life of the Buddhist community. We read in later works[2] of a succession of Elders who are sometimes called Patriarchs[3] but it would be erroneous to think of them as possessing episcopal authority. They were at most the chief teachers of the order. From the death of the Buddha to Asoka only five names are mentioned[3]. But five names can fill the interval only if their bearers were unusually long-lived. It is therefore probable that the list merely contains the names of prominent Theras who exercised little authority

[1] Cullav. XI. i. 11.

[2] Especially in Chinese works.

[3] Upâli, Dasaka, Sonaka, Siggava (with whom the name of Candravajji is sometimes coupled) and Tissa Moggaliputta. This is the list given in the Dîpavaṃsa.

in virtue of any office, though their personal qualities assured them respect. Upâli, who comes first, is called chief of the Vinaya but, so far as there was one head of the order, it seems to have been Kassapa. He is the Brahman ascetic of Uruvelâ whose conversion is recorded in the first book of the Mahâvagga and is said to have exchanged robes with the Buddha[1]. He observed the Dhutângas and we may conjecture that his influence tended to promote asceticism. Dasaka and Sonaka are also designated as chiefs of the Vinaya and there was perhaps a distinction between those who studied (to use modern phrases) ecclesiastical law and dogmatic theology.

The accounts[2] of the second Council are as abrupt as those of the first and do not connect it with previous events. The circumstances said to have led to its meeting are, however, probable. According to the Cullavagga, a hundred years after the death of the Buddha certain Bhikkhus of Vajjian lineage resident at Vesâlî upheld ten theses involving relaxations of the older discipline. The most important of these was that monks were permitted to receive gold and silver, but all of them, trivial as they may seem, had a dangerous bearing for they encouraged not only luxury but the formation of independent schools. For instance they allowed pupils to cite the practice of their preceptors as a justification for their conduct and authorized monks resident in one parish to hold Uposatha in separate companies and not as one united body. The story of the condemnation of these new doctrines contains miraculous incidents but seems to have a historical basis. It relates how a monk called Yasa, when a guest of the monks of Vesâlî, quarrelled with them because they accepted money from the laity and, departing thence, sought for support among the Theras or elders of the south and west. The result was a conference at Vesâlî in which the principal figures are Revata and Sabbakâmi, a pupil of Ânanda, expressly said to have been ordained one hundred and twenty years earlier[3]. The ten theses

[1] Sam. Nik. XVI. 11. The whole section is called Kassapa Saṃyutta.

[2] They are to be found chiefly in Cullavagga, XII., Dîpavaṃsa, IV. and V. and Mahâvaṃsa, IV.

[3] The Dîpavaṃsa adds that all the principal monks present had seen the Buddha. They must therefore all have been considerably over a hundred years old so that the chronology is open to grave doubt. It would be easier if we could suppose the meeting was held a hundred years after the enlightenment.

were referred to a committee, which rejected them all, and this rejection was confirmed by the whole Sangha, who proceeded to rehearse the Vinaya. We are not however told that they revised the Sutta or Abhidhamma.

Here ends the account of the Cullavagga but the Dîpavaṃsa adds that the wicked Vajjian monks, to whom it ascribes wrong doctrines as well as errors in discipline, collected a strong faction and held a schismatic council called the Mahâsangîti. This meeting recited or compiled a new version of the Dhamma and Vinaya[1]. It is not easy to establish any facts about the origin and tenets of this Mahâsangîtika or Mahâsanghika sect, though it seems to have been important. The Chinese pilgrims Fa Hsien and Hsüan Chuang, writing on the basis of information obtained in the fifth and seventh centuries of our era, represent it as arising in connection with the first council, which was either that of Râjagaha or some earlier meeting supposed to have been held during the Buddha's lifetime, and Hsüan Chuang[2] intimates that it was formed of laymen as well as monks and that it accepted additional matter including dhâraṇîs or spells rejected by the monkish council. Its name (admitted by its opponents) seems to imply that it represented at one time the opinions of the majority or at least a great number of the faithful. But it was not the sect which flourished in Ceylon and the writer of the Dîpavaṃsa is prejudiced against it. It may be a result of this animus that he connects it with the discreditable Vajjian schism and the Chinese tradition may be more correct. On the other hand the adherents of the school would naturally be disposed to assign it an early origin. Fa Hsien says[3] that the Vinaya of the Mahâsanghikas was considered "the most complete with the fullest explanations." A translation of this text is contained in the Chinese Tripitaka[4].

[1] They are said to have rejected the Parivâra, the Paṭisambhidâ, the Niddesa and parts of the Jâtaka. These are all later parts of the Canon and if the word rejection were taken literally it would imply that the Mahâsangîti was late too. But perhaps all that is meant is that the books were not found in their Canon. Chinese sources (*e.g.* Fa Hsien, tr. Legge, p. 99) state that they had an Abhidhamma of their own.

[2] *Buddhist Records of the Western World*, vol. II. pp. 164–5; Watters, *Yüan Chwang*, pp. 159–161.

[3] Cap. XXXVI. Legge, p. 98.

[4] See I-tsing's *Records of the Buddhist Religion*, trans. by Takakusu, p. XX. and Nanjio's *Catalogue of the Buddhist Tripitaka*, nos. 1199, 1105 and 1159.

Early Indian Buddhism is said to have been divided into eighteen sects or schools, which have long ceased to exist and must not be confounded with any existing denominations. Fa Hsien observes that they agree in essentials and differ only in details and this seems to have been true not only when he wrote (about 420 A.D.) but throughout their history. In different epochs and countries Buddhism presents a series of surprising metamorphoses, but the divergences between the sects existing in India at any given time are less profound in character and less violent in expression than the divisions of Christianity. Similarly the so-called sects[1] in modern China, Burma and Siam are better described as schools, in some ways analogous to such parties as the High and Low Church in England. On the other hand some of the eighteen schools exceeded the variations permitted in Christianity and Islam by having different collections of the scriptures. But at the time of which we are treating these collections had not been reduced to writing: they were of considerable extent compared with the Bible or Koran and they admitted later explanatory matter. The record of the Buddha's words did not profess to be a miraculous revelation but merely a recollection of what had been said. It is therefore natural that each school should maintain that the memory of its own scholars had transmitted the most accurate and complete account and that tradition should represent the successive councils as chiefly occupied in reciting and sifting these accounts.

It is generally agreed that the eighteen[2] schools were in existence during or shortly before the reign of Asoka, and that six others[3] arose about the same period, but subsequently to them. The best materials for a study of their opinions are afforded by the text and commentary[4] of the Kathâ-vatthu, a treatise attributed to Tissa Moggaliputta, who is said to have been President of the Third Council held under Asoka. It is

[1] An exception ought perhaps to be made for the Japanese sects.

[2] The names are not quite the same in the various lists and it seems useless to discuss them in detail. See Dîpavaṃsa, v. 39–48, Mahâvaṃsa, v. *ad in.*, Rhys Davids, *J.R.A.S.* 1891, p. 411, Rockhill, *Life of the Buddha*, chap. VI., Geiger, *Trans. of Mahâvaṃsa*, App. B.

[3] The Hemavatikas, Râjagirikas, Siddhattas, Pubbaselikas, Aparaselikas and Aparar̂ajagirikas.

[4] Published in the *J.P.T.S.* 1889. Trans. by S. Z. Aung and Mrs Rhys Davids, 1915. The text mentions doctrines only. The names of the sects supposed to hold them are supplied by the commentary.

an examination and refutation of heretical views rather than a description of the bodies that held them but we can judge from it what was the religious atmosphere at the time and the commentary gives some information about various sects. Many centuries later I-ching tells us that during his visit to India (671–695 A.D.) the principal schools were four in number, with eighteen subdivisions. These four[1] are the Mahâsanghika, the Sthavira (equivalent to the old Theravâda), the Mûlasarvâstivâda and the Sammitiya, and from the time of Asoka onwards they throw the remaining divisions into the shade[2]. He adds that it is not determined which of the four should be grouped with the Mahâyâna and which with the Hînayâna, that distinction being probably later in origin. The differences between the eighteen schools in I-ching's time were not vital but concerned the composition of the canon and details of discipline. It was a creditable thing to be versed in the scriptures of them all[3]. It is curious that though the Kathâvatthu pays more attention to the opinions of the six new sects than to those held by most of the eighteen, yet this latter number continued to be quoted nearly a thousand years later, whereas the additional six seem forgotten. It may be that they were more unorthodox than the others and hence required fuller criticism. Five of their names are geographical designations, but we hear no more of them after the age of Asoka.

The religious horizon of the heretics confuted in the Kathâvatthu does not differ materially from that of the Pitakas. There are many questions about arhatship, its nature, the method of obtaining it and the possibility of losing it. Also we find registered divergent views respecting the nature of knowledge and sensation. Of these the most important is the doctrine attributed to the Sammitiyas, that a soul exists in the highest and truest sense. They are also credited with holding that an arhat can fall from arhatship, that a god can enter the paths or the Order, and that even an unconverted man can get rid of all lust and ill-will[4]. This collection of beliefs is possibly

[1] They must not be confused with the four philosophic schools Vaibhâshika, Sautrântika, Yogâcâra and Mâdhyamika. These came into existence later.

[2] But the Vetulyakas were important in Ceylon.

[3] See Paramârtha's *Life of Vasabandhu*, Toung Pao, 1904, p. 290.

[4] See Rhys Davids in *J.R.A.S.* 1892, pp. 8–9. The name is variously spelt. The P.T.S. print Sammitiya, but the Sanskrit text of the Madhyamakavṛitti (in

explicable as a result of the view that the condition of the soul, which is continuous from birth to birth, is stronger for good or evil than its surroundings. The germs of the Mahâyâna may be detected in the opinions of some sects on the nature of the Buddha and the career of a Bodhisattva. Thus the Andhakas thought that the Buddha was superhuman in the ordinary affairs of life and the Vetulyakas[1] held that he was not really born in the world of men but sent a phantom to represent him, remaining himself in the Tusita heaven. The doctrines attributed to the Uttarâpathakas and Andhakas respectively that an unconverted man, if good, is capable of entering on the career of a Bodhisattva and that a Bodhisattva can in the course of his career fall into error and be reborn in state of woe, show an interest in the development of a Bodhisattva and a desire to bring it nearer to human life which are foreign to the Pitakas. An inclination to think of other states of existence in a manner half mythological half metaphysical is indicated by other heresies, such as that there is an intermediate realm where beings await rebirth, that the dead benefit by gifts given in the world[2], that there are animals in heaven, that the Four Truths, the Chain of Causation, and the Eightfold Path, are self-existent (asankhata).

The point of view of the Kathâ-vatthu, and indeed of the whole Pali Tripitaka, is that of the Vibhajjavâdins, which seems to mean those who proceed by analysis and do not make vague generalizations. This was the school to which Tissa Moggaliputta belonged and was identical with the Theravâda (teaching of the elders) or a section of it. The prominence of this sect in the history of Buddhism has caused its own view, namely that it represents primitive Buddhism, to be widely accepted. And this view deserves respect for it rests on a solid historical basis, namely that about two and a half centuries after the

Bibl. Buddh.) has Sâmmitîya. Sanskrit dictionaries give Sammatîya. The Abhidharma section of the Chinese Tripitaka (Nanjio, 1272) contains a śâstra belonging to this school. Nanjio, 1139 is apparently their Vinaya.

[1] Kern (*Versl. en Med. der K. Akad. van Wetenschappen Letterk.* 4. R. D. VIII. 1907, pp. 312–319, cf. *J.R.A.S.* 1907, p. 432) suggested on the authority of Kashgarian MSS. that the expression Vailpulya sûtra is a misreading for Vaitulya sûtra, a sûtra of the Vetulyakas. Ânanda was sometimes identified with the phantom who represented the Buddha.

[2] It is remarkable that this view, though condemned by the Kathâ-vatthu, is countenanced by the Khuddaka-pâṭha.

Buddha's death and in the country where he preached, the Vibhajjavâdins claimed to get back to his real teaching by an examination of the existing traditions[1]. This is a very early starting-point. But the Sarvâstivâdins[2] were also an early school which attained to widespread influence and had a similar desire to preserve the simple and comparatively human presentment of the Buddha's teaching as opposed to later embellishments. Only three questions in the Kathâ-vatthu are directed against them but this probably means not that they were unimportant but that they did not differ much from the Vibhajjavâdins. The special views attributed to them are that everything really exists, that an arhat can fall from arhatship, and that continuity of thought constitutes Samâdhi or meditation. These theses may perhaps be interpreted as indicative of an aversion to metaphysics and the supernatural. A saint has not undergone any supernatural transformation but has merely reached a level from which he can fall: meditation is simply fixity of attention, not a mystic trance. In virtue of the first doctrine European writers often speak of the Sarvâstivâdins as realists but their peculiar view concerned not so much the question of objective reality as the difference between being and becoming. They said that the world *is* whereas other schools maintained that it was a continual process of becoming[3]. It is not necessary at present to follow further the history of this important school. It had a long career and flourished in Kashmir and Central Asia.

Confused as are the notices of these ancient sects, we see with some clearness that in opposition to the Theravâda there was another body alluded to in terms which, though hostile, still imply an admission of size and learning, such as Mahâsanghika or Mahâsangîtika, the people of the great assembly, and Âcâryavâda or the doctrine of the Teachers. It appears to have originated in connection with some council and to embody a popular protest against the severity of the doctrine there laid down. This is natural, for it is pretty obvious that many found the argumentative psychology of the Theravâdins arid and

[1] The Kathâ-vatthu constantly cites the Nikâyas.

[2] Pali Sabbatthivâdins.

[3] Cf. the doctrine of the Sânkhya. For more about the Sarvâstivâdins see below, Book IV. chap. XXII.

wearisome. The Dîpavaṃsa accuses the Mahâsanghikas of garbling the canon but the Chinese pilgrims testify that in later times their books were regarded as specially complete. One well-known work, the Mahâvastu, perhaps composed in the first century B.C., describes itself as belonging to the Lokuttara branch of the Mahâsanghikas. The Mahâsanghikas probably represent the elements which developed into the Mahâyâna. It is not possible to formulate their views precisely but, whereas the Theravâda was essentially teaching for the Bhikkhu, they represented those concessions to popular taste from which Buddhism has never been quite dissociated even in its earliest period.

2

For some two centuries after Gotama's death we have little information as to the geographical extension of his doctrine, but some of the Sanskrit versions of the Vinaya[1] represent him as visiting Muttra, North-west India and Kashmir. So far as is known, the story of this journey is not supported by more ancient documents or other arguments: it contains a prediction about Kanishka, and may have been composed in or after his reign when the flourishing condition of Buddhism in Gândhâra made it seem appropriate to gild the past. But the narratives about Muttra and Kashmir contain several predictions relating to the progress of the faith 100 years after the Buddha's death and these can hardly be explained except as references to a tradition that those regions were converted at the epoch mentioned. There is no doubt of the connection between Kashmir and the Sarvâstivâdins nor anything improbable in the supposition that the first missionary activity was in the direction of Muttra and Kashmir.

But the great landmark in the earlier history of Buddhism is the reign of Asoka. He came to the throne about 270 B.C. and inherited the vast dominions of his father and grandfather. Almost all that we know of the political events of his reign is that his coronation did not take place until four years later, which may indicate a disputed succession, and that he rounded off his possessions by the conquest of Kalinga, that is the country between the Mahanadi and the Godavari, about 261 B.C.

[1] See especially Le Nord-Ouest de l'Inde dans le Vinaya des Mûlasarvâstivâdins by Przyluski in *J.A.* 1914, II. pp. 492 ff.

This was the end of his military career. Nothing could be gained by further conquests, for his empire already exceeded the limits set to effective government by the imperfect communications of the epoch, seeing that it extended from Afghanistan to the mouths of the Ganges and southwards almost to Madras. No evidence substantiates the later stories which represent him as a monster of wickedness before his conversion, but according to the Dîpavaṃsa he at first favoured heretics.

The general effect of Asoka's rule on the history of Buddhism and indeed of Asia is clear, but there is still some difference of opinion as to the date of his conversion. The most important document for the chronology of his reign is the inscription known as the first Minor Rock Edict[1]. It is now generally admitted that it does not state the time which has elapsed since the death of the Buddha, as was once supposed, and that the King relates in it how for more than two and a half years after his conversion to Buddhism he was a lay-believer and did not exert himself strenuously, but subsequently joined the Sangha[2] and began to devote his energies to religion rather more than a year before the publication of the edict. This proclamation has been regarded by some as the first, by others as the last of his edicts. On the latter supposition we must imagine that he published a long series of ethical but not definitely Buddhist ordinances and that late in life he became first a lay-believer and then a monk, probably abdicating at the same time. But the King is exceedingly candid as to his changes of life and mind: he tells us how the horrors of the war with Kalinga affected him, how he was an easygoing layman and then a zealous monk. Had there been a stage between the war and his acceptance of Buddhism as a layman, a period of many years in which he devoted himself to the moral progress of his people without being himself a Buddhist, he would surely have explained it. Moreover in the Bhâbrû edict, which is distinctly ecclesiastical and deals with the Buddhist scriptures, he employs his favourite word Dhamma in the strict Buddhist sense, without indicating that he is giving it an unusual or new meaning.

[1] See articles by Fleet in *J.R.A.S.* of 1903, 1904, 1908–1911 and 1914: Hultzsch in *J.R.A.S.* 1910–11: Thomas in *J.A.* 1910: S. Lévi, *J.A.* 1911.

[2] Asoka's statement is confirmed (if it needs confirmation) by the Chinese pilgrim I-ching who saw in India statues of him in monastic costume.

I therefore think it probable that he became a lay Buddhist soon after the conquest of Kalinga, that is in the ninth or tenth year after his accession, and a member of the Sangha two and a half years later. On this hypothesis all his edicts are the utterances of a Buddhist.

It may be objected that no one could be a monk and at the same time govern a great empire: it is more natural and more in accordance with Indian usage that towards the end of his life an aged king should abdicate and renounce the world. But Wu Ti, the Buddhist Emperor of China, retired to a monastery twice in the course of his long reign and the cloistered Emperors of Japan in the eleventh and twelfth centuries continued to direct the policy of their country, although they abdicated in name and set a child on the throne as titular ruler. The Buddhist Church was not likely to criticize Asoka's method of keeping his monastic vows and indeed it may be said that his activity was not so much that of a pious emperor as of an archbishop possessed of exceptional temporal power. He definitely renounced conquest and military ambitions and appears to have paid no attention to ordinary civil administration which he perhaps entrusted to Commissioners; he devoted himself to philanthropic and moral projects "for the welfare of man and beast," such as lecturing his subjects on their duties towards all living creatures, governing the Church, building hospitals and stûpas, supervising charities and despatching missions. In all his varied activity there is nothing unsuitable to an ecclesiastical statesman: in fact he is distinguished from most popes and prelates by his real indifference to secular aspirations and by the unusual facilities which he enjoyed for immediately putting his ideals into practice.

Asoka has won immortality by the Edicts which he caused to be engraved on stone[1]. They have survived to the present day and are the most important monuments which we possess for the early history of India and of Buddhism. They have a character of their own. A French writer has said "On ne bavarde pas sur la pierre," and for most inscriptions the saying holds good, but Asoka wrote on the rocks of India as if he were

[1] For a bibliography of the literature about these inscriptions see Vincent Smith, *Early History of India*, 3rd ed. 1914, pp. 172–4.

dictating to a stenographer. He was no stylist and he was somewhat vain although, considering his imperial position and the excellence of his motives, this obvious side of his character is excusable. His inscriptions give us a unique series of sermons on stones and a record, if not of what the people of India thought, at least of what an exceptionally devout and powerful Hindu thought they ought to think.

Between thirty and forty of these inscriptions have been discovered, scattered over nearly the whole of India, and composed in vernacular dialects allied to Pali[1]. Many of them are dated by the year of the King's reign and all announce themselves as the enactments of Piyadassi, the name Asoka being rarely used[2]. They comprise, besides some fourteen single edicts[3], two series, namely:

(1) Fourteen Rock Edicts, dating from the thirteenth and fourteenth years of Asoka's reign[4] and found inscribed in seven places but the recensions differ and some do not include all fourteen edicts.

(2) Seven Pillar Edicts dating from the 27th and 28th years, and found in six recensions.

The fourteen Rock Edicts are mostly sermons. Their style often recalls the Pitakas verbally, particularly in the application of secular words to religious matters. Thus we hear that righteousness is the best of lucky ceremonies and that whereas former kings went on tours of pleasure and hunting, Asoka prefers tours of piety and has set out on the road leading to true knowledge. In this series he does not mention the Buddha and in the twelfth edict he declares that he reverences all sects. But what he wished to preach and enforce was the *Dhamma*.

[1] The dialect is not strictly speaking the same in all the inscriptions.

[2] Piyadassi, Sanskrit Priyadarsin. The Dîpavaṃsa, VI. 1 and 14, calls Asoka Piyadassi and Piyadassana. The name Asoka has hitherto only been found in one edict discovered at Hyderabad, *J.R.A.S.* 1916, p. 573.

[3] The principal single edicts are (1) that known as Minor Rock Edict I. found in four recensions, (2) The Bhâbrû (or Bhâbrâ) Edict of great importance for the Buddhist scriptures, (3) Two Kalinga Edicts, (4) Edicts about schism, found at Sarnath and elsewhere, (4) Commemorative inscriptions in the Terâi, (5) Dedications of caves.

[4] Asoka came to the throne about 270 B.C. (268 or 272 according to various authorities) but was not crowned until four years later. Events are generally dated by the year after his coronation (abhisheka), not after his accession.

It is difficult to find an English equivalent for this word[1] but there is no doubt of the meaning. It is the law, in the sense of the righteous life which a Buddhist layman ought to live, and perhaps religion is the simplest translation, provided that word is understood to include conduct and its consequences in another world but not theism. Asoka burns with zeal to propagate this Dhamma and his language recalls[2] the utterances of the Dhammapada. He formulates the law under four heads[3]: "Parents must be obeyed: respect for living creatures must be enforced: truth must be spoken...the teacher must be reverenced by the pupil and proper courtesy must be shown to relations." In many ways the Sacred Edict of the Chinese Emperor K'ang Hsi resembles these proclamations for it consists of imperial maxims on public morality addressed by a Confucian Emperor to a population partly Buddhist and Taoist, just as Asoka addressed Brahmans, Jains and other sects as well as Buddhists. But when we find in the thirteenth Rock Edict the incidental statement that the King thinks nothing of much importance except what concerns the next world, we feel the great difference between Indian and Chinese ideas whether ancient or modern.

The Rock Edicts also deal with the sanctity of animal life. Asoka's strong dislike of killing or hurting animals cannot be ascribed to policy, for it must have brought him into collision with the Brahmans who offered animals in sacrifice, but was the offspring of a naturally gentle and civilized mind. We may conjecture that the humanity of Buddhism was a feature which attracted him to it. In Rock Edict i. he forbids animal sacrifices and informs us that whereas formerly many thousand animals were killed daily for the royal kitchens now only three are killed, namely two peacocks and a deer, and the deer not always. But in future even these three creatures will not be slaughtered. In Rock Edict ii. he describes how he has cared for the comfort of man and beast. Wells have been dug; trees, roots and healing herbs have been planted and remedies—possibly hospitals—have been provided, all for animals as well

[1] I must confess that Law of Piety (Vincent Smith) does not seem to me very idiomatic.

[2] See Senart, *Inscrip. de Piyadassi*, ii. pp. 314 ff.

[3] The Second Minor Rock Edict.

as for men, and this not only in his own dominions but in neighbouring realms. In the fourteenth year of his reign he appointed officers called Dhamma-mahâmâtâ, Ministers or Censors of the Dhamma. Their duty was to promote the observance of the Dhamma and they also acted as Charity Commissioners and superintendents of the households of the King's relatives. We hear that "they attend to charitable institutions, ascetics, householders and all the sects: I have also arranged that they shall attend to the affairs of the Buddhist clergy, as well as the Brahmans, the Jains, the Âjîvikas and in fact all the various sects." Further he tells us that the local authorities[1] are to hold quinquennial assemblies at which the Dhamma is to be proclaimed and that religious processions with elephants, cars, and illuminations have been arranged to please and instruct the people. Similar processions can still be seen at the Perahera festival in Kandy.

The last Rock Edict is of special interest for the light which it sheds both on history and on the King's character. He expresses remorse for the bloodshed which accompanied the conquest of Kalinga and declares that he will henceforth devote his attention to conquest by the Dhamma, which he has effected "both in his own dominions and in all the neighbouring realms as far as six hundred leagues (?), even to where the Greek King named Antiochus dwells and beyond that Antiochus to where dwell the four kings named Ptolemy, Antigonus, Magas and Alexander[2], and in the south the kings of the Colas and Pandyas[3] and of Ceylon and likewise here in the King's dominions, among the Yonas[4] and Kâmbojas[5] in Nâbhaka of the Nâbhitis[6] among the Bhojas and Pitinikas, among the Ândhras and Pulindas[7]. Asoka thus appears to state that he has sent missionaries to (1) the outlying parts of India, on the borders of his own dominions, (2) to Ceylon, (3) to the Hellenistic Kingdoms of Asia, Africa and Europe.

This last statement is of the greatest importance, but no

[1] Râjûka and pradesika.

[2] *I.e.* Syria, Egypt, Macedonia, Cyrene and Epirus.

[3] Kingdoms in the south of India.

[4] The inhabitants of the extreme north-west of India, not necessarily Greeks by race.

[5] Possibly Tibet.

[6] Or Nâbhapamtis. In any case unknown.

[7] All these appear to have been tribes of Central India.

record has hitherto been found of the arrival of these missionaries in the west. The language of the Edict about them is not precise and in fact their despatch is only an inference from it. Of the success of the Indian missions there is no doubt. Buddhism was introduced into southern India, where it flourished to some extent though it had to maintain a double struggle against Jains as well as Brahmans. The statement of the Dîpa and Mahâ-vaṃsas that missionaries were also sent to Pegu (Suvaṇṇabhûmi) is not supported by the inscriptions, though not in itself improbable, but the missions to the north and to Ceylon were remarkably successful.

The Sinhalese Chronicles[1] give the names of the principal missionaries despatched and their statements have received confirmation in the discoveries made at Sanchi and Sonari where urns have been found inscribed with the names of Majjhima, Kassapa, and Gotiputta the successor of Dundhubhissara, who are called teachers of the Himalaya region. The statement in the Mahâ and Dîpa-vaṃsas is that Majjhima was sent to preach in the Himalaya accompanied by four assistants Kassapa, Mâlikâdeva, Dundhâbhinossa and Sahassadeva.

About the twenty-first year of his reign Asoka made a religious tour and under the guidance of his preceptor Upagupta, visited the Lumbini Park (now Rummindei) in the Terâi, where the Buddha was born, and other spots connected with his life and preaching. A pillar has been discovered at Rummindei bearing an inscription which records the visit and the privileges granted to the village where "the Lord was born." At Niglîva a few miles off he erected another inscribed pillar stating that he had done reverence to the stûpa of the earlier Buddha Konâgamana and for the second time repaired it.

During this tour he visited Nepal and Lalitpur, the capital, founding there five stûpas. His daughter Cârumatî is said to have accompanied him and to have remained in Nepal when he returned. She built a convent which still bears her name and lived there as a nun. It does not appear that Asoka visited Kashmir, but he caused a new capital (Srînagar) to be built there, and introduced Buddhism.

In the 27th and 28th year of his reign he composed another series of Edicts and this time had them carved in pillars not

[1] Dîpav. VIII.; Mahâv. XII.

on rocks. They are even more didactic than the Rock Edicts and contain an increasing number of references to the next world, as well as stricter regulations forbidding cruelty to animals, but the King remains tolerant and says[1] that the chief thing is that each man should live up to his own creed. It is probable that at this time he had partially abdicated or at least abandoned some of the work of administration, for in Edict IV. he states that he has appointed Commissioners with discretion to award honours and penalties and that he feels secure like a man who has handed over his child to a skilful nurse.

In the two series of Rock and Pillar Edicts there is little dogmatic Buddhism. It is true that the King's anxiety as to the hereafter of his subjects and his solicitude for animals indicate thoughts busy with religious ideas, but still his Dhamma is generally defined in terms which do not go beyond morality, kindness and sympathy. But in the Bhâbrû (less correctly Bhâbrâ) Edict he recommends for study a series of scriptural passages which can be identified more or less certainly with portions of the Pali Pitakas. In the Sarnath Edict he speaks not only as a Buddhist but as head of the Church. He orders that monks or nuns who endeavour to create a schism shall put on lay costume and live outside their former monastery or convent. He thus assumes the right to expel schismatics from the Sangha. He goes on to say that a similar edict (*i.e.* an edict against schism) is to be inscribed for the benefit of the laity who are to come and see it on Uposatha days. "And on the Uposatha days in all months every officer is to come for the Uposatha service to be inspired with confidence in this Edict and to learn it." Thus the King's officers are to be Buddhists at least to the extent of attending the Uposatha ceremony, and the edict about schismatics is to be brought to the notice of the laity, which doubtless means that the laity are not to give alms to them.

It is probable that many more inscriptions remain to be discovered but none of those known allude to the convening of a Council and our information as to this meeting comes from the two Sinhalese Chronicles and the works of Buddhaghosa. It is said to have been held two hundred and thirty-six years

[1] Pillar Edict VI.

after the death of the Buddha[1] and to have been necessitated by the fact that the favour shown to the Sangha induced heretics to become members of it without abandoning their errors. This occasioned disturbances and the King was advised to summon a sage called Tissa Moggaliputta (or Upagupta) then living in retirement and to place the affairs of the church in his hands. He did so. Tissa then composed the Kathâ-vatthu and presided over a council composed of one thousand arhats which established the true doctrine and fixed the present Pali Canon.

Even so severe a critic of Sinhalese tradition as Vincent Smith admits that the evidence for the council is too strong to be set aside, but it must be confessed that it would be reassuring to find some allusion to it in Asoka's inscriptions. He did not however always say what we should expect. In reviewing his efforts in the cause of religion he mentions neither a council nor foreign missions, although we know from other inscriptions that such missions were despatched. The sessions of the council may be equally true and are in no way improbable, for in later times kings of Burma, Ceylon and Siam held conventions to revise the text of the Tripitaka. It appeared natural that a pious King should see that the sacred law was observed, and begin by ascertaining what that law was.

According to tradition Asoka died after reigning thirty-eight or forty years but we have no authentic account of his death and the stories of his last days seem to be pure legends. The most celebrated are the pathetic tale of Kunâla which closely resembles a Jâtaka[2], and the account of how Asoka vowed to present a hundred million gold pieces to the Sangha and not being able to raise the whole sum made a gift of his dominions instead.

3

Asoka had a decisive effect on the history of Buddhism, especially in making it a world religion. This was not the

[1] Perhaps meant to be equivalent to 251 B.C. Vincent Smith rejects this date and thinks that the Council met in the last ten years of Asoka's reign. But the Sinhalese account is reasonable. Asoka was very pious but very tolerant. Ten years of this regime may well have led to the abuse complained of.

[2] Jâtaka, no. 472.

accidental result of his action in establishing it in north-west India and Ceylon, for he was clearly dominated by the thought that the Dhamma must spread over the whole world and, so far as we know, he was the first to have that thought in a practical form. But we could estimate his work better if we knew more about the religious condition of the country when he came to the throne. As it is, the periods immediately before and after him are plunged in obscurity and to illuminate his reign we have little information except his own edicts which, though copious, do not aim at giving a description of his subjects. Megasthenes who resided at Pataliputra about 300 B.C. does not appear to have been aware of the existence of Buddhism as a separate religion, but perhaps a foreign minister in China at the present day might not notice that the Chinese have more than one religion. On the other hand in Asoka's time Buddhism, by whatever name it was called, was well known and there was evidently no necessity for the King to explain what he meant by Dhamma and Sangha. The Buddha had belonged to a noble family and was esteemed by the aristocracy of Magadha; the code of morality which he prescribed for the laity was excellent and sensible. It is therefore not surprising if the Kshatriyas and others recognized it as their ideal nor if Asoka found it a sound basis of legislation. This legislation may be called Buddhist in the sense that in his edicts the King enjoins and to some extent enforces *sîlam* or morality, which is the indispensable beginning for all spiritual progress, and that his enactments about animals go beyond what is usual in secular law. But he expressly refrains from requiring adherence to any particular sect. On the other hand there is no lack of definite patronage of Buddhism. He institutes edifying processions, he goes on pilgrimages to sacred sites, he addresses the Sangha as to the most important parts of the scriptures, and we may infer that he did his best to spread the knowledge of those scriptures. Though he says nothing about it in the Edicts which have been discovered, he erected numerous religious buildings including the Sanchi tope and the original temple at Bodh-Gaya. Their effect in turning men's attention to Buddhism must have been greatly enhanced by the fact that so far as we know no other sect had stone temples at this time. To such influences, we must add the human element. The example and well-known wishes of a great king, supported by a numerous and learned clergy, could not fail to attract crowds to the faith, and the faith itself—for let us not forget Gotama while we give credit to his follower—was satisfying. Thus Asoka probably found Buddhism in the form of a numerous order of monks, respected locally and exercising a considerable power over the minds and conduct of laymen. He left it a great church spread from the north to the south of India and even beyond, with an army of officials to assist its progress, with sacred buildings and monasteries, sermons and ceremonies. How long his special institutions lasted we do not know, but no one acquainted with India can help feeling that his system of inspection was liable to grave abuse. Black-mailing and misuse of authority are ancient faults of the Indian police and we may surmise that the generations which followed him were not long in getting rid of his censors and inspectors.

Christian critics of Buddhism are apt to say that it has a paralyzing effect on the nations who adopt it, but Asoka's edicts teem with words like energy and strenuousness. "It is most necessary to make an effort in this world," so he recounts the efforts which he has himself made and wants everybody else to make an effort. "Work I must for the public benefit—and the root of the matter is in exertion and despatch of business than which nothing is more efficacious for the general welfare." These sound like the words of a British utilitarian rather than of a dreamy oriental emperor. He is far from pessimistic: indeed, he almost ignores the Truth of Suffering. In describing the conquest of Kalinga he speaks almost in the Buddha's words of the sorrow of death and separation, but instead of saying that such things are inevitable he wishes his subjects to be told that he regrets what has happened and desires to give them security, peace and joy.

Asoka has been compared with Constantine but it has been justly observed that the comparison is superficial, for Constantine (more like Kanishka than Asoka) merely recognized and regulated a religion which had already won its way in his empire. He has also been compared with St Paul and in so far as both men transformed a provincial sect into a religion for all mankind the parallel is just, but it ends there. St Paul was a constructive theologian. For good or evil he greatly developed and complicated the teaching of Christ, but the Edicts of Asoka if compared with the Pitakas seem to curtail and simplify their doctrines. No inscription has yet been found mentioning the four truths, the chain of causation and other familiar formulæ. Doubtless Asoka duly studied these questions, but it was not theology nor metaphysics which drew him towards religion. In the gallery of pious Emperors—a collection of dubious moral and intellectual value—he stands isolated as perhaps the one man whose only passion was for a sane, kindly and humane life, neither too curious of great mysteries nor preoccupied with his own soul but simply the friend of man and beast.

For the history of doctrine the inscription at Rummindei is particularly important. It merely states that the King did honour or reverence to the birthplace of the Buddha, who receives no titles except Sakyamuni and Bhagavan here or elsewhere in the inscriptions. It is a simple record of respect paid to a great human teacher who is not in any way deified nor does Asoka's language show any trace of the doctrines afterwards known under the name of Mahayana. He does not mention nirvana or even transmigration, though doubtless what he says about paradise and rewards hereafter should be read in the light of Indian doctrines about karma and samsâra.

CHAPTER XIII

THE CANON

1

THERE are extant in several languages large collections of Buddhist scriptures described by some European writers as the Canon. The name is convenient and not incorrect, but the various canons are not altogether similar and the standard for the inclusion or exclusion of particular works is not always clear. We know something of four or five canons.

(1) The Pali Canon, accepted by the Buddhists of Ceylon, Burma and Siam, and rendered accessible to European students by the Pali Text Society. It professes to contain the works recognized as canonical by the Council of Asoka and it is reasonably homogeneous, that is to say, although some ingenuity may be needed to harmonize the different strata of which it consists, it does not include works composed by several schools.

(2) The Sanskrit Canon or Canons.

(*a*) Nepalese scriptures. These do not correspond with any Pali texts and all belong to the Mahayana. There appears to be no standard for fixing the canonical character of Mahayanist works. Like the Upanishads they are held to be revealed from time to time.

(*b*) Buddhist texts discovered in Central Asia. Hitherto these have been merely fragments, but the number of manuscripts found and not yet published permits the hope that longer texts may be forthcoming. Those already made known are partly Mahayanist and partly similar to the Pali Canon though not a literal translation of it. It is not clear to what extent the Buddhists of Central Asia regarded the Hina and Mahayanist scriptures as separate and distinct. Probably each school selected for itself a small collection of texts as authoritative[1].

(3) The Chinese Canon. This is a gigantic collection of Buddhist works made and revised by order of various Emperors.

[1] See for instance the *Life of Hsüan Chuang*; Beal, p. 39; Julien, p. 50.

The imperial imprimatur is the only standard of canonicity. The contents include translations of works belonging to all schools made from the first to the thirteenth century A.D. The originals were apparently all in Sanskrit and were probably the texts of which fragments have been found in Central Asia. This canon also includes some original Chinese works.

(4) There is a somewhat similar collection of translations into Tibetan. But whereas the Chinese Canon contains translations dated from 67 A.D. onwards, the Tibetan translations were made mainly in the ninth and eleventh centuries and represent the literature esteemed by the mediæval Buddhism of Bengal. Part at least of this Tibetan Canon has been translated into Mongol.

Renderings of various books into Uigur, Sogdian, Kuchanese, "Nordarisch" and other languages of Central Asia have been discovered by recent explorers. It is probable that they are all derived from the Sanskrit Canon and do not represent any independent tradition. The scriptures used in Japan and Korea are simply special editions of the Chinese Canon, not translations.

In the following pages I propose to consider the Pali Canon, postponing until later an account of the others. It will be necessary, however, to touch on the relations of Pali and Sanskrit texts.

The scriptures published by the Pali Text Society represent the canon of the ancient sect called Vibhajjavâdins and the particular recension of it used at the monastery in Anuradhapura called Mahâvihâra. It is therefore not incorrect to apply to this recension such epithets as southern or Sinhalese, provided we remember that in its origin it was neither one nor the other, for the major part of it was certainly composed in India[1]. It was probably introduced into Ceylon in the third century B.C. and it is also accepted in Burma, Siam and Camboja[2]. Thus in a considerable area it is the sole and undisputed version of the scriptures.

[1] I consider it possible, though by no means proved, that the Abhidhamma was put together in Ceylon.

[2] For the Burmese Canon see chap. XXVI. Even if the Burmese had Pali scriptures which did not come from Ceylon, they sought to harmonize them with the texts known there.

The canon is often known by the name of Tripiṭaka[1] or Three Baskets. When an excavation was made in ancient India it was the custom to pass up the earth in baskets along a line of workmen[2] and the metaphorical use of the word seems to be taken from this practice and to signify transmission by tradition.

The three Pitakas are known as Vinaya, Sutta, and Abhidhamma. Vinaya means discipline and the works included in this division treat chiefly of the rules to be observed by the members of the Sangha. The basis of these rules is the Pâtimokkha, the ancient confessional formula enumerating the offences which a monk can commit. It was read periodically to a congregation of the order and those guilty of any sin had to confess it. The text of the Pâtimokkha is in the Vinaya combined with a very ancient commentary called the Sutta-vibhanga. The Vinaya also contains two treatises known collectively as the Khandakas but more frequently cited by their separate names as Mahâvagga and Cullavagga. The first deals with such topics as the rules for admission to the order, and observance of fast days, and in treating of each rule it describes the occasion on which the Buddha made it and to some extent follows the order of chronology. For some parts of the master's life it is almost a biography. The Cullavagga is similar in construction but less connected in style[3].

[1] Pali Tipiṭaka.

[2] So in Maj. Nik. XXI. a man who proposes to excavate comes Kuddalapiṭakam âdâya, "With spade and basket."

[3] The list of the Vinaya books is:

Pârâjikam, Pacittiyam } together constituting the Sutta-vibhanga.

Mahâvagga, Cullavagga } together constituting the Khandakas.

Parivâra-pâṭha: a supplement and index. This book was rejected by some schools.

Something is known of the Vinaya of the Sarvâstivâdins existing in a Chinese translation and in fragments of the Sanskrit original found in Central Asia. It also consists of the Pâtimokkha embedded in a commentary called Vibhâga and of two treatises describing the foundation of the order and its statutes. They are called Kshudrakavastu and Vinayavastu. In these works the narrative and anecdotal element is larger than in the Pali Vinaya. See also my remarks on the Mahâvastu under the Mahayanist Canon. For some details about the Dharmagupta Vinaya, see *J.A.* 1916, II. p. 20: for a longish extract from the Mûlasarv. Vinaya, *J.A.* 1914, II. pp. 493–522.

The Vinaya contains several important and curious narratives and is a mine of information about the social conditions of ancient India, but much of it has the same literary value as the book of Leviticus. Of greater general interest is the Sutta Pitaka, in which the sermons and discourses of the Buddha are collected. Sutta is equivalent to the Sanskrit word Sûtra, literally a thread, which signifies among the Brahmans a brief rule or aphorism but in Pali a relatively short poem or narrative dealing with a single object. This Sutta Pitaka is divided into five collections called Nikâyas. The first four are mainly in prose and contain discourses attributed to Gotama or his disciples. The fifth is mostly in verse and more miscellaneous.

The four collections of discourses bear the names of Dîgha, Majjhima, Saṃyutta and Anguttara. The first, meaning long, consists of thirty-four narratives. They are not all sermons and are of varying character, antiquity and interest, the reason why they are grouped together being simply their length[1]. In some of them we may fancy that we catch an echo of Gotama's own words, but in others the legendary character is very marked. Thus the Mahâsamaya and Aṭânâṭiya suttas are epitomes of popular mythology tacked on to the history of the Buddha. But for all that they are interesting and ancient.

Many of the suttas, especially the first thirteen, are re-arrangements of old materials put together by a considerable literary artist who lived many generations after the Buddha. The account of the Buddha's last days is an example of such a compilation which attains the proportions of a Gospel and shows some dramatic power though it is marred by the juxtaposition of passages composed in very different styles.

The Majjhima-Nikâya is a collection of 152 discourses of moderate (majjhima) length. Taken as a whole it is perhaps the most profound and impassioned of all the Nikâyas and also the oldest. The sermons which it contains, if not verbatim reports of Gotama's eloquence, have caught the spirit of one who urged with insistent earnestness the importance of certain difficult truths and the tremendous issues dependent on right conduct and right knowledge. The remaining collections, the

[1] I find it hard to accept Francke's view that the Dîgha should be regarded as the Book of the Tathâgata, deliberately composed to expound the doctrine of Buddhahood. Many of the suttas do not deal with the Tathâgata.

Saṃyutta and Anguttara, classify the Buddha's utterances under various headings and presuppose older documents which they sometimes quote[1]. The Saṃyutta consists of a great number of suttas, mostly short, combined in groups treating of a single subject which may be either a person or a topic. The Anguttara, which is a still longer collection, is arranged in numerical groups, a method of classification dear to the Hindus who delight in such computations as the four meditations, the eightfold path, the ten fetters. It takes such religious topics as can be counted in this way and arranges them under the numbers from one to eleven. Thus under three, it treats of thought, word and deed and the applications of this division to morality; of the three messengers of the gods, old-age, sickness and death; of the three great evils, lust, ill-will and stupidity and so on.

The fifth or Khuddaka-Nikâya is perhaps the portion of the Pali scriptures which has found most favour with Europeans, for the treatises composing it are short and some of them of remarkable beauty. They are in great part composed of verses, sometimes disconnected couplets, sometimes short poems. The stanzas are only imperfectly intelligible without an explanation of the occasion to which they refer. This is generally forthcoming, but is sometimes a part of the accepted text and sometimes regarded as merely a commentary. To this division of the Pitaka belong the Dhammapada, a justly celebrated anthology of devotional verses, and the Sutta-Nipâta, a very ancient collection of suttas chiefly in metre. Other important works included in it are the Thera and Therî-gâthâ or poems written by monks and nuns respectively, and the Jâtaka or stories about the Buddha's previous births[2]. Some of the rather miscellaneous contents of this Nikâya are late and do not belong to the same epoch of thought as the discourses

[1] The Saṃyutta quotes by name a passage from the Dîgha as "spoken by the Lord": compare Sam. Nik. XXII. 4 with Dig. Nik. 21. Both the Anguttara and Saṃyutta quote the last two cantos of the Sutta-Nipâta.

[2] It appears that the canonical book of the Jâtaka consists only of verses and does not include explanatory prose matter. Something similar to these collections of verses which are not fully intelligible without a commentary explaining the occasions on which they were uttered may be seen in Chândogya Up. VI. The father's answers are given but the son's questions which render them intelligible are not found in the text but are supplied in the commentary.

attributed to Gotama. Such are the Buddha-vaṃsa, or lives of Gotama and his twenty-four predecessors, the Cariyâ-Piṭaka, a selection of Jâtaka stories about Gotama's previous births and the Vimâna and Peta-vatthus, accounts of celestial mansions and of the distressful existence led by those who are condemned to be ghosts[1].

Though some works comprised in this Nikâya (*e.g.* the Sutta-nipâta) are very ancient, the collection, as it stands, is late and probably known only to the southern Church. The contents of it are not quite the same in Ceylon, Burma and Siam, and only a small portion of them has been identified in the Chinese Tripitaka. Nevertheless the word *pañcanekâyika*, one who knows the five Nikâyas, is found in the inscriptions of Sanchi and five Nikâyas are mentioned in the last books of the Cullavagga. Thus a fifth Nikâya of some kind must have been known fairly early.

The third Pitaka is known by the name of Abhidhamma.

[1] The following is a table of the Sutta Pitaka:

I. Dîgha-Nikâya
II. Majjhima-Nikâya
III. Samyutta-Nikâya
IV. Anguttara-Nikâya
} Collections of discourses mostly attributed to the Buddha.

V. Khuddaka-Nikâya: a collection of comparatively short treatises, mostly in poetry, namely:

1. Dhammapada.
2. Udâna
3. Itivuttakam
} Utterances of the Buddha with explanations of the attendant circumstances.
4. Khuddaka-pâtha: a short anthology.
5. Sutta-nipâta: a collection of suttas mostly in verse.
*6. Thera-gâthâ: poems by monks.
*7. Therî-gâthâ: poems by nuns.
8. Niddesa: an old commentary on the latter half of the Sutta-nipâta, ascribed to Sâriputta.
*9. The Jâtaka verses.
10. Paṭisambhidâ.
*11. Apadâna.
*12. Buddha-vaṃsa.
*13. Vimâna-vatthu.
*14. Peta-vatthu.
*15. Cariyâ-piṭaka.

The works marked * are not found in the Siamese edition of the Tripiṭaka but the Burmese editions include four other texts, the Milinda-pañha, Petakopadesa, Suttassanigaha, and Nettipakaraṇa.

The Khuddaka-Nikâya seems to have been wanting in the Pitaka of the Sarvâstivâdins or whatever sect supplied the originals from which the Chinese Canon was translated, for this Canon classes the Dhammapada as a miscellaneous work outside the Sutta Pitaka. Fragments of the Sutta-nipâta have been found in Turkestan but it is not clear to what Pitaka it was considered to belong. For mentions of the Khuddaka-Nikâya in Chinese see *J.A.* 1916, pp. 32–3.

Dhamma is the usual designation for the doctrine of the Buddha and Buddhaghosa[1] explains the prefix abhi as signifying excess and distinction, so that this Pitaka is considered pre-eminent because it surpasses the others. This pre-eminence consists solely in method and scope, not in novelty of matter or charm of diction. The point of view of the Abhidhamma is certainly later than that of the Sutta Pitaka and in some ways marks an advance, for instead of professing to report the discourses of Gotama it takes the various topics on which he touched, especially psychological ethics, and treats them in a connected and systematic manner. The style shows some resemblance to Sanskrit sûtras for it is so technical both in vocabulary and arrangement that it can hardly be understood without a commentary[2]. According to tradition the Buddha recited the Abhidhamma when he went to heaven to preach to the gods, and this seems a polite way of hinting that it was more than any human congregation could tolerate or understand. Still throughout the long history of Buddhism it has always been respected as the most profound portion of the scriptures and has not failed to find students. This Pitaka includes the Kathâ-vatthu, attributed to Tissa Moggaliputta who is said to have composed it about 250 B.C. in Asoka's reign[3].

There is another division of the Buddhist scriptures into nine *angas* or members, namely: 1. Suttas. 2. Geyya: mixed prose and verse. 3. Gâthâ: verse. 4. Udâna: ecstatic utterances. 5. Veyyâkaraṇa: explanation. 6. Itivuttaka: sayings beginning with the phrase "Thus said the Buddha." 7. Jâtaka: stories of former births. 8. Abbhutadhamma: stories of wonders. 9. Vedalla: a word of doubtful meaning, but perhaps questions

[1] See *J.R.A.S.* 1891, p. 560. See too *Journal P.T.S.* 1919, p. 44. Lexicographical notes.

[2] Mrs Rhys Davids' *Translations of the Dhamma-sangaṇi* give a good idea of these books.

[3] The works comprised in this Pitaka are:

1. Dhamma-sangaṇi.
2. Vibhanga.
3. Kathâ-vatthu.
4. Puggala-paññatti.
5. Dhâtu-kathâ.
6. Yamaka.
7. Paṭṭhâna. The Abhidhamma of the Sarvâstivâdins was entirely different. It seems probable that the Abhidhamma books of all schools consisted almost entirely of explanatory matter and added very little to the doctrine laid down in the suttas. It would appear that the only new topic introduced in the Pali Abhidhamma is the theory of relations (paccaya).

and answers. This enumeration is not to be understood as a statement of the sections into which the whole body of scripture was divided but as a description of the various styles of composition recognized as being religious, just as the Old Testament might be said to contain historical books, prophecies, canticles and so on. Compositions in these various styles must have been current before the work of collection began, as is proved by the fact that all the *angas* are enumerated in the Majjhima-Nikâya[1].

2

This Tripitaka is written in Pali[2] which is regarded by Buddhist tradition as the language spoken by the Master. In the time of Asoka the dialect of Magadha must have been understood over the greater part of India, like Hindustani in modern times, but in some details of grammar and phonetics Pali differs from Mâgadhî Prakrit and seems to have been influenced by Sanskrit and by western dialects. Being a literary rather than a popular language it was probably a mixed form of speech and it has been conjectured that it was elaborated in Avanti or in Gândhâra where was the great Buddhist University of Takshaśîlâ. Subsequently it died out as a literary language in India[3] but in Ceylon, Burma, Siam and Camboja it became the vehicle of a considerable religious and scholastic literature. The language of Asoka's inscriptions in the third century B.C. is a parallel dialect, but only half stereotyped. The language of the Mahâvastu and some Mahayanist texts, often called the language of the Gâthâs, seems to be another vernacular brought more or less into conformity with Sanskrit. It is probable that

[1] Maj. Nik. XXII. and Angut. Nik. IV. 6.

[2] Pali means primarily a line or row and then a text as distinguished from the commentary. Thus Pâlimattam means the text without the commentary and Palibhâsâ is the language of the text or what we call Pali. See *Pali and Sanskrit*, R. O. Franke, 1902. Windisch, "Ueber den sprachlichen Character des Pali," in *Actes du XIVme Congrès des Orientalistes*, 1905. Grierson, "Home of Pali" in *Bhandarkar Commemorative Essays*, 1917.

[3] It is not easy to say how late or to what extent Pali was used in India. The Milinda-Pañha (or at least books II. and III.) was probably composed in North Western India about the time of our era. Dharmapâla wrote his commentaries (c. 500 A.D.) in the extreme south, probably at Conjeevaram. Pali inscriptions of the second or third century A.D. have been discovered at Sarnath but contain mistakes which show that the engraver did not understand the language (*Epig. Ind.* 1908, p. 391). Bendall found Pali MSS. in Nepal, *J.R.A.S.* 1899, p. 422.

in preaching the Buddha used not Pali in the strict sense but the spoken dialect of Magadha[1], and that this dialect did not differ from Pali more than Scotch or Yorkshire from standard English, and if for other reasons we are satisfied that some of the suttas have preserved the phrases which he employed, we may consider that apart from possible deviations in pronunciation or inflexion they are his *ipsissima verba*. Even as we have it, the text of the canon contains some anomalous forms which are generally considered to be Magadhisms[2].

The Cullavagga relates how two monks who were Brahmans represented to the Buddha that "monks of different lineage... corrupt the word of the Buddha by repeating it in their own dialect. Let us put the word of the Buddhas into *chandas*[3]." No doubt Sanskrit verse is meant, *chandas* being a name applied to the language of the Vedic verses. Gotama refused: "You are not to put the word of the Buddhas into *chandas*. Whoever does so shall be guilty of an offence. I allow you to learn the word of the Buddhas each in his own dialect." Subsequent generations forgot this prohibition, but it probably has a historical basis and it indicates the Buddha's desire to make his teaching popular. It is not likely that he contemplated the composition of a body of scriptures. He would have been afraid that it might resemble the hymns of the Brahmans which he valued so little and he wished all men to hear his teaching in the language they understood best. But when after his death his disciples collected his sayings it was natural that they should make at least one version of them in the dialect most widely spoken and that this version should be gradually elaborated in what was considered the best literary form of that dialect[4]. It is probable that the text underwent several linguistic revisions before it reached its present state.

Pali is a sonorous and harmonious language which avoids

[1] Magadha of course was not his birth-place and the dialect of Kosala must have been his native language. But it is not hinted that he had any difficulty in making himself understood in Magadha and elsewhere.

[2] *E.g.* nominatives singular in *e*. For the possible existence of scriptures anterior to the Pali version and in another dialect, see S. Lévi, *J.A.* 1912, II. p. 495.

[3] Cullavag. v. 33, chandaso âropema.

[4] Although Pali became a sacred language in the South, yet in China, Tibet and Central Asia the scriptures were translated into the idioms of the various countries which accepted Buddhism.

combinations of consonants and several difficult sounds found in Sanskrit. Its excellence lies chiefly in its vocabulary and its weakness in its syntax. Its inflexions are heavy and monotonous and the sentences lack concentration and variety. Compound words do not assume such monstrous proportions as in later Sanskrit, but there is the same tendency to make the process of composition do duty for syntax. These faults have been intensified by the fact that the language has been used chiefly for theological discussion. The vocabulary on the other hand is copious and for special purposes admirable. The translator has to struggle continually with the difficulty of finding equivalents for words which, though apparently synonymous, really involve nice distinctions and much misunderstanding has arisen from the impossibility of adequately rendering philosophical terms, which, though their European equivalents sound vague, have themselves a precise significance. On the other hand some words (*e.g. dhamma* and *attho*) show an inconveniently wide range of meaning. But the force of the language is best seen in its power of gathering up in a single word, generally a short compound, an idea which though possessing a real unity requires in European languages a whole phrase for its expression. Thus the Buddha bids his disciples be *attadîpâ atta-saraṇâ, anañña-saraṇâ: dhammadîpâ dhammasaraṇâ*[1]. "Be ye lamps unto yourselves. Be ye a refuge unto yourselves. Betake yourselves to no external refuge. Hold fast to the truth as a lamp. Hold fast to the truth as a refuge." This is Rhys Davids' translation and excellent both as English and as giving the meaning. But the five Pali words compel attention and inscribe themselves on the memory in virtue of a monumental simplicity which the five English sentences do not possess.

But the feature in the Pali scriptures which is most prominent and most tiresome to the unsympathetic reader is the repetition of words, sentences and whole paragraphs. This is partly the result of grammar or at least of style. The simplicity of Pali syntax and the small use made of dependent sentences, lead to the regular alignment of similar phrases side by side

[1] Mahâparinibbâna-sutta, II. 26. Another expressive compound is Dhûmakâlikam (Cullav. XI. 1. 9) literally smoke-timed. The disciples were afraid that the discipline of the Buddha might last only as long as the smoke of his funeral pyre.

like boards in a floor. When anything is predicated of several subjects, for instance the five Skandhas, it is rare to find a single sentence containing a combined statement. As a rule what has to be said is predicated first of the first Skandha and then repeated *totidem verbis* of the others. But there is another cause for this tedious peculiarity, namely that for a long period the Pitakas were handed down by oral tradition only. They were first reduced to writing in Ceylon about 20 B.C. in the reign of Vaṭṭagâmani, more than a century and a half after their first importation in an oral form. This circumstance need not throw doubt on the authenticity of the text, for the whole ancient literature of India, prose as well as verse, was handed down by word of mouth and even in the present day most of it could be recovered if all manuscripts and books were lost. The Buddhists did not, like the Brahmans, make minute regulations for preserving and memorizing their sacred texts, and in the early ages of the faith were impressed with the idea that their teaching was not a charm to be learnt by heart but something to be understood and practised. They nevertheless endeavoured, and probably with success, to learn by heart the words of the Buddha, converting them into the dialect most widely understood. It was then a common thing (and the phenomenon may still be seen in India) for a man of learning to commit to memory a whole Veda together with subsidiary treatises on ritual, metre, grammar and genealogy. For such memories it was not difficult to retain the principal points in a series of sermons. The Buddha had preached day by day for about forty-five years. Though he sometimes spoke with reference to special events he no doubt had a set of discourses which he regularly repeated. There was the less objection to such repetition because he was continually moving about and addressing new audiences. There were trained Brahman students among his disciples, and at his death many persons, probably hundreds, must have had by heart summaries of his principal sermons.

But a sermon is less easy to remember than a poem or matter arranged by some method of *memoria technica*. An obvious aid to recollection is to divide the discourse into numbered heads and attach to each certain striking phrases. If the phrases can be made to recur, so much the better, for there is a guarantee of correctness when an expected formula appears at appropriate points.

It may be too that the wearisome and mechanical iteration of the Pali Canon is partly due to the desire of the Sinhalese to lose nothing of the sacred word imparted to them by missionaries from a foreign country, for repetition to this extent is not characteristic of Indian compositions. It is less noticeable in Sanskrit Buddhist sûtras than in the Pali but is very marked in Jain literature. A moderate use of it is a feature of the Upanishads. In these we find recurring formulæ and also successive phrases constructed on one plan and varying only in a few words[1].

But still I suspect that repetition characterized not only the reports of the discourses but the discourses themselves. No doubt the versions which we have are the result of compressing a free discourse into numbered paragraphs and repetitions: the living word of the Buddha was surely more vivacious and plastic than these stiff tabulations. But the peculiarities of scholars can often be traced to the master and the Buddha had much the same need of mnemonics as his hearers. For he had excogitated complicated doctrines and he imparted them without the aid of notes and though his natural wit enabled him to adapt his words to the capacity of his hearers and to meet argument, still his wish was to formulate a consistent statement of his thoughts. In the earliest discourse ascribed to him, the sermon at Benares, we see these habits of numbering and repetition already fully developed. The next discourse, on the absence of a soul, consists in enumerating the five words, form, sensation, perception, sankhâras, and consciousness three times, and applying to each of them consecutively three statements or arguments, the whole concluding with a phrase which is used as a finale in many other places. Artificial as this arrangement sounds when analyzed, it is a natural procedure for one who wished to impress on his hearers a series of philosophic propositions without the aid of writing, and I can imagine that these

[1] Winternitz has acutely remarked that the Pali Pitaka resembles the Upanishads in style. See also Keith, *Ait. Ar.* p. 55. For repetitions in the Upanishads, see Chând. v. 3. 4 ff., v. 12 ff. and much in VII. and VIII., Brihad.-Âr. III. ix. 9 ff., VI. iii. 2, etc. This Upanishad relates the incident of Yâjñavalkya and Maitreyî twice. So far as style goes, I see no reason why the earliest parts of the Vinaya and Sutta Pitaka should not have been composed immediately after the Buddha's death.

rhythmical formulæ uttered in that grave and pleasant voice which the Buddha is said to have possessed, seemed to the leisurely yet eager groups who sat round him under some wayside banyan or in the monastery park, to be not tedious iteration but a gradual revelation of truth growing clearer with each repetition.

We gather from the Pitakas that writing was well known in the Buddha's time[1]. But though it was used for inscriptions, accounts and even letters, it was not used for books, partly because the Brahmans were prejudiced against it, and partly because no suitable material for inditing long compositions had been discovered. There were religious objections to parchment and leaves were not employed till later. The minute account of monastic life given in the Vinaya makes it certain that the monks did not use writing for religious purposes. Equally conclusive, though also negative, is the fact that in the accounts of the assemblies at Râjagaha and Vesâlî[2] when there is a dispute as to the correct ruling on a point, there is no appeal to writing but merely to the memory of the oldest and most authoritative monks. In the Vinaya we hear of people who know special books: of monks who are preachers of the Dhamma and others who know the Sutta: of laymen who have learnt a particular suttanta and are afraid it will fall into oblivion unless others learn it from them. Apprehensions are expressed that suttas will be lost if monks neglect to learn them by heart[3]. From inscriptions of the third century B.C.[4] are quoted words like Petakî, a reciter of the Pitakas or perhaps of one Pitaka: Suttântika and Suttântakinî, a man or woman who recites the suttantas: Pancanekâyika, one who recites the five Nikâyas. All this shows that from the early days of Buddhism onwards a succession of persons made it their business to learn and recite the doctrine and disciplinary rules and, considering the retentiveness of trained memories, we have no reason to doubt that the doctrine and rules have been preserved without much loss[5].

[1] *E.g.* Mahâv. 1. 49, Dig. Nik. I. 14, Sut. Vib. Bhikkhunî, LXIX., Sut. Vib. Pârâj. III. 4. 4.

[2] Cullav. IV. 15. 4.

[3] Ang. Nik. IV. 100. 5, ib. V. lxxiv. 5.

[4] See Bühler in *Epigraphia Indica*, vol. II. p. 93.

[5] Even at the time of Fa Hsien's visit to India (c. 400 A.D.) the Vinaya of the Sarvâstivâdin school was preserved orally and not written. See Legge's trans. p. 99.

Not, however, without additions. The disadvantage of oral tradition is not that it forgets but that it proceeds snowball fashion, adding with every generation new edifying matter. The text of the Vedic hymns was preserved with such jealous care that every verse and syllable was counted. But in works of lesser sanctity interpolations and additions were made according to the reciters' taste. We cannot assign to the Mahâbhârata one date or author, and the title of Upanishad is no guarantee for the age or authenticity of the treatises that bear it. Already in the Anguttara-Nikâya[1], we hear of tables of contents and the expression is important, for though we cannot give any more precise explanation of it, it shows that care was taken to check the contents of the works accepted as scripture. But still there is little doubt that during the two or three centuries following the Buddha's death, there went on a process not only of collection and recension but also of composition.

An account of the formation of the canon is given in the last two chapters of the Cullavagga[2]. After the death of the Buddha his disciples met to decide what should be regarded as the correct doctrine and discipline. The only way to do that was to agree what had been the utterances of the master and this, in a country where the oral transmission of teaching was so well understood, amounted to laying the foundations of a canon. Kassapa cross-examined experts as to the Buddha's precepts. For the rules of discipline Upâli was the chief authority and we read how he was asked where such and such a rule—for instance, the commandment against stealing—was promulgated.

"At Râjagaha, sir."

"Concerning whom was it spoken?"

"Dhaniya, the potter's son."

"In regard to what matter?"

"The taking of that which had not been given."

For collecting the suttas they relied on the testimony of Ânanda and asked him where the Brahmajâla[3] was spoken. He replied "between Râjagaha and Nâlanda at the royal rest-house at Ambalatthika." "Concerning whom was it spoken?"

[1] Ang. Nik. IV. 160. 5, Bhikkhû bahussutâ......mâtikâdharâ monks who carry in memory the indices.

[2] Cullavag. XI., XII.

[3] Dig. Nik. 1.

"Suppiya, the wandering ascetic and Brahmadatta the young Brahman."

Then follows a similar account of the Sâmaññaphala sutta and we are told that Ânanda was "questioned through the five Nikâyas." That is no doubt an exaggeration as applied to the time immediately after the Buddha's death, but it is evidence that five Nikâyas were in existence when this chapter was written[1].

3

Lines of growth are clearly discernible in the Vinaya and Sutta Pitakas. As already mentioned, the Khuddaka-Nikâya is, as a collection, later than the others although separate books of it, such as the Sutta-nipâta (especially the fourth and fifth books), are among the earliest documents which we possess. But other books such as the Peta-[2] and Vimâna-vatthu show a distinct difference in tone and are probably separated from the Buddha by several centuries. Of the other four Nikâyas the Saṃyutta and Anguttara are the more modern and the Anguttara mentions Munda, King of Magadha who began to reign about forty years after the Buddha's death. But even in the two older collections, the Dîgha and the Majjhima, we have not reached the lowest stratum. The first thirteen suttantas of the Dîgha all contain a very ancient tractate on morality, and the Sâmaññaphala and following sections of the Dîgha and also some suttas of the Majjhima contain either in whole or in part a treatise on progress in the holy life. These treatises were probably current as separate portions for recitation before the suttas in which they are now set were composed.

Similarly, the Vinaya clearly presupposes an old code in the form of a list of offences called the Pâtimokkha. The Mahâvagga contains a portion of an ancient word-for-word explanation of this code[3] and most of the Sutta-vibhanga is an amplification and exposition of it. The Pâtimokkha was already in existence when these books were composed, for we hear[4] that if in a

[1] It is remarkable that this account contemplates five Nikâyas (of which the fifth is believed to be late) but only two Pitakas, the Abhidhamma not being mentioned.

[2] It refers to a king Pingalaka, said to have reigned two hundred years after the Buddha's time.

[3] Mahâv XI. 3.

[4] Mahâv. II. 17.

company of Bhikkhus no one knows the Pâtimokkha, one of the younger brethren should be sent to some better instructed monastery to learn it. And further we hear[1] that a learned Bhikkhu was expected to know not merely the precepts of the Pâtimokkha but also the occasion when each was formulated. The place, the circumstances and the people concerned had been in each case handed down. There is here all the material for a narrative. The reciter of a sutta simply adopts the style of a village story-teller. "Thus have I heard. Once upon a time the Lord was dwelling at Râjagaha," or wherever it was, and such and such people came to see him. And then, after a more or less dramatic introduction, comes the Lord's discourse and at the end an epilogue saying how the hearers were edified and, if previously unconverted, took refuge in the true doctrine.

The Cullavagga states that the Vinaya (but not the other Pitakas) was recited and verified at the Council of Vesâlî. As I have mentioned elsewhere, Sinhalese and Chinese accounts speak of another Council, the Mahâsangha or Mahâsangîti. Though its date is uncertain, there is a consensus of tradition to the effect that it recognized a canon of its own, different from our Pali Canon and containing a larger amount of popular matter.

Sinhalese tradition states that the canon as we now have it was fixed at the third Council held at Pataliputra in the reign of Asoka (about 272–232 B.C.). The most precise statements about this Council are those of Buddhaghosa who says that an assembly of monks who knew the three Pitakas by heart recited the Vinaya and the Dhamma.

But the most important and interesting evidence as to the existence of Buddhist scriptures in the third century B.C. is afforded by the Bhâbrû (or Bhâbrâ) edict of Asoka. He recommends the clergy to study seven passages, of which nearly all can be identified in our present edition of the Pitakas[2]. This edict

[1] Cullav. IX. 5.

[2] The passages are:

1. The Vinaya-Samukasa. Perhaps the sermon at Benares with introductory matter found at the beginning of the Mahâvagga. See Edmunds, in *J.R.A.S.* 1913, p. 385.
2. The Alia-Vâsâni (Pali Ariya-Vâsâni) = the Samgîti-sutta of the Dîgha Nikâya.
3. The Anâgata-bhayâni = Anguttara-Nikâya, v. 77–80, or part of it.

does not prove that Asoka had before him in the form which we know the Dîgha and other works cited. But the most cautious logic must admit that there was a collection of the Buddha's sayings to which he could appeal and that if most of his references to this collection can be identified in our Pitakas, then the major part of these Pitakas is probably identical in substance (not necessarily verbally) with the collection of sayings known to Asoka.

Neither Asoka nor the author of the Kathâ-vatthu cites books by name. The latter for instance quotes the well-known lines "anupubbena medhavi" not as coming from the Dhammapada but as "spoken by the Lord." But the author of the Questions of Milinda, who knew the canonical books by the names they bear now, also often adopts a similar method of citation. Although this author's probable date is not earlier than our era his evidence is important. He mentions all five Nikâyas by name, the titles of many suttas and also the Vibhanga, Dhâtu-kathâ, Puggala-Paññatti, Kathâ-vatthu, Yamaka and Paṭṭhâna.

Everything indicates and nothing discredits the conclusion that this canon of the Vibhajjavâdins was substantially fixed in the time of Asoka, so far as the Vinaya and Sutta Pitakas are concerned. Some works of minor importance may have had an uncertain position and subsequent revisions may have been made but the principal scriptures were already recognized and contained passages which occur in our versions. On the other hand this recension of the scriptures was not the only one in existence. If the patronage of Asoka gave it a special prestige in his lifetime, it may have lost it in India after his death and for many centuries the Buddhist Canon, like the list of the Upanishads, must have been susceptible of alteration. The Sarvâstivâdins compiled an Abhidhamma Pitaka of their own, apparently in the time of Kanishka, and the Dharmagupta school also seems to have had its own version of this Pitaka[1].

4. The Munigâtha = Sutta-Nipâta, 206–220.
5. The Moneyasute = Moneyya-sutta in the Itivuttakam, 67: see also Ang. Nik. III. 120.
6. The Upatisapasine. The question of Upatissa: not identified.
7. The Lâghulovâde musâvâdam adhigicya. The addresses to Râhula beginning with subject of lying = Maj. Nik. 61.

[1] See *J.A.* 1916, II. pp. 20, 38.

The date of the Pali Abhidhamma is very doubtful and I do not reject the hypothesis that it was composed in Ceylon, for the Sinhalese seem to have a special taste for such literature. But there is no proof of this Sinhalese origin.

According to Sinhalese tradition all three Pitakas were introduced into Ceylon by Mahinda in the reign of Asoka, but only as oral tradition and not in a written form. They received this latter about 20 B.C., as the result of a dispute between two monasteries[1]. The controversy is obscure but it appears that the ancient foundation called Mahâvihâra accepted as canonical the fifth book of the Vinaya called Parivâra, whereas it was rejected by the new monastery called Abhayagiri. The Sinhalese chronicle (Mahâvamsa XXXIII. 100–104) says somewhat abruptly "The wise monks had hitherto handed down the text of the three Pitakas (Piṭakattayapâlim) as well as the commentary by word of mouth. But seeing that mankind was becoming lost, they assembled together and wrote them in books in order that the faith might long endure." This brief account seems to mean that a council was held not by the whole clergy of Ceylon but by the monks of the Mahâvihâra at which they committed to writing their own version of the canon including the Parivâra. This book forms an appendix to the Vinaya Pitaka and in some verses printed at the conclusion is said to be the work of one Dîpa. It is generally accepted as a relatively late production, composed in Ceylon. If such a work was included in the canon of the Mahâvihâra, we must admit the possibility that other portions of it may be Sinhalese and not Indian.

But still the *onus probandi* lies with those who maintain the Sinhalese origin of any part of the Pali Canon and two strong arguments support the Indian origin of the major part. First, many suttas not only show an intimate knowledge of ancient Indian customs but discuss topics such as caste, sacrifice, ancient heresies, and the value of the Veda which would be of no interest to Sinhalese. Secondly, there is no Sinhalese local colour and no Sinhalese legends have been introduced. Contrast with this the Dîpa- and Mahâ-vaṃsa both of which open with accounts of mythical visits paid by the Buddha to Ceylon[2].

[1] For the date see the chapter on Ceylon.

[2] S. Lévi gives reasons for thinking that the prohibitions against singing sacred texts (ayataka gîtassara, Cullavag. v. 3) go back to the period when the Vedic accent was a living reality. See *J.A.* 1915, I. pp. 401 ff.

In Ceylon versions of the scriptures other than that of the Mahâvihâra were current until the twelfth century when uniformity was enforced by Parâkrama Bâhu. Some of these, for instance the Pitaka of the Vetulyakas, were decidedly heretical according to the standard of local orthodoxy but others probably presented variations of reading and arrangement rather than of doctrine. Anesaki[1] has compared with the received Pali text a portion of the Saṃyuktâgama translated by Guṇabhadra into Chinese. He thinks that the original was the text used by the Abhayagiri monastery and brought to China by Fa Hsien.

The Sinhalese ecclesiastical history, Nikâya-Sangrahawa, relates[2] that 235 years after the Buddha's death nine heretical fraternities were formed who proceeded to compose scriptures of their own such as the Varṇapiṭaka and Angulimâla-Piṭaka. Though this treatise is late (*c.* 1400 A.D.) its statements merit attention as showing that even in orthodox Ceylon tradition regarded the authorized Pitaka as one of several versions. But many of the works mentioned sound like late tantric texts rather than compositions of the early heretics to whom they are attributed.

Ecclesiastical opinion in Ceylon after centuries of discussion ended by accepting the edition of the Mahâvihâra as the best, and we have no grounds for rejecting or suspecting this opinion. According to tradition Buddhaghosa was well versed in Sanskrit but deliberately preferred the southern canon. The Mahayanist doctor Asanga cites texts found in the Pali version, but not in the Sanskrit[3]. The monks of the Mahâvihâra were probably too indulgent in admitting late scholastic treatises, such as the Parivâra. On the other hand they often showed a critical instinct in rejecting legendary matter. Thus the Sanskrit Vinayas contain many more miraculous narratives than the Pali Vinaya.

[1] *Muséon*, 1905, p. 23. Anesaki thinks the text used by Guṇabhadra was in Pali but the Abhayagiri, which had Mahayanist proclivities, may have used Sanskrit texts.

[2] Nikâya-Ṣangrahawa. Fernando, *Govt. Record Office*, Colombo, 1918.

[3] See Mahâyâna-sûtrâlankâra, XVI. 22 and 75, with Lévi's notes.

4

European critics have rarely occasion to discuss the credibility of Sanskrit literature, for most of it is so poetic or so speculative that no such question arises. But the Pitakas raise this question as directly as the Gospels, for they give the portrait of a man and the story of a life, in which an overgrowth of the miraculous has not hidden or destroyed the human substratum. How far can we accept them as a true picture of what Gotama was and taught?

Their credibility must be judged by the standard of Indian oral tradition. Its greatest fault comes from that deficiency in historic sense which we have repeatedly noticed. Hindu chroniclers ignore important events and what they record drifts by in a haze in which proportion, connection, and dates are lost. They frequently raise a structure of fiction on a slight basis of fact or on no basis at all. But the fiction is generally so obvious that the danger of historians in the past has been not to be misled by it but to ignore the elements of truth which it may contain. For the Hindus have a good verbal memory; their genealogies, lists of kings and places generally prove to be correct and they have a passion for catalogues of names. Also they take a real interest in describing doctrine. If the Buddha has been misrepresented, it is not for want of acumen or power of transmitting abstruse ideas. The danger rather is that he who takes an interest in theology is prone to interpret a master's teaching in the light of his own pet views.

The Pitakas illustrate the strong and weak points of Hindu tradition. The feebleness of the historical sense may be seen in the account of Devadatta's doings in the Cullavagga[1] where the compiler seems unable to give a clear account of what he must have regarded as momentous incidents. Yet the same treatise is copious and lucid in dealing with monastic rules, and the sayings recorded have an air of authenticity. In the suttas the strong side of Hindu memory is brought into play. Of consecutive history there is no question. We have only an introduction giving the names of some characters and localities followed by a discourse. We know from the Vinaya that the monks were expected to exercise themselves in remembering

[1] Cullav. VII. 3.

these things, and they are precisely the things that they would get rightly by heart. I see no reason to doubt that such discourses as the sermon preached at Benares[1] and the recurring passages in the first book of the Dîgha-Nikâya are a Pali version of what was accepted as the words of the Buddha soon after his death. And the change of dialect is not of great importance. Asoka's Bhâbrû Edict contains the saying: *Thus the good law shall long endure,* which is believed to be a quotation and certainly corresponds pretty closely with a passage in the Anguttara-Nikâya[2]. The King's version is *Saddhamma cilathitike hasati*: the Pali is *Saddhammo ciratthitiko hoti.* Somewhat similar may have been the differences between the Buddha's speech and the text which we possess. The importance of the change in language is diminished and the facility of transmission is increased by the fact that in Pali, Sanskrit and kindred Indian languages ideas are concentrated in single words rather than spread over sentences. Thus the principal words of the sermon at Benares give its purport with perfect clearness, if they are taken as a mere list without grammatical connection. Similarly I should imagine that the recurring paragraphs about progress in the holy life found in the early Suttas of the Dîgha-Nikâya are an echo of the Buddha's own words, for they bear an impress not only of antiquity but of eloquence and elevation. This does not mean that we have any sermon in the exact form in which Gotama uttered it. Such documents as the Sâmaññaphala-sutta and Ambaṭṭha-sutta probably give a good idea of his method and style in consecutive discourse and argument. But it would not be safe to regard them as more than the work of compilers who were acquainted with the surroundings in which he lived, the phrases he used, and the names and business of those who conversed with him. With these they made a picture of a day in his life, culminating in a sermon[3].

Like the historical value of the Pitakas, their literary value can be justly estimated only if we remember that they are not books in our sense but treatises handed down by memory and

[1] In the first book of the Mahâvagga.

[2] Ang. Nik. v. 201 and VI. 40.

[3] It may be objected that some Suttas are put into the mouths of the Buddha's disciples and that their words are very like those of the Master. But as a rule they spoke on behalf of him and the object was to make their language as much like his as possible.

that their form is determined primarily by the convenience of the memory. We must not compare them with Plato and find them wanting, for often, especially in the Abhidhamma, there is no intention of producing a work of art, but merely of subdividing a subject and supplying explanations. Frequently the exposition is thrown into the form of a catechism with questions and answers arranged so as to correspond to numbered categories. Thus a topic may be divided into twenty heads and six propositions may be applied to each with positive or negative results. The strong point of these Abhidhamma works—and of Buddhist philosophy generally—lies in careful division and acute analysis but the power of definition is weak. Rarely is a definition more than a collection of synonyms and very often the word to be defined is repeated in the definition. Thus in the Dhamma-saṅgaṇi the questions, what are good or bad states of mind? receive answers cast in the form: when a good or bad thought has arisen with certain accompaniments enumerated at length, then these are the states that are good or bad. No definition of good is given.

This mnemonic literature attains its highest excellence in poetry. The art of composing short poems in which a thought, emotion or spiritual experience is expressed with a few simple but pregnant words in the compass of a single couplet or short hymn, was carried by the early Buddhists to a perfection which has never been excelled. The Dhammapada[1] is the best known specimen of this literature. Being an anthology it is naturally more suited for quotation or recitation in sections than for continuous reading. But its twenty-five chapters are consecrated each to some special topic which receives fairly consecutive treatment, though each chapter is a mosaic of short poems consisting of one or more verses supposed to have been uttered by the Buddha or by arhats on various occasions. The whole work combines literary beauty, depth of thought and human feeling in a rare degree. Not only is it irradiated with the calm light of peace, faith and happiness but it glows with sympathy, with the desire to do good and help those who are struggling in the mire of passion and delusion. For this reason it has found more favour with European readers than the detached and

[1] The Pali anthology known by this name was only one of several called Dhammapada or Udâna which are preserved in the Chinese and Tibetan Canons.

philosophic texts which simply preach self-conquest and aloofness. Inferior in beauty but probably older is the Sutta-nipâta, a collection of short discourses or conversations with the Buddha mostly in verse. The rugged and popular language of these stanzas which reject speculation as much as luxury, takes us back to the life of the wanderers who followed the Buddha on his tours and we may imagine that poems like the Dhaniya sutta would be recited when they met together in a rest-house or grove set apart for their use on the outskirts of a village.

The Buddhist suttas are interesting as being a special result of Gotama's activity; they are not analogous to the Brahmanic works called sûtras, and they have no close parallel in later Indian literature. There is little personal background in the Upanishads, none at all in the Sânkhya and Vedânta sûtras. But the Sutta Pitaka is an attempt to delineate a personality as well as to record a doctrine. Though the idea of writing biography has not yet been clearly conceived, yet almost every discourse brings before us the figure of the Lord: though the doctrine can be detached from the preacher, yet one feels that the hearers of the Pitaka hungered not merely for a knowledge of the four truths but for the very words of the great voice: did he really say this, and if so when, where and why? Most suttas begin by answering these questions. They describe a scene and report a discourse and in so doing they create a type of literature with an interest and individuality of its own. It is no exaggeration to say that the Buddha is the most living figure in Hindu literature. He stands before us more distinctly not only than Yâjñavalkya and Śankara, but than modern teachers like Nanak and Râmânuja and the reason of this distinctness can I think be nothing but the personal impression which he made on his age. The later Buddhists compose nothing in the style of the Nikâyas: they write about Gotama in new and fanciful ways, but no Acts of the Apostles succeed the Gospels.

Though the Buddhist suttas are *sui generis* and mark a new epoch in Indian literature, yet in style they are a natural development of the Upanishads. The Upanishads are less dogmatic and show much less interest in the personality of their sages, but they contain dialogues closely analogous to suttas.

Thus about half of the Bṛihad-Âraṇyaka is a philosophic treatise unconnected with any particular name, but in this are set five dialogues in which Yâjñavalkya appears and two others in which Ajâtaśatru and Pravâhaṇa Jaivali are the protagonists.

Though many suttas are little more than an exposition of some doctrine arranged in mnemonic form, others show eloquence and dramatic skill. Thus the Sâmaññaphala-sutta opens with a vivid description of the visit paid one night by Ajâtasattu to the Buddha[1]. We see the royal procession of elephants and share the alarm of the suspicious king at the unearthly stillness of the monastery park, until he saw the Buddha sitting in a lighted pavilion surrounded by an assembly of twelve hundred and fifty brethren, calm and silent as a clear lake. The king's long account of his fruitless quest for truth would be tiresome if it were not of such great historic interest and the same may be said of the Buddha's enumeration of superstitious and reprehensible practices, but from this point onwards his discourse is a magnificent crescendo of thought and language, never halting and illustrated by metaphors of great effect and beauty. Equally forcible and surely resting on some tradition of the Buddha's own words is the solemn fervour which often marks the suttas of the Majjhima such as the descriptions of his struggle for truth, the admonitions to Râhula and the reproof administered to Sâti.

5

As mentioned above, our Pali Canon is the recension of the Vibhajjavâdins. We know from the records of the Chinese pilgrims that other schools also had recensions of their own, and several of these recensions—such as those of the Sarvâstivâdins, Mahâsanghikas, Mahisâsakas, Dhammaguttikas, and Sammitîyas—are still partly extant in Chinese and Tibetan translations. These appear to have been made from the Sanskrit and fragments of what was probably the original have been preserved in Central Asia. A recension of the text in Sanskrit probably implies less than what we understand by a translation. It may mean that texts handed down in some Indian dialect

[1] The work might also be analyzed as consisting of three old documents (the tract on morality, an account of ancient heresies, and a discourse on spiritual progress) put together with a little connecting matter, and provided with a prologue and epilogue.

which was neither Sanskrit nor Pali were rewritten with Sanskrit orthography and inflexions while preserving much of the original vocabulary. The Buddha allowed all men to learn his teaching in their own language, and different schools are said to have written the scriptures in different dialects, *e.g.* the Mahâsanghikas in a kind of Prakrit not further specified and the Mahâsammatîyas in Apabhramsa. When Sanskrit became the recognized vehicle for literary composition there would naturally be in India (though not in Ceylon) a tendency to rewrite books composed in other dialects[1]. The idea that when any important matter is committed to writing it should be expressed in a literary dialect not too intelligible to the vulgar is prevalent from Morocco to China. The language of Bengal illustrates what may have happened to the Buddhist scriptures. It is said that at the beginning of the nineteenth century ninety per cent. of the vocabulary of Bengali was Sanskrit, and the grammatical construction sanskritized as well. Though the literary language now-a-days is less artificial, it still differs widely from the vernacular. Similarly the spoken word of the Buddha was forced into conformity with one literary standard or another and ecclesiastical Pali became as artificial as Sanskrit. The same incidents may be found worked up in both languages. Thus the Sanskrit version of the story of Pûrṇâ in the Divyâvadâna repeats what is found in Pali in the Saṃyutta-Nikâya[2] and reappears in Sanskrit in the Vinaya of the Mûlasarvâstivâdin school.

The Chinese Tripitaka has been catalogued and we possess some information respecting the books which it contains, though none of them have been edited in Europe. Thus we know something[3] of the Sarvâstivâdin recension of the Abhidhamma. Like the Pali version it consists of seven books of which one, the Jñâna-prasthâna by Kâtyâyanîputra, is regarded as the principal, the rest being supplementary. All the books are attributed to human authors, and though some of these bear the names of the Buddha's immediate disciples, tradition connects Kâtyâyanîputra with Kanishka's council. This is not

[1] But in Ceylon there was a decided tendency to rewrite Sinhalese treatises in Pali.

[2] Cf. Divyâv. ed. Cowell, p. 37 and Sam. Nik. *P.T.S.* edition, vol. IV. p. 60.

[3] See Takakusu on the Abhidharma literature of the Sarvâstivâdins in the *Journ. of the Pali Text Society*, 1905, pp. 67–147.

a very certain date, but still the inference is that about the time of the Christian era the contents of the Abhidhamma-Pitaka were not rigidly defined and a new recension was possible.

The Sanskrit manuscripts discovered in Central Asia include Sûtras from the Saṃyukta and Ekottara Âgamas (equivalent to the Saṃyutta and Anguttara Nikâyas), a considerable part of the Dharmapada, fragments of the Sutta-Nipâta and the Prâtimoksha of the Sarvâstivâdin school. These correspond fairly well with the Pali text but represent another recension and a somewhat different arrangement. We have therefore here fragments of a Sanskrit version which must have been imported to Central Asia from northern India and covers, so far as the fragments permit us to judge, the same ground as the Vinaya and Suttas of the Pali Canon. Far from displaying the diffuse and inflated style which characterizes the Mahâyâna texts it is sometimes shorter and simpler than our Pali version[1].

When was this version composed and what is its relation to the Pali? A definite reply would be premature, for other Sanskrit texts may be discovered in Central Asia, but two circumstances connect this early Buddhist literature in Sanskrit with the epoch of Kanishka. Firstly the Sanskrit Abhidharma of the Sarvâstivâdins seems to date from his council and secondly a Buddhist drama by Aśvaghosha[2] of about the same time represents the Buddha as speaking in Sanskrit whereas the inferior characters speak Prakrit. But these facts do not prove that Sanskrit was not the language of the canon at an earlier date[3] and it is not safe to conclude that because Asoka did not employ it for writing edicts it was not the sacred language of any section of Indian Buddhists. On the other hand some of the Sanskrit texts contain indications that they are a translation from Pali or some vernacular[4]. In others are found historical allusions which suggest that they must have received additions after our era[5].

[1] But not always. See S. Lévi, *J.A.* 1910, p. 436.

[2] See Lüders, *Bruchstücke Buddhistischer Dramen*, 1911 and ib. *Das Sâri putra-prakaraṇa*, 1911.

[3] Inscriptions from Swat written in an alphabet supposed to date from 50 B.C. to 50 A.D. contain Sanskrit verses from the Dharmapada and Mahâparinirvânasûtra. See *Epig. Indica*, vol. IV. p. 133.

[4] *E.g.* The Sanskrit version of the Sutta-Nipâta. See *J.R.A.S.* 1916, pp. 719–732.

[5] See the remarks on the Saṃyuktâgama in *J.A.* 1916, II. p. 272.

I have already raised the question of the relative value attaching to Pali and Sanskrit texts as authorities for early history. Two instances will perhaps illustrate this better than a general discussion. As already mentioned, the Vinaya of the Mûlasarvâstivâdins makes the Buddha visit north-western India and Kashmir, whereas the Pali texts do not represent him as travelling further west than the country of the Kurus. The Sanskrit account is not known to be confirmed by more ancient evidence, but there is nothing impossible in it, particularly as there are periods in the Buddha's long life filled by no incidents. The narrative however contains a prediction about Kanishka and therefore cannot be earlier than his reign. Now there is no reason why the Pali texts should be silent about this journey, if the Buddha really made it, but one can easily imagine reasons for inventing it in the period of the Kushan kings. North-western India was then full of monasteries and sacred sites and the same spirit which makes uncritical Buddhists in Ceylon and Siam assert to-day that the master visited their country impelled the monks of Peshawar and Kashmir to imagine a not improbable extension of his wanderings[1].

On the other hand this same Vinaya of the Mûlasarvâstivâdins probably gives us a fragment of history when it tells us that the Buddha had three wives, perhaps too when it relates how Râhula's paternity was called in question and how Devadatta wanted to marry Yaśodharâ after the Buddha had abandoned worldly life[2]. The Pali Vinaya and also some Sanskrit Vinayas[3] mention only one wife or none at all. They do not attempt to describe Gotama's domestic life and if they make no allusion to it except to mention the mother of Râhula, this is not equivalent to an assertion that he had no other wife. But when one Vinaya composed in the north of India essays to give a biography of the Buddha and states that he had three wives, there is no reason for doubting that the compiler was in touch with good local tradition.

[1] In the same spirit, the Chinese version of the Ekottara (sec. 42) makes the dying Buddha order his bed to be made with the head to the north, because northern India will be the home of the Law. See *J.A.* Nov., Dec. 1918, p. 435.

[2] See for the whole question, Péri, Les Femmes de Çâkya Muni, *B.E.F.E.O.* 1918, No. 2.

[3] Those of the Dharmaguptas, Mahâsânghikas and Mahîśâsakas.

CHAPTER XIV

MEDITATION

INDIAN religions lay stress on meditation. It is not merely commended as a useful exercise but by common consent it takes rank with sacrifice and prayer, or above them, as one of the great activities of the religious life, or even as its only true activity. It has the full approval of philosophy as well as of theology. In early Buddhism it takes the place of prayer and worship and though in later times ceremonies multiply, it still remains the main occupation of a monk. The Jains differ from the Buddhists chiefly in emphasizing the importance of self-mortification, which is put on a par with meditation. In Hinduism, as might be expected in a fluctuating compound of superstition and philosophy, the schools differ as to the relative efficacy of meditation and ceremonial, but there is a strong tendency to give meditation the higher place. In all ages a common characteristic appears in the most divergent Indian creeds—the belief that by a course of mental and physical training the soul can attain to a state of bliss which is the prelude to the final deliverance attained after death.

1

We may begin by examining Brahmanic ideas as to meditation. Many of them are connected with the word Yoga, which has become familiar to Europe. It has two meanings. It is applied first to a definite form of Indian philosophy which is a theistic modification of the Sânkhya and secondly to much older practices sanctioned by that philosophy but anterior to it.

The idea which inspires these theories and practices is that the immaterial soul can by various exercises free itself from the fetters of matter. The soul is distinguished from the mind which, though composed of the subtlest matter, is still material. This presupposes the duality of matter and spirit taught by Jainism and the Sânkhya philosophy, but it does not necessarily presuppose the special doctrines of either nor do Vedântists object to the practice of the Yoga. The systematic prosecution of mental concentration and the idea that supernatural powers can be acquired thereby are very old—certainly older than Buddhism. Such methods had at first only a slight philosophic substratum and were independent of Sânkhya doctrines, though these, being a speculative elaboration of the same fundamental principles, naturally commended themselves to those who practised Yoga. The two teachers of the Buddha, Âlâra and Uddaka, were Yogis, and held that beatitude or emancipation consisted in the attainment of certain trances. Gotama, while regarding their doctrine as insufficient, did not reject their practices.

Our present Yoga Sûtras are certainly much later than this date. They are ascribed to one Patañjali identified by Hindu tradition with the author of the Mahâbhâshya who lived about 150 B.C. Jacobi[1] however is of opinion that they are the work of an entirely different person who lived after the rise of the philosophy ascribed to Asanga sometimes called Yogâcâra. Jacobi's arguments seem to me suggestive rather than conclusive but, if they are confirmed, they lead to an interesting deduction. There is some reason for thinking that Śankara's doctrine of illusion was derived from the Buddhist Śûnyavâda. If Patañjali's sûtras are posterior to Asanga, it also seems probable that the codification of the Yoga by the Brahmans was connected with the rise of the Yogâcâra among the Buddhists[2].

The Sûtras describe themselves as an exposition of Yoga, which has here the meaning not of union with God, but rather of effort. The opening aphorisms state that "Yoga is the suppression of the activities of the mind, for then the spectator abides in his own form: at other times there is identity of form with the activities." This dark language means that the soul in its true nature is merely the spectator of the mind's activity, consciousness being due, as in the Sânkhya, to the union of the soul with the mind[3] which is its organ. When the mind is active,

[1] See *J.A.O.S.* Dec. 1910, p. 24.

[2] Jacobi considers the Yoga Sûtras later than 450 A.D. but if we adopt Péri's view that Vasubandhu, Asanga's brother, lived from about 280–360, the fact that they imply a knowledge of the Vijnânavâda need not make them much later than 300 A.D. It is noticeable that both Asanga and the Yoga Sûtras employ the word *dharma-megha*.

[3] Called Citta in the Yoga philosophy.

the soul appears to experience various emotions, and it is only when the mind ceases to feel emotions and becomes calm in meditation, that the soul abides in its own true form. The object of the Yoga, as of the Sânkhya, is Kaivalya or isolation, in which the soul ceases to be united with the mind and is dissociated from all qualities (guṇas) so that the shadow of the thinking principle no longer falls upon it. This isolation is produced by performing certain exercises, physical as well as mental, and, as a prelude to final and complete emancipation, superhuman powers are acquired. These two ideas, the efficacy of physical discipline and the acquisition of superhuman powers, have powerfully affected all schools of religious thought in India, including Buddhism. They are not peculiar to the Yoga, but still it is in the Yoga Sûtras that they find their most authoritative and methodical exposition.

The practice of Yoga has its roots in the fact that fasting and other physical mortifications induce a mental state in which the subject thinks that he has supernatural experiences[1]. Among many savage tribes, especially in America, such fasts are practised by those who desire communication with spirits. In the Yoga philosophy these ideas appear in a refined form and offer many parallels to European mysticism. The ultimate object is to dissociate the soul from its material envelopes but in the means prescribed we can trace two orders of ideas. One is to mortify the body and suppress not only appetite and passion but also discursive thought: the other is to keep the body in perfect health and ease, so that the intelligence and ultimately the soul may be untroubled by physical influences. These two ideas are less incongruous than they seem. Many examples show that extreme forms of asceticism are not unhealthy but rather conducive to long life and the Yoga in endeavouring to secure physical well-being does not aim at pleasure but at such a purification of the physical part of man that it shall be the obedient and unnoticed servant of the other parts. The branch of the system which deals with method and discipline is called Kriyâ-yoga and in later works we also find the expression Haṭha-yoga, which is specially used to designate

[1] See Tylor, *Primitive Culture*, vol. II. pp. 410 ff. Savages often supplement fasting by the use of drugs and the Yoga Sûtras (IV. 1) mention that supernatural powers can be obtained by the use of herbs.

mechanical means (such as postures, purification, etc.) prescribed for the attainment of various mental states. In contrast to it is Râja-yoga, which signifies ecstasy and the method of obtaining it by mental processes. The immediate object of the Kriyâ-yoga is to destroy the five evils[1], namely ignorance, egoism, desire, aversion and love of life: it consists of asceticism, recitations and resignation to God, explained as meaning that the devotee fasts, repeats mantras and surrenders to God the fruit of all his works and, feeling no more concern for them, is at peace. Though the Yoga Sûtras are theistic, theism is accessory rather than essential to their teaching. They are not a theological treatise but the manual of an ancient discipline which recognizes devotional feelings as one means to its end. The method would remain almost intact if the part relating to the deity were omitted, as in the Sânkhya. God is not for the Yoga Sûtras, as he is for many Indian and European mystics, the one reality, the whence and whither of the soul and world.

Eight branches of practice[2] are enumerated, namely:—

1. Yama or restraint, that is abstinence from killing, lying, stealing, incontinence, and from receiving gifts. It is almost equivalent to the five great precepts of Buddhism.

2. Niyama or observance, defined as purification, contentment, mortification, recitation and devotion to the Lord.

Purification is treated at great length in the later treatises on Haṭha-yoga under the name of Shaṭ-karma or sixfold work. It comprises not only ordinary ablutions but cleansing of the internal organs by such methods as taking in water by the nostrils and discharging it by the mouth. The object of these practices which, though they assume queer forms, rest on sound therapeutic principles, is to remove adventitious matter from the system and to reduce the gross elements of the body[3].

3. Âsanam or posture is defined as a continuous and pleasant attitude. It is difficult to see how the latter adjective

[1] Kleśa: Kilesa in Pali.

[2] The practices systematized in the Yoga Sûtras are mentioned even in the older Upanishads such as the Maitrâyaṇa, Śvetâśvatara and Chândogya.

[3] An extreme development of the idea that physical processes can produce spiritual results is found in Raseśvara Darśana or the Mercurial System described in the Sarva-Darśana-Sangraha chap. IX. *Marco Polo* (Yule's Edition, vol. II. pp. 365, 369) had also heard of it.

applies to many of the postures recommended, for considerable training is necessary to make them even tolerable. But the object clearly is to prescribe an attitude which can be maintained continuously without creating the distracting feeling of physical discomfort and in this matter European and oriental limbs feel differently. All the postures contemplated are different ways of sitting cross-legged. Later works revel in enumerations of them and also recognize others called Mudrâ. This word is specially applied to a gesture of the hand but is sometimes used in a less restricted sense. Thus there is a celebrated Mudrâ called Khecharî, in which the tongue is reversed and pressed into the throat while the sight is directed to a point between the eye-brows. This is said to induce the cataleptic trance in which Yogis can be buried alive.

4. Prâṇayama or regulation of the breath. When the Yogi has learnt to assume a permanent posture, he accustoms himself to regulate the acts of inspiration and expiration so as to prolong the period of quiescence between the two. He will thus remove the veils which cover the light within him. This practice probably depends on the idea which constantly crops up in the Upanishads that the breath is the life and the soul. Consequently he who can control and hold his breath keeps his soul at home, and is better able to concentrate his mind. Apart from such ideas, the fixing of the attention on the rhythmical succession of inspirations and expirations conduces to that peaceful and detached frame of mind on which most Indian sects set great store. The practice was greatly esteemed by the Brahmans, and is also enjoined among the Taoists in China and among Buddhists in all countries, but I have found no mention of its use among European mystics.

5. Pratyâhâra, the retraction or withdrawing of the senses. They are naturally directed outwards towards their objects. The Yogi endeavours to bring them into quiescence by diverting them from those objects and directing them inwards. From this, say the Sûtras, comes complete subjugation of the senses[1].

6–8. The five kinds of discipline hitherto mentioned constitute the physical preparation for meditation comprising in

[1] It seems to me analogous to the *introversion* of European mystics. See Underhill, *Mysticism*, chaps. VI. and VII.

succession (*a*) a morality of renunciation, (*b*) mortification and purification, (*c*) suitable postures, (*d*) regulation of the breathing, (*e*) diversion of the senses from their external objects. Now comes the intellectual part of the process, consisting of three stages called Dhâraṇâ, Dhyâna and Samâdhi. Dhâraṇâ means fixing the mind on a particular object, either a part of the body such as the crown of the head or something external such as the sky. Dhyâna[1] is the continuous intellectual state arising out of this concentration. It is defined as an even current of thought undisturbed by other thoughts. Samâdhi is a further stage of Dhyâna in which the mind becomes so identified with the thing thought of that consciousness of its separate existence ceases. The thinking power is merged in the single thought and ultimately a state of trance is induced. Several stages are distinguished in this Samâdhi. It is divided into conscious and unconscious[2] and of the conscious kind there are four grades[3], analogous, though not entirely corresponding to the four Jhânas of Buddhism. When the feeling of joy passes away and is lost in a higher sense of equanimity, there comes the state known by the remarkable name of Dharma-megha[4] in which the isolation of the soul and its absolute distinctness from matter (which includes what we call mind) is realized, and Karma is no more. After the state of Dharma-megha comes that of unconscious Samâdhi, in which the Yogi falls into a trance and attains emancipation which is made permanent by death.

The methods of the Kriyâ-yoga can be employed for the attainment not only of salvation but of miraculous powers[5]. This subject is discussed in the third book of the Yoga Sûtras

[1] Jhâna in Pali.

[2] Samprajñâta and Asamprajñâta, called also sa- and nirbīja, with and without seed.

[3] Savitarka and Savicâra, in which there is investigation concerned with gross and subtle objects respectively: Sânanda, in which there is a feeling of joy: Sasmitâ, in which there is only self-consciousness. The corresponding stages in Buddhism are described as phases of Jhâna not of Samâdhi.

[4] It is not easy to translate. *Megha* is cloud and *dharma* may be rendered by righteousness but has many other meanings. For the metaphor of the cloud compare the title of the English mystical treatise *The Cloud of Unknowing*.

[5] Siddhi, vibhûti, aiśvarya. A belief in these powers is found even in the Rig Veda where it is said (x. 136) that munis can fly through the air and associate with gods.

where it is said that such powers are obstructions in the contemplative and spiritual life, though they may lead to success in waking or worldly life. This is the same point of view as we meet in Buddhism, viz. that though the miraculous powers resulting from meditation are real, they are not essential to salvation and may become dangerous hindrances[1].

They are attained according to the Yoga Sûtras by the exercise of saṃyama which is the name given conjointly to the three states of dhâraṇâ, dhyâna and samâdhi when they are applied simultaneously or in immediate succession to one object of thought[2]. The reader will remember that this state of contemplation is to be preceded by pratyâhâra, or direction of the senses inwards, in which ordinary external stimuli are not felt. It is analogous to the hypnotic state in which suggestions made by the hypnotizer have for the subject the character of reality although he is not conscious of his surroundings, and autosuggestions—that is the expectations with which the Yogi begins his meditation—apparently have the same effect. The trained Yogi is able to exercise saṃyama with regard to any idea—that is to say his mind becomes identified with that idea to the exclusion of all others. Sometimes this saṃyama implies simply a thorough comprehension of the object of meditation. Thus by making saṃyama on the saṃskâras or predispositions existing in the mind, a knowledge of one's previous births is obtained; by making saṃyama on sound, the language of animals is understood. But in other cases a result is considered to be obtained because the Yogi in his trance thinks it is obtained. Thus if saṃyama is made on the throat, hunger and thirst are subdued; if on the strength of an elephant, that strength is obtained: if on the sun, the knowledge of all worlds

[1] So too European mystics "are all but unanimous in their refusal to attribute importance to any kind of visionary experience" (Underhill, *Mysticism*, p. 335). St John of the Cross, Madame Guyon and Walter Hilton are cited as severe critics of such experience.

[2] Cf. Underhill's remarks about contemplation (*Mysticism*, p. 394). "Its results feed every aspect of the personality: minister to its instinct for the Good, the Beautiful and the True. Psychologically it is an induced state in which the field of consciousness is greatly contracted: the whole of the self, its conative power, being sharply focussed, concentrated upon one thing. We pour ourselves out or, as it sometimes seems to us, *in* towards this overpowering interest: seem to ourselves to reach it and be merged with it. Whatever the thing may be, in this act we *know* it, as we cannot know it by any ordinary devices of thought."

is acquired. Other miraculous attainments are such that they should be visible to others, but are probably explicable as subjective fancies. Such are the powers of becoming heavy or light, infinitely large or infinitely small and of emitting flames. This last phenomenon is perhaps akin to the luminous visions, called photisms by psychologists, which not infrequently accompany conversion and other religious experiences and take the form of flashes or rays proceeding from material objects[1]. The Yogi can even become many persons instead of one by calling into existence other bodies by an effort of his will and animating them all by his own mind[2].

Europeans are unfavourably impressed by the fact that the Yoga devotes much time to the cultivation of hypnotic states of doubtful value both for morality and sanity. But the meditation which it teaches is also akin to aesthetic contemplation, when the mind forgets itself and is conscious only of the beauty of what is contemplated. Schopenhauer[3] has well expressed the Indian idea in European language. "When some sudden cause or inward disposition lifts us out of the endless stream of willing, the attention is no longer directed to the motives of willing but comprehends things free from their relation to the will and thus observes them without subjectivity purely objectively, gives itself entirely up to them so far as they are ideas, but not in so far as they are motives. Then all at once the peace which we were always seeking, but which always fled from us on the former path of the desires, comes to us of its own accord and it is well with us." And though the Yoga Sûtras represent superhuman faculties as depending chiefly on the hypnotic condition of saṃyama, they also say that they are obtainable—at any rate such of them as consist in superhuman knowledge—by pratibhâ or illumination. By this term is meant a state of enlightenment which suddenly floods the mind prepared by the Yoga discipline. It precedes emancipation as the morning star precedes the dawn. When

[1] See instances quoted in W. James, *Varieties of Religious Experience*, pp. 251–3.

[2] This curious idea is also countenanced, though not much emphasized, by the Brahma Sûtras, IV. 4. 15. The object of producing such bodies is to work off Karma. The Yogi acquires no new Karma but he may have to get rid of accumulated Karma inherited from previous births, which must bear fruit. By "making himself many" he can work it off in one lifetime.

[3] *World as Will and Idea*, Book III. p. 254 (Haldane and Kemp's translation).

this light has once come, the Yogi possesses all knowledge without the process of saṃyama. It may be compared to the Dibba-cakkhu or divine eye and the knowledge of the truths which according to the Pitakas[1] precede arhatship. Similar instances of sudden intellectual enlightenment are recorded in the experiences of mystics in other countries. We may compare the haplosis or ekstasis of Plotinus and the visions of St Theresa or St Ignatius in which such mysteries as the Trinity became clear, as well as the raptures in which various Christian mystics[2] experienced the feeling of levitation and thought that they were being literally carried off their feet.

The practices and theories which are systematized in the Yoga Sûtras are known to the Upanishads, particularly those of the Atharva Veda. But even the earlier Upanishads allude to the special physical and mental discipline necessary to produce concentration of mind. The Maitrâyana Upanishad says that the sixfold Yoga consists of restraint of the breath, restraint of the senses, meditation, fixed attention, investigation, absorption. The Śvetâśvatara Upanishad speaks of the proper places and postures for meditation, and the Chândogya[3] of concentrating all the senses on the self, a process which is much the same as the pratyâhâra of the Yoga.

A later and mysterious but most important method of Yoga is known to the Tantras[4] as Shaṭcakrabheda or piercing of the six cakras. These are dynamic or nervous centres distributed through the human body from the base of the spinal cord to the eyebrows. In the lowest of them resides the Devî Kuṇḍalinî, a force identical with Śakti, who is the motive power of the universe. In ordinary conditions this Kuṇḍalinî is pictured as lying asleep and coiled like a serpent. But appropriate exercises cause her to awake and ascend until she reaches the highest cakra when she unites with Śiva and ineffable bliss

[1] *E.g.* Dig. Nik. II. 95, etc.

[2] St Theresa, St Catharine of Siena and Rudman Merswin. Cf. 1 John ii. 20, 27. 'Ye know all things."

[3] Chândog. Up. VIII. 15.

[4] As also to the Saṃhitâs of the Vaishṇavas and the Âgamic literature of the Śaivas. The six cakras are: (1) Mûladhâra at the base of the spinal cord, (2) Svâdhishṭhâna below the navel, (3) Maṇipûra near the navel, (4) Anâhata in the heart, (5) Viśuddha at the lower end of the throat, (6) Âjñâ between the eyebrows. See Avalon, *Tantric Texts*, II. Shaṭcakranirûpana. Ib. *Tantra of Great Liberation*, pp. lvii ff., cxxxii ff. Ib. *Principles of Tantra*, pp. cvii ff. Gopinatha Ras, *Indian Iconography*, pp. 328 ff. See also "Manual of a Mystic" (*Pali Text Soc.*) for something apparently similar, though not very intelligible, in Hinayanist Buddhism.

and emancipation are attained. The process, which is said to be painful and even dangerous to health, is admittedly unintelligible without oral instruction from a Guru and, as I have not had this advantage, I will say no more on the topic except this, that strange and fanciful as the descriptions of Shaṭcakrabheda may seem, they can hardly be pure inventions but must have a real counterpart in nervous phenomena which apparently have not been studied by European physiologists or psychologists[1].

2

When we turn to the treatment of meditation and ecstasy in the earlier Buddhist writings we are struck by its general resemblance to the programme laid down in the Yoga Sûtras, and by many coincidences of detail. The exercises, rules of conduct, and the powers to be incidentally obtained are all similar. The final goal of both systems also seems similar to the outsider, although a Buddhist and a Yogi might have much to say about the differences, for the Yoga wishes to isolate a soul which is complete and happy in its own nature if it can be disentangled from its trammels, whereas Buddhism teaches that there is no such soul awaiting release and that religious discipline should create and foster good mental states. Just as the atmosphere of the Pitakas is not that of the Brâhmaṇas or Sûtras, so are their ideas about Jhâna and Samâdhi somewhat different. Though hypnotic and even cataleptic phases are not wanting, the journey of the religious life, as described in the Pitakas, is a progress of increasing peace, but also of increasing intellectual power and activity. Gotama did not hold Jhâna or regulated meditation to be essential to nirvana or arhatship, for that state was attainable by laymen and apparently through sudden illumination. But such cases were the exception. His own mental evolution which culminated in enlightenment comprised the four Jhânas[2]. Also in the eightfold path which is essential to arhatship and nirvana the last and highest stage is sammâsamâdhi, right rapture or ecstasy.

[1] For the later Yoga see further Book v. I have recently received A. Avalon, *The Serpent Power*, from which it appears that the danger of the process lies in the fact that as Kuṇḍalinî ascends, the lower parts of the body which she leaves become cold. The preliminary note on Yoga in Grierson and Barnett's Lallâ-Vâkyâni (*Asiat. Soc.'s Monographs*, vol. XVII. 1920) contains much valuable information, but both works arrived too late for me to make use of them.

[2] Maj. Nik. 36 and 85, but not in 26.

Jhâna is difficult for laymen, but it was the rule of the order to devote at least the afternoon to it. We might compare this with the solitary prayer of Christians, and there is real similarity in the process and the result. It brought peace and strength to the mind and we hear of the bright clear faces and the radiantly happy expression of those who returned to their duties after such contemplation. But Christian prayer involves the idea of self-surrender and throwing open the doors and windows of the soul to an influence which streams into it. Buddhist meditation is rather the upsoaring of the mind which rises from ecstasy to ecstasy until it attains not some sphere where it can live *in* bliss but a state which is in itself satisfying and all-comprising.

All mental states to which such names as ecstasy, trance, and vision can be applied involve a dangerous element which, if not actually pathological, can easily become so. But the account of meditation put in the Buddha's own mouth does not suggest either morbid dejection or hysterical excitement[1] and it is stated expressly that the exercise should be begun after the midday meal so that any visions which may come cannot be laid to the charge of an empty stomach. Jhâna is not the same as Samâdhi or concentration, though the Jhânas may be an instance of Samâdhi. This latter is capable of marvellous extension and development, but essentially it is a mental quality like Sammâsati or right mindfulness, whereas Jhâna is a mental exercise or progressive rapture passing through defined stages.

Any system which analyzes and tabulates stages of contemplation and ecstasy may be suspected of being late and of having lost something of the glow and impetus which its cold formulæ try to explain. But the impulse to catalogue is old in Buddhism[2] and one important distinction in the various mental states lumped together under the name of meditation deserves attention, namely that according to the oldest documents some of them are indispensable preliminaries to nirvana and some are not. Buddhaghosa reviewing the whole matter in scholastic

[1] Dig. Nik. 2. For the methods of Buddhist meditation, the reader may consult the "Manual of a Mystic," edited (1896) and translated (1916) by the *Pali Text Society*. But he will not find it easy reading.

[2] See Ang. Nik. 1. 20 for a long list of the various kinds of meditation. A conspectus of the system of meditation is given in Seidenstücker, *Pali-Buddhismus*, pp. 344–356.

fashion in his Way of Purity divides the higher life into three sections, firstly conduct or morality as necessary foundation, secondly *adhicitta*, higher consciousness or concentration which leads to *samatho* or peace and thirdly *adhipaññâ* or the higher wisdom which leads to *vipassanâ* or insight. Of these *adhipaññâ* and *vipassanâ* are superior inasmuch as nirvana cannot be obtained without them but the methods of *adhicitta*, though admirable and followed by the Buddha himself, are not equally indispensable: they lead to peace and happiness but not necessarily to nirvana. It is probably unwise (at any rate for Europeans) to make too precise statements, for we do not really know the nature of the psychical states discussed. *Adhipaññâ* assuredly includes the eightfold path ending with *samâdhi* which is defined by the Buddha himself in this connection in terms of the four *Jhânas*[1]. On the other hand the doctrine that nirvana is attainable merely by practising the *Jhânas* is expressly reprobated as a heresy[2]. The teaching of the Pitakas seems to be that nirvana is attainable by living the higher life in which meditation and insight both have a place. In normal saints both sides are developed: raptures and trances are their delight and luxury. But in some cases nirvana may be attained by insight only: in others meditation may lead to ecstasy and more than human powers of mind but yet stop short of nirvana. The distinction is not without importance for it means that knowledge and insight are indispensable for nirvana: it cannot be obtained by hypnotic trances or magical powers.

The Buddha is represented as saying that in his boyhood when sitting under a tree he once fell into a state of contemplation which he calls the first Jhâna. It is akin to a sensation which comes to Europeans most frequently in childhood, but sometimes persists in mature life, when the mind, usually under the influence of pleasant summer scenery, seems to identify itself with nature, and on returning to its normal state asks with surprise, can it be that what seems a small distant personality is really I? The usual form of Jhâna comprises four stages[3]. The first is a state of joy and ease born of detachment, which

[1] Dig. Nik. XXII. *ad. in.*

[2] Dig. Nik. I. 21–26.

[3] See, for instance, Dig. Nik. II. 75. Sometimes five Jhânas are enumerated. This means that reasoning and investigation are eliminated successively and not simultaneously, so that an additional stage is created.

means physical calm as well as the absence of worldly desires and irrelevant thoughts. It is distinguished from the subsequent stages by the existence of reasoning and investigation, and while it lasts the mind is compared to water agitated by waves. In the second Jhâna reasoning and investigation cease: the water becomes still and the mind set free rises slowly above the thoughts which had encumbered it and grows calm and sure, dwelling on high[1]. In this Jhâna the sense of joy and ease remains, but in the third stage joy disappears, though ease remains. This ease (sukham) is the opposite of dukkham, the discomfort which characterizes all ordinary states of existence. It is in part a physical feeling, for the text says that he who meditates has this sense of ease in his body. But this feeling passes away in the fourth Jhâna, in which there is only a sense of equanimity. This word, though perhaps the best rendering which can be found for the Pali upekkhâ, is inadequate for it suggests merely the absence of inclination, whereas upekkhâ represents a state of mind which, though rising above hedonistic views, is yet positive and not merely the negation of interest and desire.

In the passage quoted the Buddha speaks as if only an effort of will were needed to enter into the first Jhâna, but tradition, supported by the Pitakas[2], sanctions the use of expedients to facilitate the process. Some are topics on which attention should be concentrated, others are external objects known as Kasina. This word (equivalent to the Sanskrit kṛitsna) means entire or total, and hence something which engrosses the attention. Thus in the procedure known as the earth Kasina[3] the Bhikkhu who wishes to enter into the Jhâna makes a small circle of reddish clay, and then gazes at it fixedly. After a time he can see it as plainly when his eyes are closed as when they are open[4]. This is followed by entry into Jhâna and he should not continue looking at the circle. There are ten kinds of Kasina differing from that described merely in substituting for the earthen circle

[1] See *Dhamma-Sangaṇi*; Mrs Rhys Davids' translation, pp. 45–6 and notes. Also *Journal of Pali Text Society*, 1885, p. 32, for meaning of the difficult word Ekodibhâva.

[2] *E.g.* Maj. Nik. 77; Ang. Nik. 1. xx. 63.

[3] Hardy, *Eastern Monachism*, pp. 252 ff.

[4] But also without shape, colour or outward appearance, so this statement must not be taken too literally.

some other object, such as water, light, gold or silver. The whole procedure is clearly a means of inducing a hypnotic trance[1].

The practice of tranquillizing the mind by regulating the breathing is recommended repeatedly in Suttas which seem ancient and authentic; for instance, in the instruction given by the Buddha to his son Râhula[2]. On the other hand, his account of his fruitless self-mortification shows that the exercise even in its extreme forms is not sufficient to secure enlightenment. It appears to be a method of collecting and concentrating the mind, not necessarily hypnotic. All Indian precepts and directions for mental training attach far more importance to concentration of thought and the power of applying the mind at will to one subject exclusively than is usual in Europe.

Buddhaghosa at the beginning of his discussion of *adhicitta* enumerates forty subjects of meditation namely, "the ten Kasinas, ten impurities, ten reflections, four sublime states (Brahmâ-vihâra), the four formless states, one perception and one analysis[3]." The Kasinas have been already described. The ten impurities are a similar means of inducing meditation. The monk fixes his attention on a corpse in some horrible stage of decay and thus concentrates his mind on the impermanence of all things. The ten recollections are a less gloomy exercise but similar in principle, as the attention is fixed on some religious subject such as the Buddha, his law, his order, etc.

The Brahmâ-vihâras[4] are states of emotional meditation which lead to rebirth in the heavens of Brahmâ. They are attained by letting love or some other good emotion dominate the mind, and by "pervading the whole world" with it. This language about pervading the world with kindly emotion is common in Buddhist books though alien to European idiom. The mind must harbour no uncharitable thought and then its

[1] Such procedure has not received much countenance in Christian mysticism but the contemplation of a burnished pewter dish and of running water induced ecstasy in Jacob Boehme and Ignatius Loyola respectively. See Underhill, *Mysticism*, p. 69.

[2] Maj. Nik. 62 end.

[3] The analysis means to analyze all things as consisting alike of the four elements. The one perception is the perception that all nourishment is impure.

[4] See Dig. Nik. 13 and Rhys Davids' introduction to it. In spite of their name, they seem to be purely Buddhist and have not been found in Brahmanic literature. The four states are characterized respectively by love, sympathy with sorrow, sympathy with joy, and equanimity.

benevolence becomes a psychic force which spreads in all directions, just as the sound of a trumpet can be heard in all four quarters.

These Brahmâ-vihâras are sometimes represented as coming after the four Jhânas[1], sometimes as replacing them[2]. But the object of the two exercises is not the same, for the Brahmâ-vihâras aim at rebirth in a better world. They are based on the theory common to Buddhism and Hinduism that the predominant thoughts of a man's life, and especially his thoughts when near death, determine the character of his next existence.

The trances known as the four formless states are analogous to the Brahmâ-vihâras, their object being to ensure rebirth not in the heaven of Brahmâ but in one of the heavens known as Formless Worlds where the inhabitants have no material form[3]. They are sometimes combined with other states into a series of eight, known as the eight deliverances[4]. The more advanced of these stages seem to be hypnotic and even cataleptic. In the first formless state the monk who is meditating rises above all idea of form and multiplicity and reaches the sphere in which the infinity of space is the only idea present to his mind. He then passes to the sphere where the infinity of thought only is present and thence to the sphere in which he thinks "nothing at all exists[5]," though it would seem that the consciousness of his own mental processes is undiminished. The teaching of Alâra Kâlâma, the Buddha's first teacher, made the attainment of this state its goal. It is succeeded by the state in which neither any idea nor the absence of any idea is specially present to the mind[6]. This was the goal of Uddaka Râmaputta, his second teacher, and is illustrated by the simile of a bowl which has been smeared with oil inside. That is to say, consciousness is reduced to a minimum. Beyond these four stages is yet another[7], in which a complete cessation of perception and feeling is

[1] Dig. Nik. XIII. 76.

[2] Dig. Nik. XVII. 2–4.

[3] Christian mystics also, such as St Angela and St Theresa, had "formless visions." See Underhill, *Myst.* pp. 338 ff.

[4] Attha vimokkhâ. See Mahâparinib. sut. in Rhys Davids' *Dialogues of the Buddha*, II. 119.

[5] Akiñcaññâyatanam.

[6] Nevasaññânâsaññâyatanam.

[7] Saññavedâyita nirodhasamâpatti. The Buddha when dying (Dig. XVI. v. 8, 9) passes through this state, but does not go from it to Parinibbâna. This perhaps means that it was regarded as a purification of the mind, but not on the direct road to the final goal.

attained[1]. This state differs from death only in the fact that heat and physical life are not extinct and while it lasts there is no consciousness. It is stated that it could continue during seven days but not longer. Such hypnotic trances have always inspired respect in India but the Buddha rejected as unsatisfying the teaching of his masters which made them the final goal.

But let us return to his account of Jhâna and its results. The first of these is a correct knowledge of the body and of the connection of consciousness with the body. Next comes the power to call up out of the body a mental image which is apparently the earliest form of what has become known in later times as the astral body. In the account of the conversion of Angulimâla the brigand[2] it is related that the Buddha caused to appear an image of himself which Angulimâla could not overtake although he ran with all his might and the Buddha was walking quietly.

The five states or faculties which follow in the enumeration are often called (though not in the earliest texts) abhiññâ, or transcendental knowledge. They are *iddhi*, or the wondrous gift: the heavenly ear which hears heavenly music[3]: the knowledge of others' thoughts: the power of remembering one's own previous births: the divine eye, which sees the previous births of others[4]. It would appear that the order of these states is not important and that they do not depend on one another. Iddhi, like the power of evoking a mental image, seems to be connected with hypnotic phenomena. It means literally power, but is used in the special sense of magical or supernatural gifts such as

[1] See Maj. Nik. 43. But the point of the discussion seems to be not so much special commendation of this form of trance as an explanation of its origin, namely that it, like other mental states, is bound to ensue when certain preliminary conditions both moral and intellectual have been realized. See also Sam. Nik. XXXVI. ii. 5. See for examples of this cataleptic form of Samâdhi Max Müller's *Life of Ramakrishna*, pp. 49, 59, etc. Christian mystics (*e.g.* St Catharine of Siena and St Theresa) were also subject to deathlike trances lasting for hours and St Theresa is said once to have been in this condition for some days.

[2] Maj. Nik. 86.

[3] This is known to European mystics, particularly Suso. St Francis of Assisi, St Catharine of Siena and Richard Rolle are also cited. See Underhill, *Mysticism*, p. 332.

[4] Christian visions of Hell, Purgatory and Paradise are another instance of the divine eye, which thinks it can see the whole scheme of things.

ability to walk on water, fly in the air, or pass through a wall[1]. Some of these sensations are familiar in dreams and are probably easily attainable as subjective results in trances. I am inclined to attribute accounts implying their objective reality to the practice of hypnotism and to suppose that a disciple in a hypnotic state would on the assurance of his teacher believe that he saw the teacher himself, or some person pointed out by the teacher, actually performing such feats. Of iddhi we are told that a monk can practise it, just as a potter can make anything he likes out of prepared clay, which is a way of saying that he who has his mind perfectly controlled can treat himself to any mental pleasure he chooses. Although the Buddha and others are represented as performing such feats as floating in the air whenever it suits them, yet the instruction given as to how the powers may be acquired starts by bidding the neophyte pass through the four stages of Jhâna or meditation in which ordinary external perception ceases. Then he will be able to have the experiences described. And it is probable that the description gives a correct account of the sensations which arise in the course of a trance, particularly if the trance has been entered upon with the object of experiencing them. In other words they are hypnotic states and often the result of suggestion, since he who meditates knows what the result of his meditation should be. Sometimes, as mentioned, Jhâna is induced by methods familiar to mesmerists, such as gazing at a circle or some bright object but such expedients are not essential and with this European authorities agree. Thus Bernheim states that even when a subject is hypnotized for the first time, no gestures or passes are necessary, provided he is calm. It suffices to bid him look at the operator and go to sleep. He adds that those who are most susceptible to the hypnotic influence are not nervous and hysterical subjects but docile and receptive natures who can concentrate their attention[2]. Now it is hardly possible to imagine better hypnotic

[1] Tales about such powers are still very common in the East, for instance the Chinese story (in the *Liao Chai*) of the man who learnt from a Taoist how to walk through a wall but failed ignominiously when he tried to give an exhibition to his family. Educated Chinese seem to think there is something in the story and say that he failed because his motives were bad.

[2] Bernheim, *La Suggestion*, chap. I. Quand j'ai éloigné de son esprit la préoccupation que fait naître l'idée de magnétisme...je lui dis "Regardez-moi bien

subjects than the pupils of an Indian religious teacher. They are taught to regard him with deep respect and complete confidence: they are continually in a state of expectant receptivity, assimilating not only the texts and doctrines which he imparts, but his way of life: their training leads them to believe in the reality of mental and physical powers exceeding those of ordinary mankind and indeed to think that if they do not have such experiences it is through some fault of their own. The teachers, though ignorant of hypnotism as such, would not hesitate to use any procedure which seemed to favour progress in meditation and the acquisition of supernatural powers. Now a large number of Indian marvels fall under two heads. In the first case Buddha, Krishna, or any personage raised above the ordinary human level points out to his disciples that wonders are occurring or will occur: he causes people to appear or disappear: he appears himself in an amazing form which he explains. In the other case the possessor of marvellous powers has experience which he subsequently relates: he goes up to heaven or flies to the uttermost parts of the earth and returns. Both of these cases are covered by the phenomena of hypnotism. I do not mean to say that any given Indian legend can be explained by analyzing it as if it were a report of a hypnotic operation, but merely that the general character of these legends is largely due to the prevalence of hypnotic experiences among their composers and hearers[1]. Two obscure branches of hypnotism are probably of great importance in the religious history of the human race, namely self-hypnotization without external suggestion and the hypnotization of crowds. India affords plentiful materials for the study of both.

There is no reason to doubt that the Buddha believed in the existence of these powers and countenanced the practices supposed to lead to them. Thus Moggallâna, second only to

et ne songez qu'à dormir. Vous allez sentir une lourdeur dans les paupières, une fatigue dans vos yeux: ils clignotent, ils vont se mouiller; la vue devient confuse: ils se ferment." Quelques sujets ferment les yeux et dorment immédiatement.... *C'est le sommeil par la suggestion, c'est l'image du sommeil* que je suggère, que j'insinue dans le cerveau. Les passes, la fixation des yeux ou des doigts de l'opérateur, propres seulement à concentrer l'attention, ne sont pas absolument nécessaires.

[1] Thus in the drama Ratnâvalî a magician makes the characters see an imaginary conflagration of the palace and also a vision of heaven. His performance seems to be accepted as merely a remarkable piece of conjuring.

Sâriputta among his disciples, was called the master of iddhi[1], and it is mentioned as a creditable and enjoyable accomplishment[2]. But it is made equally plain that such magical or hypnotic practices are not essential to the attainment of the Buddha's ideal. When lists of attainments are given, iddhi does not receive the first place and it may be possessed by bad men: Devadatta for instance was proficient in it. It is even denounced in the story of Piṇḍola Bhâradvâja[3] and in the Kevaddha sutta[4]. In this curious dialogue the Buddha is asked to authorize the performance of miracles as an advertisement of the true faith. He refuses categorically, saying there are three sorts of wonders namely iddhi, that is flying through the air, etc.: the wonder of manifestation which is thought-reading: and the wonder of education. Of the first two he says "I see danger in their practice and therefore I loathe, abhor and am ashamed of them." Then by one of those characteristic turns of language by which he uses old words in new senses he adds that the true miracle is the education of the heart.

Neither are the other transcendental powers necessary for emancipation. Sâriputta had not the heavenly eye, yet he was the chief disciple and an eminent arhat. This heavenly eye (dibba-cakkhu) is not the same as the eye of truth (dhamma-cakkhu). It means perfect knowledge of the operation of Karma and hence a panoramic view of the universe, whereas the eye of truth is a technical phrase for the opening of the eyes, the mental revolution which accompanies conversion. But though transcendental knowledge is not indispensable for attaining nirvana, it is an attribute of the Buddha and in most of its forms amounts to an exceptional insight into human nature and the laws of the universe, which, though after the Indian manner exaggerated and pedantically defined, does not differ essentially from what we call genius.

The power of recollecting one's previous births, often mentioned in the Pitakas, has been described in detail by Buddhist writers and Buddhaghosa[5] distinguishes between the

[1] Ang. Nik. XVI. 1. In spite of his magic power he could not prevent himself being murdered. The Milinda-Pañha explains this as the result of Karma, which is stronger than magic and everything else.

[2] *E.g.* Maj. Nik. 77.

[3] Cullavag. v. 8.

[4] Dig. Nik. XI.

[5] Visuddhi Magga, XIII. in Warren, *Buddhism in Translation*, pp. 315 ff.

powers possessed by various persons. The lowest form of recollection merely passes from one mental state to a previous mental state and so on backwards through successive lives, not however understanding each life as a whole. But even ordinary disciples can not only recollect previous mental states but can also travel backwards along the sequence of births and deaths and bring up before their minds the succession of existences. A Buddha's intelligence dispenses with the necessity of moving backwards from birth to birth but can select any point of time and see at once the whole series of births extending from it in both directions, backwards and forwards. Buddhaghosa then goes on to prescribe the method to be followed by a monk who tries for the first time to recollect previous births. After taking his midday meal he should choose a quiet place and sitting down pass through the four Jhânas in succession. On rising from the fourth trance he should consider the event which last took place, namely his sitting down; and then in retrograde order all that he did the day and night before and so backwards month after month and year after year. A clever monk (so says Buddhaghosa) is able at the first trial to pass beyond the moment of his conception in the present existence and to take as the object of his thought his individuality at the moment of his last death. But since the individuality of the previous existence ceased and another one came into being, therefore that point of time is like thick darkness. Buddhaghosa goes on to explain, if I apprehend his meaning rightly, that the proper recollection of previous births involves the element of form and the mind sharpened by the practice of the four trances does not merely reproduce feelings and impressions but knows the name and events of the previous existence, whereas ordinary persons are apt to reproduce feelings and impressions without having any clear idea of the past existence as a whole. This, I believe, corresponds with the experience of modern Buddhists. It is beyond doubt that those who attempt to carry their memory back in the way described are convinced that they remember existences before the present life. As a rule it takes from a fortnight to a month to obtain such a remembrance clearly, and every day the aspirant to a knowledge of previous births must carry his memory further and further back, dwelling less and less on the details of recent events. When he reaches the time of his birth, he feels as if there were a curtain of black darkness before him, but if the attention is concentrated, this curtain is rent and the end of the previous life is recovered behind it. The process is painful for it involves the recollection of death and the even greater pains of birth and many have not courage to go beyond this point. It is not uncommon in Ceylon, Burma, Siam and probably in all parts of the Far East, to find people who are persuaded they can remember previous births in this way, but I have never met anyone who professed to recall more than two or three. There is no room in these modest modern visions for the long vistas of previous lives seen by the earlier Buddhists.

Meditation also plays a considerable part in the Buddhism of the Far East under the name of Ch'an or Zen of which we shall have something to say when we treat of China and Japan.

As already indicated the methods and results of meditation as practised by Brahmanic Hindus and by Buddhists show considerable resemblance to the experiences of Christian mystics. The coincidences do not concern mere matters of detail, although theology has done its best to make the content and explanation of the experiences as divergent as possible. But the essential similarity of form remains and there is clearly no question of borrowing or direct influence. It is certain that what is sometimes called the Mystic Way is not only true as a succession of psychic states but is, for those who can walk in it, the road to a happiness which in reality and power to satisfy exceeds all pleasures of the senses and intellect, so that when once known it makes all other joys and pains seem negligible. Yet despite the intense reality of this happy state, despite the illumination which floods the soul and the wide visions of a universal plan, there is no agreement as to the cause of the experience nor, strange to say, as to its meaning as opposed to its form. For many both in the east and west the one essential and indubitable fact throughout the experience is God, yet Buddhists are equally decided in holding that the experience has nothing to do with any deity. This is not a mere question of interpretation. It means that views as to theism and pantheism are indifferent for the attainment of this happy state.

The mystics of India are sometimes contrasted with their fellows in Europe as being more passive and more self-centred:

they are supposed to desire self-annihilation and to have no thought for others. But I doubt if the contrast is just. If Indian mysticism sometimes appears at a disadvantage, I think it is because it is popular and in danger of being stereotyped and sometimes vulgarized. Nowadays in Europe we have students of mysticism rather than mystics, and the mystics of the Christian Church were independent and distinguished spirits who, instead of following the signposts of the beaten track, found out a path for themselves. But in India mysticism was and is as common as prayer and as popular as science. It was taught in manuals and parodied by charlatans. When mysticism is the staple crop of a religion and not a rare wild flower, the percentage of imperfect specimens is bound to be high. The Buddha, Śankara and a host of less well-known teachers were as strenuous and influential as Francis of Assisi or Ignatius Loyola. Neither in Europe nor in Asia has mysticism contributed much directly to political and social reform. That is not its sphere, but within the religious sphere, in preaching, teaching and organization, the mystic is intensely practical and the number of successes (as of failures) is greater in Asia than in Europe. Even in theory Indian mysticism does not repudiate energy. No one enjoyed more than the Buddha himself what Ruysbroeck calls "the mysterious peace dwelling in activity," for before he began his mission he had attained nirvana and such of his disciples as were arhats were in the same case. Later Buddhism recognizes a special form of nirvana called apratishṭhita: those who attain it see that there is no real difference between mundane existence and nirvana and therefore devote themselves to a life of beneficent activity.

The period of transition and trial known to European mystics as the Dark Night of the Soul, is not mentioned in Indian manuals as an episode of the spiritual life, for such an interruption would hardly harmonize with their curriculum of regular progress towards enlightenment. But mystic poetry testifies that in Asia as in Europe this feeling of desertion and loneliness is a frequent experience in the struggles and adventures of the soul. It is apparently not necessary, just as the incidental joys and triumphs of the soul—strains of heavenly music, aerial flights, and visions of the universal scheme—are also not essential. The essential features of the mystic way, as well as its usual incidents, are common to Asia and Europe, and in both continents are expressed in two forms. One view contrasts the surface life and a deeper life: when the intellect ceases to plague and puzzle, something else arises from the depth and makes its unity with some greater Force to be felt as a reality. This idea finds ample expression in the many Brahmanic systems which regarded the centre and core of the human being as an *âtman* or *purusha*, happy when in the undisturbed peace of its own nature but distracted by the senses and intellect. The other view of mystic experiences regards them as a remaking of character, the evolution of a new personality and in fact a new birth. This of course need not be a denial of the other view: the emergence of the latent self may effect a transformation of the whole being. But Buddhism, at any rate early Buddhism, formulates its theory in a polemical form. There is no ready-made latent self, awaiting manifestation when its fetters and veils are removed: man's inner life is capable of superhuman extension but the extension is the result of enlargement and training, not of self-revelation.

CHAPTER XV

MYTHOLOGY IN HINDUISM AND BUDDHISM

1

The later phases of Buddhism, described as Mahâyâna, show this feature among many others, that the supernatural and mythological side of religion becomes prominent. Gods or angels play an increasingly important part, the Buddha himself becomes a being superior to all gods, and Buddhas, gods and saints perform at every turn feats for which miracle seems too modest a name. The object of the present chapter is to trace the early stages of these beliefs, for they are found in the Pali Canon, although it is not until later that they overgrow and hide the temple in whose walls they are rooted.

It may be fairly said that Buddhism is not a miraculous religion in the sense that none of its essential doctrines depend on miracles. It would seem that such a religion as Mormonism must collapse if it were admitted that the Book of Mormon is not a revelation delivered to Joseph Smith. But the content of the Buddha's teaching is not miraculous and, though he is alleged to have possessed insight exceeding ordinary human knowledge, yet this is not exactly a miracle and it is a question whether an unusual intelligence disciplined by meditation might not attain to such knowledge. Still, though the essence of the doctrine may be detachable from miracles and even be scientific, one cannot read very far in the Vinaya or the Sutta Pitaka without coming upon unearthly beings or supernatural occurrences.

The credibility of miracles is to my mind simply a question of evidence. Any extraordinary event, such as a person doing a thing totally foreign to his character, is improbable *a priori*. But the law does not allow that the best of men is incapable of committing the worst of crimes, if the evidence proves he did. Nor can the most extraordinary violation of nature's laws be pronounced impossible if supported by sufficient evidence, only the evidence must be strong in proportion to the strangeness of the circumstances. But I cannot see that the uniformity of nature is any objection to the occurrence of miracles, for as a rule a miracle is regarded not as an event without a cause, but as due to a new cause, namely the intervention of a superhuman person. Many of the best known miracles are such that one may imagine this person to effect them by understanding and controlling some unknown natural force, just as we control electricity. Only evidence is required to show that he can do so. But on the other hand the weakness of every religion which depends on miracles is that their truth is contested and not unreasonably. If they are true, why are they not certain? Of all the phenomena described as miracles, ghosts, fortune telling, magic, clairvoyance, prophesying, and so on, none command unchallenged acceptance. In every age miracles, portents and apparitions have been recorded, yet none of them with a certainty that carries universal conviction and in many ages contemporary scepticism was possible. Even in Vedic times there were people who did not believe in the existence of Indra[1].

It is clear that some miracles require more evidence than others and many old stories are so fantastic that they may justly be put aside because those who reported them did not see, as we can, what difficulties they involve and hence felt no need for caution in belief. Among ancient Indians or Hebrews tales of seven headed snakes or of stopping the sun did not arouse the critical spirit, for the phenomena did not seem much more extraordinary than centipedes or eclipses. Only those who understand that such stories upset all we know of anatomy and astronomy can realize their improbability and the weight of evidence necessary to make them credible. The most important distinction in miracles (I use the word as a popular description of extraordinary events which is readily understood though hard to define) is whether they are in any way subjective, that is to say that they depend in the last resort on an impression produced in certain, but not all, human minds or whether they are objective, that is to say that all witnesses would have seen them like any other event. A man rising into the air would be an objective miracle if it were admitted that this levitation was as real as the flight of a bird, and very strong evidence would be necessary to make us believe that such a movement had really

[1] R.V. II. 12. 5.

been executed. But the case is different if we are dealing with the conviction of an enthusiast that he rose aloft or even with the conviction of his disciples, that they, being in an ecstasy, saw him do so. There is no reason to doubt the subjective reality of well-authenticated visions and as motives and stimuli to action they may have real objective importance. Miracles of healing are not dissimilar. A man's mind can affect his body, either directly through his conviction that certain physical changes are about to take place or indirectly as conveying the influence of some powerful external mind which may be either calming or stimulating. That some persons have a special power of healing nervous or mental diseases can hardly be doubted and I am not disposed to reject any well-authenticated miraculous cure, believing that sudden mental relief or acute joy can so affect the whole frame that in the improved physical conditions thus caused even diseases not usually considered as nervous may pass away. But though there is no reason to discredit miracles of healing, it is clear that they are not only exaggerated but also distorted by reporters who do not understand their nature. Those who chronicle the cures supposed to be effected at Lourdes at the present day keep within the bounds of what is explicable, but a Hindu who had seen a cripple recover some power of movement might be equally ready to believe that when a man's leg had been cut off the stump could grow into a complete limb.

The miraculous events recorded in the Pitakas differ from those of later works, whether Mahayanist literature or the Hindu Puranas and Epics, chiefly in their moderation. They may be classified under several heads. Many of them are mere embroidery or embellishment due to poetical exuberance, esteemed appropriate in those generous climates though repugnant to our chilly tastes. In every country poetry is allowed to overstep the prosaic borders of fact without criticism. When an English poet says that—

> The red rose cries She is near, she is near:
>   And the white rose weeps She is late:
> The larkspur listens, I hear, I hear:
>   And the lily whispers, I wait—

no one thinks of criticizing the lines as absurd because flowers cannot talk or of trying to prove that they can. Poetry can take liberties with facts provided it follows the lines of metaphors which the reader finds natural. The same latitude cannot be allowed in unfamiliar directions. Thus though a shower of flowers from heaven is not more extraordinary than talking flowers and is quite natural in Indian poetry, it would probably disconcert the English reader[1]. An Indian poet would not represent flowers as talking, but would give the same idea by saying that the spirits inhabiting trees and plants recited stanzas. Similarly when a painter draws a picture of an angel with wings rising from the shoulder blades, even the very scientific do not think it needful to point out that no such anatomical arrangement is known or probable, nor do the very pious maintain that such creatures exist. The whole question is allowed to rest happily in some realm of acquiescence untroubled by discussions. And it is in this spirit that Indian books relate how when the Buddha went abroad showers of flowers fell from the sky and the air resounded with heavenly music, or diversify their theological discussions with interludes of demons, nymphs and magic serpents. And although this riot of the imagination offends our ideas of good sense and proportion, the Buddhists do not often lose the distinction between what Matthew Arnold called Literature and Dogma. The Buddha's visits to various heavens are not presented as articles of faith: they are simply a pleasant setting for his discourses.

Some miracles of course have a more serious character and can be less easily separated from the essentials of the faith. Thus the Pitakas represent the Buddha as able to see all that happens in the world and to transport himself anywhere at will. But even in such cases we may remember that when we say of a well-informed and active person that he is omniscient and ubiquitous, we are not misunderstood. The hyperbole of Indian legends finds its compensation in the small importance attached to them. No miraculous circumstance recorded of the Buddha has anything like the significance attributed by Christians to the virgin birth or the resurrection of Christ. His superhuman powers are in keeping with the picture drawn of his character. They are mostly the result of an attempt to

[1] Yet Tennyson can say "And at their feet the crocus brake like fire," but in a mythological poem.

describe a mind and will of more than human strength, but the superman thus idealized rarely works miracles of healing. He saves mankind by teaching the way of salvation, not by alleviating a few chance cases of physical distress. In later works he is represented as performing plentiful and extraordinary miracles, but these are just the instances in which we can most clearly trace the addition of embellishments.

2

The elaboration of marvellous episodes is regarded in India as a legitimate form of literary art, no more blameable than dramatization, and in sacred writings it flourishes unchecked. In Hinduism, as in Buddhism, there is not wanting a feeling that the soul is weary of the crowd of deities who demand sacrifices and promise happiness, and on the serener heights of philosophy gods have little place. Still most forms of Hinduism cannot like Buddhism be detached from the gods, and no extravagance is too improbable to be included in the legends about them. The extravagance is the more startling because their exploits form part of quasi-historical narratives. Râma and Krishna seem to be idealized and deified portraits of ancient heroes, who came to be regarded as incarnations of the Almighty. This is understood by Indians to mean not that the Almighty submitted consistently to human limitations, but that he, though incarnate, exercised whenever it pleased him and often most capriciously his full divine force. With this idea before them and no historical scruples to restrain them, Indian writers tell how Krishna held up a mountain on his finger, Indian readers accept the statement, and crowds of pilgrims visit the scene of the exploit.

The later Buddhist writings are perhaps not less extravagant than the Puranas, but the Pitakas are relatively sober, though not quite consistent in their account of the Buddha's attitude to the miraculous. Thus he encourages Sâgata[1] to give a display of miracles, such as walking in the air, in order to prepare the mind of a congregation to whom he is going to preach, but in other narratives[2] which seem ancient and authentic, he expresses his disapproval of such performances (just as Christ

[1] Mahâv. v. i.

[2] *E.g.* Dig. Nik. XI. and Cullavag. v. 8.

refused to give signs), and says that they do not "conduce to the conversion of the unconverted or to the increase of the converted." Those who know India will easily call up a picture of how the Bhikkhus strove to impress the crowd by exhibitions not unlike a modern juggler's tricks and how the master stopped them. His motives are clear: these performances had nothing to do with the essence of his teaching. If it be true that he ever countenanced them, he soon saw his error. He did not want people to say that he was a conjurer who knew the Gândhâra charm or any other trick. And though we have no warrant for doubting that he believed in the reality of the powers known as iddhi, it is equally certain that he did not consider them essential or even important for religion.

Somewhat similar is the attitude of early Buddhism to the spirit world—the hosts of deities and demons who people this and other spheres. Their existence is assumed, but the truths of religion are not dependent on them, and attempts to use their influence by sacrifices and oracles are deprecated as vulgar practices similar to juggling. Later Buddhism became infected with mythology and the critical change occurs when deities, instead of being merely protectors of the church, take an active part in the work of salvation. When the Hindu gods developed into personalities who could appeal to religious and philosophic minds as cosmic forces, as revealers of the truth and guides to bliss, the example was too attractive to be neglected and a pantheon of Bodhisattvas arose. But it is clear that when the Buddha preached in Kosala and Magadha, the local deities had not attained any such position. The systems of philosophy then in vogue were mostly not theistic, and, strange as the words may sound, religion had little to do with the gods. If this be thought to rest on a mistranslation, it is certainly true that the *dhamma* had very little to do with *devas*. The example of Rome under the Empire or of modern China makes the position clearer. In neither would a serious enquirer turn to the ancient national gods for spiritual help.

Often as the Devas figure in early Buddhist stories, the significance of their appearance nearly always lies in their relations with the Buddha or his disciples. Of mere mythology, such as the dealings of Brahmâ and Indra with other gods, there is little. In fact the gods, though freely invoked as accessories, are not taken seriously[1], and there are some extremely curious passages in which Gotama seems to laugh at them, much as the sceptics of the eighteenth century laughed at Jehovah. Thus in the Kevaddha sutta[2] he relates how a monk who was puzzled by a metaphysical problem applied to various gods and finally accosted Brahmâ himself in the presence of all his retinue. After hearing the question, which was Where do the elements cease and leave no trace behind? Brahmâ replies, "I am the Great Brahmâ, the Supreme, the Mighty, the All-seeing, the Ruler, the Lord of all, the Controller, the Creator, the Chief of all, appointing to each his place, the Ancient of days, the Father of all that are and are to be." "But," said the monk, "I did not ask you, friend, whether you were indeed all you now say, but I ask you where the four elements cease and leave no trace." Then the Great Brahmâ took him by the arm and led him aside and said, "These gods think I know and understand everything. Therefore I gave no answer in their presence. But I do not know the answer to your question and you had better go and ask the Buddha." Even more curiously ironical is the account given of the origin of Brahmâ[3]. There comes a time when this world system passes away and then certain beings are reborn in the World of Radiance and remain there a long time. Sooner or later, the world system begins to evolve again and the palace of Brahmâ appears, but it is empty. Then some being whose time is up falls from the World of Radiance and comes to life in the palace and remains there alone. At last he wishes for company, and it so happens that other beings whose time is up fall from the World of Radiance and join him. And the first being thinks that he is Great Brahmâ, the Creator, because when he felt lonely and wished for companions other beings appeared. And the other beings accept this view. And at last one of Brahmâ's retinue falls from that state and is born in the human world and, if he can remember his previous birth, he reflects that he is transitory but that Brahmâ still remains and from this he draws the erroneous conclusion that Brahmâ is eternal.

[1] Even in the Upanishads the gods are not given a very high position. They are powerless against Brahman (*e.g.* Kena Up. 14–28) and are not naturally in possession of true knowledge, though they may acquire it (*e.g.* Chând. Up. VIII. 7).

[2] Dig. Nik. XI.

[3] Dig. Nik. I. chap. 2, 1–6. The radiant gods are the Abhassara, cf. Dhammap. 200.

He who dared to represent Brahmâ (for which name we might substitute Allah or Jehovah) as a pompous deluded individual worried by the difficulty of keeping up his position had more than the usual share of scepticism and irony. The compilers of such discourses regarded the gods as mere embellishments, as gargoyles and quaint figures in the cathedral porch, not as saints above the altar. The mythology and cosmology associated with early Buddhism are really extraneous. The Buddha's teaching is simply the four truths and some kindred ethical and psychological matter. It grew up in an atmosphere of animism which peopled the trees and streams and mountains with spirits. It accepted and played with the idea, just as it might have accepted and played with the idea of radio-activity. But such notions do not affect the essence of the Dharma and it might be preached in severe isolation. Yet in Asia it hardly ever has been so isolated. It is true that Indian mythology has not always accompanied the spread of Buddhism. There is much of it in Tibet and Mongolia but less in China and Japan and still less in Burma. But probably in every part of Asia the Buddhist missionaries found existing a worship of nature spirits and accepted it, sometimes even augmenting and modifying it. In every age the elect may have risen superior to all ideas of gods and heavens and hells, but for any just historical perspective, for any sympathetic understanding of the faith as it exists as a living force to-day, it is essential to remember this background and frame of fantastic but graceful mythology.

Many later Mahayanist books are full of dhâraṇîs or spells. Dhâraṇîs are not essentially different from mantras, especially tantric mantras containing magical syllables, but whereas mantras are more or less connected with worship, dhâraṇîs are rather for personal use, spells to ward off evil and bring good luck. The Chinese pilgrim Hsüan Chuang[1] states that the sect of the Mahâsanghikas, which in his opinion arose in connection with the first council, compiled a Pitaka of dhâraṇîs. The tradition cannot be dismissed as incredible for even the Dîgha-Nikâya relates how a host of spirits visited the Buddha in order to impart a formula which would keep his disciples safe from harm. Buddhist and Brahmanic mythology represent two methods of working up popular legends. The Mahâbhârata and

[1] Watters, II. p. 160.

Puranas introduce us to a moderately harmonious if miscellaneous society of supernatural personages decently affiliated to one another and to Brahmanic teaching. The same personages reappear in Buddhism but are analogous to Christian angels or to fairies rather than to minor deities. They are not so much the heroes of legends, as protectors: they are interesting not for their past exploits but for their readiness to help believers or to testify to the true doctrine. Still there was a great body of Buddhist and Jain legend in ancient India which handled the same stories as Brahmanic legend—*e.g.* the tale of Krishna—but in a slightly different manner. The characteristic form of Buddhist legend is the Jâtaka, or birth story. Folk-lore and sagas, ancient jokes and tragedies, the whole stock in trade of rhapsodists and minstrels are made an edifying and interesting branch of scripture by simply identifying the principal characters with the Buddha, his friends and his enemies in their previous births[1]. But in Hinayanist Buddhism legend and mythology are ornamental, and edifying, nothing more. Spirits may set a good example or send good luck: they have nothing to do with emancipation or nirvana. The same distinction of spheres is not wholly lost in Hinduism, for though the great philosophic works treat of God under various names they mostly ignore minor deities, and though the language of the Bhagavad-gîtâ is exuberant and mythological, yet only Krishna is God: all other spirits are part of him.

The deities most frequently mentioned in Buddhist works are Indra, generally under the name of Sakka (Śakra) and Brahmâ. The former is no longer the demon-slaying soma-drinking deity of the Vedas, but the heavenly counterpart of a pious Buddhist king. He frequently appears in the Jâtaka stories as the protector of true religion and virtue, and when a good man is in trouble, his throne grows hot and attracts his attention. His transformation is analogous to the process by which heathen deities, especially in the Eastern Church, have been accepted as Christian saints[2]. Brahmâ rules in a much higher heaven than Sakka. His appearances on earth are rarer and more weighty, and sometimes he seems to be a personifica-

[1] The legends of both Râma and Krishna occur in the *Book of Jâtakas* in a somewhat altered form, nos. 641 and 454.

[2] Thus Helios the Sun passes into St Elias.

tion of whatever intelligence and desire for good there is in the world[1]. But in no case do the Pitakas concede to him the position of supreme ruler of the Universe. In one singular narrative the Buddha tells his disciples how he once ascertained that Brahmâ Baka was under the delusion that his heaven was eternal and cured him of it[2].

3

All Indian religions have a passion for describing in bold imaginative outline the history and geography of the universe. Their ideas are juster than those of Europeans and Semites in so far as they imply a sense of the distribution of life throughout immensities of time and space. The Hindu perceived more clearly than the Jew and Greek that his own age and country were merely parts of a much longer series and of a far larger structure or growth. He wished to keep this whole continually before the mind, but in attempting to describe it he fell into that besetting intellectual sin of India, the systematizing of the imaginary. Ages, continents and worlds are described in detailed statements which bear no relation to facts. Thus, Brahmanic cosmogony usually deals with a period of time called Kalpa. This is a day in the life of Brahmâ, who lives one hundred years of such days, and it marks the duration of a world which comes into being at its commencement and is annihilated at its end. It consists of 4320 times a million years and is divided into fourteen smaller periods called manvantaras each presided over by a superhuman being called Manu[3]. A manvantara contains about seventy-one mahâyugas and each mahâyuga is what men call the four ages

[1] He is often called Brahmâ Sahampati, a title of doubtful meaning and not found in Brahmanic writings. The Pitakas often speak of Brahmâs and worlds of Brahmâ in the plural, as if there were a whole class of Brahmâs. See especially the Suttas collected in book I, chap. vi. of the Saṃyutta-Nikâya where we even hear of Pacceka Brahmâs, apparently corresponding in some way to Pacceka Buddhas.

[2] Maj. Nik. 49. The meaning of the title Baka is not clear and may be ironical. Another ironical name is manopadosikâ (debauched in mind) invented as the title of a class of gods in Dig. Nik. I. and XX. The idea that sages can instruct the gods is anterior to Buddhism. See *e.g.* Bṛihad-Âr. Up. II. 5. 17, and ib. IV. 3. 33, and the parallel passage in the Tait. Chând. Kaush. Upanishads and Śat. Brâhmaṇa for the idea that a Śrotriya is equal to the highest deities.

[3] Six Manvantaras of the present Kalpa have elapsed and we are in the seventh.

of the world[1]. Geography and astronomy show similar precision. The Earth is the lowest of seven spheres or worlds, and beneath it are a series of hells[2]. The three upper spheres last for a hundred Kalpas but are still material, though less gross than those below. The whole system of worlds is encompassed above and below by the shell of the egg of Brahmâ. Round this again are envelopes of water, fire, air, ether, mind and finally the infinite Pradhâna or cause of all existing things. The earth consists of seven land-masses, divided and surrounded by seven seas. In the centre of the central land-mass rises Mount Meru, nearly a million miles high and bearing on its peaks the cities of Brahmâ and other gods.

The cosmography of the Buddhists is even more luxuriant, for it regards the universe as consisting of innumerable spheres (cakkavâlas), each of which might seem to a narrower imagination a universe in itself, since it has its own earth, heavenly bodies, paradises and hells. A sphere is divided into three regions, the lowest of which is the region of desire. This consists of eleven divisions which, beginning from the lowest, are the hells, and the worlds of animals, Pretas (hungry ghosts), Asuras (Titans)[3] and men. This last, which we inhabit, consists of a vast circular plain largely covered with water. In the centre of it is Mount Meru, and it is surrounded by a wall. Above it rise six devalokas, or heavens of the inferior gods. Above the realms of desire there follow sixteen worlds in which there is form but no desire. All are states of bliss one higher than the other and all are attained by the exercise of meditation. Above these again come four formless worlds, in which there is neither desire nor form. They correspond to the four stages of Arûpa trances and in them the gross and evil elements of existence are reduced to a minimum, but still they are not permanent and cannot be

[1] We are in the Kali or worst age of the present mahâyuga. The Kali lasts 432,000 years and began 3102 B.C.

In their number and in many other points of cosmography the various accounts differ greatly. The account given above is taken from the Vishnu Purâna, book II. but the details in it are not entirely consistent.

[2] The detailed formulation of this cosmography was naturally gradual but its chief features are known to the Nikâyas. Dig. Nik. XIV. 17 and 30 seem to imply the theory of spheres. For Heavens, see Maj. Nik. 49, Dig. Nik. XI. 68–79 and for Hells Sut. Nip. III. 10, Maj. Nik. 129. See too De la Vallée Poussin's article, *Cosmology Buddhist*, in *E.R.E.*

[3] See for the Asuras Sam. Nik. I. xi. 1.

regarded as final salvation. We naturally think of this series of worlds as so many storeys rising one above the other and they are so depicted[1] but it will be observed that the animal kingdom is placed between the hells and humanity, obviously not as having its local habitation there but as better off than the one, though inferior to the other, and perhaps if we pointed this out to the Hindu artist he would smile and say that his many storeyed picture must not be taken so literally: all states of being are merely states of mind, hellish, brutish, human and divine.

Grotesque as Hindu notions of the world may seem, they include two great ideas of modern science. The universe is infinite or at least immeasurable[2]. The vision of the astronomer who sees a solar system in every star of the milky way is not wider than the thought that devised these Cakkavâlas or spheres, each with a vista of heavens and a procession of Buddhas, to look after its salvation. Yet compared with the sum of being a sphere is an atom. Space is filled by aggregates of them, considered by some as groups of three, by others as clusters of a thousand. And secondly these world systems, with the living beings and plants in them, are regarded as growing and developing by natural processes, and, equally in virtue of natural processes, as decaying and disintegrating when the time comes. In the Aggañña-Sutta[3] we have a curious account of the evolution of man which, though not the same as Darwin's, shows the same idea of development or perhaps degeneration and differentiation. Human beings were originally immaterial, aerial and self-luminous, but as the world gradually assumed its present form they took to eating first of all a fragrant kind of earth and then plants with the result that their bodies became gross and differences of sex and colour were produced.

No sect of Hinduism personifies the powers of evil in one figure corresponding to Satan, or the Ahriman of Persia. In proportion as a nation thinks pantheistically it is disinclined to regard the world as being mainly a contest between good and evil. It is true there are innumerable demons and innumerable good spirits who withstand them. But just as there is no

[1] See a Tibetan representation in Waddell's *Buddhism of Tibet*, p. 79.

[2] The question of whether the universe is infinite in space or not is according to the Pitakas one of those problems which cannot be answered.

[3] Dig. Nik. XXVII.

finality in the exploits of Râma and Krishna, so Râvaṇa and other monsters do not attain to the dignity of the Devil. In a sense the destructive forces are evil, but when they destroy the world at the end of a Kalpa the result is not the triumph of evil. It is simply winter after autumn, leading to spring and another summer.

Buddhism having a stronger ethical bias than Hinduism was more conscious of the existence of a Tempter, or a power that makes men sin. This power is personified, but somewhat indistinctly, as Mâra, originally and etymologically a god of death. He is commonly called Mâra the Evil One[1], which corresponds to the Mrityuh pâpmâ of the Vedas, but as a personality he seems to have developed entirely within the Buddhist circle and to be unknown to general Indian mythology. In the thought of the Pitakas the connection between death and desire is clear. The great evils and great characteristics of the world are that everything in it decays and dies and that existence depends on desire. Therefore the ruler of the world may be represented as the god of desire and death. Buddha and his saints struggle with evil and overcome it by overcoming desire and this triumphant struggle is regarded as a duel with Mâra, who is driven off and defeated[2].

Even in his most mythological aspects, Mâra is not a deity of Hell. He presides over desire and temptation, not over judgment and punishment. This is the function of Yama, the god of the dead, and one of the Brahmanic deities who have migrated to the Far East. He has been adopted by Buddhism, though no explanation is given of his status. But he is introduced as a vague but effective figure—and yet hardly more than a metaphor—whenever it is desired to personify the inflexible powers that summon the living to the other world and there make them undergo, with awful accuracy, the retribution due

[1] Mâro pâpimâ. See especially Windisch, *Mâra and Buddha*, 1895, and Sam. Nik. I. iv.

[2] We sometimes hear of Mâras in the plural. Like Brahmâ he is sometimes a personality, sometimes the type of a class of gods. We also hear that he has obtained his present exalted though not virtuous post by his liberality in former births. Thus, like Sakka and other Buddhist Devas, Mâra is really an office held by successive occupants. He is said to be worshipped by some Tibetan sects. It is possible that the legends about Mâra and his daughters and about Krishna and the Gopîs may have a common origin for Mâra is called Kaṇha (the Prakrit equivalent of Krishna) in Sutta-Nipâta, 439.

for their deeds. In a remarkable passage[1] called Death's Messengers, it is related that when a sinner dies he is led before King Yama who asks him if he never saw the three messengers of the gods sent as warnings to mortals, namely an old man, a sick man and a corpse. The sinner under judgment admits that he saw but did not reflect and Yama sentences him to punishment, until suffering commensurate to his sins has been inflicted.

Buddhism tells of many hells, of which Avîci is the most terrible. They are of course all temporary and therefore purgatories rather than places of eternal punishment, and the beings who inhabit them have the power of struggling upwards and acquiring merit[2], but the task is difficult and one may be born repeatedly in hell. The phraseology of Buddhism calls existences in heavens and hells new births. To us it seems more natural to say that certain people are born again as men and that others go to heaven or hell. But the three destinies are really parallel[3].

The desire to accommodate influential ideas, though they might be incompatible with the strict teaching of the Buddha, is well seen in the position accorded to spirits of the dead. The Buddha was untiring in his denunciation of every idea which implied that some kind of soul or double escapes from the body at death and continues to exist. But the belief in the existence of departed ancestors and the presentation of offerings to them have always formed a part of Hindu domestic religion. To gratify this persistent belief, Buddhism recognized the world of Petas, that is ghosts or spirits. Many varieties of these are described in later literature. Some are as thin as withered leaves and suffer from continual hunger, for their mouths are so small that they can take no solid food. According to strict theology, the Petas are a category of beings just above animals and certain forms of bad conduct entail birth among them. But in popular estimation, they are merely the spirits of the

[1] Ang. Nik. III. 35.

[2] This seems to be the correct doctrine, though it is hard to understand how the popular idea of continual torture is compatible with the performance of good deeds. The Kathâ-vatthu, XIII. 2, states that a man in purgatory can do good. See too Ang. Nik. I. 19.

[3] But even the language of the Pitakas is not always quite correct on this point, for it represents evil-doers as falling down straight into hell.

dead who can receive nourishment and other benefits from the living. The veneration of the dead and the offering of sacrifices to or for them, which form a conspicuous feature in Far Eastern Buddhism, are often regarded as a perversion of the older faith, and so, indeed, they are. Yet in the Khuddaka-pâṭha[1], which if not a very early work is still part of the Sutta Pitaka, are found some curious and pathetic verses describing how the spirits of the departed wait by walls and crossways and at the doors, hoping to receive offerings of food. When they receive it their hearts are gladdened and they wish their relatives prosperity. As many streams fill the ocean, so does what is given here help the dead. Above all, gifts given to monks will redound to the good of the dead for a long time. This last point is totally opposed to the spirit of Gotama's doctrine, but it contains the germ of the elaborate system of funeral masses which has assumed vast proportions in the Far East.

4

What then is the position of the Buddha himself in this universe of many worlds and multitudinous deities? European writers sometimes fail to understand how the popular thought of India combines the human and superhuman: they divorce the two aspects and unduly emphasize one or the other. If they are impressed by the historical character of Gotama, they conclude that all legends with a supernatural tinge must be late and adventitious. If, on the other hand, they feel that the extent and importance of the legendary element entitles it to consideration, they minimize the historical kernel. But in India, reality and fancy, prosaic fact and extravagant imagination are found not as successive stages in the development of religious ideas, but simultaneously and side by side. Keshub Chunder Sen was a Babu of liberal views who probably looked as prosaic a product of the nineteenth century as any radical politician.

[1] Khud. Path. 7. In this poem, the word Peta (Sk. Preta) seems to be used as equivalent to departed spirits, not necessarily implying that they are undergoing punishment. In the *Questions of Milinda* (IV. 8. 29) the practice of making offerings on behalf of the dead is countenanced, and it is explained exactly what classes of dead profit by them. On the other hand the Kathâ-vatthu states that the dead do not benefit by gifts given in this world, but two sects, the Râjagirika and Siddhattika, are said by the commentary to hold the contrary view.

Yet his followers were said to regard him as a God, and whether this is a correct statement or not, it is certain that he was credited with superhuman power and received a homage which seemed even to Indians excessive[1]. It is in the light of such incidents and such temperaments that we should read the story of the Buddha. Could we be transported to India in the days of his preaching, we should probably see a figure very like the portrait given in the more sober parts of the Pitakas, a teacher of great intelligence and personal charm, yet distinctly human. But had we talked about him in the villages which lay along his route, or even in the circle of his disciples, I think we should have heard tales of how Devas visited him and how he was wont to vanish and betake himself to some heaven. The Hindu attributes such feats to a religious leader, as naturally as Europeans would ascribe to him a magnetic personality and a flashing eye.

The Pitakas emphasize the omniscience and sinlessness of the Buddha but contain no trace of the idea that he is God in the Christian or Mahommedan sense. They are consistently non-theistic and it is only later that Buddhas and Bodhisattvas become transformed into beings about whom theistic language can be used. But in those parts of the Pitakas which may be reasonably supposed to contain the ideas of the first century after the Buddha's death, he is constantly represented as instructing Devas and receiving their homage[2]. In the Khuddaka-pâṭha the spirits are invited to come and do him reverence. He is described as the Chief of the World with all its gods[3], and is made to deny that he is a man. If a Buddha cannot be called a Deva rather than a man, it is only because he is higher than both. It is this train of thought which leads later Buddhists[4] to call him Devâtideva, or the Deva who is above all other Devas, and thus make him ultimately a being comparable with Siva or Vishnu.

The idea that great teachers of mankind appear in a regular series and at stated intervals is certainly older than Gotama,

[1] See Max Müller's *Ramakrishna*, p. 40, for another instance.

[2] In a passage of the Mahâparinib. Sut. (III. 22) which is probably not very early the Buddha says that when he mixes with gods or men he takes the shape of his auditors, so that they do not know him.

[3] Sam. Nik. II. 3. 10. Sadevakassa lokassa aggo.

[4] *E.g.* in the Lotus Sutra.

but it is hard to say how far it was systematized before his time. The greatness of the position which he won and the importance of the institutions which he founded naturally caused his disciples to formulate the vague traditions about his predecessors. They were called indifferently Buddha, Jina, Arhat, etc., and it was only after the constitution of the Buddhist church that these titles received fixed meanings.

Closely connected with the idea of the Buddha or Jina is that of the Mahâpurusha or great man. It was supposed that there are born from time to time supermen distinguished by physical marks who become either universal monarchs (cakravartin) or teachers of the truth. Such a prediction is said to have been made respecting the infant Gotama and all previous Buddhas. The marks are duly catalogued, as thirty-two greater and eighty[1] smaller signs. Many of them are very curious. The hair is glossy black: the tongue is so long that it can lick the ears: the arms reach to the knees in an ordinary upright position: the skin has a golden tinge: there is a protuberance on the skull and a smaller one, like a ball, between the eyebrows. The long arms may be compared with the Persian title rendered in Latin by Longimanus[2] and it is conceivable that the protuberances on the head may have been personal peculiarities of Gotama. For though the thirty-two marks are mentioned in the Pitakas as well-known signs establishing his claims to eminence, no description of them has been found in any pre-Buddhist work[3], and they may have been modified to suit his personal appearance. At any rate it is clear that the early generations of Buddhists considered that the Master conformed to the type of the Mahâpurusha and attached importance to the fact[4]. The Pitakas repeatedly allude to the knowledge of

[1] One hundred and eight marks on the sole of each foot are also enumerated in later writings.

[2] Artaxerxes Longimanus. Cf. the Russian princely name Dolgorouki. The Chinese also attribute forty-nine physical signs of perfection to Confucius, including long arms. See Doré, *Recherches sur les Superstitions en Chine*, vol. XIII. pp. 2–6.

[3] Though Brahmans are represented as experts in these marks, it seems likely that the idea of the Mahâpurusha was popular chiefly among the Kshatriyas, for in one form, at any rate, it teaches that a child of the warrior caste born with certain marks will become either a universal monarch or a great teacher of the truth. This notion must have been most distasteful to the priestly caste.

[4] See Dig. Nik. 3. The Lakkhana Suttanta (Dig. Nik. 30) contains a discussion of the marks.

these marks as forming a part of Brahmanic training and in the account of the previous Buddha Vipassî they are duly enumerated. These ideas about a Great Man and his characteristics were probably current among the people at the time of the Buddha's birth. They do not harmonize completely with later definitions of a Buddha's nature, but they show how Gotama's contemporaries may have regarded his career.

In the older books of the Pitakas six Buddhas are mentioned as preceding Gotama[1], namely Vipassî, Sikhî, Vessabhû, Kakusandha, Konâgamana and Kassapa. The last three at least may have some historical character. The Chinese pilgrim Fa Hsien, who visited India from 405 to 411 A.D., saw their reputed birthplaces and says that there still existed followers of Devadatta (apparently in Kosala) who recognized these three Buddhas but not Gotama. Asoka erected a monument in honour of Konâgamana in Nepal with a dedicatory inscription which has been preserved. In the Majjhima-Nikâya[2] we find a story about Kakusandha and his disciples and Gotama once gave[3] an extended account of Vipassî, whose teaching and career are represented as almost identical with his own. Different explanations have been given of this common element. There is clearly a wish to emphasize the continuity of the Dhamma and the similarity of its exponents in all ages. But are we to believe that the stories, true or romantic, originally told of Gotama were transferred to his mythical forerunners or that before his birth there was a Buddha legend to which the account of his career was accommodated? Probably both processes went on simultaneously. The notices of the Jain saints show that there must have been such legends and traditions independent of Gotama. To them we may refer things like the miracles attending birth. But the general outline of the Buddha's career, the departure from home, struggle for enlightenment and hesitation before preaching, seem to be a reminiscence of Gotama's actual life rather than an earlier legend.

There is an interesting discourse describing the wonders that attend the birth of a Buddha[4], such as that he passes from the Tusita heaven to his mother's womb; that she must die seven

[1] See Dik. Nig. 14, Mahâpadânasutta: Therag. 490; Sam. Nik. XII. 4–10.
[2] Maj. Nik. 50, Mâratajjaniyasuttam.
[3] Dig. Nik. 14.
[4] Maj. Nik. 123. See also Dig. Nik. 14.

days after his birth: that she stands when he is born: and so on. We may imagine that the death of the mother is due to the historical fact that Gotama's mother did so die, while the other circumstances are embellishments of the old Buddha and Mahâpurusha legend. But the construction of this sutta is curious. The monks in the Jetavana are talking of the wondrous powers possessed by Buddhas. Gotama enters and asks what is the subject of their discourse. They tell him and he bids Ânanda describe more fully the wondrous attributes of a Buddha. Ânanda gives a long list of marvels and at the end Gotama observes, "Take note of this too as one of the wondrous attributes of a Buddha, that he has his feelings, perceptions and thoughts under complete control[1]."

No passage has yet been adduced from the suttas mentioning more than seven Buddhas but later books, such as the Buddhavaṃsa and the introduction to the Jâtaka, describe twenty-five[2]. There are twenty-four Jain Tîrthankaras and according to some accounts twenty-four incarnations of Vishnu. Probably all these lists are based on some calculation as to the proper allowance of saints for an aeon. The biographies of these Buddhas are brief and monotonous. For each sage they record the number of his followers, the name of his city, parents, and chief disciples, the tree under which he attained enlightenment, his height and his age, both in extravagant figures. They also record how each met Gotama in one of his previous births and prophesied his future glory. The object of these biographies is less to give information about previous Buddhas than to trace the career of Gotama as a Bodhisattva. This career began in the time of Dîpankara, the first of the twenty-five Buddhas, incalculable ages ago, when Gotama was a hermit called Sumedha. Seeing that the road over which Dîpankara had to pass was dirty, he threw himself down in the mire in order that the Buddha might tread on him and not soil his feet. At the same time he made a resolution to become a Buddha and received from Dîpankara the assurance that ages afterwards his

[1] More literally that he knows exactly how his feelings, etc., arise, continue and pass away and is not swayed by wandering thoughts and desires.

[2] Three extra Buddhas are sometimes mentioned but are usually ignored because they did not, like the others, come into contact with Gotama in his previous births.

wish would be fulfilled. This incident, called praṇidhâna or the vow to become a Buddha, is frequently represented in the frescoes found in Central Asia.

The history of this career is given in the introduction to the Jâtaka and in the late Pali work called the Cariyâ-piṭaka, but the suttas make little reference to the topic. They refer incidentally to Gotama's previous births[1] but their interest clearly centres in his last existence. They not infrequently use the word Bodhisattva to describe the youthful Gotama or some other Buddha before the attainment of Buddhahood, but in later literature it commonly designates a being now existing who will be a Buddha in the future. In the older phase of Buddhism attention is concentrated on a human figure which fills the stage, but before the canon closes we are conscious of a change which paves the way for the Mahâyâna. Our sympathetic respect is invited not only for Gotama the Buddha, but for the struggling Bodhisattva who, battling towards the goal with incredible endurance and self-sacrifice through lives innumerable, at last became Gotama.

It is only natural that the line of Buddhas should extend after as well as before Gotama. In the Pitakas there are allusions to such a posterior series, as when for instance we hear[2] that all Buddhas past and to come have had and will have attendants like Ânanda, but Metteya the Buddha of the future has not yet become an important figure. He is just mentioned in the Dîgha Nikâya and Buddha-Vaṃsa and the Milinda Pañha quotes an utterance of Gotama to the effect that "He will be the leader of thousands as I am of hundreds," but the quotation has not been identified.

The Buddhas enumerated are supreme Buddhas (Sammâ-sam-buddha) but there is another order called Pacceka (Sanskrit Pratyeka) or private Buddhas. Both classes attain by their own exertions to a knowledge of the four truths but the Pacceka Buddhas are not, like the supreme Buddhas, teachers of mankind and omniscient[3]. Their knowledge is confined to what is necessary for their own salvation and perfection. They are

[1] *E.g.* Ang. Nik. III. 15 and the Mahâ-Sudassana Sutta (Dig. Nik. x.) in which the Buddha says he has been buried at Kusinâra no less than six times.

[2] Dig. Nik. XVI. v. 15.

[3] The two kinds of Buddhas are defined in the Puggala-Pannatti, IX. 1. For details about Pratyeka-Buddhas see De La Vallée Poussin's article in *E.R.E.*

mentioned in the Nikâyas as worthy of all respect[1] but are not prominent in either the earlier or later works, which is only natural, seeing that by their very definition they are self-centred and of little importance for mankind. The idea of the private Buddha however is interesting, inasmuch as it implies that even when the four truths are not preached they still exist and can be discovered by anyone who makes the necessary mental and moral effort. It is also noticeable that the superiority of a supreme Buddha lies in his power to teach and help others. A passionless and self-centred sage falls short of the ideal.

[1] Thus in Dig. Nik. xvi. 5. 12 they are declared worthy of a Dâgaba or funeral monument and Sam. Nik. iii. 2. 10 declares the efficacy of alms given to them.